Silver Screen in the Silver City

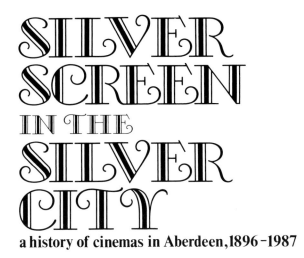

SILVER SCREEN IN THE SILVER CITY

a history of cinemas in Aberdeen, 1896-1987

MICHAEL THOMSON

ABERDEEN UNIVERSITY PRESS

First published 1988
Aberdeen University Press
A member of the Pergamon Group

© Michael Thomson 1988

British Library Cataloguing in Publication Data

Thomson, Michael
   Silver screen in the silver city: a
   history of cinemas in Aberdeen, 1896-1987.
   1. Scotland. Grampian region. Aberdeen.
   Cinemas to 1987
   I. Title
   791.43′09412′35

ISBN 0 08 036402 0

Cover illustration
Capitol auditorium, 1930s.

PRINTED IN GREAT BRITAIN
THE UNIVERSITY PRESS
ABERDEEN

Contents

List of Illustrations

Preface

In 1939, just before the Second World War, Aberdeen possessed no less than 19 cinemas, serving a population of 175,000 in an area more or less bounded by Torry to the South, Ruthrieston and Mannofield to the West, and Woodside and Old Aberdeen to the North. Both Aberdeen and Glasgow have been claimed as possessing the highest ratio of cinema seats per head of population in Scotland at that time, and one would suspect a very close tie between the two centres. On a national scale, Aberdeen was one of the very best-served communities for cinema accommodation, and spent more on screen entertainments than any other city of comparable size.

This book is the first-ever attempt to trace comprehensively the growth and decline (but not disappearance) of the cinema industry in Aberdeen, and is based upon contemporary newspaper reports and the personal reminiscences of a large number of people who were either involved in the business or were its frequent customers in this most cinema-minded of cities.

For those who remember the hey-day of cinema-going in Aberdeen, it is hoped that many pleasant memories may be evoked. For those who (like the author) are of a later generation, it is hoped that this book might help to explain how and why it happened...

Acknowledgements

The author would like to express gratitude to the many who, in a great number of ways, have given help and encouragement in this work, particularly:

Aberdeen Journals, Ltd., James Brooks, Isabella Deans, Department Of Planning And Conservation, St Nicholas House, Aberdeen, Herbert M. Donald, Herbert W.G. Donald, Frank Donnelly, Charles Elder, The late Bert Ewen, Alex Garden, The late Meyer Kalson, Janet McBain, Ian Main, Bobby Pagan, John K.S. Poole, Scottish Film Council, Glasgow, John Soutar, The late George Walker jnr, Susan K. Weddle, The late Jack Wright

Special thanks to Aberdeen City Libraries (City Librarian—Peter Grant, ALA) for access to archive materials.

Chapter 1

Beginnings 1896

Photographs of Aberdeen in the 1890s show a rather small, crowded city, mainly clustered around its harbour and the Union Street area, with new residential schemes just beginning to make serious encroachments on the surrounding countryside. Futtie, Torry and Woodside are virtually separate communities, and the day of Cults, Bieldside, Culter, Bucksburn and Dyce as commuter suburbs is far in the future. Carriages and carts rattle over the cobbled streets, and the tram-cars are still horse-drawn. Domestic electricity is also in the future—gas, instead, is very much the order of the day. Union Street is already becoming a thoroughfare of shops and offices, and in other areas tenements proliferate as the 'granite city' takes shape.

The city's main theatre is Her Majesty's Theatre in Guild Street (replaced in 1906 by the new His Majesty's Theatre in Rosemount Viaduct). The Palace Theatre in Bridge Place, still popularly known by its old names of Cooke's Circus or the People's Palace, is the centre for music hall entertainment, while for those so minded there are occasional performances of classical music at another Music Hall—the concert hall in Union Street. The days of touring orchestras are yet to come, and much music-making is done at a purely domestic level; a piano or harmonium in the parlour is a prized possession.

Let us suppose this to be 1896, 18 September to be exact, and that you are engrossed in a copy of the Aberdeen Free Press for that date. Having read the latest local gossip, Empire news and reports of mass killing in Armenia you turn to the advertisements (on the front page) to find a new entry amid the familiar columns:

Music Hall, September 28th, 29th 30th:
ANIMATED PHOTOGRAPHS

What will they think of next? Enquiry yields the information that these 'animated photographs' are a new invention that has become quite a fad in the great city of London. Your curiosity may be further aroused when you see the large advertisement in the *Free Press* of Monday the 28th, the day of the show's premiere:

1

Scenes reproduced on a canvas screen with all the actual movements of REAL
LIFE. A selection will be made from a collection of 86 pictures including

Arrival Of Paris Express
Sea Bathing
The Serpentine Dance (in brilliant colour)
Cycling In Hyde Park
A Highland Dance
Westminster Bridge
Coronation Of The Czar
The Wedding
An Engineer's Workshop
The Boulevards, Paris Etc, Etc.

This 'most amusing and delightful' entertainment, 'all the rage in London
and Paris', is to be supplemented with conjuring and musical sketches by Mr
Douglas Beaufort, 'the Prince of Conjurors'. Taking part in the show will be
pianists H.G. Newsam and Burwood Nicholls. Organist of Rubislaw Church
since 1890, Mr Nicholls is already well known for his music at all sorts of
functions in the Music Hall.

If, appetite whetted, you have not already visited the Union Street music
shop of Marr Wood & Co to reserve your two-shilling seat, you may go along
to the Music Hall for doors-open at 7.30 p.m., pay your 1s. 6d. (a very
substantial sum in 1896) and find your place among an excited, curious
crowd. Looking around, you will see a good number of University folk,
come to witness man's latest feat of ingenuity in this marvellous nineteenth
century.

The first part of the programme is a virtuoso display of sleight-of-hand by
the smooth-talking Mr Beaufort, who, using such mundane objects as candles,
cards and pieces of paper, performs astonishing tricks interlaced with refined
witty chat. When he tells of how once, at the behest of the Foreign Office, he
went all the way to Fez to confound the magicians of no less than the Sultan
of Morocco, you may be quite prepared to believe it, especially if the language
barrier had allowed him such an infectious line of 'patter'. In his singing and
ventriloquism act there is a particularly funny song, 'The Oldest Inhabitant',
in which his great talent for mimicry would steal the show at any variety
theatre. The same goes for another ludicrous song about some private dance,
but the audience is restive. The remainder of his act, good as it is, even begins
to mildly 'get the bird' from some quarters, although no doubt realising why,
Mr Beaufort doesn't seem to mind too much and the first part of the show is
concluded with grace.

At last, down go the Music Hall's gas lights to a glow, and an odd-looking
machine standing in the middle of the hall is cranked into life by its operator.
It looks like a magic lantern of the type now long familiar, with the usual
lamp-box containing lime-light (calcium carbonate rods made incandescent
in an acetylene flame) but instead of a slide carriage on the front it has a
system of cogs which carry past the lens hundreds of successive black and

white photographs on transparent celluloid film. This film comes from a reel surmounting the machine, and once it has gone through the wheels it falls into a box on the floor to be rewound. When each image is in the right position behind the lens, a special rotating shutter admits a blink of light from the lamp-box. Flashed at the rate of some twenty to thirty per second on to a big canvas screen on the stage, the projected pictures come uncannily to life—a bit flickery, but moving nevertheless. The scenes shown are everyday ones, but the great thing is that those scenes can be watched again and again, as many times as you wish. Amazing!

Of the 18 short films that you see that night, those that seem to make the greatest impression are the most prosaic ones. There, recorded for all to see, is the Boulevarde des Italiens in far-off Paris, with its crowds, the carriages of the fashionable, and the loungers watching them. There is a pleasure boat coming to shore at Brighton, with the boatmen wading through the surf to lift the trippers off just as in real life, and all of a sudden everyone notices just how the ladies whisk their skirts when put down, and how 'Arry gets carried ashore waving his stick. There is a train drawing into a station, with the station master hurrying on to the platform to meet it. The train disgorges, with porters bounding across the line and ladies fussing over their luggage. The Skirt Dance film is in a sort of unsteady colour, laboriously stencilled on to the print frame by frame. You watch a French wedding scene in which there looms on the right hand side of the picture a slightly officious-looking gent who keeps the crowd back so that the wedding procession is clearly visible. This gentleman, you are told, is Mr Robert W. Paul, inventor of the intriguing machine of which tonight you are seeing the most that anyone has been shown so far, only eight of these films having been given at one time even in London.

There is no music during the films, but some are accompanied by a commentary from Mr Beaufort. The audience watches quite silently, but the applause afterwards is terrific. Those life-size figures coming towards you on the screen can be just a little worrying until you get used to the effect, but you come out determined to see the show again. You may with some justification harbour a suspicion that while this could be just a flash in the pan, a passing showman's gimmick, it could turn into a great deal more than that.

Such, according to contemporary press reporting, might have been your reaction to Aberdeen's first ever sight of the culmination of many years' hard work by various inventors on devices that used the phenomenon called 'persistence of vision' (characteristic of the human eye) to produce the illusion of movement from drawings or photographs. Much intensive experimentation had been carried out during the 1880s, and the man who got it right was the great Thomas Alva Edison. In 1889, Edison, with the help of his assistants and aided by the timely availability of long strips of film, found a practical and reliable way of moving successive pictures through a lens system with a synchronizing shutter that separated each frame. What he came out with commercially, however, was not a projector but a peep-show for fairgrounds. Using continuous film loops, this was patented in 1891 as the 'Kinetoscope' but due to the number of other projects in progress it was not marketed until 1894. Even then, commercial development came about only at the urging of some businessmen who became Edison's partners in the Kinetoscope Company.

Edison considered screen projection to be 'killing the goose that laid the golden egg', and despite pressure from his partners he dragged his feet over perfecting it. This was something of a tactical error, as one of his customers, a New York Kinetoscope exhibitor called Major Woodville Latham, stepped in and on Sunday, 21 April 1895 gave the very first demonstration of a projector. This was built for him in the manner of a reversed Kinetoscope by a freelance engineer with the help of one of Edison's ex-assistants—and with a long legal battle to follow.

As the Latham family worked to put their moving pictures on a commercial footing, others were realising the possibilities inherent in the Kinetoscope. In Lyons, France, the aptly named brothers Louis and August Lumière, inspired by the Kinetoscopes that arrived in Paris in 1894, started work on their own camera and projector. As manufacturers of photographic materials they were in a position to obtain and coat their own celluloid, and their hard work was rewarded by the great success of what is believed to be the world's first public picture show, given in the Indian Salon of the Grand Café, Boulevarde des Capucines, Paris, on 28 December 1895. The Lumières' 'Cinématograph' (the name was soon to become a generic one) was taken to London and exhibited to the Press at the Empire Theatre, Leicester Square, on 7 February 1896. It was later demonstrated in private at the Regent Street Polytechnic and was quickly booked as part of the bill at the Empire, which itself became one of the country's most luxurious picture palaces about thirty years later.

Edison, meanwhile, had made more trouble for himself through inadequate patenting of the Kinetoscope. He had not, despite warnings, taken steps to protect his rights outwith the U.S.A., and he had failed to take out any patent at all on a projection model. It was therefore with intentions quite within the law that a couple of Greek businessmen visited the Hatton Garden premises of scientific instrument-maker Robert Paul, to see if he would copy the Edison machines in their London peep-show arcade so that their business could expand at reasonable cost. Paul, amazed to find the copyright situation as it was, not only quickly fulfilled their order but also entered successfully into production on his own account. On hearing of this the Edison Company cut off Paul's supply of ready-made films, but they were only locking the stable door after the horse had bolted. Paul made a camera of his own, for which he invented a new intermittent action to move the film along frame by frame. Next he made a projector using that same mechanism, the 'Maltese Cross', which has remained standard ever since. This machine he patented as the

'Theatrograph', followed a while later by an improved model named the 'Animatograph'.

On the same day as the Lumières gave their first London show, the Theatrograph was unveiled in a demonstration at Finsbury Technical College. This was followed on 28 February by a demonstration at the Royal Institution of Science, in accordance with Paul's original concept of moving pictures as belonging to the world of science rather than that of entertainment. Things changed that March, however, when a Theatrograph was installed at the Olympia exhibition hall in London, and instantly proved that if the machine's maker needed persuasion of its entertainment value, the public did not. Soon, Paul's pictures were on the bill at the Alhambra Theatre, Leicester Square, where the huge Odeon cinema of the 1930s now stands. He was given space on the Alhambra's flat roof to set up a little studio, from whence came many short rather elementary films over the next few years. Ranging from only about half a minute to just over a minute in duration, these covered a variety of subjects. Some were of the daily scenes that constituted the staple fare of the cinematograph's infancy, some featured early examples of trick-photography, while others ranked as Britain's first little screen narratives. Paul's trade in equipment and films (the latter increasing in length, of course) continued until 1910 when the motion picture became big business and he was obliged to return to the manufacture of optical instruments.

With the availability of Paul's and, soon, other makes of equipment to add films to the bills of music halls and to enliven any other kind of show, the entertainment industry began to take a close interest in the novelty. Within only two days of the Lumière Cinématograph's opening at the Empire, the great conjuror and showman J. Nevil Maskelyne installed a Paul Theatrograph at the Egyptian Hall, 'England's Home Of Mystery', in Piccadilly. Prime mover behind this was a young conjuror named David Devant, an associate of Maskelyne's and, as of 1905, partner in Maskelyne's entertainment company.

David Devant it was who put the cinematograph show on the road, giving the provinces their first sight of films by Robert Paul, Lumière, and another French picture pioneer, Georges Méliès. Next stop after Aberdeen was Brechin on 2 October. Montrose followed on the 3rd, then up to Inverness for the 6th, across to Macduff and Elgin for the next two days, and back to Aberdeen for a return performance on 8 October in the Albert Hall, Huntly Street. The Albert Hall was the original Gilcomston South Church, vacated in 1868 when the present Union Street building was completed. It then existed for many years as the Philharmonic Hall (home of Aberdeen Philharmonic Society) before changing its name once again, and it will figure later in our narrative.

Aberdeen's second cinematograph show also included a contribution by Douglas Beaufort, although whether his reception was any better than before is not recorded. There were also several new films, including Sea Bathing at Trouville, the recent Derby (shown specially to the Prince of Wales, whose own horse was the winner) and a very early comedy centring upon a gardener pictured peacefully watering plants with a hose. A small boy steps on the hose, stopping the water; as the puzzled gardener looks down the end, the boy raises his foot and the gardener receives a face-full. The fleeing boy is caught, given the same treatment and thrown out. This historic film, originally entitled *L'Arroseur Arrosé* (literally *The Waterer Watered*), was made by Georges Méliès, and as *Teasing The Gardener* was considered screamingly funny in 1896—surely the oldest screen gag of all.

That Music Hall show on 28 September was Aberdeen's first taste of a means of communication that was already being joyously hailed as the ultimate one, requiring neither knowledge of language or even basic literacy. However, the very first cinematograph show in the North of Scotland was a private one for the Duke and Duchess of York (later King George V and Queen Mary) in the drawing room of Glenmuick House on Royal Deeside. At the behest of Lord and Lady Glenesk, Devant's cinematograph was booked for a special performance on the night of Saturday, 26 September to entertain a large house party which included the Russian Ambassador Monsieur de Staal and his wife, the Earl and Countess of Clanwilliam, the Princess of Hohenlohe, Father Meany of St Mary's R.C. Cathedral in Aberdeen, and several other distinguished guests visiting Deeside while the Queen was at Balmoral.

As the Duke and Duchess had been invited to dine at Balmoral that night, a special preview of the cinematograph was given for them before they left. The company that assembled in the drawing room for the full show at 9 p.m. saw a two-hour version of what was planned for Aberdeen on the Monday, complete with contribution by Douglas Beaufort who, as one of the foremost society drawing-room conjurors of the day, with regular appearances at Maskelyne's Egyptian Hall to his credit, would have been quite in his element. Lord Glenesk (Sir Algernon Borthwick, philanthropist and proprietor of the *London Morning Post*), had a long lease of Glenmuick and Invercauld Houses, hence the connection with Deeside and with the Royal Family. Prominent in the Garrick Club, he was very interested in theatrical matters, and it would have been quite natural for him to have seized the opportunity to test out the capabilities as well as the novelty value of an invention which seemed to hold such enormous potential for the future.

Chapter 2

Pioneering Days   1896—1899

Among the spectators at those first Lumière Brothers' shows in February 1896 was a prominent Aberdeen bookseller named William Walker. Beginning as an apprentice at the age of 13, Walker had worked his way up to become proprietor of his own bookshop at No.36 Bridge Street while still a very young man. From there he moved in 1885 to four-storey premises at No.19 Bridge Street, and as his business expanded he opened subsidiary shops at 41 and 43 Bridge Street and at 71 Schoolhill. He was the largest supplier of educational works outwith Edinburgh, and in addition to books he carried on a flourishing trade in stationery, photographic services and equipment, teaching and drawing supplies, typewriters, cameras, and magic lantern shows.

Lantern shows were a great favourite of the day, and by this time Walker possessed a collection of more than 10,000 slides. He employed teams of lanternists to travel Scotland giving displays for any and every occasion, be it historical lecture, drawing-room party, church fête, society gathering or even, on occasion, an appearance before Royalty at Balmoral Castle. He sent lanterns and boxes of slides to places which were too small for the more extensive exhibitions, he supplied educational slides to School Boards throughout the north of Scotland, he sold slides and equipment—and all while still in his thirties.

Lantern slides, often illustrating stories or events, were produced either photographically or by hand drawing, and could be very elaborate. Made of glass, they were often hand painted in beautiful colours, and some would incorporate little movable sections. 'Limelight Views' were a sort of slide travelogue of places afar, and the effect of a 'Tableau Vivant', in which a series of gracefully posed human groups, abstract patterns or floral designs dissolved from one to the other, could be quite lovely.

Any new development that might have a bearing on trade was worth investigating, and in London for the occasion were not only Walker and his wife but also his chief technician Paul Robello, a trainee of the great Aberdeen photographer George Washington Wilson, and a member of the Walker team since 1892. What the three saw was not easy on the eye, but even in that crude, unsteady form it was interesting. What really swayed Walker, as a Company Sergeant Major in Aberdeen Artillery Volunteers, was a short film of the Royal Field Artillery at practice. Immediate inquiries brought only the information that Lumière's machines were subject to a year's waiting list. An approach to Robert Paul was no more fruitful, but it so happened that a firm

1   William Walker (*BA* 29 Dec. 1904)

called Wrench & Sons was in process of making its first projector. Walker eagerly bought the machine, which, together with a cinematograph camera and some films, arrived in Aberdeen on Wednesday, 30 September 1896.

Along with Paul Robello, one of the earliest of Walker's associates was another pioneer in Aberdeen cinema circles—Alexander (Joe) Gray. Born in Longside, Joe Gray spent his younger days in the usual educational round, but preparatory to leaving school at the age of 14 he began evening classes with the local Episcopal minister Dean McKay. McKay encouraged Joe to take an interest in the magic lantern after the boy had found a piece of broken slide left behind at a Walker visit. Fascinated, the young lad went to every lantern show that he could in order to learn more. His lucky break came in April 1895 when, seeking employment, he answered an advertisement for an apprentice to a bookseller in town. That bookseller was William Walker, a fellow native of Longside where his grandfather was kirk bellman; Joe and his father made the trip to Bridge Street, and the job was secured at the handsome salary of five shillings per week. Although his lodgings cost him half that again, it was a beginning!

Joe lost no time in learning the secrets of the lantern from his new employer, and within only a couple of months he achieved proficiency. His first solo engagement was an evening performance at Portlethen Kirk. A little nervous, he arrived at the church during the day and set up his equipment. The lantern was powered not by gas but by a large paraffin burner that required warming up in advance for it to work cleanly and efficiently—a procedure which entailed the lighting of small paraffin wicks under the main one. Having carried out this duty Joe adjourned to the manse for a welcome cup of tea with the minister, Dr Grant. Returning to the church, Joe was met by the sight of smoke pouring from the building. Convinced that he must have set the place on fire, the horrified young lanternist rushed inside to discover to his intense relief that the smoke came only from his heater wicks, which he had set too high! This alarming incident always remained in his memory as his 'baptism of fire'. No doubt he was also faced with quite some cleaning before that particular show could go on!

William Walker's unpacking of his cinematograph gear that September day is an important enough event in our story, but in the broader history of Aberdeen the date stands out for another reason. At about ten minutes past eight that night a performance at the Palace Theatre was in full swing. With the manager Ernest Sheldon away in Dundee, the theatre's affairs were being looked after by the stage manager Harry Russell, who was just then on stage with his staff preparing for the next act, a sketch called 'The Barmaid' by lady and gentleman duettists and dancers Spry and Monti. Its bar-room background was just being moved into place when somehow one of the wood and canvas upper borders of the heavy piece of scenery brushed a gas light in the flies above the stage and started to burn. Almost immediately the flames spread to the surrounding woodwork; assistant stage manager James Macaulay went up to try to extinguish them but had to beat a hasty retreat.

The Palace building had been erected in 1887 for John Henry Cooke (proprietor of several very popular indoor Circuses) as an improvement on his original crude wooden premises on the reclaimed ground at the foot of Market Street. After Cooke's day it passed to trustees and was leased out first to a concern which ran it as 'The Jollity', then to Livermore Brothers under whom it became 'The People's Palace'. Within only a few more days Livermore's were to have purchased it outright in order to build in its place an up-to-date music hall, and with good reason. Into the structure had gone a large quantity of old materials and fittings, flimsy and inflammable, and it would be no exaggeration to call the place jerry-built. The ceiling of the auditorium consisted of nothing more than packsheet stretched over a light frame, covered with paper and painted. Originally it had extended to the back of the stage, but so that scenery could be hung from the rafters above, the overstage area had been opened up, forming a natural funnel into the roof wherein lay not only plenty of dust to conduct fire but also the network of lead gas pipes that supplied all parts of the house.

So it was that Harry Russell found himself having to call upon every ounce of simulated calm as he alerted the performers in the dressing rooms and then attempted to clear the hall in an orderly fashion while behind him the stage area went up like a torch. The safety curtain was not down, and it could not be lowered in time. Fire precautions were non-existent, and there were no emergency exits.

Some members of the audience had already realised what was happening and were on their way out of the building. When the alarm was raised the hall began to empty without too much panic, but almost immediately afterwards flames burst through the curtains and swept along the insubstantial ceiling at incredible speed. It was then a question of survival of the fittest as those of the audience that were left fled for the exits on Bridge Place, fire literally at their heels. The theatre did, of course, have back doors—locked, as Spry and Monti discovered on trying to escape via a passageway under the side galleries. Fortunately the two managed to scramble out through a fanlight. Many of the audience were injured in doors and stairways, some fell and were trampled on, and some at the back of the crush suffered severe burns from falling debris, but miraculously the majority escaped unharmed.

The performers were safe, although some had had a close call. They had lost all of their precious music and all of their personal possessions bar the stage costumes in which they stood. The pit musicians, who escaped unscathed, were more fortunate in being able to save the instruments on which their livelihoods depended. Shocked and confused, they and the stage party were taken in at the nearby Royal Hotel. Harry Russell, who had initially attempted to fight the fire, was on the injured list, while a deeply shocked Ernest Sheldon, arriving back in Aberdeen post-haste, suffered an immediate setback to the already indifferent health that he had been away nursing. Never the same again, he had to retire prematurely within a few years.

Firemaster Inkster and his brave volunteer crew, willingly aided by young men of the town and by a group of soldiers that had been in the audience, could only endeavour to save surrounding properties as best they could. In just twenty minutes the Palace was an inferno (someone likened it to a train of gunpowder), burning so fiercely that by 9.30 p.m. the fire had expended itself, consuming everything but the outer walls which, left unsafe, had to be demolished forthwith.

In the ruins, the charred remains were found of three young lads of 13 or 14 who had been overcome by smoke only feet away from safety. Of the thirty injured who had to be taken to hospital some of the worst cases later died, but it was a wonder that the number of casualties was not much higher. The Palace fire was a harsh lesson on the safety of buildings of this type. Fortunately there had been only about 500 in the 2,000-seater auditorium; a full house would have meant catastrophe, and it was resolved by the City Fathers that far more stringent regulations would be imposed in future. Also, the need for a properly trained full-time fire service was brought to public consciousness. As there were no back-up facilities, part of the fire team had at one point been obliged to go to Marischal Street and answer what proved to be a false alarm—a fact that did not go unnoted. The events of that evening did at least serve to mobilise local opinion and to initiate pressure for the formation of the Municipal Fire Brigade that had long been the dream of Mr Inkster.

The Palace's limelight had been fuelled by bottles of acetylene supplied by Walker, and in the furnace heat these, as might be expected, exploded like bombs. Aberdeen in those days was quiet enough for the sound to carry as far as Queen's Cross where Joe Gray and Paul Robello were walking back into town after a lantern show. Robello remarked, 'That sounded like cannon-fire', but Joe, sensing trouble, replied 'Na, na,—that's the cylinders exploding at the Palace!' The two took off at the run for the centre of town and for the blaze, which by then could be seen from all over Aberdeen. Fearing for the safety of the brand-new cinematograph equipment in Walker's Bridge Street basement store, Joe dashed down the shop stairs to find the place serene and intact as one of Aberdeen's most famous—or infamous—fires raged only a matter of yards away.

In the course of reporting over the years, an erroneous impression seems to have formed that Walker was actually on the bill of the Palace with his cinematograph that night. In fact, William Walker's moving pictures were first demonstrated on Friday, 16 October 1896, when a 'trial run' was given for the press in the Music Saloon of Messrs Marr Wood at 183 Union Street. Aberdeen's weekly *Bon-Accord* magazine said that the occasion

> ...barring the small hitches peculiar to tests, was an unqualified success, various comical pictures being depicted

and it seemed that Walker had found a good formula.

Another of Walker's team, Hamish Beveridge, gave lime-light views and an illustrated description of Dr L. Starr Jamieson's dash to start an Uitlander rising in Johannesburg—part of the lead-up to the Boer War. To Joe Gray fell the duty of turning the cinematograph handle while Walker and Robello saw to the lantern and the film respectively. Messrs Burwood Nicholls and Robert Newsam played the piano, and the films were interspersed with songs from Miss Jessie Robertson, Miss Mary Burnett and Mr William Arthur (principal bass in Nicholls' choir at Rubislaw Church and well known locally in oratorio work.)

The first Walker advertisement to mention pictures appeared in the papers two days before the press show, proclaiming:

A Sparkling Entertainment.
The Cinematograph.
Moving Photographs.
Movements on the screen as in real life.
10,000 lantern slides for hire.
Agents for Acetylene Gas Generators,
    the light of the future for country houses.

Exactly when and where Walker gave his first fully public show is not known, but the great interest and excitement sparked off by the Devant visit (for which, incidentally, Walker had supplied acetylene and some lenses) guaranteed a prosperous new line of business. Engagements took him further and further afield until soon his company was touring extensively in Scotland.

As early as 24 November 1896 he gave an ambitious programme in the Music Hall, entitled 'A Night With Charles Dickens'. Devised and recited by an associate, Alfred McLeod, this included 160 'electro-drama' slides, films, songs by Miss Florence Christie from London, Burwood Nicholls at the piano, and violin music from Mr James Cassie, leader of Aberdeen Orchestral Society Orchestra. The event was well remembered by Joe Gray, who recalled a turn-out of over 2,000, and despite the fact that the old Wrench projector could not be placed more than 20 feet away from the screen, limiting the size of the picture to only 12 feet square, there were rave reviews in the press. The lenses and lighting available to Walker at that time were soon improved upon, and a new 'guire jet' lighting unit was fitted, giving about 2,000 candle power.

However rudimentary may have been Walker's first major exposition of the new medium compared to his own standards of a year or two later, it attracted inquiries from all quarters. Ambitiously, he arranged booking facilities with the Lecture Agency at 38 The Outer Temple, Strand, London, and soon 19 Bridge Street was a hive of activity.

To supplement the films that he bought, Walker used his cinematograph camera to capture footage of local scenes and events. His first experiments in newsreel work were by way of commercials for McMillan's large hardware and fancy goods shop at Union Bridge. By means of a Philip's camera positioned on the other side of Union Street, he filmed his family emerging from the shop doorway (try doing that in Union Street now!), and following on the success of this trial he fulfilled a similar commission for Marr Wood's. Very soon local films, referred to from this time onwards as 'topicals', were the most popular part of his programmes. The mainstay among his staff was undoubtedly Paul Robello who was even at that time hailed as indispensable, looking after the technical details while Walker concentrated on the business side of the venture.

Others were far from backward in introducing the great novelty. The old Alhambra Theatre on the corner of Guild Street and Exchange Street, converted long before from Trinity Chapel Of Ease, had in latter years been run by Livermore Brothers as a cheaper companion hall to the Palace, but had closed in the early 1890s. With the burning down of the Palace, however, business was transferred to the much smaller Alhambra, which reopened in October 1896 as temporary—and rather cramped—quarters until a new Palace could be built. A Paul Theatrograph was brought in for the week of Monday, 26 October, rounding off the show with about a dozen short pictures that included Blackfriars Bridge, London, the coloured Serpentine Dance once again, and an opportunity for Aberdonians to see history in the making with a visit to Paris of the Czar of Russia, although for some reason there seems to have been a possibility that the Chief Constable might order the latter subject to be withdrawn! The next month brought a fortnight's visit by Morrit's Lifeograph, showing still more new pictures.

The cinematograph made its appearance at this time as part of theatre programmes throughout the country, but it was not long before the newness wore off and in some halls unwatchable films, badly made or poorly projected, were put on, apparently to chase people out between houses! Moving pictures were also adopted for use in fair-ground side-shows. Farther south, many 'Biographs' toured the countryside in marquees, accompanied by barkers, fair-ground organs, dancers, etc, and such associations did nothing for the cinematograph's chances of acceptance as a legitimate pastime and form of communication. The cinema men of this country and the USA had ahead of them much hard work and investment before the motion picture gained general recognition as anything much more than a diverting toy.

In view of the long shadow cast by the near-calamity at the Palace, it may be no coincidence that Aberdeen saw little if any of the 'Biograph' variety of cinema activity. William Walker went out of his way to foster a responsible, safe, high-class image so that not only was enthusiasm stimulated in a wide section of the public, but Royalty extended its patronage anew—as we shall shortly see. Bright as his prospects looked as the end of 1896 approached, however, it soon became apparent that he was not to have the stage all to himself. In the *Evening Express* of 16 December, beside Walker's advertisements for shows at the Victoria Hall, Ballater and Aboyne Town Hall, and the availability of his pictures for Christmas parties, there appeared the following announcement:

> A new and novel entertainment.
> Cinematographic moving photographs and floral tableaux vivants representations. Largest and finest display of living pictures ever shown in the North of Scotland.
> Robert Calder, lanternist, 93A Queen Street, Aberdeen, is prepared to give exhibitions of above and invites correspondence regarding same.

It must surely have been in anticipation of this impending competition that Walker changed the form of his newspaper advertising the previous week to include the phrase 'Scotland's greatest cinematograph', offering floral tableaux (which he described as 'enchanting transformation scenes'), and stressing his agency for the best Paris, London and American films. New pictures were quoted as being available every week, with 'smart operators, polished lecturers, popular vocalists and musicians', and in that same advertisement Walker made his first claim to Royal patronage. Quite early on, news of his recent achievements had reached Queen Victoria at Balmoral, resulting in a special appearance there. Of this Walker was extremely proud, and from then on he dubbed his company 'Walker's Royal Cinematograph'.

Of Robert Calder little background information comes down to us, but it is known that he was born at Moss-Side Farm, Glassel. After leaving school he trained as a joiner, entering lantern work as a side-line in 1893. Many of his

2   Robert Calder (Cinematograph Exhibition Programme, 1900)

bookings were handled through the agency of Messrs Collie & Taylor, fancy warehousemen, 123 Union Street. Very soon he was established as a top lanternist, so much so, it has been said, that William Walker actually 'farmed out' work to him—a rumour that was always denied by Calder partisans! A highly entertaining man, his puckish sense of humour was seen at an early age when he terrorised Glassel Station with a mechanical snake. The station-master took refuge in his booking office and refused to budge until the 'creature' was removed!

Calder quickly followed the trends by setting up in business as a cine-matographer along much the same lines as Walker, with films, slides, and a concert party to provide musical turns, resting the audience's eyes from the flickering of the screen. While no firm evidence exists as to which of the two showmen was the first to take the motion picture on tour, advertisements seem to suggest that Walker lead by about a fortnight, already travelling Deeside while Calder was still setting up. Calder's activities are not as well documented as Walker's, but it seems certain that while both men were hailed as 'cinematograph kings' their approaches were different enough to make the championing of one or the other very much a matter of taste, Walker's style being considered a little more 'cultural' than Calder's, whose emphasis was more on pure entertainment.

Robert Calder's young daughter Sarah travelled with her father's show, acting as cashier and working the projector for the floral tableaux and Scottish scenery slides that provided continuity while the films were being changed over. She also possessed considerable talent as an elocutionist, and when one day the idea occurred of having her speak lines from behind the screen to heighten the effect of a picture, the germ was born of what was to be an extremely popular part of Aberdeen film presentation in years to come.

Calder was at that time beadle of the old North Church in Queen Street, and the address from which he operated was the beadle's flat attached to the church, but as his cinematograph business grew he gave up that post and moved to No.57 Rose Street, the base for his operations from then on. He also later abandoned his joinery work to concentrate on entertainment, vying for scope of territory and variety of programme with Walker, who he possibly outshone in size of concert party. Calder's excellent range of variety acts included comedian Dufton Scott and the great 'Strathspey King' James Scott Skinner, inspiration of many a Scots fiddler. Violet Davidson, on her way to becoming one of Aberdeen's favourite singers, was frequently on the bill, and other Calder regulars were pianist Jessie Cosgrove and dancer Jeannie Hendry, who in later years was to be one of the city's best known dancing teachers.

On Thursday, 21 January 1897, William Walker and Alfred McLeod consolidated their earlier success with another even more ambitious Music Hall show, 'A Nicht Wi' Burns', which was hailed as the climax of all that had gone before. This time the programme had two cinematograph sections instead of one, and Burns songs and poems were intermingled to great effect with floral tableaux and electro-drama slides. Walker couldn't fail; the picture part of the evening was supported in style by the soloists and by Burwood Nicholls at the piano and the Music Hall Grand Organ, and the show was a sell-out at the customary shilling or so per head. *Bon-Accord*, which was not a paper to mince words, had this to say in its issue for 28 January:

> The most successful cinematographic exhibition yet given in Aberdeen was provided by Messrs Walker & Co., Bridge Street, last Thursday.
>
> It was on the occasion of 'A Nicht Wi' Burns', and a capital programme of songs was contributed by Miss Florence Christie, Miss Jessie S. Robertson, Miss Mary Burnett, Mr Goodlad and Mr Arthur. These singers are well known in the city as capable exponents of our national songs, and on Thursday they ably maintained their reputation. Mr Alfred MacLeod's polished recitations were appreciated, but the same cannot be said of his address. It was an able appreciation of Robert Burns, but a lecture at a concert is out of place. Miss L. Christie and Mr Burwood Nicholls' accompaniments were tastefully played.
>
> The moving photographs were particularly good, and Mr Walker's faith in them has not been misplaced. One never gets tired of them. There are several good new ones. The lovely floral tableaux were as popular as ever. Messrs Marr

Wood's arrangements were, as usual, perfect. Messrs Walker & Co. are to be thanked for providing such a high class entertainment.

Other more traditional entertainments were having to be up-dated and improved to compete with the cinematograph. One of these was Hamilton's Diorama, founded as far back as 1848 by a Dundee family of showmen. Dioramas, in which large vertical rolls with scenes painted on them unwound horizontally to reveal a constantly changing picture (sometimes with additional moving figures), had been very popular during the nineteenth century, and this particular one, which had been a frequent visitor to the Music Hall over a good many years, travelled far and wide as 'Hamilton's Excursions', specialising in scenic views. Now, on arrival in Aberdeen that February, it brought moving pictures in addition to its usual fare. It had a concert party which included the Royal Navy Ladies' Orchestra, and in charge of the tour was William Hamilton, sole survivor among the original founders of the firm. His son Victor was also active in the business, entering the cinema trade in Dundee when, in 1911, the company finally disbanded in the face of competition from the cinema hall.

With everybody seemingly jumping on the cinematograph bandwagon, moving pictures were the talk of the day. Someone calling himself 'Eye Tee' wrote thus in *Bon-Accord* of 25 February 1897:

> Animation!
>
> About twenty years ago, a humorous writer put it on paper that 'the art of printing will never be complete till Professor Edison or someone else invents a means of conveying to readers' ears the peculiar whistle that escapes a husband's lips when he first learns that his wife has had twins.' With the help of type we can read his words, and by the cinematograph we can see the shape of his mouth and the sickly smile on his face.
>
> Animation is in the air; and for an old song the old maid may have an animated picture of a—well, of a gentleman who can while away the tedium that is inseparable from the dignity of an attic!
>
> Even a batchelor is not woman proof, for some roguish Miss may send him a present of a very animated wife to bestir the sluggish action of his indifferent heart. Yes, animation is on the list of 'up-to-dates'. Let it stay.

Walker's big show for March 1897 was a cinematograph and slide lecture entitled 'With Nansen In The Polar Seas'. Captain Brown of the ship *Windward* spoke on the subject of the recent polar exhibition, specially painted slides of polar scenery were shown, and a packed Music Hall was the first to hear this personal account of the far North, its flora and its fauna.

That April, Paul's Theatrograph was still in evidence at the Alhambra, while on the Inches at the foot of Market Street was H. McIndoe's touring X.L.C.R. Variety Pavilion in which Renny's Marvellous Cinematograph, advertised as the only machine of its kind, gave 'The Railway Scene', 'The Lover's Quarrel', 'Leap Frog' and 'The Great Steamboat Scene', all in quick succession and concluding (to quote its billing in the *Aberdeen Free Press* of 29 April) with a 'laughable farce'. Operator was a Mr Fred Gray, and in charge was a Mr George Devant (whether or not he was related to the Devant that we have already met is not clear). Admission was 1s. for the front seats and 3d. for the gallery, with the remainder at 6d.—the nearer to the screen the better in those days!

Queen Victoria's Jubilee in June 1897 was the occasion of many a special event, often with cinematograph show. For example, a Trade, Industrial and Art Exhibition in the Music Hall sported films, music from the Red Hussar Band of Ladies, acrobatics from 'The Flying Lady', and yet another new attraction, the 'wonder of wonders', X-Rays. Walker, who was doing a roaring trade in Jubilee photographs and stationery, journeyed to Deeside to make two films of the Queen's Guard of Honour at Ballater, her departure for Balmoral, and the Artillery on inspection with the band, showing the big guns and prominent men in the battalion. By this time his rather imperfect Wrench machine had given place to a Paul Theatrograph, and Paul Robello and a joiner had organised a removable projection box to fit against the back wall of the Music Hall at floor level, keeping machine and operator out of sight and earshot.

So brisk was business that by August he was able to give only a few vacant dates for the following month, and already it was necessary to book early for shows over the winter. *Bon-Accord* noted how captivated a Stonehaven audience was by a Walker show on 19 August, and how younger lads took the opportunity, with the lights down low and with their elders gaping at the marvellous moving figures on the screen, to 'do a bit of spooning with their best girls'!

On 16 September, after a very successful visit to Dundee, Walker's Jubilee films constituted an early opener for the Aberdeen winter season. The stage turns included Mr and Mrs Dickson Moffat (singers and elocutionists who soon became Walker regulars) and although the quality of the acts seems to have been considered somewhat patchy this time, no-one really minded. It was Walker's own 'topicals' that made even standing room scarce in the Music Hall and drew great cheers from the crowd when well-known local figures appeared on the screen. So many people had to be turned away from the doors that a special repeat performance was held the following Thursday, with a new concert programme and what appears to have been the first-ever children's matinee. *Bon-Accord* of that same day reported:

Some ill-grained 'letter-to-the-editor' writer has been finding fault with Messrs Walker and Company for over-crowding the Music Hall last Saturday. Messrs Walker and Company have promptly answered the aggrieved party by offering back the money of disappointed ones, or giving tickets for a repetition of the cinematograph exhibition and concert tonight. The pictures are wonderfully fine, the company select, and we have no doubt that Messrs Walkers' efforts to amuse will be eminently successful.

With films taken locally and in London, not only was Walker's Jubilee show his performance of the year, but it was also the first recorded instance of a programme being taken on an extended tour, calling at Dingwall, Dundee, Huntly, Elgin, Nairn, Inverness, Keith, Fraserburgh, Peterhead and Arbroath, plus the Aberdeen repeat. For a special performance at the Music Hall on 2 October in aid of Powis Clock Fund, he managed to lure Scott Skinner away from Calder. Also on the bill was an elocutionist named William Dove Paterson, who had been making a good name for himself on the stage of the Alhambra and at performances in connection with the Temperance Movement; we will encounter him again.

On 21 October 1897, as Walkers went their triumphant way to Ballater, Braemar and their third Balmoral visit, another newcomer to the cinematograph fraternity received his first mention in the press. Mr J. Lizars of the well-known photographic and optical firm, then situated near to Walker in Bridge Street, was to be showing films at a special demonstration of the Edison Phonograph two days later, given by the machine's local licensed dealer, Mr J. Leith. J. Scott Skinner was in the concert party, there was a 'splendid orchestra', and on the Phonograph were played brass band music and speeches and songs by the greatest orators and singers of the day. Films included the London Jubilee Procession, the Greco-Turkish war (or at least enactments of it), comic scenes, and local views taken specially by Lizars. Lanternist was a Mr Hunter.

Although not even the introduction in December of 'new pictures, life size' could quite bring Lizars' Cinematograph to the high standard of Walker's or Calder's, it still proved popular enough to do the rounds of gatherings and functions of all kinds, at the fee of 25 shillings upwards per show. This may well have continued right into the permanent cinema era, and in later years when portable projectors and safety film became available the company returned to its old role of purveyor of private film shows. Lizars also became actively connected with cinematography through a film processing agency run from his shop in Shandwick Place, Edinburgh.

No doubt encouraged by the above publicity, the popularity of the Phonograph grew rapidly, and by December Walker was using one in his travelling show. His moving pictures continued to delight and bamboozle country audiences; *Bon-Accord* of 23 December 1897 reported on an evening in Turriff when:

> Walker and Company's cinematograph and phonograph fairly startled the eyes and ears of a 'hall-thronged' audience..... 'Man, that's grand!', 'Splendid, min!', 'Lorie, leuk, Jinny! Sic a funny ane's that is. Feth, 'oman, that's up to the point o' perfection!'

Bon-Accord (6 January, 1898) also eavesdropped on a visit by Walker's 'sinny-mattygraf' to New Deer and the showing of a film of the Gordon Highlanders on parade. During this:

...an old man from the outlying farming districts was gazing at the long array of soldiers issuing from the barracks with open eyes. When the pictures came to an end he drew a long breath, turned to his nearest neighbour and exclaimed 'Man, Jock, but it maun hae ta'en a heap o' siller to fess a' thae sodgers fae Aiberdeen to here. I canna see through't ava', min!'.

Typical of Walker's town shows was one in November 1897, when his company was the principal attraction of the choir concert at the church of St George In The West (now long closed). Interspersing the solos and partsongs of the choir were his latest films and an illustrated lecture by Hamish Beveridge on the Nansen Expedition.

Worthy of note was a film that he made of that year's Braemar Gathering. Not only did this enjoy great public popularity, but it also occasioned further Royal interest. According to Joe Gray, Walker gave a total of eleven performances for Queen Victoria over the last years of her reign, and was subsequently invited to give cinematograph shows for King Edward VII and Queen Alexandra.

The end of the first full year of motion pictures in Aberdeen brought to all of the city's cinematographers their first taste of a really busy Christmas season. Not only were Walker's lantern teams working to capacity as usual, but his cinematograph was working to its tightest schedule yet, with a performance at Skene House on 27 December, one the next day for Sir William Cunliffe Brooks of Glen Tanar, plus another that evening in nearby Aboyne, then on 29 December a show for Sir Allan MacKenzie. On 30 December it was in the precincts of Balmoral Castle, on 31 December at Altries, Maryculter, then on to Perth for New Year's Day 1898 and two shows under the auspices of the Lord Provost and Magistrates. Back in Aberdeen that same day, there was an evening performance at the Cafe Hall, as St Katherine's Hall in the Shiprow was then known. It had been a hectic twelve months, and there was much more to come.

William Walker's first brain-child for 1898 was a Burns and Byron concert in the Music Hall on 20 January, with a concert party that included The Moffats, Florence Christie (just back from a tour of South Africa) and violinist James Cassie (soon to travel to Germany for study). The first half of the evening consisted of Burns songs and recitations illustrated by lantern slides, while the second half was devoted to Byron. Naturally, there were films, and as usual Burwood Nicholls was at the piano and organ. All this came on the crest of a vogue for the above two authors, of whose works a good choice would certainly have been available at 19 Bridge Street. Burns themes were always a sure winner, and Walker repeated them constantly on his journeys, with modifications here and there as required. Audiences never seemed to tire of Rabbie's poems, songs and writings, enlivened by the presenter's virtuosity with slide and dissolving view.

Calder's work was surrounded by less publicity than Walker's, but it was in just as wide demand—he is recorded as having given a particularly successful performance in Saltcoats, Ayrshire, that March. Like Walker, he made his own 'topicals', and from quite early on his picture shows were enhanced by an important new technical refinement—electric arc lighting powered by a small portable generator, an advance on the cumbrous and rather unpleasant acetylene limelight still employed by his rivals. On 2 May 1898, Calder, in conjunction with Dove Paterson, presented the first of Aberdeen's tremendously popular Cinematograph Carnivals which, under one local exhibitor or another, filled the Music Hall every public holiday week-end until the coming of the permanent picture house.

Monday, 11 May brought a week's visit to the Music Hall by the Gloucester-based Charles W. Poole's 'Royal Myriorama'. This was another diorama-type scenic exhibition, of which, in the book 'Picture Pioneers' by G.J. Mellor, an eye-witness account states that an 'immense vertical scroll, lighted from the front or back, or both, slowly unwound to show fresh delights', with the showman pointing out features of interest. Poole's 'Eventograph Or Improved Cinematograph' was the latest addition to this 'Amazing Amusement Aggregation', the 60-year pedigree of which was a matter of great pride. The films were of the Gordons at Dargai, the inevitable Jubilee celebrations, the American-Spanish war, Bombardment of Manilla, Nansen's latest journey, and the Klondike, while the Myriorama was a special edition showing events and places of note during the Jubilee. In addition, there were performing dogs, negro comedians, dancers, gymnasts, singers and all sorts of other variety turns.

Walker's 'topicals' were the main attraction of that year's September Holiday Carnival, at which was shown film of an annual event known as 'MacGregor's Gathering', in which a certain Captain MacGregor took an official party from Aberdeen on a visit to one place or another in his ship the *Caledonian*. This year the trip was to the Clyde, and various city notables were faithfully recorded on celluloid. Audiences also saw the Scots Greys, Cavalry sports, Hospital Saturday, Fife and Forfar Light Horse, the Cameron Highlanders at the charge, Great North of Scotland Railway scenes, and Aberdeen's Volunteers. There were yet more new pictures at a repeat of the Carnival show later that month, including scenes at the Beach Bathing Station, police sports, a tug-of-war, and Glasgow v. Aberdeen—apparently the first football match to be filmed in the city. There was a concert party, and the pipes and drums of the Gordon Highlanders were on hand to play stirring accompaniments to the military films that were Walker's speciality.

The mention, in *Bon-Accord*, of the pipe band's contribution is the earliest reference yet found to the playing of music during the public showing of a film in Aberdeen. This suggests (although proof is lacking) that Walker, and perhaps Calder as well, may previously have followed the pattern of the 1896 Devant show, in which no music at all was played during pictures. In any case, the introduction of the pipes and drums was more than just a piece of good showmanship on Walker's part; it was an important advance in picture presentation, and the idea was immediately copied by his competitors. Not that music was the main concern to those who flocked to cinematograph shows in 1898—the real attraction was the chance of spotting a friend, someone well known, or even oneself in the 'topicals', a fact not lost on Walker who added at the foot of his advertisements that year the line 'Have You Been Cinematographed?'

3   George W. Walker, *c.*1920

On Saturday, 17 September 1898, the Music Hall was the venue for the public debut of yet another new arrival on the picture scene. Namesake of William Walker but in no way related to him, George W. Walker had been a member of Calder's concert party virtually from the beginning, and his fine baritone voice and handsome appearance (often in Highland dress) made him quite a favourite in the city, especially among the ladies. As of February 1897 he had worked in partnership with Calder, for whom he had supervised an additional touring company, and for a while the two had traded as 'Calder, Walker & Company', causing William Walker enough anxiety to place a whole series of notices and announcements in the press denying any involvement in the concern. Typical among these notices was one prominently displayed in the *Evening Express* over an entire week that February:

A Warning to the public.
Walker and Company, 19 Bridge Street, and the cinematograph.
Notice is hereby given that we have no connection with any other cinematograph exhibition and we warn the public against all misleading advertisements and announcements which may be an attempt to make the public believe that we have amalgamated with any other exhibition.
The only address of our firm for cinematograph exhibitions is 19 Bridge Street, Aberdeen.

By 1898 George W. Walker was out on his own with his 'Favourite Cinematograph', his own local films, illustrated songs, dissolving views from all over the world, and a large concert party consisting of Mr Leo Rippin (cornettist), Mary Burnett, Mr Tom Milner (comedian from Glasgow), Miss Jennie Thomson (leader of Aberdeen Mandoline Band), Mr James Fleming, bass (from Paisley), the Pirie Family (dancers), Miss Mary Gellatly, 'the piper's lass' from Dundee (skirt dancer), and her brother David, champion step dancer of Scotland.

The pictures that he showed on that first night included footage of the disastrous launch of the *HMS Albion* which left hundreds struggling in the water, the unloading of a trawler at Aberdeen Fish Market, the Co-op sports, a cricket match (Caledonia v. Stonehaven), the fishing fleet leaving Aberdeen, 'Grand Sensational Bull Fight', a 'Splendid Military Obstacle Race', and many others. Aberdeen Mandoline Band played under the direction of its conductor G. Glen Turriff, and at the organ and piano was Mr J.R. Brooke. Chief operator was George Walker himself. For 2s., 1s. or 6d., patrons could see a show which if perhaps not remarkable was certainly highly competent; its enthusiastic reception signalled wide travels for a company soon popularly known as the 'Other Walkers'.

For the 1898 Braemar Gathering, William Walker (no word of Calder) was in attendance as usual. Also present was Lizars, whose 'Great Cinematograph' subsequently travelled with what was claimed to be the only complete set of pictures of the Gathering and of the arrival of Queen Victoria. Shown first in the Trades Hall, Belmont Street, on 29 September, with concert party that included Violet Davidson, and supplemented with pipe and drum music, these films gave Lizars a place alongside Walker as purveyor of cinematograph entertainment to the Royal Family, a distinction conferred on 26 October by a special show at Balmoral. Local footage had been taken specially for the occasion, and as part of the entertainment a demonstration was given of the Phonograph's rival, the Gramophone. From then on it was 'Lizars' Royal Cinematograph', taking the Braemar pictures to places great and small throughout the area, doubtless to the intense annoyance of William Walker, who, so proud of his 'Royal' status, vigorously claimed a special showing of his own work at the Music Hall on 1 October to be the only complete account of the event. 'Any other firm advertising this', read his publicity, 'is not in accordance with fact'.

The Highland Association Concert in November was a collaboration between William Walker and Dove Paterson, while Walker's Cinematograph played a large part in the 1st Aberdeen Volunteer Artillery Naval and Military Display that December. (*Bon-Accord* noted a good sprinkling of 'big guns' in the front seats!) By late 1898 or early 1899 Walker had made visits to London, appearing at the Royal Polytechnic and, more prestigiously still, at the Queen's Hall in Langham Place, one of the country's premier concert halls. As of this time Walker had a new accompanist, Mr John Allan, as Burwood Nicholls had to some extent transferred his allegiance to Calder, floating between the two cinematographers from then on!

The sparkling new electrically-lit Palace Theatre rose out of the ashes of the old to open its doors on Monday, 24 October 1898. On the bill (presumably as a closing act) was the Edison-Rodgers 'Electrographe', which would appear to have been subject to certain teething troubles. *Bon-Accord* noted how the films seemed to be shown at too high a speed, spoiling the viewing quality, but technology triumphed in the end—by the following April the Electrographe had become 'The finest and steadiest machine before the public'!

January 1899 brought the now customary Walker celebration of the life of Burns, with demand for seats in the Music Hall far exceeding supply. Another evening with the cinematograph and lantern was promised soon, and this arrived the following month with a programme consisting of new films, pictorial sketches by lantern operator Hamish Beveridge, and a contingent of pipers from the Gordon Highlanders. With a fair proportion of the audience from the Regiment itself, Beveridge's pictorial sketches 'The Sudan Reconquered', 'Khartoum Occupied' and 'Gordon Revenged' were quite the highlight of the evening, and they were much repeated on subsequent tours. In March, Walker continued this very successful theme in his next show, a 'Military Entertainment', which featured the pipes and band of the Gordon Highlanders from Edinburgh Castle—the 'Dargai Heroes' themselves.

With Walker spending a great deal of time out of town throughout 1899, others took on the Holiday Carnivals, Lizars doing the honours in May, and Calder in September. The Lizars show had Scott Skinner, Jessie Cosgrove at the piano, and a sketch called 'The Funnygraph'—an amusing send-up of the Edison Phonograph by Dove Paterson and his son Leo.

Calder's Carnival had in it over fifty films, notably ones of the Prince of Wales in Edinburgh, 'The Fire Dance', 'The Astronomer's Dream', the 6,000-strong Highland Brigade camp at Fochabers (wherein were seen all the Volunteers between Banffshire and Caithness), and a tournament between golfers Vardon and Park—the latter footage said to be unique.

Walker's spring visit to the Music Hall on 27 April 1899, which featured the famous illusionist Herr Ludwig Dobler (a favourite at Balmoral) carried the bonus of a real scoop—an exciting extra-long film of a spectacular fire that destroyed Bisset's Warehouse in Windmill Brae, very close to the Palace Theatre with its memories of that fateful night not so long before. Here was another major blaze that had to be left more or less to burn itself out for lack of proper fire-fighting facilities, but this time enough pressure was brought to bear on the authorities for Aberdeen at last to gain a professional fire-service. For some time after the event, Walker had on sale photographic enlargements made from this film, and crowds gathered just to gaze at the prints prominently displayed in his shop window. One wonders if any copies survive.

In time for two nights of 'Evening Entertainments' at the Music Hall over the first weekend of October, Walker acquired a new 20-foot screen (paltry perhaps by today's standards, but quite an innovation in 1899) and converted his projectors, of which he now had at least two, to electric lighting. His films were of the usual military camps and parades, and of events from the Boer War—a subject with which film makers were starting to busy themselves, producing chiefly propaganda material and mock-up newsreels. Aberdeen Musical Institute's 'Grand Nautical Concert and Cinematograph' in honour of Trafalgar Day featured cinematograph work by Walker, who must certainly have been delighted at the high-class nature of a programme in which an entire opera company sang on the Music Hall stage!

Motion picture entertainment was now firmly established in the Granite City. Despite its rather elementary nature, it could be counted as one of the great success stories of its time, and the scene was set for the hey-day of Aberdeen's early picture showmen.

Chapter 3

Seeds Take Root   1900—1907

The new century was greeted in up-to-date fashion with a New Year Festival in the Music Hall on 1 January 1900. Given under the auspices of Aberdeen Temperance Society, its organiser was Dove Paterson and its bill included the Patersons, Scots fiddler Mackenzie Murdoch, and cinematograph work by Lizars.

With the Boer War the great news subject of the day, Walker booked the Music Hall that March for a special 'theme' show entitled 'The Fight For The Flag In South Africa', presenting all the newest war pictures that he had been able to lay hands on. Even the programme sheet was printed in khaki, with illustrations of British Generals and the two sections of Volunteers then fighting at the front. Younger people were catered for with another special children's matinee. With Walker on his travels again over the latter part of the year, Calder covered the September holiday week-end Carnival, showing films of the Paris Exhibition, the Queen in Ireland and many other subjects on a new 900 square-feet screen which he claimed as the largest yet in Aberdeen. So popular was the show that a repeat performance was held a month later on 20 April.

The day after Calder's September triumph, Walker was in the Music Hall with an even bigger screen—this time of 1,200 square feet and billed as 'the largest picture in existence'! Among his films was another of the Paris Exhibition, a ballet, and shots of the return home of soldiers from South Africa. Lizars was at work enlivening many of the regular Saturday night City Concerts (a series of entertainments founded at the Music Hall four years previously), while the Palace Theatre hosted visits by Hillcoats' Famous Cinematograph and the 'Bio-Tableaux' of Walter Gibbons, a Wolverhampton entrepreneur who dealt in Paul Animatographs.

Thursday, 17 January 1901 brought another winner for Walker—a Grand 'Scotch' Concert with illustrated works of Burns, lots of new pictures, the band of the Aberdeen Volunteers, pipes and drums of the Gordon Highlanders, Dove Paterson, and violinist Patti Hicks. John Allan provided the accompaniments, and so well received was the entertainment that concerts on this theme joined the list of annual fixtures.

Queen Victoria died in January 1901, and when the proclamation of the

4   A Calder Programme Cover, 1900

new King was made at the Castlegate on 26 January, Walker was on the scene with his motion picture camera. The film that he took was shown along with footage of the Queen's funeral at a two-night Grand Exhibition in the hall of the old YMCA building in Union Street, the Music Hall being unavailable. This presentation summarised in picture, song and story the reign of the greatly-loved Victoria, who during the last years of her life had taken such an interest in the infant cinematograph.

The 'Phono' part of Walter Gibbons' Phono-Bio-Tableaux, which arrived at the Music Hall for a ten-day run just after Calder's Spring Holiday concert in May 1901, referred to a brand new invention first shown at the Paris Exhibition that year as the 'Cine-Phono-Matograph'. Roughly synchronising moving pictures with records, to which the performers had been filmed miming, it was popular as a means of showing music hall personalities in action, and Gibbons brought to Aberdeen 'Singing Pictures' of Lil Hawthorne giving 'Kitty Malone', the American Comedy Four singing 'Sally In Our Alley', Alec Hurley in 'The Lambeth Walk', and songs by Vesta Victoria and Vesta Tilley. The rest of the films consisted of the usual scenes in factories and of schools coming out, plus a 'Phantom Ride On An Aberdeen Electric Car', 'Sheffield United v. Tottenham Hotspur', 'Sunderland v. Newcastle United', *Cinderella* Pantomime and 'An Attack On A Chinese Mission Station—Handyman To The Rescue'. These could be seen each afternoon at 3 p.m. and each evening at 8 p.m., at admission prices ranging from 4*d*. to 2*s*. Managing the show was a Mr Fred Nestor, who doubled as singer, and between 12 noon and 1 o'clock each day the phonograph played in the Music Hall vestibule.

Unfortunately the visit took place immediately after a holiday weekend, and of the resulting thin turn-out *Bon-Accord* observed:

> This week festivity reaches the low water mark of its career in Aberdeen—the Holiday is over, the Purse is correspondingly low, the rent has just been paid— or otherwise ...

but added:

> ...(The) Cinematograph does its automatic best to give a faithful rendering of how those MATCHLESS Vestas, if we may use the phrase, Vesta Tilley and Vesta Victoria, would sing 'The Midnight Sun' and 'Our Lodger's Such A Nice Young Man' if they had the good fortune to be in Aberdeen personally.

The Alhambra, given up by Livermores on the opening of the new Palace, had for a while housed MacLeod's Waxwork, but as of 13 May 1901 (the same day as the Walter Gibbons company came to the Music Hall) it became a theatre again under Arthur Hillcoats' Star Company and Cinematograph. Hillcoats gave place a couple of weeks later to Mr Hugh Dempsey's 'Stars Of The Night', most notable among whose films (which were shown on an Edison machine) was a prize boxing match between J. Corbett and Kid McKoy. During the next month the 'American Biograph' was there, operated by G.W. Walker or by some company for whom he was acting as promoter in his growing capacity as concert agent. The Alhambra petered out again at the end of the year, but this was not to be the last of it.

William Walker's success with his 'Scotch' concert was later matched by Calder, who on Saturday 10 August put on a Scottish concert of his own with Jessie N. MacLachlan ('The Scottish Prima Donna'), Patti Hicks and G.W. Walker. The film programme consisted of a new pantomime *Little Red Riding Hood*, made in twelve scenes (films were now becoming longer), local subjects, and an assortment of other items with a Scottish flavour. The evening put a sizeable feather in Calder's cap; *Bon-Accord*, who particularly liked Miss MacLachlan's Scots songs, remarked:

> ...as if a most attractive programme, an array of talent and that hardy annual the cinematograph were not enough to secure a good attendance, the very rain must needs smile on Mr Calder, till a bumper house was the inevitable result. And they were wise in their generation who came, for the concert itself was worth the money. Then there was the cinematograph—but if there is anyone who can say anything new about the cinematograph let him not hide his light under a bushel, for the pages of 'Bon-Accord' are open to him. Personally we confess that we are unequal to the occasion. So just say that Mr Calder has added to the many laurels that already crowd his cinematograph brow.

George W. Walker was not the only Aberdeen entertainer to double as impresario. Dove Paterson also brought stage acts to Aberdeen for the increasing number of concerts with which he was connected. Ambitiously, he took the Music Hall for a whole week that September, presenting 'Madame Lloyd's Grand Musical And Scenic Company', a variety show in which all kinds of musical acts, dances and tableaux vivants were performed by a company consisting mainly of attractive young ladies. The balance of the programme consisted of Diorama trips and 'The King Of Cinematographs'. On the Sunday the company gave a sacred concert in the Trades Hall, but whether the cinematograph was used there is not recorded. If it was, then this must have been Aberdeen's first sight of it at a public religious event outwith a church.

The cinematograph was by this time a fairly regular part of the City Concerts. One of these in November 1901, evidently a somewhat highbrow affair, was wittily commented upon by *Bon-Accord*:

> A mixture of Tannhäuser and the Cinematograph is just the sort of thing to suit the palate of a Music Hall audience. They are highly educated, you can see that by the look of blasé composure with which Wagner's amazing music is received, but at the same time you must understand that a little innocent frivolity is not beneath their attention. Hence the rapture with which Mr David Thomson [Well known Aberdeen comedian, later of the Beach Pavilion] is greeted. Mr Thomson tells of the troubles of a certain McCallum who objected to being called Callum. Mr Thomson says he could write a column about McCallum. We deeply sympathise with Mr Thomson. We sometimes write columns ourselves. They never pass the editor unscathed. This is the mutilated remains of one of the finest criticisms (ahem!) dictated to our secretary.
>
> Miss Davidson [Violet Davidson, who was now married to David Thomson] sang the usual thing about the sailor boy on a raft right out in the middle of the

big damp ocean. The sailor boy came out all right. Miss Davidson sings excellently well, as we all know. She smiled in our direction once...

The Cinematograph Exhibition was quite of the manner of its kind, highly amusing to the less cultured portion of the audience. We enjoyed it immensely.

Between 28 December 1901 and 4 January 1902, William Walker was busy with his first New Year Holiday Carnival, this time in the Union Hall, Skene Terrace—the first recorded use for cinematographic purposes of what was later to become the Cinema House. On the programme was Scott Skinner and a conjurer named Harry Marvello, who was at this time often appearing in Walker shows.

Hamilton's Excursions' visit to the Music Hall in January 1902 was accompanied by their 'Eragraph' (it seems to have been called something different each time!), but the old Diorama show still retained a great deal of popularity '...despite', as *Bon-Accord* put it, 'the advent of the various things that end in 'graph'. The 'Edison Animated Pictures' from the Operetta House, Edinburgh, visited the old Her Majesty's Theatre, Guild Street the following month, bringing films of 'An Inspection Of The Scottish Horse', Scotland v. Ireland in a League National, a pantomime *Bluebeard*, a stag hunt, *Winter Sports On The Engadine*, and local views. Among the supporting acts was the rather precarious-sounding Jones-Hilliard Patent Stage Cycle Track!

The major historical event of 1902 was King Edward's accession to the throne, in connection with which Calder's May holiday concert was a special Coronation edition, organised in association with Dove Paterson and pre-saging the big Coronation Exhibitions that were to follow. These began on Thursday, 4 August with Walker's Special Coronation Exhibition, showing films of the great State processions, scenes in Westminster Abbey, and the decorations and celebrations in London and Aberdeen. Other items included Indian and Colonial troops being reviewed, a group of Fijians visiting Aberdeen, a Maori war dance, a Grand Naval Review, the Duke of Cambridge's unveiling of the Gordon Statue in Aberdeen, the return of the Highlanders after the end of the Boer War, and *Home Sweet Home*, sub-titled the 'old mother's reception'! Finally came scenes of the eruption of Mount Pélée, with the organist, Mr Allan, using the Music Hall instrument to produce appropriately mighty sounds.

A month later a rival Calder show, not greatly different from the Walker one, also attracted a full Music Hall. Competition among Aberdeen's cine-matographers had always been intense, but on Saturday, 6 September 1902 it reached a new level when G.W. Walker set up a season of Saturday night 'Trades Concerts' at the Trades Hall in direct opposition to the Music Hall's regular City Concerts. He also gave his own September Holiday show with the Anglo-American Bioscope, himself as singer, and tricks by well-known ventriloquist 'Professor' James Montague and his Merry Family.

Having spent the summer down south looking for talent for his thriving concert agency, G.W. Walker had already been commissioned to supply artists for promoters in Dundee, Greenock, Kirkcaldy and other places. He was therefore able to bring to the Trades Concerts an interesting mixture of local and visiting artistes. As with the American Biograph before it, the identity of the Anglo-American Bioscope is obscure—either Walker was trading under different names at different times, or this was one of his outside bookings.

The primary function of the Concerts was to raise money to meet costs still outstanding on the Trades Hall premises, the construction of which in 1896 was a unique venture for the labour movement. The building provided much-needed accommodation for meetings, social events and lectures, and although it was hardly a structure of beauty (*Bon-Accord* called its arrival 'the permanent disfigurement of one of the finest building sites in the city'), it did have in its main hall some fine ceiling paintings by Douglas Strachan, creator also of the now largely vanished murals in the Music Hall and better known for his superb later work in stained glass. The project was a courageous one, but unfortunately the Trades Hall's financial affairs seem always to have been a trifle precarious, and this will have important bearings on our story.

William Walker's Holiday Carnival on Hogmanay Night of 1902-3 offered something quite new—a special midnight recital for those who wished to stay on after the main show and welcome in the New Year. Over 1903 the rather military atmosphere of Walker's previous shows gave place to a royal theme that started in March with 'Round The British Empire', the programme notes of which contained a coloured map of the travelogue route and interesting descriptions of all the places visited. In May the theme continued with a 'Royal Cinematic Exhibition' of films depicting the King and Queen in Glasgow and Edinburgh (filmed by Paul Robello) and the King in Paris. One of Walker's greater honours at time was an engagement at the Royal Court Theatre, London, on Friday, 26 August 1903, to show films taken that very same day at the annual Kew Dog Show. Undertaken at the behest of the Dog Show's chairman and organiser the Countess of Aberdeen, and given as a special benefit for the Ladies Kennel Association, this novelty added greatly to Walker's fame and distinction.

Walker's 'topical' filming continued with such items as the annual Braemar Gathering and a society garden party at Devanha House. One great cinematic 'capture' was the felling that September of a 175-feet chimney stalk at the defunct Torry premises of the Seaton Brick & Tile Company. The toppling of the chimney provided capital entertainment, with more than a few members of the audience quite plainly making ready to dodge flying bricks as the structure hit the ground in a cloud of dust!

Improvement of film projection using the 'only example in existence' of 'Walker & Co.'s Flickerless, Steadfast Machine', and the giving to date of no less than eight Royal performances and four public ones in London, were the main points of a sudden burst of trumpet-blowing in the press that November. This, it seems, was occasioned by the continuing activities of 'the other Walkers', who were obviously something of an embarrassment. 'Our Mr Walker', it was felt necessary to point out in *Bon-Accord* of 26 November, 'is not connected with any other cinematograph. Warning is given against colourable announcements.'

Robert Calder took a trip to the Queen's Hall, London in 1903, showing all his newest and finest films to an audience that included the Prince of Wales, the Duke of Argyll, Lord Strathcona and other distinguished personages. In August, Aberdonians were given the opportunity of seeing a repeat of this programme, which, Calder claimed, 'actually brought Canada to Scotland'. Among its many subjects were President Loubet of Canada, the King and Queen in Scotland, in Ireland and at the London Show, Irish Motor Car Week, a recent major fire in London, demolition of a chimney (which chimney is not made clear, but the film seems to have predated Walker's), tobogganing, sheep shearing, Niagara Falls, and elephants stacking timber ('Wonderful Sagacity'). Finally there were local pictures by Calder himself and a new pantomime production *Sleeping Beauty*, which ran to twenty scenes and cost all of £50 to buy. At an average price of 6*d*. per foot, this makes it a very long film for the time, although perhaps being 'gorgeously coloured' made it more expensive. As usual, the films were supplemented by a large concert party, and due no doubt to demand for seats that night, another major performance followed in November.

Visiting cinematographs centred mainly on the Trades Hall concert season, which lasted until April. Perhaps most notable among these visitors was the travelling team of Dundee exhibitor Charles Feathers, while rather more obscure is Calverto's Royal Cinematograph (yet another 'Royal' one—poor old Walker).

At the beginning of 1904 the Palace Theatre was billing Raymond's Vivagraph, followed as of 1 February by its own 'Palace Cinematograph', more commonly described from August onwards as the 'Palace Bioscope'. Here we encounter something of a puzzle, as over the next three winters or so there was apparently in residence a second cinematograph team, called Vernon's Imperial Bioscope. It existed as a separate company and carried out off-season specialist work such as pantomime film shows for the amazing Dr Walford Bodie, but exactly how it inter-related with the Palace's own team, and just who was showing the Palace's films at any one time during the period 1904-1908 remains a matter of some confusion.

The Burns Anniversary of 1904 was celebrated by Walker in his usual way, although this time G.W. Walker was hot on his heels with a rival performance at the Trades Hall, featuring Feathers' Cinematograph. Hamilton's Excursions, which arrived on their annual visit that February, were a special edition centring around the Russo-Japanese war, and in the wake of the interest generated William Walker's Music Hall concert the following month took the theme of 'Japan And The Japanese'. Planned as a scenic tour through Japan and the Far East, its mood was reinforced with 'Japanese' songs sung by the costumed Misses Hendry and McAdam, and the films dealt with the current war situation. Every aspect of the show followed the theme, right down to the design of the programme sheets, and the subject recurred in most of Walker's performances in the course of the year. For his May

Holiday Carnival he had more war scenes, Jeannie Hendry in a Butterfly Dance, and more 'scenic effects'; the whole show went on tour around Inverurie, Fraserburgh and Peterhead.

Calder showed similar films and scenes at a big Music Hall performance in August, and (a measure of the vigour with which the cinematograph's two main protagonists rivalled each other) opened a show called 'The Wild West' in the YMCA Hall, right next door to Walker's September Carnival and on the same day!

Burwood Nicholls, one of Aberdeen's most distinguished and popular musical figures, was given a 'complimentary concert' in the Music Hall in October 1904. A large orchestra and choir was conducted by Mr James Wood, and leader of the orchestra was Mr J.M. Riach, who was to become prominent in the cinema orchestras of later times. Organists included G.C. Dawson of St Machar's Cathedral, and among the accompanists was A.O. Henry, who had played for both sets of Walkers and had been in charge of the music for the Trades Hall concerts. Calder's Cinematograph turned out to participate in this event, given in honour of a man who contributed much to the early picture show in Aberdeen.

5   Burwood Nicholls (*BA* 13 Oct. 1904)

The New Century Company's 10,000 Animated Pictures spent a week at the Music Hall in November, following a successful engagement in Liverpool. Burwood Nicholls was in charge of the music, and there was a contribution from the local Engineers' Band under Mr William Stavert. The most important films on the programme were of Russo-Japanese war scenes and the Hull Fishing Fleet disaster of that year, mostly shown in logical succession rather than the more usual flitting from one subject to another. This was something that *Bon-Accord* particularly liked—praise indeed! The New Century company was based in Bradford, and its proprietors were theatre manager Sydney Carter, Birmingham showman Walter Jeffs and, as backer and financial controller, Bradford fish merchant F.D. Sutherland. This kind of arrangement was becoming increasingly common as investment was directed towards picture entertainments, and businessmen came to play an ever more important role in them.

By this time the Co-operative movement could provide a cinematograph show in addition to its famous range of wares and services that covered everything from shoes to funerals; among the Trades Hall concert engagements of late 1904 was a visit by the Scottish Co-operative Wholesale Society Royal (weren't they all?) Bioscope.

Walker's Burns Concert for 1905 was a bumper affair, this time featuring (among many others) Dufton Scott and special guest Mr Ross Campbell 'late Professor of elocution at St Andrew's University' (a likely story!) This programme, like its predecessors, was taken on tour, calling at Fraserburgh, Maud, Ellon, then south to Kirkcaldy. Though the work was hard, there was a great deal of fun and adventure to be had on a trip of this kind, and not everyone would welcome the advent of the picture hall—not far around the corner as 1906 dawned.

The first cinematographic event of 1906 was a visit to the Union Hall, Skene Terrace, between 1 and 3 January, of the Anglo-Scots Cinematograph Company from London. This was the year of the great San Francisco earthquake, filmed by plucky cinematographers as buildings around them crumbled and burned. Even now these early documents are quite spectacular to watch, and it would be nice to think that they were the actual pictures shown by William Walker on Saturday, 1 September 1906 at one of his special concerts. Unfortunately, the 'harrowing scenes' which came as the show's main attraction are clearly stated in the advertisements as having been taken before and after the earthquake—no mention of during it! To lend extra excitement, however, action footage was shown of Mount Vesuvius in eruption.

The opening of the new Marischal College that same month was the occasion of a Royal visit, and Walker, Joe Gray and Paul Robello arranged to be on the spot with their cameras to cover the event. Joe Gray was detailed to take up a vantage point at Holburn Street Station to catch the Royal Party disembarking from the Deeside train. The camera was discreetly hidden behind a tree, and to Joe's assistant George Emslie went the glamorous job of holding back the branches. After that, the two went by cab along Holburn Street and Nellfield Place, through Claremont Street and into Albyn Place, where special permission had been given to cut a hole in the wire crowd barriers so that filming could proceed unobstructed. Next, they made a quick journey on horseback through the back streets to the Wallace Statue—where their well-planned schedule struck a hitch. A table had been set up to raise the camera above the heads of the crowd, and on this table a group of pensioners had comfortably ensconced themselves. Much argument and negotiation was necessary before they would move over and the camera could be set up just in time to finish the work. But the end product was well worth all the trouble; it was given an immediate Royal showing and was Walker's pride and joy for many months.

In the summer of 1906, a young animal trainer named John Sinclair set up a small zoo at the beach. Proving popular, it was enlarged and made permanent for the summer season of 1907. Next, Sinclair made his operation an all-year-round one by taking a three year lease on the then untenanted Alhambra, which he reopened on Monday, 14 October 1907 as the WINTER ZOO.

A new main entrance was made through the former Guild Street shop of George S. Mackay. Inside, the gallery that extended round the south and east sides was made into a promenade with side-shows, novelty machines and stalls, one of which was shortly to be occupied by a tattooist! An Imhof & Mukle Orchestrion (a small automatic organ brought all the way from Hamburg) tooted out the latest tunes from punched patterns on a paper roll, while round the walls at floor level were animal cages, one containing a fine lion and lioness, Chaka and Sheba.

At the west end of the building was the small stage, built into an extension which jutted out into Exchange Street behind it. Over the proscenium was painted a huge mural of an Eastern procession with elephants, lions, camels, tigers, bears, snake-charmers and dancing girls, and round the gallery was a series of allegorical murals four feet in depth and totalling 70 feet in length, the work of Mr Charles of decorative artists Crawford & Charles. All these wonders were open to the public between the hours of 10 a.m. and 10 p.m. at an admission charge of 3d. (later 4d.), reduced to 2d. for juveniles. There was another attraction—regular quarter-hour shows by the Electro-Graphic Cinematograph of Dove Paterson.

For years Paterson had been an enthusiastic champion of motion pictures as a feature of the concerts in which he was involved, and at last in 1905 he became a cinematographer in his own right, displaying great skill in the medium. His contribution to the Zoo's entertainments was a major factor in ensuring that the Alhambra, in its latest incarnation, was continually packed to the doors, with hundreds turned away on Saturday nights. As a result his initial booking for just a fortnight was extended to a month, and soon a still

6   Dove Paterson, 1890s

longer-term arrangement was entered into with Sinclair and his assistant Jim Richardson, from Barbados.

Apart from being credited with a period as a high-class 'barker' at 'Raggie' Morrison's Economic Stores in St Nicholas Street, Paterson's earlier history is rather obscure. A native of Newburgh, he is shown in the pages of the Aberdeen Directory as having been active in the city as early as 1882, teaching elocution in a studio at No. 1 Black's Buildings (a rather grim pile by Schoolhill, demolished in the 1950's), while his dwelling house was at No. 26 Catherine Street. Apparently something of a bird of passage, he changed his address the next year to No. 26 Jute Street. By 1885 he was at No. 2 Eden Place, his studio being by then at No. 101 Union Street; in 1886 he was living at No. 7 Cherrybank (now also vanished) where he set up his studio as well. By 1891 he and his studio were at No. 65 Rosemount Viaduct, then the next year his studio was at No. 22 St Nicholas Street while he lived at No. 32 Ashvale Place. In 1893 he was at No. 24 Jamaica Street, but in 1895 or 1896 he settled at Trilby Cottage (which he renamed Crighton Cottage), 38 Erskine Street, centring all operations there by 1901. On the adoption of his new line of work he began to advertise himself as 'Elocutionist and

Cinematographer', providing film shows under the name of 'Aberdeen Cine-matograph Bureau', and entering into the local 'topicals' market.

Some of his history and philosophy are outlined in an article published in the trade paper *Kinematograph and Lantern Weekly* for 2 July 1908 under the title 'How I Handle Pictures—By Dove Paterson, The Northern Picture Specialist'. It reads:

> My living picture life has only just begun in earnest. Until three years ago I was quite unknown in 'Screenland', though since the early eighties I had been before the public in one function or another, more especially the Scottish public, as an elocutionist and concert promoter. In this capacity I toured the United States and Canada in 1892-3 with the Royal Edinburgh Concert Company, and perhaps I then absorbed a little of the hustling propensities of the Yankee—which are very useful in making my picture shows a success at the present time.
>
> At the time when the kinematograph first became a feature on concert pro-grammes, I foresaw its drawing powers and great possibilities, and often wished that I might at some future time adopt what I quickly realised was to many 'the hen that laid the golden eggs'. This hope was destined to be realised in a curious and unexpected way. I had become a camera fiend, contributing snapshots to the local press and taking the 'shooter' with me on many Continental trips. About that time the illustrated lantern lecture was in great demand by the public, and on one eventful engagement at the Scottish National Salon in 1906, held in Dundee, I gave a Pictorial Trip to Belgium, with kinematograph pictures inter-spersed. The innovation was a marked success, and I lost no time in acquiring plant of the very best and latest type. Fortunately, in my own son I had a very skilled electrician and lantern operator, who quickly mastered the bioscope, and as we worked in perfect harmony our entertainment soon became favourably known.
>
> Our first big hit was at the Royal Horticultural Society's Show three years ago. Here I gave my first *al fresco* entertainment for three nights, drawing £357 for the Society. I hope to repeat my success with them on many occasions.
>
> Another notable incident in my living picture life led to my present engagement, which started in October last year and looks like running on indefinitely. The proprietor of the Aberdeen Beach Zoo attracted my attention while amusing himself, when quite a lad, with a baby bear, and I engaged him to give a show at a youngsters' matinee: the booming I gave the 'baby' did us both good. The youthful animal trainer has now developed into a successful Zoo exhibitor, and on acquiring the Alhambra Music Hall last year he very kindly remembered his first engagement and made me an offer for my show as a permanent feature of his, which has turned out to be a most successful venture, and he thanks the Electro-Graphic pictures accordingly.
>
> My success I attribute to the following elements to be found in my pro-gramme:— The high ideal of giving only the best of everything, knowing that only the good lasts; changing subjects every week; providing an intelligent dialogue for every picture I show; demanding and commanding perfect silence and attention from the audience during dramatic stories; and joining with real gusto in the fun and acting in my comics. Every week a pictorial trip is given to some place of interest; the slides rest the eyes between the animated films, and also serve to give my voice a rest. I see that local pictures of the moment are made specialities.
>
> I always welcome my audiences with a special curtain slide, and bid them au

revoir by film. I tolerate no show of white sheet or 'blanking', but keep the screen continually aglow with hand-painted title-slides; in short, I endeavour to keep my audience in Pictureland when once the spell is cast. Should a break occur when running a film my operator flashes the following polite intimation, 'A film slip, please excuse a moment'. 'Ere the audience has time to read the request we are off again, the smart idea is commented on, and the sympathy is never broken. The best possible music by the best possible musicians accompanies all my pictures. Being a methodical man and a strict disciplinarian, I insist on the sobriety of my whole staff. I have been a life-long abstainer, and Lady Nicotine claims none of my affections, and it is simply by adherence to those (some would think minor) details that I have been able to handle the pictures so successfully, and retain the favour and confidence of the public so far.

Paterson's first projector (replaced by a better one in December 1907) already incorporated several safety patents of his own. With it he showed such films as Carl Hagenbeck's famous 'Hamburg Animal Park' and novelties like *The Hen Which Laid The Golden Egg, Bobbie's Birthday, The Fatal Sneeze,* and *Red Sceptre: Or The Devil And The Dancing Cat,* to the music of pianist Miss Lily Wallace. Other examples such as *The Greek Slave: Or The Power Of Love, Accidents Will Happen* (a 'screaming skit' on the new Employers' Liability Act), and *The Fearful Adventures Of Sarah On Her First Cycle Run: Or Needs Must When The Devil Drives* reflected early attempts at working a real plot into narratives and comedies, the duration of which was growing as their subject matter developed.

Leo Paterson replaced the original lanternist and operator Tom Beattie in November 1907, and the father-and-son team thus formed was a first-rate one. In providing pictures with 'intelligent dialogues' Dove Paterson followed the Calder example, improvising (with the assistance of a Mr Simpson) script and sound effects behind the screen. This soon became one of the most talked-of features of the Winter Zoo, and before long Paterson's films had become quite the centrepiece there.

In the summer of 1907 Robert Calder's pictures were frequently to be seen as part of the entertainments at the old wooden Beach Pavilion, precursor of the well-known seaside theatre which flourished between the wars. About September the 'Pavilion Cinematograph' was left in the hands of a Mr Mollison, who continued it until the end of the season. One might assume that Calder had left to continue on his rounds, but with the onset of winter he put aside his engagement book and took a lease on the Northern Friendly Society's 'Northern Hall' at 217 George Street, opening it in December as the EMPIRE MUSIC HALL, with films and varieties.

One deciding factor in this must have been the popularity of the Winter Zoo. Also, Calder's daughter Sarah, main helper out of his family of ten, now had a fiancé, Robert Abercrombie, from whom she was not at all happy to be so frequently parted in the course of the company's annual itinerary. (They were married in March 1908.) To go indoors was therefore an astute move from more than one point of view. The family rallied round, and sons William and (a year or so later) Alexander proved more than proficient as operators, while another daughter, May, became pianist. Her deputies included a Mr Bright and John O. Kynoch, who was a veteran of the Beach Pierrot shows and an experienced accompanist in all kinds of entertainments.

Among the great many new acts that 'Pa' Calder introduced at the Empire was a very professional young cross-talk comedy duo called the Twin Savoys, consisting of a 17 year old lad named Jack Mitchell and another boy aged about 14 or 15—obviously the leading light—whose perfectionism was immediately noticed. Whether the word 'Savoys' was intended as some pun on the name of a famous London theatre versus a type of cabbage is something that history has not handed down to us, but considering the younger boy's sense of humour anything is possible. Even in 1908 or so it looked as if Harry Gordon would be 'going places'.

The Empire's manager was James (Monty) Montague, who we have already encountered as a member of G.W. Walker's team at the Trades Hall concerts years before. One-time director of the Beach Pierrots, he had been prominent on the bill of the Winter Zoo at its inception, and was now general mainstay of the Empire along with an aspiring young comedian named Dan Fraser, who, although a lesser light than Harry Gordon, had a good stage career ahead of him.

Calder's little music hall lasted for three winter seasons, between which the company was able to resume touring. Both sets of Walkers remained resolutely on a travelling basis, with William Walker's Music Hall shows continuing as usual, but before long the pattern of cinema exhibition in Aberdeen was to undergo a transformation.

Chapter 4

The Picture Hall Arrives   1908—1911

Early 1908 saw the further spread of Cinematograph 'fever' in Aberdeen. Between 1905 and 1910 an Englishman, William Humber, operated Humber's Art Waxwork at 112 George Street, presenting nightly varieties in which his own conjuring acts played a prominent part. In January 1908 these varieties were brought up to date by the addition of Humber's A1 Cinematograph, worked by William Calder with the help of the proprietor himself.

The film part of the programme consisted of short comedies, shown one at a time at various points in the proceedings when sufficient patrons had collected. The light from the projector, which stood in full view on a high platform, was rather poor, but admission prices were a mere 2*d*. for adults and 1*d*. for children. If the cinematograph or varieties failed to please, there was always Professor Whittingham who, like his counterpart at the Alhambra, would, for a small fee, embellish one's epidermis with a tasteful tattoo.

Motion pictures came to His Majesty's Theatre in May 1908 when William (later Sir William) Jury's Imperial Pictures spent a week there as an off-season attraction. Jury's chief claim to a place in cinema history lies in his being among the first of a new breed—the large-scale film renter. Whereas travelling exhibitions could get by on a few films shown over and over again, permanent picture halls required a steady supply of material to show week by week. Films were expensive to buy and agencies like Jury's were able to make a good living by offering them for hire rather than for sale.

During the summer months when John Sinclair moved his animals back to the beach, the Winter Zoo reverted to the name Alhambra, its film and variety entertainments continuing as before. Sinclair fully appreciated the value of Dove Paterson's constant efforts towards improvement of picture quality and presentation, and gave him every encouragement. When, in June 1908, the balcony was provided with separate 'up' and 'down' staircases at the back, opportunity was taken to move the hot, cramped little iron operating box forwards towards the stage.

Shortly after, Paterson redesigned and improved his projection apparatus, fitting a new, brighter lamp and moving its electrical resistor unit to a shelf outside the box. This gave the resistor free ventilation while lowering the temperature inside the box by about 60 degrees Fahrenheit! His projector already had a new gyroscopic shutter which prevented the celluloid film from catching fire, and around early August 1908 an electric motor was fitted to replace the machine's manual cranking. This reduced tiresome flicker and made the picture more watchable over long periods—a development which allowed him to dispense with 'live' acts as a relief from the screen.

With one of his '*al fresco* entertainments' lined up for London's great Crystal Palace, Paterson now considered himself to have made enough headway to open a hall of his own, concentrating entirely on films, slides and pictorial views.

Occupying a prominent site on the corner of the Shiprow between Union Street and Provost Ross's House, St Katherine's Hall at No.10 Shiprow (dating from 1878 and named after the hill on which the east end of Union Street was built) was by this time vacant, although its ancillary rooms still housed the headquarters of the Central United Mission and the St Katherine's Club For Girls. The main hall, though small and plain, with the view from the back interrupted by the pillars that supported the horseshoe balcony, was neverthless very suitable for Paterson's purposes. On Saturday, 5 September 1908 he gave his last performance at the Alhambra, and on the following Monday he was sole proprietor of Aberdeen's very first permanent cinema, the GAIETY. The house was declared open that evening by Baillie Alex Wilkie, who started the first film.

Of the concert party of old, all that Paterson retained was the slide-illustrated song and an occasional variety act. With the majority of films rented rather than bought, and with few additional acts to hire, the Gaiety's economics (even allowing for rent, etc) were of a quite different order from those of the travelling show. A decade before, admission to a Walker or Calder show had cost 1s. or so, but Paterson was able to charge only 3d. or 6d., thereby vastly extending the availability of screen entertainment to an Aberdeen public who found picture-going both enthralling and habit-forming.

Film fare during the Gaiety's first week was of the interest and early narrative kind, including such titles as *The Great Marathon Race*, *The Pearl Fisher*, *Bringing Home The Mattress*, *The Little Savoyard*, *The Stolen Duck*, *False Coiners* and *Oh, Those Boys!*. The illustrated song was the already-venerable ballad 'The Village Blacksmith', a most amenable vehicle for such treatment. Later in the month, a film of the renowned Scots comedian Harry Lauder, entitled *Harry In A Hurry*, was a great attraction, especially as it was well known that Harry never hurried unless, as in this picture, he was to meet someone like King Edward! For such a session of uncharacteristic haste the astute Mr Lauder received a commission of 2d. for every foot of film sold. Operator was Leo Paterson, and pianist was John O. Kynoch.

From the very start it seemed that the Patersons could do no wrong. Their five-year lease on the hall was taken with the intention of opening over winter seasons only, but the public's terrific enthusiasm for pictures soon changed that, land the Gaiety stayed open all year round.

At the Alhambra, the space left by the Patersons' departure was immediately filled by John Sinclair himself and his new manager as of that year, George B. Lee. A native of Virginia, Lee had been an associate of Sinclair's in the early days of the Beach Zoo and had subsequently spent some time as manager and advance agent for operatic and dramatic companies in England. He also possessed considerable ability as an electrician, and so the two men were able to keep the cinematograph going until, a fortnight later, it was put in the hands of Mr J. MacKenzie Fraser, whose Star Cinematograph Company operated from his tobacconist's shop at 13 Regent Quay. The programmes were filled out with illustrated songs sung by Mr Alexander Smith, and a little orchestra played under the direction of Mr George Donald. Care of the cinematograph passed next to a Mr Kennedy who remained associated with the Alhambra for quite some time. The evening variety performances, stage-managed by George Lee, had at first been the work of local amateurs, but by the middle of 1908 the show was entirely professional.

As of 25 January 1909, an arrangement was arrived at between Sinclair at the Alhambra and Calder at the Empire whereby the halls would run in conjunction, sharing a single augmented company which travelled between the two each evening under the organising hand of James Montague. At the Alhambra, seating room was expanded and the cinematograph box was removed from the balcony altogether; reinstalled at floor level, its new straight 'throw' to the screen greatly improved the picture. A new orchestra under Mr A. Bannerman (already involved with the Alhambra's music at some previous time) was brought in to replace George Donald who had gone to play for Dove Paterson. Solo pianist was Miss Marguerite Lowe, long associated with the Calders.

If this link-up came about for purely economic reasons, it must have paid off well enough—on busy nights many were still being turned away. However, in May 1910, at the end of the winter season, both theatres closed for good. Sinclair's Beach Zoo opened as usual, but the Alhambra's lease was up, and one must assume that the same situation pertained at the Empire. Since then the building has served a variety of purposes and the interior has been extensively rebuilt. At the end of 1987 it was made into a restaurant.

The year 1909 brought no new competition for Dove Paterson. William Walker was still going strong with his touring company and Music Hall shows, and G.W. Walker was also back on the road, having, in 1907, handed over management of the Trades Hall concerts to a Mr George Park. In early 1909 Mr Park was replaced by a young entertainer from Hertfordshire working under the name 'Vulcaris'. Vulcaris (real name Albert Worthing) had, like many of his local stage contemporaries, first come to notice at the Beach Pierrot Garden, recently opened at the foot of Bannermill Road. Over the summer of 1908 Vulcaris (not 'Vulgaris' as he was once misprinted!) had made a good name for himself as director of the Beach Pavilion entertainments, which included pictures by the London Safety Bioscope. Now he

7   The Alhambra in the 1970s as a food store (James Brooks)

was promoting, stage-managing and playing the piano for the Trades' variety shows in which the cinematograph featured prominently, drawing on material from the catalogue of another very early (and long-lived) renter, Walturdaw.

Between 10 January and 20 February 1909 the Union Hall was the venue for a visit by a travelling team from BB Pictures of Glasgow. Proprietor of BB ('Bright and Beautiful') Pictures was a man by the name of J.J. Bennell, one-time touring manager for Sydney Carter's New Century Pictures, and supervisor of their Aberdeen visit back in 1904. At the end of 1908, he had become proprietor of the Palace, Wellington, in Glasgow's Gorbals, and had since acquired other cinema halls in that city. His shows are reputed to have been of very high standard for their day; those given in Aberdeen consisted of such titles as *The Rent Collection*, *The Martyrdom Of Thomas A Becket*, *Love On A Farm* and *If Women Were Policemen*, each having explanatory notes penned by Bennell himself. In addition there was Mr Frank Stavert, entertainer, and xylophone and dulcimer solos by Mr Willie Hayward. Admission cost 1*s*., 6*d*. or 3*d*., and the visiting company was under the supervision of a Mr Lunn. As at Bennell's Glasgow halls, sacred shows were given on Sundays, one of these including a very early film of the Passion Play. This offering would be unlikely to cut much ice these days, with costumes a mixture of Greek, Roman and pantomime, and with 'angels' dressed in tights, knee-length laced boots and 'halos' made from the sides of film reels!

After BB Pictures, the Union Hall had a brief visit from the World's Animated Picture Company, owned by James Atroy of Sheffield. Operator was Mr Jack Paterson, and pianist was J.O. Kynoch.

The Beach Esplanade in those days was a far less extensive affair than it is now, and had few entertainments for the summer crowds, but in the spring and summer of 1909 William Humber's ELECTRIC HIPPODROME brought films and varieties to the seaside, establishing a popular seasonal diversion. One example of the type of act presented by Humber was 46-stone Miss Lucy Moore, who, as 'Heaviest Woman In The World' spent alternate fortnights at the beach and the Waxwork that May.

Many authors on the history of the cinema in Britain write of the crudity of the very earliest picture houses in major cities. Often formed from converted shops in varying degrees of conversion and salubriety, these were known in the London area, from where the term seems to have spread, as 'Penny Gaffs'. Probably rather less respectable than their American cousin the 'Nickelodeon', Penny Gaffs did nothing to dispel the fair-ground associations that the cinematograph still evoked in many people's minds, but in 1904 Col. A.C. Bromhead (later to co-found the huge Gaumont-British company) showed the way by opening a greatly superior 'Daily Bioscope' in London's Bishopsgate Street.

Rivals followed in the Daily Bioscope's wake, and as films became longer and better the demand increased for better places in which to watch them. Exhibitors addressed themselves to meeting this demand, and all over the country cinemas opened with names like 'Globe', 'Bijou', 'Star', 'Gem', 'Electric Theatre' or 'Electric Palace', in accordance with the genteel image that their owners were anxious to cultivate. Many of these cinemas were newly built, but it was also common for exhibitors to look for existing buildings to buy or lease. Hundreds of public halls and theatres throughout Britain went over to films as the motion picture made ever deeper inroads into traditional entertainment patterns. But no sooner was the early picture hall movement under way than there appeared on the scene a competitor which looked as if it might destroy the budding cinema business before it had even properly begun.

That competitor was roller-skating, a craze which produced a crop of rinks in virtually every city and major township. In Aberdeen during 1909, skating premises opened at Canal Road (the Bon Accord), Sunnybank Road, Great Northern Road (the Woodside), Justice Mill Lane (the Olympia), Union Street (the Arcade), Sinclair Road (the Torry), the beach (the Beach Rink), Forbesfield Road (the gigantic Forbesfield, later renamed the Glaciarium) and even in the Trades Hall, where a beautiful maple floor was laid to form the Trades Hall Rink.

Skates were made available for hire, sweets and soft drinks put on sale and bands taken on, but the craze quickly faded. As early as March 1910 some rinks were in trouble, and by 1912 the only one still in operation in Aberdeen was the well-equipped Olympia, which seems to have survived up to the outbreak of war in 1914 (its site is now covered by a large garage). By and large the picture trade went its way untouched, actually buying over many former rinks for its own purposes. Investors who put their money into skating had their fingers burned, and one may well surmise that the whole affair increased the attractiveness of pictures to those seeking a 'safe bet'.

Along with the permanent cinema came an important piece of legislation governing it—the first Cinematograph Films Act, which took effect on 1 January 1910. The Act's chief concern was with safety in places of cinematograph entertainment. The 'celluloid' of which films were made in those days was a compound more properly called cellulose nitrate, and was a close relative of gun cotton—too close for comfort, in fact. If overheated, it gave off inflammable vapour and was likely to burst violently into flames without warning. In the UK, accidents involving nitrate film had so far been confined to a few alarming incidents, but on the Continent there had been some horrific occurrences, and it would doubtless have been with these facts in mind that the Government made compulsory the provision of a fireproof operating box entered from outwith the auditorium. The projector beams had to shine through small ports fitted with thick metal shutters. Firefighting equipment (principally a bucket of water and a water-soaked blanket) had to be kept at the ready inside the box, and emergency exits and staffing levels had to be up to standard. Local authorities were given the responsibility of enforcing the Act and issuing Cinematograph Licences once premises had been inspected and approved. Such buildings as schools, while not requiring a licence in order to show films, were also subject to scrutiny.

The picture trade, feeling itself to have officially 'arrived' at last, welcomed the new regulations, although exhibitors in some parts of the country were not so pleased when local authorities, choosing to interpret 'public safety' as 'public well-being', immediately imposed censorship on the material being shown. Such matters apart, the 1909 Act, amended and extended over the years, remains the basis of cinema law to this day.

1910 saw the true start of the picture trade's expansion in Aberdeen. In May of that year the Torry Skating Rink Syndicate tried out its Sinclair Road premises as the TORRY PICTURE PALACE, with films courtesy of Paterson's Aberdeen Cinematograph Bureau. Operator was W.B. Black, and general manager was Robertson Prosser, an associate of Paterson's in the running of the Gaiety halls, which were by this time all under Paterson's control. The 'Picture Palace Band' (presumably an alias for the rink band) played every night under its director Walter Bromby, and as at the Gaiety 'singing pictures' were an integral part of the programme. These were nothing new in the city; Walter Gibbons had had them in 1901, and Vernon's Imperial Bioscope at the Palace Theatre had tried them out briefly in 1906, using one of the Gaumont Company's Chronophones (a sound reproducer actuated by air pressure), but Paterson made a lasting success of them, using the then very popular Cinephone synchronising device to match the speed of film and record.

Shows at the Torry Picture Palace were given twice each evening, with two Saturday matinees. Typical of the kind of programme was that of the first week:

Supreme Recognition (a play about Russian anarchists); *Aspirants For The Hand Of Ellen* (farce); *A Day Off* (comedy); *The Amateur Pugilist* (farce); *An Indian's Trust* (Western); *The King's Command* (in colour); *The Disappearing Burglar* (trick film); *Miss Annette Kellerman* (channel swimmer).

A selection of coloured or tinted slides, mainly of (landscapes, provided continuity between films.

8   Dove Paterson's Beach Bijou (*EE* 30 April 1910)

At noon on 30 April 1910, Dove Paterson assumed the role of provider of summer entertainments at the beach with his own BEACH BIJOU, a little semi-permanent wood and canvas structure situated a short distance to the south of the Bathing Station. The Bijou accommodated up to 200 patrons at eight sessions per day according to demand, each session being announced by a bell outside. Its inauguration ceremony was chaired by a local councillor, deputising for the indisposed Provost Mearns, who sent a letter expressing hope that one day the Beach Esplanade might be carried along to the Bridge of Don with a tramway, accumulating attractions 'which, if they were on the educative lines of the Beach Bijou, would turn the sea beach into an educative influence in our midst'. How much one would necessarily have wished to be educated while relaxing at the beach may be open to debate, but there is no doubt that the motion picture's instructional possibilities constituted an important weapon in the belt of those who struggled to give it respectability and recognition.

Prices of admission to the Beach Bijou were 1*d*. for 'little folks' and 2*d*. for adults, and programmes were much the same as those at the Gaiety and the Torry Picture Palace, but with music from an automatic player-piano instead of a 'live' pianist. The Bijou's educational potential does indeed seem to have been appreciated, as school parties from Glentanar and Dinnet came all the way there on a special excursion that July! Shows ran until September, and the Bijou's success was repeated the following summer.

In July 1910 Paterson, always recognising the need to stay ahead technically, acquired for the Gaiety one of the first examples (if not the very first) in Scotland of a new type of projector designed by a young German, Louis Kamm, founder of a firm well known in the field of advanced optical manufacture. The Kamm projector, which gave further reduction in jumpiness and flicker, won Paterson even more acclaim; his 'singing pictures' were subsequently improved by the replacement of the Cinephone by one of the much-imitated Vivaphones of the pioneering Cecil Hepworth Company. Audiences joined heartily in the choruses, and it is clear that Paterson knew exactly how to give the most fun with a film show. He even had his own little 'teaser' film in which the words 'Dove Paterson's Pictures' appeared to squirt from a hose-pipe on to the screen!

That same year, a young elocutionist named Marie Pascoe came to the Gaiety on a four-week engagement and ended up with a different kind of engagement—to her employer. Information on Paterson's first marriage is lacking, but his marriage to Marie (who was reported as being a descendent of the Admiral that hoisted the historic 'England Expects' signal for Nelson at the Battle of Trafalgar) took place in February 1911, and the family settled down at Crighton House (later Crightonville), 33 Leslie Road. The 'Crighton' connection is obscure, but when, in 1912 or 1913, the Patersons moved to 24 Powis Terrace, they named the house 'Crighton Villa', a name which went with them when they moved again in 1914 to No.46 Powis Terrace.

Precisely why a Londoner should have come all the way to Aberdeen to start a picture house when there was still so much unconquered territory in between is not easy to deduce, but that was what happened when, in late June 1910, a certain Mr Henry N. Phillips set up business in the Union Hall, which became Aberdeen's second permanent cinema, the PICTUREDROME. The Union Hall was built in 1897-98 to the design of Arthur H.L. Mackinnon as part of a new £10,000 headquarters for the Aberdeen Unionist Club at 42 Union Terrace. Occupying part of a former piece of croft ground called Longlands, the block, which is still very much extant, replaced old houses on the corner of Union Terrace and Skene Terrace, an area which had undergone

9   Dove and Marie Paterson (*BA* 2 Feb. 1911)

great change since the construction of Rosemount Viaduct a few years previously. Its imposing granite frontage, with shops at street level, rounds the
corner into Skene Terrace where, in a separate wing of the building and
bounded by North Silver Street at the side, there stands the main hall at
ground level, with two smaller rooms above. One of these, overlooking Skene
Terrace, is an assembly hall with a tiny stage, while the other, at the back of
the building, used to be designated 'Dance Hall'. Both are lit by an unusual
glazed roof and ceiling.

Phillips' venture did well, and 'British Animated Pictures', the company
that he formed to administer it, was soon firmly established. First manager
at the Picturedrome was Mr Harry Fenton, who also appeared on stage as
singer. Pianist was Harry (Hal) Scott, who played background music for the
films, accompanied the slide-illustrated songs, and gave interludes during the
showing of limelight views. A new manager, Frank Walker, took over in

September, and must have made many friends, as a year later a large benefit concert was held in his honour. Many local artistes took part in this concert, among them a baritone by the name of D. Brown McGill, whose closer acquaintance we shall later make. Productions by the Edison film company were often advertised at the Picturedrome in those early days, and when other cinemas arrived to compete for the best variety acts as well as the best pictures, the ' 'Drome' kept itself well in the forefront with regular stage turns. In August 1911 a full cine-variety policy was put into operation, although at most halls this was considered less essential now that films and their presentation were becoming more sophisticated.

In nearby Belmont Street, the Trades Council still owed a great deal of money on its building, despite all fund-raising efforts. As early as 1907 a letter was published in *Bon-Accord*, claiming that the premises were being allowed to fall into disrepair. 'The big hall', wrote the contributor under the pseudonym En Avant, 'is not let as it should be; the concerts are a scandal—the happy hunting-ground for the hooligans of the city. Some Saturday nights the singers can hardly be heard through the noise and horseplay of the gammons (*sic*) of the city. Unions complain about being shoved from hall to hall instead of having one room set aside for their use.'

The skating rink had brought some financial solace for a while, and its failure was bad news indeed, but fortunately a solution to the Trades Council's problems was at hand. Up until the summer of 1910 the Trades Hall's longest run of pictures had been a few days' showing of films of King Edward's funeral early in the year; now, however, the building was to enter upon a long life as a permanent cinema. On Monday, 22 August 1910 William Walker, abandoning his travels at last, opened the main Trades Hall as the COLISEUM with a programme consisting of *Robinson Crusoe, Cinematograph News Of The World* (the very latest cinematographic development, presenting film of international events within only two days of their occurrence) and 'other pictures of travel, wit and wisdom'. This latter category included *The Brussels Exhibition On Fire: Terrible Disaster, Record Air-ship Flight*, colour footage of a 2,800 mile journey in Tibet, sensational drama with *The Brother, Sister And The Cow-Puncher*, and humour with *Wanted, A Bath-Chair Attendant* and *Betty Goes From Bad To Worse*.

Great interest was still engendered by Walker's 'topicals', and anyone spotting themselves in these during the first week or so could claim a free mounted enlargement of their screen debut! The Coliseum's pianist was John Kynoch, while the 'singing pictures', obligatory over the three or four years that they remained in favour, featured great singers, music hall stars, and instrumentalists.

At first only one performance was given each night, at 8 o'clock, but by April 1911 there were separate houses at 7 p.m. and 9 p.m. To control any rowdy element there were constables on duty; the seating of patrons was in the charge of lady attendants, 'following the example now set at other first-class places of entertainment'.

When it came to 'first-class' aspirations, there was no cinema in the city quite like the one that commenced business on Monday, 29 October 1910 in the old Arcade Skating Rink at the west end of Union Street. The Arcade Rink had, like most, survived for only about a year. The building had been erected as a replacement for the New Market when the latter burned down in 1882, but even in those days shoppers preferred the very centre of the city, and as a market its life was short. It then housed a succession of different traders, including from about 1905 an early motor car dealer, but now the west-end placing that had proved so unfavourable to it in the past was to work to its advantage. Under new lessee Mr H. Bannister Howard (of the Howard family of Howard & Wyndham theatres), the former Arcade, after suitable alterations, became the NEW ELECTRIC, its first programme including a long picture of the launching of HMS *Olympic* (then the largest steam-ship in the world), and singing pictures on an Animatophone.

The New Electric (its name soon curtailed to simply the ELECTRIC) was aimed

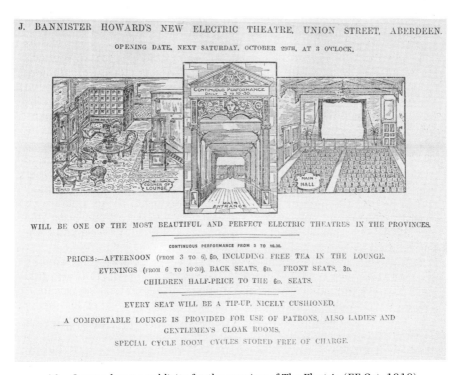

10   Some advance publicity for the opening of The Electric (*EE* Oct. 1910)

at the West-End audience, pursuing a policy of daily matinees during which patrons could partake of free tea in a large lounge attached to the hall. Although not uncommon elsewhere, this method of encouraging a select image was new to Aberdeen, and Howard was very successful in giving the Electric an almost club-room-like atmosphere. Cigars, sweets and cakes were on sale in the lounge, and for the reasonable sum of sixpence one could have not only pictures and tea, but also papers and magazines to read. Headed writing paper was available for those who just had to dash off a little note from this the very top drawer of picture houses, 'largely frequented', to quote local news reports, 'by the leisured and fashionable'.

Film programmes, advertised in advance by the Electric's own Weekly Letter, did not rely on the usual comedies, dramas or early Westerns, but specialised in seemlier fare of a documentary, biographical and literary nature. Pianist was Harry Scott, and for as long as the Electric remained under its original owners its manager was Mr Herbert Austin.

Continuous performances, already common farther south, were introduced to Aberdeen by Howard. The Electric's afternoon houses became so popular that in July 1911 a small orchestra under the leadership of J.M. Taylor, MTSA, was brought in to play between 3 p.m. and 6 p.m. each day. The quality of the 'singing pictures' was improved by the introduction of the more advanced Vivaphone, and by September it was the custom to fill in intervals between films with violin or clarinet solos or with records of such famous singers as Melba, Caruso and McCormack. As befitted the Electric's decorous mien, the type of music played was predominantly classics or light classics.

In May 1911 the famous magician Lafayette died in a disastrous fire at the Empire Theatre, Edinburgh, and the Electric was able to obtain a film of his funeral within only a very few days of its taking place. On the day of King George V's Coronation, the Electric was the only cinema to open, running a special show at 10 a.m.. At the same time the following day it was first to show film of the Coronation, and for a full fortnight thereafter it showed a complete set of Coronation newsreels.

Howard certainly seems to have had the knack for making friends and influencing people—within a few weeks of the Electric's opening, Union Street trams were setting down passengers right at its door! His method of business was to provide the initial capital to establish his cinemas (he had already started two in Bath, one in Dundee, another in Newport, Monmouthshire, and one, the Lyceum, in London), then, after recouping his outlay, to float them as local companies with himself as a shareholder. Subscriptions for an Electric Theatre Company in Aberdeen were advertised in September 1911, and on 2 October the concern was formally launched. Chairman was aerated water manufacturer William Thomson, and the directors were Howard himself and W. Stewart Thomson.

Floated on only £9,000, the Electric proved a good investment. Howard stated from the start that he saw no reason to over-capitalise, and he quickly proved himself right—such was the attraction of the Electric that by June 1911 he was able to claim that the equivalent of the entire population of the city had visited it.

In May 1911 Walker's operations at the Coliseum suddenly ceased, and with them all local references to cinematograph work by him. That October both his Bridge Street shop and his Schoolhill stationery department closed, and their entire contents—including all cinematograph and lantern equipment—were sold off. The reason for this has still to come to light, but it is known that Walker and his family then moved to Glasgow where Walker spent part of his childhood (he may even in fact have been born there), and thence to Newcastle, where they ran the Empire Cinema and carried on a film renter's business supplied from London. Their Newcastle cinema proved difficult financially, but in time they managed to build up a small circuit in the north-east of England. When wireless arrived in the very early 1920s they opened Newcastle's first radio shop, abandoning the renting side of their business soon after. By 1922 the family had returned to Aberdeen, but their picture days were over.

Walker's place at the Trades Hall was taken by Glasgow's J.J. Bennell who, by the time that he came to reopen the Coliseum on Monday, 31 July 1911, had attained the position of largest-scale picture exhibitor in Scotland. He also succeeded Walker as presenter of Music Hall film shows on high days and holidays. Under his regime, the Coliseum's programmes included many variety acts, supplemented by farcical sketches during the first few weeks. Bennell was fortunate in inheriting the services of Joe Gray who enthusiastically perpetuated the tradition of the 'topical', and among the subjects filmed during the first few weeks of the new Coliseum were the Timmer Market, and Broadford Works employees at lunch break. Gray and his camera were also regularly to be seen at Pittodrie Football Ground where BB, in return for a fee, had rights to film each week for the regular 'BB Budget Of Scottish News'. The Coliseum's manager was Mr James Gillespie.

An 'exclusive' for the 'Colly' in October 1911 was a smash-hit detective film called *Zigomar*, which attracted nearly three and a half thousand patrons over only three days. It was estimated that in a good week the 740-seater house would be visited by some 10,000 film-goers, for whom the illuminated BB sign at the door evidently meant good entertainment. BB's twenty or so cinemas, like a large number of their contemporaries, changed their programmes at the half-week. Each film had to be sent on to the next hall within the allotted time so that even the most popular picture could not be held for a full week; instead, every effort was made to arrange a prompt return showing.

A great affection for children made Bennell the benefactor of many a barefoot 'wean' who visited the Wellington Palace on Christmas Day to receive a present of free boots and socks. There is a tradition that, in Bennell's judgement, films that were not good enough to show to children were not good enough for adults either, and no film would be shown by him without a personal viewing. Children's Saturday matinees (common by this time but still not yet general) were regular fixtures for BB Cinemas, and, anticipating children's cinema clubs by a couple of decades, Bennell taught a little song to his young audiences as he stood by the screen at the Wellington Palace. Heard all over the Gorbals, it soon became current throughout his circuit:

BB Pictures, they're all right
Always beautiful and bright,
We will sing with all our might,
'Go and see them every night!'

One prestigious scoop for the Electric in early 1911 was the first-ever screen version of a Shakespeare play, *Henry VIII*, starring the celebrated actor Beerbohm Tree. With each copy of the film was sent out a special musical score by the well-known composer Edward German. *Henry VIII* created quite a vogue for Shakespearean subjects, of which there was soon a wide choice as famous theatrical figures were lured on to celluloid—often to receive a shock when they saw how exaggerated their larger-than-life stage gestures looked in a medium that was so much more intimate! Still, their efforts met with acclaim and were perfect for the upper-crust Electric. During the week preceding the above much-publicised cultural treat, the Coliseum had the temerity to show a production called *Henry VIII And Catherine Howard*. This brought forth a strong letter to the *Evening Express* from Herbert Austin, pointing out that no other film in Aberdeen had anything to do with his!

As a contingency measure, the Electric always kept a spare film programme to hand—a wise precaution, as in early 1911 a massive rail strike stopped many films and stage artistes from reaching their destinations. Aberdeen, in its northerly isolation, had a rough ride, but despite talk of closures picture hall managements were able to find enough old material to tide them over. Delays in film transport were to remain a bugbear until specialist carriers were set up by the picture industry, but that was a long way in the future, and for many years exhibitors were to be at the mercy of fire, flood and labour dispute!

There now enters an important new figure in our story—a man named Bert Hedgley Gates who, in partnership with his wife Nellie and with the financial backing of local businessmen, turned the former premises of the Aberdeen East End Mission on the corner of Park Street and South Constitution Street into what must be the most fondly remembered of all of Aberdeen's earlier cinemas—the STAR PICTURE PALACE. The Star, which began life in early March 1911, is thought to have been so called because it had a red stained glass window in the shape of a star, a legacy from the hall's mission days.

The auditorium stood on the south side of South Constitution Street, with the entrance at No.23 Park Street, a corner doorway under a block of tenements. Mid-nineteenth century maps show development on this site, although not even the city valuation rolls indicate any public function. The Mission is first indicated as having existed there in 1903, and perhaps it was then that the the the building was given the form of an upper and a lower hall, with caretaker's flat in the upstairs tenement. By 1910 the Mission had moved out and ownership of the halls had passed to the Aberdeen Property Investment Company, a group of solicitors from whom the Gates obtained the lease.

11   Bert Gates (*EE* 2 Feb. 1933)

Mr and Mrs Gates had first met at a concert in that very Mission Hall. Both having ambitions as stage artistes, they became partners, specialising in sketches written by Bert himself, and for a while they appeared in William Walker's concert party. One of their show-stoppers from those days (its nature bespeaking its period) was 'Skating Carnival', performed entirely on roller skates.

Enjoying great popularity wherever they played, both north and south of the border, the Gates were for a short while based in Bert's home town, Campbeltown. There Bert combined a stage career in Glasgow with partnership in his father's photographic business, and it would certainly have been at this time that he came into close contact with cinematography. He underwent training in London as a projectionist, then he and his wife made the journey back to Aberdeen to set up as cinema proprietors.

It took only a few weeks for a regular clientele to be heading night by night for the Star ('The People's Popular Picture Palace') to see a mixture of all the latest films and 'singing pictures', as well as to hear ex-Coliseum pianist Thomas Telfer and the 'classic overtures' in which he specialised. Taking a

12   The Star, Park Street, 1920s

leaf from the Calder/Paterson book, the Gates installed themselves behind the screen and put their stage training to good use by adding elocutions to all the important films. In so doing they took impromptu script-writing a stage further, as they also threw in topical references and amusing allusions to well-known local people. For example, when (in somewhat later years) the characters in a film included a second-hand dealer, he would immediately become Alex 'Cocky' Hunter, Aberdeen's ace second-hand man! Attempts to find professional actors and actresses to perform those speaking parts always met with failure, as no-one could stand the pace for more than a few weeks, or match the popularity of the Gates with their Scottish accents and pawky sense of humour. Working every night while bringing up a family was not easy for Bert and Nellie, but with a good house-keeper, cook and nanny they managed to continue into the next decade as 'the voices of the "Starrie"'.

Making up a film dialogue, often with little or no rehearsal, had its hazards. For the first showing of a film called *The Road To Richmond*, the Gates had no opportunity of an advance viewing, but, expecting a nice drama set in rural England, they stationed themselves out of sight as usual and waited to read the sub-titles through their special little transparent screen. When the film began, they found to their horror that the Richmond in question was the one in Virginia, USA, and that the picture was all about the American Civil War! Neither Bert nor Nellie being overly well versed in American history, their mental agility must have been put to the test on that occasion!

Screen action was pointed up by the Gates with sound effects—for instance, coconut shells were clapped together to make the sound of horses' hooves, and the sound of waves on a sea-shore was simulated by tilting a box of dried peas on to a sheet of perforated zinc. Whistles and rattles provided further 'noises off', and gunshots were real blanks fired in a rifle—until one night, after the 'Richmond' film, Mrs Gates found a bullet hole in the curtain just above her head...

THE STAR,

PARK STREET, ABERDEEN.

TO-NIGHT, ETC., THE GREATEST ANIMAL DRAMA EVER SEEN,

"'Neath the Lion's Paw."

"YOU WILL ACTUALLY HEAR THE LIONS ROAR."
TIME AND PRICES AS USUAL.

13   Advertising sound effects at the Star, May 1914 (*EE*)

Shortly after the Gates' launching of the Star, Henry Phillips of the Pic-turedrome took a lease on the Northern Friendly Society's hall where the Empire Music Hall had been, opening it on 1 May 1911 as the KING's, a companion hall to the 'Drome. Kalem and Lubin films (big names of their time) enjoyed particular popularity there, and were specially mentioned in the advertisements. In evidence too were the films of the American Biograph company, later to be famed for its association with the great producer D.W. Griffith. Pianist was Mr H. Crombie.

Situated in the farthest corner of the city centre, the King's did a brisk trade from the start, and it was not long before variety acts were introduced on its stage, newly refitted 'with charming scenery and all accessories'. Built about 1885, the Northern Hall was a fairly typical public room, quite narrow, and with a shallow gallery extending around the walls in a horse-shoe shape (as at the Gaiety). Along the narrow sides of the balcony the seats were arranged in pairs, which put them at something of a premium with courting couples!

As was the practice in many early rentings, the Northern Friendly Society reserved the right to use the hall when necessary, in which case the cinema show would have to be cancelled. This right, however, was rarely if ever exercised, and the arrangement between owner and lessee worked to their mutual benefit.

In the pay-box at the King's around this time was George W. Walker's son, George junior, who for several years had assisted the 'other Walkers' in their touring shows. Of late, the G.W. Walker company had ceased travelling and had settled for a while at the Corn Exchange, Kirkcaldy, which for the duration of the visit became the 'Pavilion'. Originally, the Pavilion was to have run for only a fortnight, but it proved so popular that it remained in operation for several months. George Walker junior recounted to the author how newsreels often had to be rushed around various cinemas in the same day, and how, braving all hazards, he cycled every day for a week between Kirkcaldy and Cowdenbeath with a film of King Edward's funeral. One very foggy night he lost his way altogether and was just on the point of panic when he saw a light approaching out of the murk. It was the cycle lantern of his brother, who had had the foresight to pedal out after him! On returning to Aberdeen, young George Walker joined the staff of Henry Phillips, in whose organisation he was to become a central figure.

Stories are told of children paying $1\frac{1}{2}d.$ admission to the King's on Saturday afternoons and being presented with an orange on the way in—possibly a slight tactical error, as a large part of the fun then lay in throwing the peel from the balcony on to the heads of those below! It has been said that a man was paid to patrol the auditorium with a long pole, tapping any juvenile miscreant on the shoulder and issuing a command to behave, but one would wonder if sooner or later the King's management may not have felt it wise to keep those particular hand-outs for the little horrors' departure!

At the Tivoli Theatre, Guild Street (reconstructed in 1910 from the old Her Majesty's Theatre) films were on the bill, but on an increasingly desultory basis. Mainly confined to Gaumont Graphic newsreels, they had all but disappeared by the time of the Great War, when they quickly came back into their own. Pictures played a much more important part at the Palace Theatre where up to 1908 Vernon's Bioscope (superseded around 1909 by something called 'Palascope') had been rounding off performances with up to three films projected on a roll-down screen. On the departure of Vernon's, the showing of pictures went into some decline, with a brief re-emergence for King Edward's funeral films, the clarity of which was described by *Bon-Accord* as 'the subject of general encomium'.

By 1911, the Palace was the property of United County Theatres, which also had houses at Bristol, Gateshead, Plymouth, Dundee (the King's) and other places, but in June of that year the company failed and the Palace was sold to Aberdeen's Tivoli Company for the reinstatement of 'High Class Variety'. Successor to the popular former manager Percy Gallagher was F. Lawson Clark, under whose supervision the Palace reopened on 17 July. For 2*d.* (Gallery), 3*d.* (Pit), 6*d.* (Stalls) or 9*d.* (Grand Circle), patrons could see, among many other acts, Sandy McNab and Company in a comedy sketch 'The Egyptian Mummy', the Celestas Quartette (comedy vocalists) and a trained dog and pony presented by a Miss Lona.

Each bill now carried quite a large film element, with such titles as *Back To The Primitive* (a UK Premier!), *The Maid Of Niagara* (drama), *His Wife's Birthday* (comedy), *The Hydraulic Lift Lock* (educational), *Scroggins Plays Golf* (comedy), and *Baden-Powell Junior* (drama). At the piano was Miss Maggie Fraser. As part of a general improvement programme a new silver screen was installed, and by the following year the Palace had garnered a good reputation for the quality of its pictures, which always included a weekly travelogue. Strangely, as late as 1914 the Palace films were still being referred to in press reporting as the 'Bioscope', long an outmoded word!

In the Union Street YMCA Hall, from 23 December 1911, there ran the very short-lived TROCADERO. Its proprietor was Henry C. Cavanagh, who in 1901 had succeeded his father as manager of the old Her Majesty's Theatre, but had returned to his original vocation in the legal profession when the new HM Theatre in Rosemount Viaduct opened in 1906. The Trocadero's prices were 3*d.*, 4*d.*, and 6*d.*, (shows in evenings only), with Saturday matinees at 1*d.* or 2*d.* and children admitted at 3*d.* during the week. Pianist was Miss Lottie Stewart (well known as pianist at the Beach Pavilion), and the programme included variety acts on stage.

Unfortunately, the Saturday night City Cinema Concerts, as the City Concerts were by then called, were still running in the Music Hall next door, and often other week-end bookings had to take priority over them. The Concerts (with cinematograph by Dove Paterson) would then be transferred to either the Albert Hall, Huntly Street, or, more commonly, the YMCA Hall, leaving poor Cavanagh in limbo. Between that and the YMCA's own requirements for use of its hall on Fridays and Saturdays, the Trocadero was crowded out after

A MODERN BRITISH THOROUGHFARE.

14   *Bon-Accord*'s view of the spread of the Picture Hall, 1911

only two or three months, and Cavanagh turned to theatre management outwith Aberdeen.

At the south end of the Beach Promenade, the BEACH PICTURE THEATRE operated in the old skating rink between June and September 1911. Problems with the power supply (a traction engine and generator) delayed its planned Saturday night opening until the following Thursday, but its brief time as a picture hall seems otherwise to have passed without incident. The structure served various purposes thereafter, including that of a dance hall. Built of wood with a canvas roof, it went up in flames in August 1924!

By 1912 all but one of Aberdeen's major local cinema exhibitors had appeared on the scene, and in the next chapter we will see how others joined them to further develop the cinema business in the city.

Chapter 5

Growth and Development   1912—1914

At the beginning of 1912, the Electric, well established as Aberdeen's most superior picture hall, underwent improvement both inside and out, with new display lights added at the entrance. At the same time the Electric Company branched out with a subsidiary house in the old rink at 407 Great Northern Road, Woodside. Opened on 1 January 1912, the WOODSIDE PICTURE PALACE soon became better known as the WOODSIDE ELECTRIC, and even better among the folk of the area as 'The Rinkie'. In his book 'Woodside Ways' (published in 1977) the late Andrew McKessock, who lived all his life in Woodside, recalled that before the 'Rinkie' was built the vacant piece of ground was often used by travelling shows of various kinds, among them the variety and dramatic company of a certain Mr and Mrs Leonard Greensmith, who toured in caravans and put on their performances in a tent. The Greensmiths were among many touring companies who gave plays and shows in the rink after it closed, and they continued their association with the place by becoming its managers when the Electric Company took it over as a cinema. This progression would have been a natural enough one; Andrew McKessock remembered a man and his wife standing at either side of the stage, adding elocutions to the pictures, and these must surely have been the Greensmiths. The 'Rinkie' gave entertainment both inside and out, as Mr McKessock recounted:

> During a Zeppelin raid in the First World War the Rinkie was cleared and we all ran home in a blackout. However, the greatest hazard we had to put up with in the Rinkie was a bombardment from outside. There were ventilation hatches along the walls near the roof, and it was very easy to climb on the roof from Smithfield Lane and open these doors. This the boys did, and in the middle of a show we were pelted with divots of grass, skins of oranges and pails of water. The pandemonium that followed was appalling, as those in direct line of the missiles broke seats as they tried to get to the corridors. The lights would go up but the pictures kept on showing.
>
> This din could only be equalled when the pictures broke down, which was quite frequently, as the films were usually old. The operator sometimes mixed the reels and we had no earthly idea what the story was about. At times the operator went to the White Horse Bar for a drink and left the machine running, with the result that the machine moved, and we had feet walking on heads and such like, and someone had to go out and fetch the operator, the din going on all the time...

Back in town, Bert and Nellie Gates, purveyors of cinema entertainment to young and old from King Street to Futtie, set about expanding their business by taking over the empty Nelson Street United Presbyterian Church, the congregation of which had amalgamated in 1909 with that of St Andrew's United Free Church on the corner of King Street and Urquhart Road to form King Street Church. The modest 1867 Nelson Street building received a new front extension containing entrance-ways and other necessary accommodation, and a new brick rear wall was built. The interior was reconstructed, with a small stage, and on 29 January 1912 the GLOBE PICTURE PLAYHOUSE opened its doors. The same general formula was used as at the Star, and its backstage elocutionists were Mr Andrew Watson (doubling as manager) and Miss E. Mann, who soon became Mrs Watson.

The Gates also consolidated their position by founding a public limited company with the businessmen who were backing them. Named Aberdeen Picture Palaces, it echoed the Electric Company in having as senior partner a mineral water manufacturer—in this instance Mr Alexander D. Hay. A native of Alford where his father had been a general merchant, Mr Hay's early career had been in the drapery trade in Glasgow. In 1876 he had returned to join other members of his family in the soft drinks business which, perhaps thanks to the efforts of the Temperance movement, burgeoned during the closing years of the nineteenth century and the earlier part of the twentieth.

When, in 1889, he set up a factory in Inverurie, his brother William, Lord Provost of that town, joined him in the firm. Later, Mr Hay became a town councillor in Inverurie, where for five years he was 'mine host' at the Kintore Arms, and for a while held the position of Burgh Treasurer. In 1896 he set up a lemonade works in College Street, Aberdeen, then in 1901 bought over the large factory of R.H. Strachan in Berryden Road. He also opened branches in Huntly and Elgin.

Since moving to Aberdeen in 1903 he had taken no part in public affairs, retaining only Masonic connections, but the formation of Aberdeen Picture Palaces appears to have provided him with quite a new direction in life. After only three years in the picture business, he retired from his very large company and devoted himself entirely to his new and absorbing interest. For hours he would stand in the vestibule of the Star, just watching patrons come and go. In order to facilitate queue control and ticket checking, the metal shutters of the entranceway were generally kept partially drawn—a practice which nowadays would be subject to strong official disapproval! Everyone knew when Mr Hay was visiting the Star, as parked somewhere close by would be his large yellow Rolls-Royce, purchased from the Cowdrays of Dunecht. Quite unmistakable as it stood by the kerb or bowled about town, it created a great impression at a time when to own a car of any sort was remarkable.

With Mr Hay as Chairman and Bert Gates as Managing Director, the other partners in Aberdeen Picture Palaces were Mr James Hill, licensee of the Eastern Star Bar, Park Street, and Mr A. Wilson, owner of a large grocer's shop in the same street. Within a year of APP's formation, Mr Hill too gave up his trade in favour of the cinema, leaving the bar to his son James B. Hill. APP's accountant was Patrick Jeffrey, C.A., and its secretary was solicitor James Clapperton of Potterton House, Belhelvie. Clapperton had established himself in Aberdeen about 1905, and his legal skills had quickly put him in great demand. His office at No.177 Union Street became the company's registered office, transferring in 1929 to No.2 West Craibstone Street, from where he ran multifarious business projects of his own and undertook legal representation for other cinema concerns in the city.

Bert Gates left no-one in doubt of his commitment to the cinema. Even his house at No.278 Broomhill Road, where he moved from No.35 Stanley Street, was called 'Kineto Villa', exchanged in 1926 for 'Hollywood', 184 Broomhill Road. (Seven years later the family was at the unnamed No.176 Broomhill Road, then in 1935 at No.289 King's Gate.) Gates' enthusiasm, the business acumen and financial resources of his backers, and the good placing of his trade contacts in Glasgow (film booking centre for Scotland) enabled him to put Aberdeen Picture Palaces right at the top, securing new releases with a promptness more than comparable with any major British provincial centre.

On the Globe's second night of business, the operator, Arthur Mann, was just changing films between performances when all of a sudden the reel that he had just removed slightly warm from the projector went up in flames, also igniting the film that he was threading up in its place. Fortunately by 1912 the best projectors incorporated a device which, in the event of fire, blew a little gun-cotton fuse, setting off a mechanism that brought down the 'dowser' (a heavy iron shutter cutting off the lamp-house from the film gate), switched off the power, and set off a built-in extinguisher. The burning reel was soon dealt with, and the safety device on the projector took care of the rest, so that damage was slight and disruption to the Globe's operations amounted only to cancellation of the second house that night. For all that, to have a reel take fire could be a rather frightening experience, and many a cinema operator had to face this emergency before inflammable stock was finally banned in the early 1950s.

When it came to ensuring the safety and adequacy of cinema buildings, Aberdeen's planning officers were in no doubt of their remit. In June 1912 a scheme was submitted by Dundee entertainer Mr Arthur Henderson for a structure which, to judge from drawings, can only be described as a classic of its kind. On an empty site on the south side of Mealmarket Street was to be erected an outsize corrugated iron shed with public access from King Street via a long and far-too-narrow passageway. The meanness of the whole was fully reflected in its seating provisions, which consisted of nothing more than rows of wooden benches separated by narrow aisles. The plans in their original form did not even show toilets, and to crown it all, the materials specified for use in the walls were inflammable.

Even after the perfunctory addition of toilets to the plans, the response to the application was strictly 'No'. Tin-shack cinemas did appear in other parts of the country, but it is worth noting that no such fourth-rate affair was ever built for cinema purposes in Aberdeen.

In January 1912, a particularly stormy month, newsreels were shown at the Coliseum of two ships, the *Argosy* and the *Lily*, which had become beached after being blown adrift from the Dee. On 18 January the steamer *Wistow Hall* was wrecked at the Bullars O' Buchan, with the loss of 37 out of the 40 crew, and great bitterness was felt when the city magistrates turned down applications by cinema managements for a special licence to hold a show on the next available Sunday in aid of the Wistow Hall orphans, especially as carriage-owners had been given permission to run Sunday trips to the two Aberdeen wrecks. The problem was solved by BB (who had been among the applicants) with a special 'sacred service' at 8 p.m. the following Sunday, including the coloured Passión Play film and with a silver collection instead of admission charge.

One outstanding 'topical' of the early part of the year was a film taken by Joe Gray of the Fire Brigade's rush to a big blaze at the Broadford Works. Picturedrome patrons that February could experience a new concept in film-making with the pioneer documentary *With Captain Scott R.N. To The South Pole*, while later a film about the Titanic disaster was on the Electric's screen within a remarkably short time of the tragedy.

That summer the beach had another little temporary cinema, the BEACH CINEMA, run by BB with James Gillespie in charge. It operated in the open air, utilising the principle of back projection upon a small translucent shaded screen (Dove Paterson had a similar portable unit), and shows ran from 2.30 p.m to 5.00 p.m. then 6.30 p.m. to 10.00 p.m., weather permitting, with programmes duplicating those at the Coliseum. Although the quality of daytime viewing left something to be desired, the Beach Cinema's popularity was never in question.

On 8 July 1912 the Albert Hall at 49 Huntly Street entered upon a sojourn as a picture hall. Its proprietors were the Glasgow-based Scottish Cine-matograph Company, and its name was the SAVOY. Any similarity to the famous London theatre of that name was entirely coincidental. A rough-and-tumble affair, the Savoy was considered to be rather in the 'hack' category, but it differed from its competitors in the regular holding of competitions with prize coupons worth as much as £40—a very tidy sum then. Even children could win prizes worth up to £10, and with that sort of incentive who needed great pictures? Supplemented by varieties, the main features on the first night of 'Aberdeen's Premier and Finest Picture Show' were *The Coward* (cowboy drama), *The Defender Of The Name* (drama), *Her Only Romance* (drama), *Lucky Beggar* (comedy) and *Only a Chiropodist* (comedy)—a very typical programme of the Savoy's first year. On the first Saturday night, Miss Annie M. Nicol,

15   The Savoy, Huntly Street, pictured in an advert in *Bon Accord*, 1912

16　Thomas Howard

'Aberdeen's favourite comedienne and dancer' entertained on stage, while a regular feature was the wide-ranging Pathé Gazette.

After four weeks or so, the Savoy's original manager, R.M. Dalzell, gave place to a remarkable fellow named Thomas Howard. A life-long member of the show business fraternity, Howard had been involved with picture halls since their very inception. Prior to that he had been manager for various entertainment concerns such as Bostock and Wombwell's Circus, becoming as a result well acquainted with Aberdeen's favourite show-ground, Central Park, Kittybrewster. *Bon-Accord* recollected how a balloonist brought by Howard on one Bostock visit made a precipitate return to earth in the grounds of the Royal Asylum! A colourful figure, Howard soon found himself very popular socially, particularly for his entertaining stories of travels all around the world.

Throughout its existence, the Savoy's chief selling point was its many and varied novelties. Apart from lotteries and competitions, amateur talent nights were commonplace, and there were regular Friday night 'Go-As-You-Please' games. Illustrated songs were as well appreciated as ever, and of the Savoy's many variety acts Miss Lillian Howard with her 'mind reading and seance' was an intriguing example. Often on Sundays there were after-church performances on religious themes, with no apparent exception taken by the local magistrates even though no formal application had been made.

In August 1912 the Coliseum introduced a series of special band and choral concerts on Wednesday nights 'so that shop assistants and the public generally will have a capital opportunity of hearing good music under the most favourable conditions' (*Bon-Accord*, 22 August 1912). Many local brass bands, choirs and soloists appeared at those enjoyable Wednesday 'pops', and for a while musical acts (no longer so common in picture halls) appeared on other days of the week as well.

One of the newest wonders of the age was the 'Kinemacolor' productions of the film maker and distributor Charles Urban, a British-domiciled American. Urban had in 1905 patented a system which gave colour projection of a sort by alternating frames of different hues on the film print. Due to the different position of the image on each frame in a motion picture, the colours tended to separate, but the general effect was there and Kinemacolor was taken seriously enough for Urban to film the whole of the 1910 Royal Durbar in India.

Aberdeen had its first sight of Kinemacolor on 10 April 1912 when *Modern Methods In A Model Factory*, a film about the National Cash Register Company's model factory in Dayton, Ohio, was given a public showing in the Music Hall. The Durbar films, entitled *With Our King And Queen In India* attracted a great deal of attention when they arrived at His Majesty's Theatre that September, and were considered remarkable enough for the quick-off-the-mark Tivoli comedians to hatch up a spoof sketch called 'Skinny-macolour', but lack of variety of scene and subject made them heavy going for audiences. Much better liked was a return visit of Kinemacolor to HM Theatre in late November 1912, when a varied programme was given, including an impressive film of Niagara Falls, animal subjects (great merriment was caused by a film of an ostrich eating five oranges so quickly that it finished up with five separate bulges in its throat!), and such stop-motion trick subjects as card-manipulation and flowers growing to full height in just five minutes. Kinemacolor had possibilities and might perhaps have been refined further, but Urban, having created a great demand for colour films, attempted to keep a monopoly on them by making his conditions of licencing highly restrictive. That was unwise, as competitors simply stepped in with their own systems. In 1914 Urban's monopoly was ended, and Kinemacolor soon disappeared.

Each winter since 1910, Torry's Sinclair Road Rink had been donning its 'Picture Palace' guise. In May 1911, the skating part of the business came under the control (or perhaps the management) of Mr J.L. Mitchell of the Olympia and (formerly) the Woodside rinks, but on 2 September 1912 films took over entirely and the premises were redecorated and reseated to become (as its publicity proclaimed) 'one of the cosiest picture halls in town'. Tea And Biscuit Matinees were held each Wednesday, and in November a new idea was tried—films from 6 p.m. until 9 p.m., followed by a dance in the back hall until 11.30. At a children's Christmas Day matinee, 'Santa Claus' gave away over 200 'good and useful presents' from the large Christmas tree, and as at other Aberdeen halls there were strong seasonal variety bills. Although a busy little concern, the Picture Palace did not survive the upheavals of 1914-1918.

Presumably Dove Paterson's connection with the former rink at Torry ceased on its attaining full cinema status, as he is not mentioned again as having any association with it. He is, however, reported as having started regular Wednesday night Cinematograph Concerts in the Music Hall that September, with a staff that included a team of smartly-dressed girls as chocolate sellers—no ice cream as yet!

In October 1912 the Bon-Accord Rink at Canal Road (one of the city's earliest) reopened under a Mr James Illingworth as the GRAND PICTURE PALACE. Shows, which featured varieties of one sort or another plus illustrated songs, were initially given at 7 p.m. and 9 p.m. each night at the rock-bottom prices of 1*d.*, 2*d.* and 3*d.*, but at the end of November this was cut to one show per night at 7.45 p.m. for 2*d.*, 3*d.* and 4*d.*, with entry at half price after 9 p.m. Already the Grand appears to have been slipping, and it lasted less than a year. Scarcely any more successful was a latter-day EMPIRE, set up (with the involvement of James Montague) in the old Sunnybank Road Rink.

However speculative, under-financed and generally makeshift these abortive ventures may have been, one would have expected that if nothing else their bargain prices would have attracted custom. Did the Grand try unsuccessfully to undercut the Globe close by? Was too much of a gamble taken for too small a return? Or (perhaps more likely) were the entertainments on offer simply not that much of a bargain? We may never know for sure, but certainly the Aberdonian likes to see value for money, and that was exactly what people like Bert Gates and Dove Paterson were in a good position to give. The young patrons of the Globe and Star's Wednesday and Saturday 'penny matinees' would, for instance, receive not only a good show but little gifts as well. Adult prices at the APP cinemas were a little higher than those at the Grand and the Empire, but then why pay 2*d.* or 3*d.* for something that may be only 'so-so' when for only a little more you can see something much better?

'Pa' Calder, meanwhile, had not attempted to open another picture or variety hall. Instead, he had struggled on determinedly with his travelling company, but the tide of change was against him and in 1912, after 16 years as a cinematograph showman of renown, he was finally forced to give up. Moving to Fraserburgh, he spent a little while as manager of a picture hall then went to manage the town's Empire Theatre. There he supervised some redesigning and modernisation, but a fire destroyed the building only a short while after, and at that point it seems that Calder retired completely, devoting himself to his garden. He died in 1928 (the year that also saw the death of his old colleague Burwood Nicholls) and was buried in Allenvale Cemetery, Aberdeen, close by the grave of that stalwart of his early picture shows, James Scott Skinner. In his obituaries the opinion was expressed that if he had not pushed himself so hard in trying to keep the travelling show alive against all odds (the mark of the man), he would certainly have enjoyed many years more. His sons remained in the cinema business as operators, and to this day descendants of Robert Calder still live in Aberdeen.

At the Savoy's special New Year children's matinees for 1912-13, some 1,700 youngsters were given presents—bangles, brooches or shell-beads for the girls, and fountain pens for the boys. So many had to be turned away that a repeat show was held soon after—with gifts, of course! Adults were not left out of the festivities—every lady in the audience on the Thursday and Friday of New Year week was presented with a brooch containing a lucky stone.

Just before Thomas Howard left in March 1913, he was treated to a huge benefit night at which 20 artistes (many of whom were appearing at the Tivoli and Palace Theatres) gave their services. Everything was done in style, with special films, a souvenir programme, and dancing from 10.30 pm until 1.30 the next morning. There was even a telegram from Queen Alexandra, addressed to 'The Wonderful Howards'. Next manager at the Savoy was Mr Tom Davis, a friend of Howard's for 35 years and formerly in charge of Pringle's Picture Palace, Cowcaddens, Glasgow, one of the many houses controlled by Ralph Pringle, a prominent cinema owner in Dundee, Edinburgh and Glasgow.

Novelties and gimmicks continued to be a notable feature of the Savoy; a snappy advert of early 1913 read:

The Savoy's programme is always	—A 1
If you are not a patron	—B 1
If you want proof of a warm and comfortable picture palace	—C 1

Interest shown by the Scottish Cinematograph Company in a site at Justice Mill Lane (the Olympia Rink?) would seem to indicate thoughts on expansion, and in Bon-Accord of 3 July 1913 the Savoy is mentioned as being about to close for 'extensive alterations and redecoration'. Tom Davis left in December and his place was taken by a Mr Longden, formerly of the Torry Picture Palace. Under Mr Longden the Savoy's activities were further revamped and revitalised, but by the end of 1914 its bustle had ceased and the building was once again the plain old Albert Hall. In 1919 it was bought by Aberdeen Motors (a business brainchild of James Clapperton) and became a workshop, giving employment to ex-servicemen. It remained in Aberdeen Motors' owner-ship until 1969 and still exists as commercial premises, its frontage cleaned and a new roof completed in mid-1981, but in 1987 it awaits a new occupant. Its original roof of large square lead panels, though for many years 'saddle-backed' and in poor condition, was an interesting and unusual feature.

On the corner of Union Street and Back Wynd there stands a fine pillared granite edifice with a wrought-iron first floor balcony overlooking the street from above shops. Erected in 1836-7 to plans by City Architect John Smith, this building housed Advocates' Hall and Library until 1872 when the learned gentlemen, desiring to move their headquarters closer to the new law courts at the Town House, departed for Concert Court, taking with them their fine fireplaces and fittings. In June 1873 the building was sold to confectioners and restaurateurs Lockhart & Salmond, in whose possession it remained until 1882. Alterations and redecoration on the most sumptuous lines were then carried out to designs by architect J. Russell MacKenzie for the incoming Conservative Club. The ornamental iron balcony was added, and what is now the adjoining public house in Back Wynd was built as the club's bar with a billiard room (now a lounge bar) below. The street frontage was revised, and the original rather discreet entranceway on Back Wynd was replaced with a larger one on Union Street. A handsome white marble stairway connected the new entrance with the club rooms on the first floor.

No expense was spared on the building, but after only eight years it was resold, becoming the Queen's Rooms. It appears in the Aberdeen Directory for 1894-5 as the Queen's Rooms & Aberdeen Auction Company, then in 1895 it became the Queen's Billiard Saloon, reverting to its former catering function four years later as the Queen's Restaurant.

By 1909 it was known as Queen's Buildings, and that year it was acquired by the auctioneer J.R. MacKenzie of Belmont Street as a new suite of salerooms. In late 1912 MacKenzie followed several of his peers in the local business community by taking a step into the picture trade. His auction company moved to the west end of Union Street, and on New Year's Eve 1912-13 the QUEEN'S CINEMA opened in the finely domed and still beautifully decorated main hall of the old building. The screen was at the Union Street end of the hall, while at the opposite end the floor was built up to form the 'Grand Circle'.

The former club dining room, the attractive French windows of which overlooked busy Union Street and Back Wynd, became a cafe which operated independently of the hall and would appear to have been the first entirely public refreshment room in an Aberdeen cinema. On the top floor was a smoking room, whose elegant lines, in common with those of the rest of the premises, still evoked an atmosphere of gentility.

Manager was Harry Wincote, giving place the following year to James Illingworth, whom we have already met in passing. In charge of the music was pianist Harry Scott, previously of the Electric. To add variety in the accompaniment of films and in the playing of interludes, a remarkable new musical instrument was introduced during the cinema's first month of operation. Supplied from London and called the 'Cinfonium', this 'orchestra in tabloid form' consisted of harmonium, piano and bells, anticipating the cinema organ of later years by putting all of these effects in the hands of one player—and at one salary! The Queen's projection equipment was advertised as being of the 'Silent Empire' marque, with no flicker.

On 19 July 1913, J.R. MacKenzie's recently-founded Queen's Rooms Cinema Syndicate opened an entirely new companion hall, also named the QUEEN's, in Allardyce Street, Stonehaven. Designed by Stonehaven architect John Ellis, it had the distinction of being the very first purpose-built cinema in the Aberdeen area, if not perhaps in the whole of the North-East. Up-to-date features included a 'raked' floor, which improved the view of the screen from the back stalls by gradually inclining to five feet above the level of the front stalls. Of the 600 seats, most were of the tip-up kind, and although the front stalls still had benches, these were fitted with back-rests and covered in nice red plush. There was a tea-room and a smoking-room, both of which could be entered directly from the beach, and the cinema's electricity came from its own generator placed outwith the main building. Much pride and effort went into the project, which was completed within only six weeks, the building being handed over to its owners on the exact day stipulated in the contract.

In the spring of 1913, James Gillespie (with the full blessing of J.J. Bennell) introduced a weekly 'Sunday At The Coliseum', consisting of religious films, slides, talks, illustrated solos, and items by an orchestra and choir. These 'Bright Musical Services' were conducted by clergy and laymen, Gillespie himself contributing an address on 'Love, Courtship and Marriage', and Mrs Gillespie an illustrated reading entitled 'How Harry Won His Wife'—one wonders how many cinemas then or since could offer a sideline in marriage counselling!

Bennell's lease on the Coliseum expired that summer, and the last news-paper advertisement for BB Pictures appeared in the *Evening Express* of 28 July. Ready and waiting was Dove Paterson who, no doubt mindful of the advance of time upon his lease at the Gaiety, and certainly keen to fulfil a long-nurtured ambition of having a picture house further up town, restarted the Coliseum on 11 August. He and his wife were personally responsible for the elocutions, leaving those at the Gaiety in the charge of another couple, Mr and Mrs Wilfrid Ewing.

The Patersons' first Coliseum programme included *The Artist's Great Madonna* (drama), *Bill's Sweetheart* (Western) and *In The Days Of Witchcraft*, plus the usual newsreels, etc. Variety acts by a resident troupe of artistes were added soon after, and remained an integral part of entertainments for the next couple of years. By the time that Paterson took over the 'Colly', his emphasis on local filming would seem to have lessened, perhaps through pressure of work or because proprietary world newsreels had begun to eclipse local subjects in the public eye. He certainly did, however, bring his camera to the 1913 Braemar Gathering, and on 17 September the film that he took was the subject of a special command showing for the Princess Royal at Mar Lodge. A special stage was set up to accommodate a large screen, on which he showed a programme consisting of his own recent 'topicals' and some other films that had been popular at the Coliseum—*Flowers And Butterflies* (Pathe colour—educative), *A Free Lunch* (Urban-comedy), *A Regiment Of*

Two (Vitagraph-comedy), *Lord Roberts Presenting The Colours To The Gordon Highlanders* (specially taken for Paterson in London), *The Fresher* (Vitagraph-drama), and *The Prize Box* (Vitagraph-comedy).

In November, a London couple, Mr and Mrs Roland Howard, came to the Coliseum to take over as elocutionists and to assist the Patersons, handing over a few months later to Miss Hilda Merrilees and Mr Philip Durham— who are *not* recorded as having ended up married! The Gaiety's band of elocutionists and entertainers was enhanced by the addition of Mr and Mrs Len Delmar, who quickly became firm favourites; at the piano was Miss Nelly Ambler, soon promoted to the Coliseum. It has been said that Alex Calder worked as operator at the Gaiety for a while—perhaps, one might guess, during this period following Paterson's move to the Coliseum. The Gaiety's prices in those days were 2*d.* and 3*d.*, with well-attended Saturday 'penny matinees' for children.

That July saw conversion of a different kind begin in the old John Street E.U. Church. Built in 1841 as the Zion Chapel of the Rev Hugh Hart, and later taken over by the Evangelical Union (a branch of the Congregational Church), the last few years of this place of worship had been most unhappy ones. Divisions within its congregation had led to unpleasant scenes at Sunday services and had finally brought about its closure on 9 July 1913. By 17 July a submission was before the Town Council's Planning Committee for the little building's adaptation as a cinema. The plans were approved, and on 18 September the LYCEUM opened to the public after expenditure reported as totalling £1,000—twice the original estimate! Proprietor was James Gillespie from the Coliseum, and with him came Joe Gray as operator. Many of Gillespie's old customers followed on to be welcomed during the first week of the 'People's Theatre De Luxe', the aim of which was to provide Union Street luxury at the modest admission prices of 2*d.*, 4*d.* or 6*d.* The Lyceum was a tiny, friendly 'neighbourhood' house, with special weekly Mothers' Afternoons consisting of films, illustrated readings and songs. On the standard programme were Joe Gray's 'topicals', a great number of comedies, illustrated songs sung by a 'live' soloist or played on a gramophone, and singing pictures on yet another synchronisation device, this one rejoicing in the name 'Painophone'. In 1914 Mr George Maitland took over as manager, and Gillespie receives no further mention in the Lyceum's reporting or publicity.

At the same time as the Lyceum scheme was submitted for approval, a set of plans was put forward detailing a new cinema, costing between £3,000 and £4,000, for a site on the west side of King Street, occupying part of the garden ground of North Lodge, 84 West North Street—a big house which about 1910 had become the Victoria Hostel, having previously been an industrial school. (It now, in 1987, houses part of Grampian Regional Council's Social Work Department.)

17   John Street E.U. Church, and (inset) carrying the bibles out (*EE* 11 July
1913)

The proposed new cinema was named PICTURE HOUSE on the plans, and this
would appear to be its true title rather than merely a working one. Its
promoter was a company called Aberdeen Picture House Syndicate, formed
by local spirits dealer Mr H. Rose and two prominent Glasgow businessmen,
Mr V. Behar and Mr W.H. Baxter. Mr Baxter was chairman of the company
that owned the recently-built La Scala, Sauchiehall Street, and which itself
was soon to launch an expansion into Aberdeen.

The plans, which were drawn up by eminent local architect Clement
George, show a narrow frontage immediately adjoining Middleton's photo-

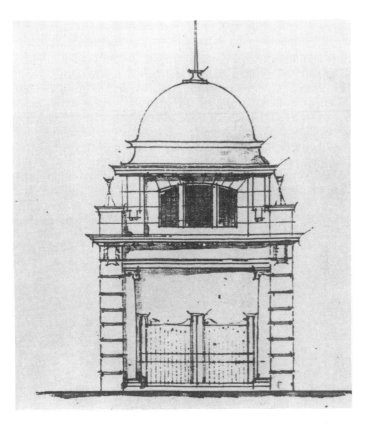

18 Clement George's proposed frontage for The Picture House, King Street,
1913 (ADC, Dept of Planning)

graphic studio (still extant as an antique shop) at No.181 King Street. Surmounted by an attractive dome and flagstaff after the manner of public
buildings of the day, the frontage was presumably intended to be finished in
stucco, pressed brick, tiling, or some other such decorative material. It would
have formed the entrance to a long, narrow, panelled corridor with paybox
and sweet counter, leading along the side of the photographic premises to a
plainish hall with some contemporary decorative detailing and the now-
standard raked floor. The remainder of the King Street gap site was to have
been left as a passageway 12 feet in width between the frontage and the
tenement building to the south. In the event, nothing came of the project.
Perhaps the hemmed-in nature of the site, with the cinema's emergency
exit opening on to narrow little Mitchell Place, did not commend it to the
authorities; at any rate, Aberdeen had to wait a little longer for its first all-
new cinema.

The Electric continued on its high-class way with such features as Sarah Bernhardt's *Queen Bess; Her Love Story*, an exclusive that January. In keeping with the importance of this production, each member of the audience received a special programme in the form of a booklet containing numerous illustrations of scenes from the play, and with a silhouette of the great Madame Bernhardt printed on its cover. Once again, the cast's gestures were stagey, but it *was* the great Bernhardt plus her entire Paris theatre company, and the film was kept for a full two weeks. In April the duties of the Electric's orchestra were extended to playing in evenings as well as in afternoons. The pianist, Arnold Matthews (from Lincoln) was apparently quite an industrious fellow, holding down an additional playing job at the Gaiety!

A new buffet opened at the Electric in August, selling mineral waters and ices. More new ground was broken in November when the first house-light dimmer in a North of Scotland cinema was installed to further enhance the presentation of screen fare in which such frivolities as singing films, travel and comedy subjects were kept as mere 'rounders off'.

> Le Roi est mort! Vive le Roi!
> Oui Oui
> The same applies to
> The Star Picture Palace
>
> The old Star is dead. Long live the new.
> The Star is supreme
> Thousands flock to its banner nightly.
> Follow the crowd down Park Street.

Such was the manner in which Aberdeen Picture Palaces proclaimed the completion of an enlarged and improved 'Starrie', in which capacity was doubled but unoccupied seats still proved scarce. That March, Aberdeen Picture Palaces had bought the building and site outright from the sequestrated estate of its previous owner, an architect named Arthur C. Bruce. (The property, incidentally, stood on part of another ancient croft land, this one with the name of Fill The Cap.) In May, the company had managed to acquire some houses at the rear of the building, allowing substantial extension of the premises. On 16 October 1913 tickets went on sale at 2*d*., 3*d*., 4*d*. and 6*d*. to what was advertised as 'Absolutely the Finest and Most Handsome Interior Out of Glasgow'. Among the attractions during the remodelled Star's first few weeks was *Sherlock Holmes*, the only Conan Doyle adaptation then approved by the author himself.

One prospective new industry for Aberdeen in 1913 was the manufacture of Cinephone sound synchronising equipment for home-made films, demonstrated to businessmen and other interested parties that July. Light in weight and reasonably priced, this was to have been made in various sizes suitable for the drawing room. Its inventor, a French-trained Italian, Ernest

19   Interior of the Star Picture Palace, 1920s

Sostantini, also showed another of his inventions, the Mega-Telephone, a development from the office Dictaphone, enabling the voice to be recorded anywhere and the message sent by wire. The 'House Cinephone Coy. Ltd' was to be floated with a capital of £200,000, the initial syndicate having been formed and half of the £1 shares already subscribed. Canny Aberdonians did not bite, though.

The great Ragtime craze arrived at the Gaiety in the early part of 1913 with a competition for the best boy or girl to perform the new dance step 'The Turkey Trot', which was demonstrated each night for a week. The hit song of the day, 'Hitchy-Koo', brought down the house when played on the Gaiety's Vivaphone (the audience joining heartily in the chorus), and Hitchy-Koo hats were much in evidence in Union Street that summer. The word 'flapper' was just beginning to be bandied about, and Suffragettes, spurred on by the militant Mrs Emily Pankhurst, were causing outrage with their fervent and disruptive demonstrations for women's votes.

The cinema was by now well established as a form of mass-entertainment, and with it came certain social questions. Its elements of newness and fantasy made it irresistible to young people, who responded by thronging picture halls in exactly the same addictive fashion that some of their descendants watch television, play computer games, or pump money into gambling machines. In the years before the First World War, children could be seen roaming the streets of Aberdeen at all hours of the night, a fact which gave rise to much public concern. That even the youngest could sit in picture halls until the end of exhibitors' licensing hours at 10.30 p.m. was seen as a serious aggravation of the problem, and nowhere can this have been more apparent than at the Savoy, whose backbone was children and whose speciality lay in dramas and the early 'Westerns' that were making their appearance in 1912-13.

Thomas Howard, replying in *Bon-Accord* of 27 January 1913 to comments voiced in the press and elsewhere regarding the presence of children in cinemas and the effect that films may be having upon their young minds, summed up what was no doubt the feeling of the majority of exhibitors— that as far as children at evening cinema performances were concerned, he would be happy to do without them.

I laid myself out to give the children an exceptional treat on the Saturday afternoons, and would much sooner have them at the matinees than in evenings. Our pictures always instruct and amuse the children at our matinees, and thereby our large attendance at the first house each evening, for they come again.

   In my opinion it is far better to have the children in a respectable picture hall, where they are properly looked after, than running about the streets at night, which, but for the picture shows, they would be doing, and at times mixing with very bad company. The pictures portrayed by any of the sensible picture palace managers should be to occupy the mind, and I for one never show murder scenes. My pictures are usually pictures shown with natural scenery, of course combined with comic element, which must be shown in order to make a variety. My experience is that the public—old and young—always like something most exciting.

   The pictures shown by me on Sunday evenings are a revelation to all educated people, for I always show the very best, and keep them in harmony with the Sabbath. We try to elevate the people's minds after coming from church, and not to prevent them from going there.

When there were ghost shows and travelling theatres playing 'Maria Martin', 'Sweeney Todd, The Barber Of Fleet Street', 'Dick Turpin' and 'Claud Duval, The Highwayman', children by the thousand visited these places. Now they can see sensible subjects with good morals at the picture shows, and I for one should be very sorry to exhibit anything tending to corrupt the morals of any child.'

Howard's successor, Tom Davis, went a stage further, turning his early houses over to children, who were then banned from all late houses unless accompanied by adults. As of October 1913 Davis made sure that the Savoy's programmes included four educational films every week, a policy that may well have been adopted in response to a well-publicised circular which Aberdeen School Board received that September from London County Council. Signed by various churchmen and dignitaries, this letter sought to indicate 'the dangers to juvenile morality from cinema over-indulgence', and asked for pressure to be brought on local authorities to counteract the influence of 'the unlicensed use of the cinematograph'. 'The cinema', said the circular, 'should be kept as a means of spiritual, intellectual and social development'.

No-one could deny that these were fine ideals, but it had long been recognised that the majority of people that went to the pictures week by week did so for amusement and thrills, not to be educated or preached to. They wanted to laugh, to have some excitement, to meet their friends and to have a good time. As for children, who could have expected them to want to see anything other than their regular adventure films?

Reaction to the circular ranged from a degree of support among local clergy, through passivity on the part of the School Board, to downright hostility from the cinema men. In an interview printed in the *Evening Express* of 25 September 1913, the 'controller of a well-known east-end picture house' (Gates?) replied:

Apparently, our careful educational authorities regard us in the light of moral lepers, battening upon a depraved public taste. There is no convincing the prudes that we are simply conducting an ordinary business in a business-like way, and, indeed, paying special attention to the needs of our juvenile patrons. We have already a strict enough censorship instituted by the film companies [the recently constituted British Board of Censors], and Mr Redford, the Censor, takes special pains to see that nothing is licensed for youthful cinema-goers which is in the least likely to contaminate their morals. The London County Council are again at the bottom of it, I see. Upon my word, we will have to apply to the L.C.C. for license to live next.

One Aberdeen minister who supported the circular wrote to the *Evening Express*, enquiring as to what could be said for the direct incentive to crime contained in many of the so-called detectives and enthralling criminal dramas? This brought a sharp retort from a Councillor who had seen the L.C.C. circular and for whom the educational value of the cinematograph was in no doubt. Those who signed the document (which the Councillor described as 'no tribute to its inditers', containing in its first sentences 'howlers' of which no schoolboy would be guilty) were, as far as he was concerned, simply busy-bodies. And so the argument raged.

It was not, in fact, so much the moral as the physical welfare of cinema-goers that was causing most concern to the city authorities at this time. Diptheria was rampant in Aberdeen all year, and the Medical Officer for the city's schools complained in a November *Evening Express* of:

> ...certain cinematograph entertainments, of which the crowded audience consists of four-fifths children of school age and under, even down to the baby in arms. When inhaling the atmosphere of tobacco smoke in a temperature of 70 degrees, young folks are in ideal conditions in such places for the spread of infection, especially when they reach the cold outside air.

The *Express* pointed out editorially that the use of disinfectants and/or the provision of adequate ventilation were conditions of licence. The 'east-end proprietor' called the attack 'unworthy of consideration' in the light of licensing regulations, which were very stringent. Trouble was taken to maintain a normal temperature in cinema halls, and some of the larger auditoria had to be heated at times. However, along with the proprietor's statement there appeared another from a city doctor who, after a recent meeting of the local Medical Association at which the matter of public health in cinemas was raised casually, had, out of curiosity, paid a visit to an Aberdeen picture hall. On entering he had been 'assailed by a most obnoxious stench of vitiated air'. The hall, as he saw it, 'must have been a veritable breeding place for disease germs', and all the greater was his disgust when he noted the proportion of children, many of them infants, in the audience.

Of course many a happy hour was spent in those cinemas of yesteryear, but might some of their less desirable aspects have been glossed over in the course of reporting and reminiscing? So far, all of the city's picture halls had been conversions from existing premises, and, with the exception of the Electric, were decidedly spartan. Few were heated in winter. Most would by this time have had some tip-up chairs (not always padded), but front stalls still generally consisted of rough wooden benches with no backs. Ventilation of a certain standard was required under the 1909 Act, but it is anybody's guess as to whether the ventilation systems of those old public buildings were really up to the new demands made upon them.

Overcrowding (illegal but not rare) could make entry and exit difficult. A full house meant children being packed like sardines along the front benches, with those at the ends quite likely to finish up on the floor in a 'shift-along' or even simply if the laughter became too boisterous. On 1 August 1913 the *Evening Express* carried a letter from a correspondent who had been in an unspecified cinema the previous Saturday night, sitting in the balcony as there was no room downstairs. After only half an hour he had been forced to leave because of the heat, and when he did so he found that the attendants had put down brown paper on the stairways to make additional seating accommodation. What, the correspondent wondered, would have happened in the event of an emergency or any situation that might cause panic? It looks as if some managements of the day were not averse to risking disaster.

The already airless atmosphere of the down-town picture house became a good deal thicker when the old worthies got out their 'cutties'. Cinemas also made ideal distribution points for man's less welcome personal companions. No cinema management appreciated having its hall referred to (in Aberdeen's picturesque local patois) as 'flechy', especially when the place itself was by no means necessarily to blame, but once the common flea became established in seats and carpeting the struggle between the cinema and insect worlds became a tough one.

Then there was the gent who, wherever one sat, always seemed to be right behind, reading out loud every sub-title on the screen. And there were discomforts of a far more deliberate nature. A report in the *Evening Express* of 13 May 1913 reads:

> One of the leading Aberdeen picture halls situated in the centre of the city [the Coliseum?] was last night the scene of a most annoying and uncomfortable experience. For some time past complaints have been made by theatre managers with regard to the nuisance, usually on a very small scale, of electric snuff [a form of sneezing powder] among the audience, but the incidence last night was by far the most serious case of the kind which has taken place recently in the city.
>
> During the second performance in the theatre, large quantities of the irritant were thrown from the gallery. The result was, of course, a constant succession of sneezes from the lower parts of the house. The attendants on duty endeavoured to clear the atmosphere by fluid sprays and opening the windows and ventilators. These means, however, proved useless, and so agitated was the state of the audience, many of whom rose and left the hall, that the performance had to be temporarily suspended. The policemen in the hall together with the fireman attempted to find the perpetrators of the foolish joke, but so unobtrusively had the powder been disseminated that they failed in their endeavours.

The *Aberdeen Journal* of 4 February 1914 carries a report of the admonition in court of a 17 year old youth caught throwing electric snuff in the Globe. Incidences of irresponsible tomfoolery were not confined to cinemas, as is shown in an *Express* report of 20 May 1913:

> Last night, a novelty in the way of nuisance was introduced at the Palace Theatre. During the performance at the first house, the stallites and occupants of the circle were treated to a shower of wire nails from the upper parts of the hall. The noise of the falling metal among the seats, and the exclamations of ladies in the circle brought a momentary stoppage of a variety 'turn' then proceeding. A few minutes later, in the course of the exhibition of a cinematograph film, more nails were rained down from the 'gods', and two police sergeants and a detective, who were in the building, promptly made a search for the practical jokers, whose pranks were causing general annoyance. The search proved unsuccessful, although two young men, seated in the gallery, whose conduct gave rise to suspicion, were asked to leave the theatre.

Pianists could make more than just good music; they also made splendid targets for any surplus orange peel, etc, that came to hand, and in some east end halls the lady or gent at the keys was the first to know if the film was not being well received. In some cinemas (not, as far as can be ascertained, in Aberdeen), a glass screen or wire netting had to be placed in front of the piano to fend off missiles!

By the end of 1913, not only were films becoming more complex and important in themselves but the people who appeared in them were receiving more and more attention. In place of the anonymity that had been general until about 1912, names were beginning to stand out—names like Florence Lawrence the original 'Biograph Girl', Mack Sennett in his early days as a comedy actor, rotund comedian John Bunny, Tom Mix in his first Western roles, handsome Francis X. Bushman, Clara Kimball Young, Louise Fazenda, Wallace Reid, Kate Bruce, and Lillian Gish. There was Lillian's sister Dorothy, who turned out to be quite a comedienne, and, perhaps most of all, there was Mary Pickford, a little girl with long fair curls, who soon earned the title of 'the world's sweetheart'.

Constant advance in all aspects of film production and projection had made the motion picture far easier and more interesting to watch over protracted periods, and extra-long 'special' films were coming into vogue. This fashion was set in the UK by the release of the very first screen 'epic', *Quo Vadis*, an Italian production which, instead of the customary one or two reels, ran to an unprecedented eight. It must also be noted that the projection speeds of silent films were relatively slow, making a reel last far longer than is the case today.

Quo Vadis was followed by another lavish production entitled *Sister Beatrice*, and both of these figured in a series of long-film programmes that Henry Phillips introduced at the Picturedrome in late 1913. Additional Saturday performances in the YMCA hall were made necessary by the great interest that the new development attracted. An important landmark historically, *Quo Vadis* proved particularly popular in Aberdeen, and made frequent returns. D.W. Griffith also entered the 'special' feature market with *Judith Of Bethulia* which enjoyed great popularity over the fateful year of 1914.

Chapter 6

Business As Usual   1914—1918

1914 began with no hint of the whirlwind to come. In February, Dove Paterson's Coliseum and Gaiety had film of the famous 'Turra Coo' incident, in which the cow's owner, Mr Robert Paterson of Lendrum, Turriff, refused to stamp the cards of his employees under the new National Insurance Act, and was forced to give up the animal for auction, causing a great stir. Paterson took the film to Turriff for a special show in aid of the Parish Church renovation scheme, and to the Victoria Hall, Ellon, where great cheers and applause greeted the appearance on screen of several well-known farmers.

The great strength of feeling surrounding the campaign for women's voting rights came to the surface on the evening of Tuesday 4 February when a German production *The Suffragette*, starring Danish beauty Asta Nielsen, played at the Queen's to an audience in which members and supporters of the Suffrage movement were present in force. Boos and hisses drowned out the music as soon as the titles came up on the screen. Peace was restored, but the sight of Asta taking a hammer to some windows brought loud scraping of shoes on the floor. Next came a scene in which Asta, refusing to eat while under arrest, was about to be force-fed, a treatment to which several members of the movement had been subjected. To quote the next day's *Evening Express*:

> Straight way several men at the back of the hall stood up and protested at the film being shown, one shouting at the pitch of his voice 'I protest against this most degrading film being shown; torture is not fun; stop it at once'. The other male suffragist loudly applauded this 'speech' but before any further disturbance took place the men left the hall, two attendants having asked them to get outside. The next picture shown was Mr Lloyd George on holiday, and this was greeted by loud hooting, and about a dozen ladies, sitting beside one another, left the hall, one being heard to exclaim passionately 'Him and his Insurance Act!', a remark which caused a ripple of laughter among the audience.

Afterwards, a somewhat astonished manager told the press that the Asta Nielsen film had 'delighted' audiences in English halls before it came to Aberdeen. Perhaps suffragists in Aberdeen were of a more militant nature than elsewhere; certainly the Queen's knew all about it that night.

As the three-to-six-reel 'special' feature film became confirmed as the main attraction in cinema programmes, supporting subjects developed along their own lines. Rudimentary colour films and early Pathé cartoons were much enjoyed in the Aberdeen of early 1914, but without doubt the most popular secondary features were serial thrillers and comedy single-reelers. Probably best known among the early serials (for which exhibitors competed vigorously) was *The Perils Of Pauline*, starring Pearl White, but there were plenty of others—for instance, *What Happened To Mary* (the first of them all, made in 1912 and starring Mary Fuller), *Adventures Of Kathlyn, Dolly Of The Dailies*, the first detective series *Stingaree*, and a series entitled *What Didn't Happen To Mary!* Each episode was guaranteed to end in a cliff-hanger situation, leaving one all agog for the following week's installment.

Leader in the comedy field was the Keystone company of the USA—a distinction due in no small part to the perfectionism of director Mack Sennett. Sennett's best-known creation was the hilarious Keystone Kops, but he masterminded a wealth of other laugh-laden material as well. Aberdeen's first advertised Keystone film was *Schnitz The Taylor*, a good example of Sennett's early work, displaying his celebrated progression from pastoral calm to sheer comic riot. It showed at the Coliseum in March 1914 and before long Keystone films were much sought after around the city's picture halls.

On Thursday 30 April 1914, motion picture exhibition in Aberdeen entered a new phase with the opening, at No.234 Union Street, of the city's first purpose-built cinema, LA SCALA. This was an event of threefold importance. For one thing, it marked the coming of large-scale investment from sources outwith Aberdeen; for another, it encouraged local taste for more elaborate cinemas, and finally it gave to the city a cinema building that was remarkable by any standards.

Behind the grand facades of many so-called 'picture palaces' of the period stood only the meagrest and cheapest of structures. Not so at La Scala. Designed jointly by architects John Ednie of Glasgow and George Sutherland of Aberdeen for the La Scala Photo Playhouse Company (Aberdeen), a branch of the Glasgow La Scala company, it reflected the desire of forward-looking managements to imbue picture-going with an aura of romance and excitement. Architectural styles and idioms of the Mediterranean and the mysterious East were borrowed to create an atmosphere of exoticism and opulence, and La Scala was an excellent example of the 'dream palace' as conceived in the years leading up to the Great War.

At a capacity of close on 1,000 La Scala was Aberdeen's largest cinema to date, and was of fair size for Scotland. After a preview of its splendours on 24 April, the *Evening Express* had this to say:

> The vestibule and foyer are resplendent with Oriental colour and reflected light. The mosaic floor, taken from the Ambassador's palace at Grenada, is full of colour and brilliancy. The leaded glass on the domes and the richly decorated ceilings recall the art of the East. Tiled and richly decorated on the walls, the main staircase leads to the paybox, which is filled with leaded glass and has a tiled roof. Decorated in a luxurious Oriental fashion, the auditorium is a delightful reminiscence of Eastern colour and effect. The walls are richly decorated with

strong contrasting colours of blue, gold, black and red, leading up to an embellished dome ceiling of similar tones...

The strains of the orchestra under the leadership of Herr Pokorny not only supply the music for the house, but permeate through into the public Chinese tea-rooms overhead. These tea-rooms, carrying forward the idea of an Eastern house, are treated in a Chinese manner in rich colours of black, gold, pink and green... A quiet smoking room, also in Chinese design, is on the floor above the Chinese tea-rooms.

Described as having been 'built and furnished by Aberdeen people for Aberdeen people', La Scala was almost entirely the work of local firms, with furnishings by Messrs J.& A. Ogilvie of Union Street, tea-room furniture by James Allan & Co, and iron-and-steelwork by the firms of James Abernethy and George Bisset.

The auditorium, whose back emergency exits opened on to Union Row, was of unique design—octagonal in plan, and surmounted by a beautiful gilt dome. Round the proscenium, which was placed across one of the angles of the octagon, were leaded glass panels, richly decorated and illuminated from behind. This style of decoration was duplicated in the tea-room, which, together with the smoking room, was situated behind the 'Moorish-style' Union Street frontage.

Tea-rooms and cafes were common adjuncts to Scottish cinemas, reflecting Scotland's 'high tea' tradition. Run separately from the pictures, they were a popular institution in themselves, and La Scala's was no exception. After only a month an extension was necessary, and premises were taken above the recently constructed bank next door. A connecting doorway was made, and the new area was opened as the Chintz Room, with a Welte Mignon automatic player-piano providing the decorous 1914 equivalent of 'muzak'. It was not necessary for patrons to climb stairs in La Scala; passenger lifts served all levels in what was justly claimed as 'The Last Word In Elegance And Comfort'.

The orchestra's leader, Herr Leon Pokorny, was a violinist of excellent repute, well known as a teacher (his studio was at 3 West Craibstone Street) and for his work in local orchestras. Now, between 3 and 5 o'clock every afternoon he could be heard at La Scala, playing in a trio with cellist L.G. Paggi (late of the Scottish National Orchestra's predecessor, the Scottish Orchestra), and pianist R.A. Chatterton, FRCO, LRAM. Between 5 p.m. and 7 p.m. a relief pianist took over, then the full orchestra—the best yet in any Aberdeen cinema—played for the rest of the evening.

Admission prices were 6d. and 1s. (children half price in afternoons), and as at the company's Glasgow hall prompt arrival could secure a table on one of the tea-terraces that occupied the back areas of the stalls and gallery. There, by the soft glow of a reading lamp, tea and dainties could be consumed while watching the pictures. This civilised arrangement met with the whole-hearted approbation of an Aberdeen public who nightly crowded La Scala under the attentive eye of its manager Mr John Anderson of Glasgow.

The first week's feature film was *A Footballer's Honour* (the 'sportsman' theme being quite in vogue at the time), and in support were local newsreels specially taken by our old friend Joe Gray, who came from the Lyceum to tend the projectors in La Scala's small operating box. The box was crammed so tightly under the balcony that special low seats had to be provided for the technical staff, but this arrangement did serve to keep the projectors level with the screen, preventing the distortion of the picture's shape which occured when machines worked at a downward angle. (This problem was solved in later years by the adoption of slightly tilted screens.) Joe Gray's topicals remained a popular feature of La Scala for several years, with any local happenings (especially accidents!) providing grist to his cinematographic mill.

La Scala's electrical power came from its own generator in the basement. The plant was driven by a 58 horse power gas engine from which a faint but unmistakable smell of coal gas seeped into the auditorium, to be countered by a pleasantly scented spray that was entirely peculiar to this cinema. The engine's constant running from morning to night (sometimes on Sundays as well) greatly annoyed La Scala's next door neighbours, the tenants at No.240 Union Street. Thinking that the noise and vibration were part of the building works, they expected that the nuisance would eventually cease. To their dismay, not only did it persist after the cinema's opening, but one Sunday it went on until 2.30 in the morning while roof repairs were being carried out. The landlord, advocate Mr John Cumine, was informed, and La Scala became the subject of Sheriff Court action until satisfactory sound-proofing was installed!

On Monday 28 June 1914, Austria's Duke Ferdinand and his wife were assassinated by a nationalist fanatic at Sarajevo in Eastern Europe, and a boiling cauldron of international tensions finally spilled over into armed conflict. German troops marched into Belgium on their way to invading France, and Britain, in an atmosphere of anti-German frenzy, mobilised on 5 August. That Kaiser would be taught a sharp lesson, and it would all be over by Christmas—or so some thought at the beginning of the First World War.

British film-makers lost no time. On only the third day of hostilities, La Scala was showing bulletins of 'Express War Telegrams', followed soon after by official 'War News'. Newsreel companies like Pathé went over almost entirely to war reporting, intrepid cameramen frequently risking their lives at the battle fronts. The first of many 'patriotic' screen productions appeared in Aberdeen at the end of August with a showing at La Scala of *Britain's Menace*—'a film that every Britisher should see. It will show you how, even now, our lively little lads in Navy blue are fighting'. War News was soon a prominent feature at the Electric, while patriotic films and scenes of military and naval manoeuvres brought rounds of applause at the Gaiety. Popular burlesque comedian Pimple 'captured the Kaiser' on screen, and war feature films proliferated.

Morale-boosting songs at the Coliseum, war fund half-crown matinees at La Scala, soldiers and sailors in uniform admitted at half price to the 3d. and 6d. seats at the Queen's, fund-raising shows with special elocutionists at the

Globe, Star, Coliseum and Gaiety—these were the stuff of cinema-going for Aberdonians during the war's opening months. Joe Gray's newsreel work for La Scala included films of the crowds attending war fund matinees, and of troops in training and under review at the Links. Many of these 'topicals' were put together in October as a 45-minute documentary of events in the city since the outbreak of war.

As the military call-up gained momentum, lack of manpower closed small cinemas in Aberdeen as it did all over the country. Larger cinemas had to bring in all manner of helpers (often retired folk) as stop-gaps. Particularly hard hit were the city's cinema orchestras, which might have disappeared altogether had not 'serious' musicians, who would otherwise have been fully occupied with teaching, been attracted into them as the number of pupils decreased. Not every orchestra could command such talent, though; an *Evening Express* correspondent wrote in late 1914 of an unspecified Aberdeen picture house where the entire musical repertoire seemed to consist of two pieces, each played twice per film!

In November, for three days beginning on Thursday 12, Mary Pickford and Charlie Chaplin received their first large-scale Aberdeen billings. Mary Pickford was in *Caprice* at the Picturedrome, and Chaplin co-starred with Mabel Normand in *Caught In A Cabaret*, at La Scala. The Pickford and Chaplin 'bugs' bit just as hard and as quickly in Aberdeen as they did wherever the two stars' films were shown.

Back in September 1913, plans had been announced for another new cinema in Aberdeen, to be built at No.181 Union Street for the rapidly-expanding English firm, Associated Provincial Picture Houses. This company was founded in 1909 by one Dr Ralph Jupp, a Boer War military medical officer who, after visiting some of the rough, badly ventilated halls in the South of England, had set out to put a good cinema in every major town and to improve the standard of picture exhibition in general. Some time later he founded London Films, and became the first large-scale British exhibitor to make his own pictures.

The war made the new cinema's construction slow and difficult, but in the spirit of 'business as usual' the best was made of what was available, and on 14 December 1914 the PICTURE HOUSE opened with an inaugural ceremony chaired by Provost Taggart. Its entrance-way was rather plain and unprepossessing, dominated by a pair of rather squat white marble-finish pillars topped by large bronze capitals, but inside its atmosphere was cosy and luxurious.

The original building on Union Street now contained the cinema's extensive foyer and waiting area, in which was retained the old large fireplace that came with the premises. Throughout the winter a cheerful coal fire burned welcomingly in the grate. The 900-seater auditorium was built side-on between Union Street and Windmill Brae, where some old houses had been demolished to leave a rectangular space. The doors at the end of the foyer opened on to the north corner of the Back Balcony, and a flight of stairs led downward from the left of the foyer (just before the auditorium doors) to the side of the Stalls—an unusual arrangement necessitated by the difference in ground levels between Union Street and the Brae.

Budgeted for at £12,000, the Picture House, one of several cinemas designed for the circuit by the south of England partnership of Robert Atkinson and George Alexander, was of an entirely different conception from La Scala. At that time Atkinson classed cinema design as a development theatre design, and the interior of the Picture House was modelled along theatre-inspired 'Classical' lines—not of the stucco-and-plaster variety, but with dark wood-panelled walls hung with French tapestries, and with a fine coffered ceiling above. The balcony, supported by pillars that continued to the full height of the auditorium, extended around the side walls in traditional fashion, and the tapestries that adorned it were of pastoral scenes. Rivalling La Scala more directly, a large tea-room called the 'Tapestry Room' took up the first floor area of the Union Street part of the building, with the manager's flat in the top storey above it. Originally there was to have been a second tea-room in the Union Street basement, but that never materialised. Embellishment of the plain granite front above the entranceway by the addition of pilasters (shallow rectangular columns) was also shown on the plans, but was not carried out.

The Picture House scored a 'first' for Aberdeen in being equipped with a central vacuum system for cleaning. Also, a Plenum system did away with draughts by supplying the auditorium with fresh air at slightly more than atmospheric pressure, and at controllable temperature.

A highly competent orchestra under the leadership of pianist W.G. Ross, FRCO (from London) put the Picture House well ahead in the musical accompaniment of films. Quite some degree of synchronisation appears to have been achieved, pointing up the action and moods of pictures instead of merely providing background music. The orchestra also played a short interlude at each performance, and requests were welcomed.

Present at the opening ceremony were magistrates, town councillors and representatives of the military and naval authorities. The evening house's proceeds, 50 guineas in all, were handed over for distribution to Aberdeen charities. The first week's programme included topical films of a naval encounter at sea and the working of a 12-inch gun, a 2-reel drama *The Chimes* (adapted from Dickens), another 2-reeler *The Call Of The Drum*, a film called *Sunshine Sue*, newsreels, and part of Lancelot Speed's popular *Bully Boy* propaganda cartoon series. After two weeks, with the Picture House securely on its feet, the first manager, Noel Hobart, moved to Wednesbury near Birmingham, where another Picture House was just being completed, and his place was taken by a Mr Russell Yeulett. Managers on this circuit tended to be frequently on the move, especially in those difficult times.

The national atmosphere was now one of such acute paranoia that even the possession of a German or a German-sounding name could be enough to bring harassment. A more subtle way in which life could be made miserable for someone was through the spreading of rumours about them, alleging Teutonic links. No-one was immune from these poisonous tissues of lies, and early on in the war Associated Provincial Picture Houses was obliged to publish statements denying tattle about the company's being German-owned or employing German staff.

The Picture House's musicians came and went constantly. In July 1915 the orchestra was under Mr F.W. Muston, then, in August, under W.J. Godden, followed a few weeks later by Braham Cowen from the Picture House, Sauchiehall Street, Glasgow. Also at this time Covent Garden baritone Norman Williams made frequent visits to sing stirring songs.

A typical Picture House musical programme of this time was:

Waltz 'The Soldier's Song' (Gung'l), Selection 'La Juive' (Halevy), Fantaisie 'La Boheme' (Puccini); Selection 'The Count Of Luxembourg' (Lehar).

For many cinema-goers the orchestral playing was as much of an attraction as the film, and in those pre-radio days, with recording still in its infancy, there is no doubt that a great deal of music was brought in a highly palatable way to a general public that might otherwise never have heard it.

Associated Provincial Picture Houses, by virtue of the number of showings that could be guaranteed for any one picture, and hence the amount of profit made for renters, was able to obtain high priority in the booking of top films. As well as giving Aberdeen a taste of the 'big circuit', it initiated more elaborate press coverage for pictures than had ever been the custom in the city before. Among the top features of January 1915 was one called *The Green Umbrella*, in connection with which the *Evening Express* printed its first-ever illustrated cinema advertisement, confirming the Picture House's status as premiere port of call for Aberdeen's screen-hungry citizens.

In the Autumn of 1914, Dove Paterson's lease on the Gaiety expired. Last mention of it under Paterson is in the *Evening Express* for 27 October, although it may have continued to operate for a short while thereafter. For some months the premises lay vacant, but on Monday 14 June 1915, after some improvements (notably in decoration and ventilation), it was reopened as the NEW GAIETY by Henry Phillips, with George W. Walker's son as manager. Unique to the New Gaiety was a weekly 'Roll Of Honour' film, for which friends and relatives were invited to lend still photographs of men on active service. Patrons were exhorted to 'roll up in thousands and give the hearty cheers when they appear on the screen', and the first of these 'Rolls' numbered close on 100. Balcony seats were 3*d.* and Stalls 2*d.* Programmes changed at mid-week, and the only afternoon performances were on Wednesdays and Saturdays.

Full-week programmes and daily matinees were to be found chiefly at the more important Union Street houses where major films had their first Aberdeen showings and where there was plenty of passing trade. At other cinemas it was more profitable to pursue the split-week policy, although a big main film could be held for a week if necessary. This had not always been universal practice—the Star ran films for full weeks when it first opened in 1911, and the Gaiety is mentioned in *Bon-Accord* of 7 August 1913 as having newly changed to two programmes per week—but by 1915 a hierarchy had been established of full-week 'first-run' and split-week 'second-run' halls. Still not every cinema ran continuous performances—these do not appear to have become general until after the war.

Already the war was forcing changes of attitude towards many aspects of life that had previously been considered beyond question. Female operators made their first appearance among cinema staffs, and tram conductresses became a common sight as the so-called 'little woman' took over in situations for which she would never before have been considered.

Another manifestation of change was a growing aura of sensationalism surrounding film promotion as producers became more daring and subjects that would never previously been discussed started to be aired and moralised upon. In 1913 there had been something of a vogue in the USA for film exposées of the white slave trade, spear-headed by a highly influential production named *Traffic In Souls*. Bearing this in mind, a side-long glance might perhaps be cast towards a Picturedrome offering of February 1915, entitled *Souls In Bondage* and claimed as 'one of the greatest moral lessons ever preached from pulpit, stage or cinema'. Its message (conveyed 'with sledge-hammer force') seems very similar to that of *Traffic In Souls*, and one wonders if it might have been a retitled version of the latter. Its plot, concerning two sisters trapped by the evil 'Vice Trust', claimed to depict 'with relentless effect...the fiendish devices which are adopted by the Western ghouls to entrap victims and increase profits.'

At quite the other end of the scale, *The Sign Of The Cross*, starring William Farnum, enjoyed great popularity at La Scala where it received its local premiere, with full musical presentation, in early 1915. A vocal quartet sang with the film at 3 p.m. and at 7 p.m. each day, and gave a varied programme at 5 and at 9 o'clock. The accompanimental music was drawn from the works of Beethoven, Mozart and Haydn, and the quartet sang excerpts from Gounod's 'Messe Solenelle', Handel's 'Hallelujah Chorus' and 'There Is A Green Hill Far Away', plus (of all things) a first-night requested encore of the finale from Bizet's opera 'Carmen'!

A further 'exclusive' for La Scala in January and February 1915 was the showing of some more of Charles Urban's 'Kinemacolor' films. This time the complicated Urban colour system, which required its own type of projector, was put to use in portraying 'the fighting forces of the civilised nations of Europe presently at war'. Described as 'the rage of London', the pictures made an impressive array:

> *The Sure Shield Of England*; *Travels In Belgium*; *Army Of France At The Front*; *Army And Navy Of Germany*; *The Kaiser At Kiel*; *The City Of Berlin*; 50,000 British and native troops under review at Delhi; Petrograd in winter, with all its palaces,

statues and cathedrals; Moscow and the Czar; *Sons Of The Empire*; Australian, Canadian, New Zealand, South African and Indian troops in London; Types of Indian Officers and Soldiers; Egyptian troops being reviewed at Khartoum; Lord Roberts inspecting the camp of the Canadian Cavalry

—and other items.

La Scala's tearoom is reputed to have enjoyed particular popularity around this time with members of the armed forces, not so much for the quality of the tea as for the qualities of certain of the ladies who consumed it. The frequenting by streetwalkers of this and (soon) other cinema cafes was encouraged by the presence of large numbers of troops in the city, and was very difficult to stamp out under war-time conditions. When, however, it was seen to persist after the war the authorities took action, a factor that has been cited as underlying the closure of some of Aberdeen's old cinema tearooms over the 1920s.

As part of its war effort, La Scala gave full publicity to the showing of a newsreel (taken by Joe Gray) of Harry Lauder leading his own Pipe Band in a big recruiting parade during a visit to His Majesty's Theatre in March 1915. In response to the new musical rivalry from the Picture House, La Scala offered culture (but not Kultur) in the shape of classical solo spots by its talented orchestral pianist, R.A. Chatterton. A series of piano recitals by Mr A.C. Stericker, blind organist of the South U.F. Church (now St Mark's), was introduced that April in the Chintz Room, beginning at 4 o'clock each afternoon and at 8 o'clock each evening. Played from a memorised repertoire of over 100 pieces, these recitals proved popular and were resumed in October after a summer break, but sadly they were cut short by Mr Stericker's death in December.

Back-stage elocutions were introduced, adding a rough-and-ready 'soundtrack' to La Scala's most important pictures. Somehow a competent orchestra was held together (although constant reorganisation was necessary), and quite often films would be interspersed with interludes by the La Scala Glasgow Vocal Quartette. The 'relief pianist' who filled in for the orchestra during breaks and minor features was a young lady named Annie S. Milne, then embarking upon a career that would take her by way of the Picture House and the Electric to the very last days of the silent film in Aberdeen. The orchestra, which in 1915 comprised a couple of violins, cello, double bass, flute, clarinet and piano (all, it was pointed out, played by British subjects) now performed in afternoons as well as in evenings, and its leaders came and went as frequently as did its rank and file. Leon Pokorny had left the scene, and among his successors was James Riach, who gave place in September 1915 to a Mr Brian O'Brien. This gentleman was himself replaced a few weeks later by well known local bandsman A. Wilfred Loseby.

The historic documentary of the 1910-13 Antarctic expedition, *With Captain Scott To The Antarctic*, had its first Aberdeen showing at La Scala that autumn, complemented by an interesting lecture on the subject. La Scala was also notable for its many special film shows in aid of wartime causes, especially the welfare of troops at the battle front and in the Navy.

Friday 12 November 1915 is an important date for our survey in that it saw the entry into full-time picture-hall proprietorship of the man in whose hands (and in the hands of whose family) lay the ultimate future of independent cinema exhibition in the city. Born in Newhills, Mr James F. Donald first arrived in Aberdeen as a youngster, and on reaching the age to learn a trade entered upon an apprenticeship with the Rose Street coachbuilders John F. Clark. After that he went to work for the Great North Of Scotland Railway Company at Kittybrewster, but before long he became his own boss with the opening of a small electro-plating and cycle business in Rosemount. This reflected his keenness for cycling, at which he was a racing champion; he was also an enthusiastic supporter of Temperance movements, but first and foremost his passion in life was for dancing.

In late 1891, he held the first meeting of his own dancing class, the Gondolier Quadrille Party, in the Lesser Albert Hall, Huntly Street (part of the building that later became the Savoy). So great was the demand for his expert tuition that he had to move to the larger Victoria Hall, Skene Terrace, of which he became Superintendent, but even the Victoria Hall was not large enough, and before long he had to expand back into the main Albert Hall. In 1905 he acquired a public hall in North Silver Street (the North Silver Street Hall) as new home of the Gondolier School Of Dancing And Deportment. He also bought the flat above the hall, moving there from No.40 Skene Terrace where he had lived since 1899 or earlier. The North Silver Street Hall became a very busy place indeed, and so far did his recognition spread that in 1921, on an all-time record vote, he was elected President of the British Association Of Teachers Of Dancing. As a sideline, he offered a well-patronised service for the booking of bands or orchestras for any sort of dancing occasion.

Entry into the picture business was not without its frustrations. An approach to Dove Paterson with a view to buying equipment brought only a flat assurance of his having 'missed the boat', but persistence paid. Projection gear was obtained from somewhere, and after a few tests in private and in public he was ready, on that day in 1915, to begin business in his very own cinema—the WEST END.

Occupying a former billiard hall above the Aberdeen Dairy at No.475 Union Street, the West End was a strictly utilitarian affair. It began with only a single projector where two was the norm for multi-reel films, and music was provided by a player-piano; an orchestra did not appear until after the war. The only heating in the hall was by means of stoves, and the presence of the dairy below earned it the nickname of 'The Tuppenny Freezer', but for 3d. or 6d. (2d. seats came a little later) its plush tip-up chairs were comfortable enough and the programme gave excellent value. The West End's first films included *Neptune's Daughter* with glamorous swimming star Annette Kellerman, *Fatty's Chance Acquaintance* starring Fatty Arbuckle, and *The Clubman*. Elocutionists (usually Mr William Pirie and Miss Frances Lawson) were brought in for important films, and among the West End's many variety acts was Willie Kemp, 'King of the Cornkisters'.

Although Mr Donald possessed no previous experience of picture hall management, he did have the able support of his wife, his manager Mr F. Humphries and (when old enough) his sons James (1901-1971), Richard, Herbert, and Peter, who left Aberdeen after the Second World War to take up a post with Howard and Wyndham Theatres in London. His success must have raised quite a few eyebrows in the trade, and if Dove Paterson did not at first take him seriously as a competitor, it cannot have been for long. James Donald and Dove Paterson did, in fact, have certain points in common. Both were strict teetotalers and of athletic inclination, Paterson being a keen all-weather swimmer. Both were of down-to-earth country origin, and both had flourishing picture businesses involving the participation of their families, the Donald company standing as an example of the family business *par excellence*.

'Festive' was scarcely the description of the depressing Christmas and New Year season of 1915-16. Even the weather was miserable and there seemed to be little or no relief from the war-time gloom. Charlie Chaplin, for all his previous popularity, became *persona non grata* in early 1916 after refusing to join the US military, and a wide taboo on his films followed, but despite that La Scala went ahead and showed all of his latest productions, starting with *Charlie At Work*. Charlie had experimented with a variety of different comic characters and had firmly settled upon the little tramp. Already his comedy touch was legendary, and no other screen comic could rival his sense of timing in what were for those days very new and sophisticated gags.

In January 1916, responsibility for the day-to-day running of La Scala passed to Boer War veteran Mr George Neill, whose grandfather, General Neill, was commemorated in his native town of Ayr for assisting in the quelling of the Indian Mutiny. Mr Neill is reported as having come to Aberdeen from a large hall near Glasgow.

La Scala was fortunate in finding adequate interim staff, but other cinemas found the going hard. Severe difficulty was caused at the Queen's when the manager, Arthur Mann (whom we have already encountered in the early days of the Globe), received his call-up papers in April 1916. He lodged an appeal for registration as a conscientous objector on grounds of loss of business, the financial responsibilities of his marriage (an experienced operator and electrician, he was earning the quite substantial sum of £3 per week), and the fact that he had already made a large contribution through war-fund entertainments, but the tribunal before which he appeared would grant him only a month's extra grace, so a replacement still had to be found. This was a Mr Simpson, who, in accord with his declared intention of 'making things hum' at the Queen's, presented such major features as the drama *Joan Of Arc*, which contained views of historic places in France—many of which were now at the heart of the battle. Successor to Mr Simpson that November was an associate of Dove Paterson's, Mr Crawford Clark, who was to remain as manager of the Queen's for several years.

In spite of all difficulties, some cinemas were able to have redecoration and improvements carried out, and it even proved possible to build a brand-new one in the city's east end. Down among the grey tenements in the network of streets behind the Castlegate, the second of Aberdeen's purpose-built halls, the CASINO, opened its doors on Monday 7 February 1916. Situated on the north side of Wales Street, it virtually backed on to the Star, for which it constituted direct competition.

Its proprietor was Mr John Peter Kilgour (1864-1920), successful dealer in waste paper, metals, flock, cloth and hay-seed from his Central Waste Factory, which occupied the site of the old slaughter-houses at Nos.42-50 Wales Street. It was on his factory yards that the Casino's 77-feet wide white stucco 'Spanish villa' front arose, unique for Aberdeen and certainly most unusual in Scotland.

The Casino was described by its architects, George Sutherland and Clement George, as their fifth cinema project, although the identities of previous schemes by the partnership are unknown; perhaps the statement really referred to the two men individually. Its frontage comprised three main features. On the corner nearest Park Street was a low square tower with a highly distinctive red-tiled roof in the shape of a concave pyramid, flattened

20   The Casino, Wales Street (*BA* 2 May 1941)

at the top and projecting over the wall heads at its base. Originally, the pyramid was intended to support an illuminating globe when war-time lighting restrictions were removed, but this part of the plan was never carried out. The central section of the frontage had a roof in similar style, but lower in elevation. Above the entranceway was a large semi-circular window filled with ruby-tinted glass which shone beautifully when lit from behind. The easternmost section of the frontage took the form of a battlemented wall, pierced by narrow windows to heighten the 'Mediterranean' flavour. All this combined to bring a welcome splash of colour and gaiety to an otherwise drab corner of the city.

Within, the pay-box was central to the main vestibule. Smaller vestibules on either side connected with the auditorium via double swing doors, each door decorated with circular panels of richly-coloured stained glass in a fan-like pattern. In the 900-seater auditorium, the crimson morroccoline padded seats faced a proscenium arch 27 feet wide, with gilt Moorish moulded capitals on its side columns. Above the proscenium was a cornice in square dentil blocks, while on either side of it was a pavilion (an ornamental structure somewhat reminiscent of a tall circular Eastern tent) with an octagonally curved roof and small gilt dome. The stage was 11 feet deep with the screen at the back, and the curtains were blue with a scalloped valance. The walls were painted with 'Moorish' motifs, and the whole scheme was set off by octagonal coloured glass light fittings suspended from the curved ceiling. Decoration work was by a new firm headed by Mr Bruce Mackenzie, who had been foreman to the well known Aberdeen painters and glaziers George 'Potty' (Putty) Donald at the time when that company decorated the new La Scala.

The Casino's general line of entertainment fare was strictly of the popular sort, with a good number of features like Blanche Sweet's *The Escape*, which was described as 'the great sensational sex problem play' but also carried the assurance of having been accorded highest approval by all teachers, parents and clergy who had seen it! Charlie Chaplin (once the fuss had died down) was staple fare, and regular community singing sessions were led by Jeannie Le Sage, the first 'chorus vocalist' to be mentioned in local cinema reports.

Perhaps most important of all, the Casino was the first Aberdeen cinema to reintroduce full-time cine-variety, which, supplemented during the first few years by miniature revues, remained a speciality right up until the end of the silent film era. One stage favourite of the Casino's early days was 'the Scottish Caruso' D. Brown McGill, who sang patriotic songs in Highland dress. These songs included a composition of his own, 'The Grand Old Flag', for the best rendition of which a prize was awarded in a special competition that continued over several Friday nights. Managing the Casino was Mr John S. Watson, who was deputised for during war service by his chief operator, Jack Willits.

The Casino's arrival at the Star's very portals called for a response from Bert Gates. Very soon he began experimenting with his own varieties and miniature revues, emulating and even surpassing those of his new neighbour by the summer of 1916. That August, Miss Madge Belmont, 'America's Handcuff Queen', amazed Star patrons by escaping from handcuffs, gyves and other assorted custodial implements. On the Friday night she gave her tour de force—an escape from an ordinary locally-provided coffin into which she was placed and the lid nailed down. Failure to emerge within the stipulated time would put £25 to charity—and nowhere is there any mention of charity having been the winner!

Another of the Star's more outstanding variety acts was Birteno's Golden Grotto, 'the most gorgeous electrical dance spectacle ever seen in Aberdeen—a display of serpentine and fire dancing by La Belle Lumière, with marvellous kaleidoscopic colour effects'. This must certainly have been in imitation of the 'electric' acts of the great Walford Bodie, M.D. (Merry Devil) who was then at the height of his career, assisted by his wife 'Princess Rubie', his sister 'Mystic Marie' and a lady called 'La Belle Electra'.

The first of several national increases in cinema and theatre admission prices was introduced on 1 May 1916, necessitated by the levying of an Entertainments Tax. A special Government-issued adhesive stamp had to be fixed on each ticket as it was sold, and anyone caught 'fiddling' (as at one Dundee hall, where it was found that patrons were being admitted on used tickets) was liable to a heavy fine. Aberdeen attendances, estimated at some 12,000 per night at an average of 6*d.* per head, seem to have remained unaffected by the tax, which was accepted as a regrettable necessity even after subsequent increases.

That October the Government put a restriction on shop opening hours, compelling closure at 8 p.m. except on Saturdays, when an extra hour was allowed. This regulation also applied to the sale of sweets and cigarettes in cinemas and theatres, and it became very common to see, at about ten minutes to the hour, an announcement flashed on the screen, warning that selling was about to stop.

Railway restrictions caused uncertainty in the booking of variety acts. Artistes could travel on Fridays only, and there was no chance of transporting scenery. Venues situated in or near to big cities were not badly affected, and older theatres with good accumulations of scenery were able to make do with what they had, but variety halls and cinemas as far north as Aberdeen did not find things easy. The one positive aspect of these stringencies was the valuable opportunity given to local talent!

As we have already noted in passing, Dove Paterson was an active man—a keen swimmer, a strict non-smoker, etc. In fact, he was something of a 'health-fiend', and it was this, through an ironic twist of fate, that led to his untimely death in the early summer of 1916. On the morning of Sunday 28

21 Letter to the School Board concerning young performers at the Star, 1916
(courtesy of Walter Watt)

Dear Sir,

    In response to your request for a letter from the Manager of the
Casino (Mr. Wells) who I regret to say is at present laid up, I, J. P.
Kilgour, Proprietor, beg to make application for the appearance of Martha
Gill at the casino for the week from 26th February to 3rd March.   Trusting
this is in order.

    A request was put in for this some time ago from Mr. De Roy from
Hamilton and no reply has yet been received.

                        Yours faithfully,

Mr. Angus,
    School Board Office,
            22 Union Terrace,

22   Casino letterhead with similar application, 1917 (courtesy of Walter Watt)

May he was having his customary swim at the beach, when, about 400 yards north of the Bathing Station, he took a severe bout of cramp and nearly drowned. Pulled out of the sea unconscious, he was taken in critical condition to the Royal Infirmary where, despite the onset of complications, he recovered enough to be looking forward to returning home. But without warning the complications (apparently pleurisy) returned in such severe form that on 16 June he succumbed. The Coliseum's affairs were wound up by his relatives, and by the end of that month all picture activity had ceased there.

The Coliseum remained closed until 18 December, when it was relaunched in a form that must have been unique in Scotland if not in Britain—a Trades Council cinema. Manager was hall-keeper Mr James Boyle. The big opening programme consisted of *The Island Of Regeneration*, starring favourite of the time Edith Storey, and *The Heart Of Sister Anne*, all in continuous performances. Unfortunately this bold attempt was doomed to failure, and after only a few months the Coliseum closed once again.

The official film of the Battle Of The Somme played for a full week at the Picture House that September and went the rounds of other city halls immediately after. Taken in the thick of fighting at the front, it was considered by some to be too harrowing in its realism, especially for relatives and friends of those 'over there', but the *Evening Express*'s film correspondent, 'Projector', spoke for many when he wrote:

> ...but why should our feelings be spared? Why should any of us be allowed to sit at home with an easy mind when men are dying for us in the trenches? We all have a stake in this great struggle, and the more the dread reality of war is brought to us, the more will we concentrate all our efforts, in the workshop and elsewhere, to bring this war to a speedy and successful conclusion. For this reason, if for no other, this film should be seen by every man, woman and child in the Kingdom.

The film consisted of five parts, and was described thus:

1. Preparatory action June 25 to 30, showing activities before Fraicourt.
2. Royal Warwickshires having a meal in camp before the great advance. High Explosive shells fired from 12 inch howitzers create havoc in enemy line; blowing up enemy trenches by a huge mine; setting up machine guns, etc.
3. The great attack.
4. British wounded and nerve-shattered prisoners arriving; more captures; scenes at the dressing station for slightly wounded at Miden Post; effect of British shell fire on German trenches between Fricourt and Mametz, etc.
5. The toll of war; seeking further laurels; a sample of the British Army, and the Worcesters off to continue the advance.

Government film was available for hire at very reasonable rates, and 40 per cent of the Somme documentary's revenue went to military charities—

£500 out of £1,300 in the first week of release. Another favourite official production of the time was *The Strafers Strafed*, showing the fate of the L21 Zeppelin shot down near London on 23 September. La Scala's rather belated Aberdeen premiering, in August 1916, of *The Perils Of Pauline* series (in which Pearl White performed all her own stunts) moved the Evening Express's 'Projector' to quote the following amusing little verse in his 'Pictures and Players' column:

> Fearless, peerless, reckless Pearl,
> More a sea-bird than a girl;
> More a wisp of flying spray,
> Than a child of mortal clay;
> Dodging bullets, hitching trains,
> Leaping slap through window panes,
> Smashing motor cars kerflop,
> Always coming out on top!
> Trapped by villains black with gore,
> Giving same the slip once more,
> Gaily facing, a la mode,
> Perils through each episode.

It must surely also have been 'Projector' who wrote a revealing account in the *Evening Express* of a press showing (at the West End on Thursday 7 September) of some preliminary studies for a film of the Cabinet at Downing Street. The full production was not given Government sanction, and perhaps with good reason; this is how the *Express* described the studies, which were eventually allowed a release under the title *Cabinet Interviews*:

> Should politics fail, film-acting as a profession is closed against politicians for aye... It is a self-conscious, hesitating, bashful, nervous display. The actors were as if put up to 'say their piece'; to obey the old injunction for elocutionary aspirants—'Hands behind, stare straight at clock, go on if you can, break down if you can't.' Some of them couldn't. They forgot their lines.

Will Crooks was the only politician to come out with much credit. Of others the report remarked:

> Mr Bonar Law—very stiff. Endeavouring to smile off his nervousness. Forgot his words once or twice. Finished with a sidelong glance and vanished.
> Sir George Askwith—Looked to Heaven for deliverance—or inspiration— muttered to himself. Again looked to Heaven. Apparently little result. Toyed with his fountain pen. Off.
> Mr Walter Long—Filmed as Scotland Yard detective—looked extremely cute and knowing. Put a leading question to the audience. Again looked darkly knowing. The mystery thickened. Off.

Some of the audience were distinguished enough to have seen themselves on the screen, and the *Express* noted as they left that many of them seemed involved in thought, if not distinctly sad!

On 23 December, only a few days after the opening of the short-lived Trades Council Coliseum, the Lyceum, after a change of ownership (to whom is not clear), entered on a new lease of life as the ROYAL. Alterations brought it up to (or returned it to?) 'Union Street standard', with tip-up chairs, new equipment, and remodelling of the decor by Bruce MacKenzie. Walls and ceiling were decorated in panels of 'pleasing tints', and a large handsome frieze ran round the whole interior. The screen was surmounted by Aberdeen's coat of arms, the architrave (a decorative moulding running round the outer edge of the stage arch) was decorated in golden dentil blocks (echoes of the Casino), and the lighting was of soft semi-direct variety. Admission cost 4*d*. and 7*d*.

The Royal did not last; in the Aberdeen Directory of 1918 the building is given as simply the 'John Street Hall' and by 1924 it was the 'South U.P. Hall'. By 1925 it was in the hands of the Salvation Army, who retained it for more than 30 years. After a sojourn as the premises of a firm of plumbers' merchants, it is currently an antiques warehouse, and nothing now remains to tell of earlier days.

Since the outbreak of war, His Majesty's Theatre had been in fairly regular use for films—chiefly war news and other special subjects, but also for a few prestigious local premieres. The first of these, in August 1915, was *Three Weeks*, based on a novel of the same name by Elinor Glyn, darling of the

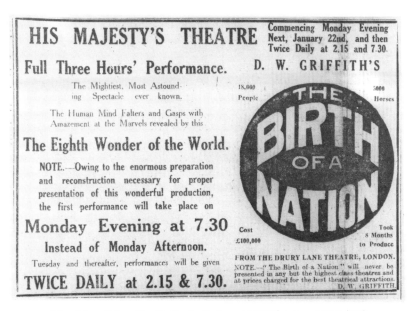

23　Advertising *The Birth of a Nation* at HM Theatre, 1917 (*EE*)

'bright young things' of the 1920s. More historically important was the first Aberdeen showing, as 1916 dragged wearily into 1917, of the great W.D. Griffith epic *Birth Of A Nation*. On this its initial release in Britain and America, it was shown not in cinemas but in theatres, at full theatre prices, in recognition of its contribution to film art. The music was specially chosen by Griffith himself, and was played by a large orchestra. Hailed as 'the eighth wonder of the world', *Birth Of A Nation* was a box-office smash and it paved the way for much further innovation by its producer.

On 10 April 1917 it was announced that La Scala had passed into the ownership of the long-established Dundee exhibitor and film renter George Green. Taking over the mantle of J.J. Bennell as largest cinema proprietor and film renter in Scotland, Green was also now the only exhibitor who still made newsreels. He was also Scottish agent for the Triangle Films company of America, which had on its roster some of the top stars of the day—much to La Scala's advantage.

Seat pricing was rearranged, with reduced admission charges until 5 p.m. during the summer months. Wounded soldiers were admitted free, and patrons of the Dress Circle and Balcony received tea at no extra charge. Large presentation advertisements in the local papers rivalled those of the Picture House as La Scala stepped firmly into the forefront among Aberdeen's picture halls.

George Neill completed his managerial term at the beginning of 1917, and his replacement was a Mr George Sinclair, who immediately took the opportunity of having the cinema's vestibules and part of the auditorium decorated in flowers to add colour and cheerfulness. In May, Mr Sinclair resigned due to ill health, and his place was taken by Mr Fred Cruickshank from the Grand Theatre, Glasgow.

Also in May, La Scala audiences were given a musical treat in the form of a week-long visit by the 16-strong St Mungo Symphony Orchestra directed by William Moore. Mr Moore was Musical Director for Green's in Glasgow, having previously occupied a similar post with Moss's Empire Theatres, for whom he had looked after the hiring of orchestras. In addition to having its own part of the programme, the St Mungo played the music for the main film, *Julius Caesar*. The week was evidently a most happy one, as at the last performance the orchestral players, the theatre staff and other friends presented Mr Moore with a silver-mounted ivory conductor's baton in a morrocco case. The baton was supplied by Marr, Wood & Co, who displayed it in their window the previous day!

By the middle of the year, La Scala's musical establishment had been greatly enhanced by the addition of Mr A. Pryor Rebecca, a musician highly respected by colleagues and pupils alike. Organist of Beechgrove Church, Mr Rebecca's first contact with the entertainment world had come about through association with some of the last Cinematograph Carnivals of William Walker; now he led La Scala's orchestra from the piano or harmonium, and was also heard

JUNE 8th, 9th, 10th,

THURSDAY, FRIDAY, and SATURDAY,

LAST THREE DAYS OF

5
Parts.

"AN AMERICAN'S HOME."

5
Parts.

Depicting a Great Invasion of America.

33rd Episode "EXPLOITS OF ELAINE,"

"THE LIFE CHAIN."

2
Parts.

A New Exclusive Keystone Comedy,

2
Parts.

"THE LITTLE TEACHER."

FIRST TIME IN ABERDEEN.

FULL PROGRAMME OF OTHER HIGH-CLASS SUBJECTS.

REVISED PRICES OF ADMISSION (Including Tax)
—STALLS, 7d; BACK STALLS, 1s 2d; BALCONY,
1s 2d.

ORCHESTRAL MUSIC.   'Phone—2814.

24   La Scala Advertisement, 1917 (*EE*)

along with the St Mungo Symphony Orchestra when it made a return visit in September.

At the Picture House that August, the orchestra gained a leader of international status when violinist David Hamburger, a member of the orchestra when the cinema first opened, returned to take charge. His early training had been as star pupil at the Amsterdam Conservatory, after which he had played in the orchestra of the great conductor Wilhelm Mengelberg, moving from there to lead an orchestra in Munich. Becoming (as the *Express* put it) 'tired of Germany and the Germans', he left to tour Europe with a string quartet. In 1909 he came to Britain as a soloist, but, like so many musicians, had to rely on the orchestra pit rather than the concert platform for a living. As soon as war broke out, he volunteered for the Dutch army, but was discharged on health grounds. The military's loss was the Picture House's gain, and music there flourished under his leadership.

So crowded was the Picture House over the winters of 1916 and 1917 that its manager, Mr Weighill, booked the Music Hall on Saturday nights to show duplicate programmes at the same admission charges—4d., 7d. and 1s. The shows in the Music Hall were accompanied by an orchestra, presumably from the Picture House. Burwood Nicholls, who was at that time a member of the Picture House orchestra, playing the Mustel organ and celesta, returned to his old seat at the Music Hall organ.

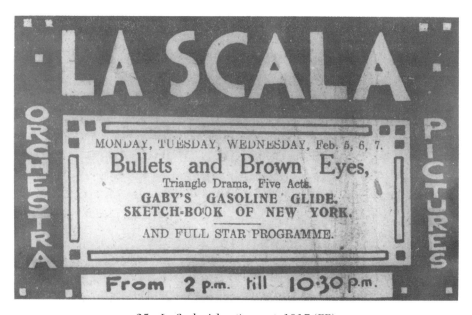

25   La Scala Advertisement, 1917 (*EE*)

℃. To-day, Friday and Saturday

POWERFUL FOUR-PART DRAMA

THE CASE OF BECKY

Featuring BLANCHE SWEET

A capital story of remarkable dramatic interest, in which the power of hypnotism over the human will is tested with results that lead to startling incidents. A photoplay you will undoubtedly like and remember.

❡ ALSO **FULL PROGRAMME COMEDY & INTEREST**

The Picture House

181 UNION STREET.

26   Picture House Advertisement, 1917 (*EE*)

27   Picture House Advertisement, 1917 (EE)

The Trades Council's attempt to run the Coliseum having foundered, next man in was concert veteran D. Brown McGill. A native of Coylton, Ayrshire, McGill appears in the Aberdeen Directory of 1907 as Superintendent of the National Benefit Trust, but by 1912 he was a 'Music Teacher and Tenor Vocalist', operating first from No.14 Thistle Street then, in 1914, from No.20 Bon Accord Street. The Coliseum's vacancy afforded him opportunities in a business with which he had already become acquainted through his singing activities, and his contacts in the entertainment world gave him access to a wide variety of live acts for what was otherwise a fairly work-a-day hall. At first McGill ran the Coliseum in partnership with a Mr W.H. Smith, acting as manager himself, but once established he handed over to deputies who looked after the cinema's day-to-day affairs during his four-year tenure.

28   D. Brown McGill, c.1912

Although now rather eclipsed by their Union Street competitors, smaller halls were still able to do a steady trade in good entertainment. The showing of Tiber Films' *Dark Souls* at the Picturedrome in April 1917 brought another clever little verse from 'Projector' of the *Evening Express*:

> Lives there a man with soul so dead,
> Who never to himself has said—
>   'I'll buy a shilling shocker;
> And roam with Doyle or Bill le Quex
> To 'Poison Belt' or far Peru
>   By submarine or Fokker;
> Or witness on the movie screen
> The daring deeds of dark Doreen,
>   And see the villain knock 'er
> Little head with knob of lead,
> Although he comes a cropper
>   In reel the last.'?
> Well, readers all, if you delight
> In thrilling tales with lots of fright,
>   Remember that on Monday,
> Good Mr Cohn, and he alone

(N.B.—Readers are requested to put another penny in the slot as the metre changes here—for the worse.)

> Will screen such a story,
> In which a pair of erring souls,
> Who get into all sorts of holes,
> Emerge at last with glory;
> And as in fairy tales of old,
> Live happily after, good as gold,
>   Till crowned with tresses hoary.

By the end of June, good Mr Cohn was in uniform, and his wife was carrying out managerial duties. He wrote from Reading, where he was stationed with the Royal Flying Corps, to say that 'every prospect pleased, and only the grub was vile,' philosophically remarking 'There's aye a something!'

Later in the year, 'Projector' noted how popular the name Mary was becoming in filmland:

> Time was when there was only one Mary worth speaking about—Mary Pickford; now there are dozens. If this continues, the old song will have to be brought up to date in something after the following fashion:—

> > Last night there were four Maries;
> > Tonight there are thirty-three;
> > And by tomorrow, if this goes on,
> >   Who knows what the total will be?

When, shortly after that, Mary Pickford was widely advertised in her latest impish juvenile role, *Poor Little Rich Girl*, 'Projector' was unable to resist remarking upon how:

> > Little socks and sandals
> > Skirts just to the knee,
> > Can't put back the hand, gals,
> > To twelve from twenty-three!'

29   Hermann Cohn

The incongruity of a grown woman's achieving world-wide fame for her impersonations of youngsters may seem amusing these days, but in 1917 it was Mary, one of the shrewdest business people in Hollywood, who was doing the laughing—all the way to the bank.

Times were right for the ascendancy of quite another kind of female screen type: the 'vampire' or 'vamp'—a *femme fatale* who lured one unsuspecting male after another to ruin and/or demise most unpleasant. The great Lorelei of them all was Theda Bara, whose so-called 'seductive' hokum provided the public with a much-needed diversion from the war's stresses. With the aid of a fabulous wardrobe and a panoply of extravagant publicity gimmicks, the rather unsylphlike Theda overplayed her 'vamping' to the point of farce, but enjoyed a brief period of great popularity, and her films were a conspicuous feature of Picturedrome programmes as 1917 drew to an end. Of her appearance in a production called *Bohemia* the *Evening Express*'s new film correspondent 'Scrutator' wrote:

Miss Bara skilfully accentuates the varying character moods desired by suiting her dresses to the part. In one scene, for instance, she appears on the stairs in a gown of orange which seems to radiate graciousness; in another, robed in a Chinese gown of blue, she creates an atmosphere of nervousness; while again a wonderful gown of deep rose throws into relief a scene instinct with impulsive fervour. Miss Bara affirms that the effect of colour vibrations serves not only to reflect her mood, but that it affects the actors with whom she is working.

And it all came out in glorious black and white.

The Great War's final year began with the first Music Hall New Year Carnival since 1914, given this time by Green's. Over a season ending in March 1918 Green's gave Saturday night shows in the Music Hall, offering continuous houses, two vocalists every week, and piano and organ music from Burwood Nicholls who had by then moved to La Scala's orchestra. Seats were 8d. for adults and 5d. for children.

For six weeks starting at New Year the Picture House emulated La Scala's earlier orchestral beanfeasts with a visit by the 40-strong Symphony Orchestra of Sgr Enrico Cinganelli, a one-time child prodigy who had studied at the College of Music in Florence. The orchestra's varied programmes embraced both classical and popular material, in accordance with Cinganelli's stated belief in getting to know the audience and feeling the pulse of its musical taste. The first week's repertoire included a symphony by Schubert, Faust selection, the overture to The Merry Wives Of Windsor, Elgar's 'Pomp And Circumstance' marches, selections from Edward German's 'Henry VIII' dances, and a lighter number entitled 'Forget-Me-Not'. For the second week it was Brahms' Second Symphony, Thomas' Mignon overture and Liszt's First Hungarian Rhapsody as music for the big picture. For interludes the orchestra played music by Bizet and Rossini, and the celebrated 'Ave Maria'. There were also violin or viola solos.

A great fund-raising campaign for armaments was then in progress, and an army tank, Tank Julian, was trundling around the country, serving as a mobile shop for War Bonds. On Tuesday 29 June it rolled into Aberdeen's Castlegate to begin selling the following day. The Lord Provost made the first purchase, and within only five minutes £100,000 worth of bonds had been handed out from within the tank's metal shell to the Corporation, local companies and private investors. A film of the tank's arrival was taken by Joe Gray for La Scala, where already prize draws could win patrons £15 worth of bonds, plus five War Certificates of 15s. 6d. each!

A conspicuous feature of Aberdeen cinema-going throughout the war had been the special charity film show, which took on a new importance in March 1918 when exhibitors joined forces to turn it into a very large-scale operation. Every Sunday for many months there was a special film evening somewhere— Picture House, Picturedrome and Royal one week, La Scala, Casino and West End the next, Electric, Queen's, Star, Globe and Coliseum the next, and so on—a generous show of co-operation between cinema proprietors that were otherwise stern rivals.

In the course of a report, in March 1918, on a Picture House programme containing a Charlie Chaplin feature and a film entitled *Would You Forgive?* (evidently something of a tear-jerker) the Express's 'Scrutator' made some interesting remarks upon contemporary film tastes in the city:

> It is a curious point in psychology how the Aberdeen cinema-goer, generally as stern and staid in ordinary life as the granite of his native city, absolutely revels in romance on the screen. The hotter the sentiment, the better it pleases.
>
> Charlie Chaplin, for example, who appeals greatly to the children and to the more frivolous members of an audience, was relished by all who saw him on the screen at the Picture House this week, and the laughter would have tickled Charlie himself even in his most lugubrious moods—if he has any.
>
> Charlie, like Harry Lauder, does occasionally make you wish you had hardened yourself against laugh-strain. In the same way, the romance in 'Would You Forgive?', which teems with sentimentality, mawkish even at times, pleased its patrons greatly.

In comparison with the above, we might take a backward glance at the *Express'* pages of almost exactly a year before—24 March 1917, when 'Scrutator''s predecessor, 'Projector' observed:

> It is interesting to note that the cinema is a tremendously popular institution in the larger towns in Russia. (Which, by the way, makes it all the more remarkable that nobody has yet blamed the movies for causing the present revolution, though I doubt this charge will be made sooner rather than later.) The Russian taste in films is peculiar. To catch the popular fancy, pictures have to be, like the old-time sermon, inordinately long and intolerably gloomy. Picture-house patrons delight in murders and suicides, and can stand anything except a happy ending. Curiously enough, farcical comedies of the knockabout type are also extremely popular, and Charlie Chaplin meets with as enthusiastic a reception in Petrograd as he does in Aberdeen.

But then, Russia took its film-going seriously. When the Czar was overthrown, the Communist regime seized the American films that were circulating in the country, but instead of destroying them put them safely away in archives. As a result, material has been preserved in the USSR that has completely vanished in the West, and exchange schemes have been enthusiastically pursued in recent times!

The Electric, in spite of its prominent Union Street location, was by 1918 suffering serious decline. Heavy competition from La Scala and the Picture House had toppled it from its former position of pre-eminence and it was now rather a second-rate house. Finally, in June or July, the Electric Company was dissolved and proprietorship of the cinema passed to Fred Cruickshank, formerly manager of La Scala, although due to war-time difficulties he had to look after both halls for a while.

The last night of the Electric in its original form was on Saturday 29 June, when its stalwart manager Herbert Austin was given a benefit concert featuring artistes from the Casino, Palace and Tivoli. Special guest performer was Mr Walter Gilbert, manager of the two latter theatres, who returned to the stage in his old capacity as operatic tenor.

Under Cruickshank, and with George Emslie as acting manager, the Electric reopened on Monday 1 July 1918. A new orchestra had been formed around a nucleus of ex-La Scala musicians, with Burwood Nicholls and Marie Sutherland playing the harmonium and piano. In preparation for the house's intended conversion for cine-varieties (with local acts in mind), new seating was installed and construction work began on a spacious waiting-room to end the necessity of queuing outside. A start was also made on the New Ritz Tearooms which would, when complete, seat 200 in 'one of the most luxurious lounges in the North of Scotland'. By October the waiting-room and the White Salon of the tearooms were ready, although Government restrictions prevented the opening of any new refreshment area. Admission prices began at 5d. for the front three rows of the Stalls, but on Saturday nights prices rose to 1s. and 1s. 6d., with seats bookable at 2s. The Woodside Electric continued as companion hall.

Propaganda films remained in full flood until the end of the war. *The Kaiser—Beast Of Berlin*, starring Rupert Julian and Elmo Lincoln, and with Lon Chaney in its cast, made an appearance at La Scala in late October 1918, just as hostilities were drawing to a close. Advertised as 'the film that made New York stand up and cheer like mad', showing the Kaiser 'as he IS', it was intended to take a tilt at Wilhelm's private life, real or supposed, and was quite typical of the product that kept film-makers on both sides of the Atlantic in top gear right up until the great day, 11 November 1918, when at last the long fight was over and peace returned.

'No Armistice Here—Good Things Continue', proclaimed La Scala as the news broke. Among those good things was a film of the official thanksgiving service in the town church, the West Church Of St Nicholas, plus one or more of the various films of the German surrender that had been immediately put on release. As a joyful rush for amusements began, the Coliseum's D. Brown McGill began combining old ideas with new. For several months starting in November 1918 the Trades Hall's fine maple floor was cleared each morning to allow the commencement of roller-skating at 11 o'clock. At 4 o'clock the seating was put back, and the picture show began at 6.45.

The Christmas of 1918 was celebrated by the city's cinemas with whatever (rather scarce) special features they could find. Cinema owners and managers could at last look forward to—well, no-one could say for sure, but few could have felt pessimistic in the 'new age' that was beginning after those long years of darkness.

Chapter 7

Towards Maturity   1919—1923

Those expecting the immediate dawn of a 'golden era' for post-war Britain were disappointed. Men returning from the forces had to seek scarce (and often badly-paid) employment amid shortages and widespread financial recession, and soon the atmosphere was one of disillusionment, discontent and social unrest.

Allied to this was a strong popular urge to get more out of life. People felt a thirst for amusements, partly as an aid towards blotting out the war's ghastly memories. Fantasy and excitement were called for, and there, waiting, was the cinema, ready to provide a world of escapism.

Well-financed and sheltered from the maelstrom, American film-making had progressed by leaps and bounds between 1914 and 1918. British production, meanwhile, had been severely hampered by lack of investment, shortage of photographic celluloid and the turning over of studios to propaganda work. Pictures from the States were highly attractive to British audiences, and were constantly improving. The American movie companies, their initial investment and main profit secure on home 'first-runs', were only too pleased at the prospect of a bonus to be made on UK releases, and made sure of offering favourable rental terms. Britain's enforced default, therefore, allowed America to consolidate an enormous head start that was never to be made up.

With the relaxation of war-time restrictions, exhibitors applied themselves in earnest to the business of capturing the cinema-going public. Cinema buildings became more elaborate, as did methods of film presentation. For a while it was fashionable to offer a short revue as part of the programme. This popular entertainment of transatlantic origin had replaced music hall at Aberdeen's Palace Theatre in 1916, and had been successfully tried at the Casino and the Star. At New Year 1919 D. Brown McGill introduced a series of mini-revues and dramas at the Coliseum, beginning with a 20-strong revue production entitled 'Hullo 1919'. 'Some of the jokes', reported the *Evening Express*, 'may have been heard before, but have lost none of their piquancy because of that.' For anyone too familiar with the gags there was always the diversion of the show's 'beauty chorus'. Another revue in the series was 'Where's The Editor?', while dramas included such well known Scots pieces as 'Jeannie Deans', 'The Mill O' Tifty's Annie' and 'Jamie Fleeman', performed by the A.W.B. Kingston Dramatic Sketch Company. Films on those nights would be kept to the ever-popular serial instalment.

Unfortunately for McGill, a detail in his billing for 'Hullo 1919' landed him in trouble. In the cast, playing a rejuvenated 'knut' (showily-dressed young fellow) of peacetime, was a man calling himself Dan Fraser. This did not amuse the now well-established and popular Scots entertainer Dan Fraser, who had up until then been a friend of McGill's and who had appeared as a member of the Coliseum's variety company only a week before. The act was a poor one, Fraser felt that his good reputation was at risk, and McGill found himself facing a court claim for £50 compensation, later restricted to £20. Maintaining that no deception had been intended, McGill held that he had not advertised the performer as a Scots comedian or put him at the top of the bill as he would certainly have done with the real Fraser. The 'imposter', who was not appearing under either his own or his normal stage name, did not imitate his 'namesake', but only played a waiter in a sketch along with five or six others.

Dan Fraser, meanwhile, had the support of some notable colleagues—Mr J. Wells, manager of the Casino, Mr Shepherd, musical director for many years at the Tivoli and at the Palace before that, and James Montague, who will be remembered from the days of the Empire and Alhambra. Matters appear to have been somewhat complicated by a statement made by Mr Shepherd to the effect that if Fraser had been on the bill it would have been disadvantageous to him as managements took cognisance of grades of hall in which artistes appeared. Fraser had of course already played at the Coliseum, which, as McGill freely admitted, was pretty unpretentious!

Still the identity of the spurious 'Fraser' seems murky, and even McGill did not apparently know that the fellow had already appeared under the name 'Jack Pearce' in a revue a fortnight before the incident. The outcome of the affair went unreported, but it seems very likely that poor old McGill simply had to pay up!

In early 1919 the Gaiety changed hands once again, reopening with regular cine-variety—a far more viable proposition now that artistes could travel freely. Its first advertisement under new management appeared on 24 February, main film during the first half of the week being an exciting five-reeler *The Conqueror Of Death*. From the Thursday the film was *A Just Deception*. The variety acts were Dan Conray the 'Great Star Comedian' ('everybody's favourite'), Lena McBean 'Vocalist and Expert Dancer' and The Famous Taffies ('Welsh harmonising and real up-to-date comedy').

Influenza was raging through a weakened Britain, and at the suggestion of the city magistrates several Aberdeen halls had curtailed their opening hours, those with matinees closing between 5 p.m. and 6 p.m., but the Gaiety, with two matinees a week, was made of sterner stuff. 'Don't be afraid of the flu', proclaimed the same advertisement as above, 'we have the most up-to-date disinfectant for killing all germs, approved by the Medical Society Of Research'. New proprietor was Mr Alexander Grant, recently retired from the Post Office. His manager, Mr Seivewright, handled the booking of stage acts which included some very unusual ones like 'Little Blind Dolly', described as a 'child psychic' who could answer questions regarding people's departed relatives, amaze with lightning arithmetical calculations, and demonstrate various forms of telepathy.

The Gaiety continued for only a matter of months in this form. On 5 May 1919 came an announcement that it had been taken over by the newly-formed Palladium Theatre Company, and exactly three weeks later, under new manager A.F. Gibson, it was renamed the PALLADIUM. Various improvements were made to the building, and new tip-up seating was installed. Continuous performances were introduced, still with cine-varieties, and these attracted substantial queues ('an unusual feature in the Shiprow', the *Evening Express* noted). The slogan 'All Cars Stop At The Palladium' quickly became a familiar one.

La Scala was one of the cinemas that trimmed its afternoon programmes to three hours, and additional precautions were taken to keep the influenza at bay. Newspaper advertisements announced that:

> Few cinemas in Scotland are better adapted to carry out the recommendations of the medical experts than La Scala. The cinema is lofty; tremendous air space; perfect ventilation. Sprayed at short intervals with the fragrant but deadly effective germ-killer, pine oil and Septol.

That same February the Picture House became one of surely very few cinemas in Britain to possess a war memorial. This took the form of a gold lettered plaque, installed in the vestibule to commemorate three members of staff killed in the recent conflict—Gunner R.W. Platt, foreman of staff; Private W.M. Crow, operator; and Private J. Morgan, a member of the orchestra. Above their names was inscribed the legend:

> This simple memorial records the names of the members of the Picture House staff who sacrificed their lives in the great cause of freedom.

It would be of interest to know what happened to the memorial—as far as can be ascertained there was no sign of it when the building was renovated in the 1950s.

The world of the cinema exhibitor was a potentially lucrative one, but it was now no longer possible to set up a business without ample capital to meet constant increases in renters' fees as film-making became more lavish, to cover other running costs both expected and unexpected, and to ride out difficult periods. This fact was rather painfully brought home to Fred S. Cruickshank, new proprietor of the Electric and possessor, it seems, of more enthusiasm than luck or judgement. When he commenced trading on 1 July 1918 his intention had been to go into partnership with his sons, drawing a basic salary of £5 per week plus commission of between £8 and £15. Green's had asked him to stay on at La Scala, but he quit because he felt that to do otherwise would be dishonest. His rent for the Electric was £14 per week, and his capital amounted to only £200 in hard cash—eaten up right away by costs. He had named his company F.S. Cruickshank And Sons, but his partnership negotiations had then failed. Still he had pressed on, taking up the lease on the Woodside Electric in October 1918 at £2. 10s. per week, plus cost of all renovations.

The 'Rinkie' turned out to be so cold and difficult to heat that audiences could not comfortably sit in it. Business was so poor that takings amounted to only £10 to £12 per week, not enough even to meet staff wages, but in the hopes of an improvement he had propped up the operation with funds from the more solvent Union Street Electric, there being no separate bank accounts. No books were kept—instead he had simply filed his receipts. He had entered into expensive film bookings with the Glasgow agencies, and then, when no upturn in trade came about at either Electric, had made frantic efforts to cancel these in favour of cheaper material, bringing claims of between £10 and £15 each for films contracted but never shown. Before long the Union Street Electric was also in trouble, taking only £40 per week as against expenses of £60 to £70.

He had also been subject to personal outlay—the cost of moving his furniture to Aberdeen from Glasgow, and of buying more locally. He had arranged (of all notions) to take over the running of La Scala's tearoom, for which he had bought from his own pocket £60 worth of plate, only to have to sell it again for £25 to meet pressing expenses. By February 1919 his liabilities were excess of £1,000. His overheads had run away with him, he had no financial backing, and his only possible recourse was to the bankruptcy court that April.

After this, Mr Cruickshank ('Cruickshank' was apparently his professional name, his real name being Davies) disappears from our sight, possibly back into the employ of Green's. At the February licensing court the Electric's licence was transferred to a man who we have already met in connection with the building and decorating of cinemas—Bruce MacKenzie.

Who were the screen-struck Aberdeen public turning out to see in those early post-war years? To tell the truth, the line-up of favourites in 1919 did not differ greatly from that of 1916—Mary Pickford, Mabel Normand, Lillian and Dorothy Gish, Marguerite Clark, W.S. Hart, etc. Up-and-coming, however, were such future stars as Gloria Swanson, Zasu Pitts, Tallulah Bankhead, Rudolph Valentino and Lon Chaney.

Then there were two films which, when they reached the Electric in mid-1919, occasioned much local pride and curiosity. These starred the Aberdeen-born opera singer Mary Garden, who, although she worked exclusively in France and America, was still affectionately regarded by many in her native city as 'our Mary'. Aberdonians followed her career with interest, and when she made periodic returns on holiday she was hailed as the city's very own celebrity.

The first film, which she made in 1918, was a silent screen version of her greatest stage success, Massenet's opera *Thais*. The second was a drama called *The Splendid Sinner*, and both films were successful wherever their star was known, although their appeal lay more in their celebrity value than in their merit as works of high screen art. As is succinctly recounted by Richard Griffith and Arthur Mayer in their book *The Movies*:

> ...(*Thais*) consisted of little more than a series of shots of Miss Garden in the statuesque poses of opera tradition, and, as a result, was a close approach to a motionless motion picture. The movie public scorned this cold stranger, trying to vamp like their Theda Bara. It was decided that for her second picture a 'modern' story might put Miss Garden over more successfully. But *The Splendid Sinner* was modern only in the details of its costume and decor. The story had Miss Garden a Parisian wanton who leaped upon a table and madly played the violin to the rich moths clustered around the flame of her sex appeal. Such abandon could not go on and leave her 'sympathetic' in the finale, so she atoned as a Red Cross nurse in a uniform which fitted as snugly as cunning could contrive. But Nurse's intellectual face did not agree with the sweet compassion written into the subtitles, and Mr Goldwyn and his backers had another load of grief on their hands.

The previous 'loads of grief' had been other famous stage personalities that Samuel Goldwyn tried to showcase in their best-known roles, but who had fared no better when it came to 'getting themselves over'. Whether Mary Garden was necessarily any more 'scorned' than Theda Bara was taken seriously is open to question, but it is certainly true that neither Miss Garden nor the majority of Goldwyn's 'Famous Players' could compete with the generation of film stars that the public had taken to its heart. Besides, it is hard to imagine anything harder to translate into the terms of silent film than an opera, with its reliance on music and singing. Miss Garden, for her part, found the whole exercise simply frustrating.

The Splendid Sinner was described in the *Evening Express* of 15 September 1919 as:

> The story of a young girl who frees herself from the hand-shackles of society life and finds happiness in the love of a young doctor, but is later pursued by her former lover, at whose hand she dies a heroic death...

Of it, Mary Garden wrote in her 1952 autobiography *The Mary Garden Story*:

> ...I made 'The Splendid Sinner' in three weeks, and I hope nobody in God's world will ever see it again. I have heard many films called the worst ever made; I am sure those who make such judgements never saw The Splendid Sinner...
> ...In the silent days we didn't say anything; we just looked. That's why there was no place for a woman like me. I had to talk. Just marching around and moving my hands smothered me as an artist...

If Aberdeen did not produce a great screen star in Miss Garden, it may at least take pleasure in having been the birthplace of one of the opera world's most captivating and popular leading ladies in the earlier part of this century.

30   Mary Garden as 'Carmen'

By the summer of 1919, Messrs Green had adopted a regular policy of pushing La Scala's weekly programmes by means of large sensationally-worded newspaper advertisements. As a standard item of publicity, La Scala calendars were presented free to patrons each January. Under a new manager, Mr Collinson (who arrived in August) local newsreels enjoyed a resurgence, the Braemar Gathering being filmed as in former years. It was also La Scala that gave the first star billings to Roscoe 'Fatty' Arbuckle, king-sized stalwart of the Keystone melee, now working on his own, and to Gloria Swanson, an ex-Mack Sennett bathing beauty then at the beginning of a brilliant career. The film in which La Scala first brought Gloria's name to the fore was *Her Decision*, shown that September. It soon had a follow-up in *Every Woman's Husband*, the subject of which was pithily described in advertisements as 'Pitfalls In Husband Handling; Or Too Much Mother-In-Law.' At the Picture House over June and July 1919, Julian Rosetti played selections on a fine Bluthner grand piano. The Palace Theatre still had a film section in its programme—mainly westerns, comedies, cartoons and Gaumont Gazette.

That September, film distribution was disrupted once again by a major rail strike that seemed set to leave Aberdeen high and dry. Things looked bad, but word reached the Picture House's manager, Mr Ling, that a consignment of programmes for Aberdeen cinemas could be collected at Perth. A few telephone calls later, a convoy of cars was on its way south to pick up the precious boxes. Even so, some less fortunate managements had to dig around for whatever they could find, with one Aberdeen hall reduced to showing films about 10 years old—their outdated costumes, etc, no doubt causing great amusement. Clearly, situations like this could not be allowed to recur, and soon films were being carried back and forth by special road hauliers.

The first screen cartoon favourites, Mutt And Jeff, were to be seen in every cinema in 1919. Syndicated from the States and perhaps a little Americanised for British tastes, the antics of the long-and-short pair were nevertheless very topical, particularly when it came to their supposed acquaintance with the great boxer Jacques Carpentier. The two would vie continually for the privilege of being Carpentier's sparring partner, but each would somehow manage to duck out at the last minute if any sort of success seemed imminent!

By October, the Electric had been considerably up-graded, and 'Scrutator' of the *Evening Express* commented that he would not be surprised to see the hall blossom into a 'marble stair and crimson carpet' one. Manager was still George Emslie, and in accordance with its new status the Electric now boasted the Select Orchestra of the veteran Mr Shepherd. Pianist was Miss Jose Squire, who had been in charge of music at the Beach Pavilion over the summer season, and who within a short while was promoted as leader of the Electric's five-piece ensemble.

'Jazz' was already *the* word in the popular vocabulary. The Palace Theatre had the Great Jazz Seven in a 'Whirlwind Of Ragtime', and at Christmas 1919 Aberdeen was given the opportunity to 'get ahead' when the Casino screened *Jazz Mania*, the orchestra doing its level best to synchronise to all the latest (silent) dance steps!

The Palladium began 1920 with a scheme of refurbishment in which separate entrances were made for Stalls and Balcony, and a new waiting room was provided. Manager was Mr Jack Francis, who up until 1912 had toured variety halls under the name 'Joe Weston' with a solo patter and trick violin-playing act. In this he performed popular melodies in all manner of contortionist's postures, his favourite tune being G.H. Chirgwin's music hall song 'My Fiddle Is My Sweetheart'. Although Mr Francis had long since given up the stage for managerial work, it seems that he could still hold the attention of an audience. That June, by request, he performed the variety act in one of his own shows; so good was his reception that several curtain-calls had to be taken before the screen could be lowered for the film, and this became the first of many such appearances. To lead the community singing (always enjoyed as part of cinema shows, but now coming more than ever into vogue) the Palladium secured the services of a regular Chorus Vocalist, Miss Lillie Currie, 'a beautiful lady attired in lovely dresses', to rest the eyes of patrons while exercising their vocal cords.

The Picture House, its pre-war slogan 'Meet Me At The Picture House' reinstated, enhanced its presentations by the augmentation of its orchestra, which was under the direction of Mr S.O. Goldsmith, formerly musical director at first-class picture halls and theatres in London. At the Coliseum, meanwhile, films and varieties were supplemented by boxing matches, drawing large crowds and attracting participants from near and far. Dances were held after the Coliseum's Monday, Wednesday and Friday shows during the early part of the year.

At the Casino that February, Elmo Lincoln starred in the very first Tarzan film, *Tarzan Of The Apes*, made in 1918. The swashbuckling screen hero was by now well established, with W.S. Hart fighting the Hun in his own fearless way, Douglas Fairbanks as the athletic young heart-throb, and the debonair Tom Mix rising to stardom as the sporty Adonis.

The war had one noticeable effect on film producers—it made them far more careful about the accuracy of military drill. Patrons were now inclined to give a hearty horse-laugh to guns that fired shot after shot without any apparent effort to load, operate the bolt, or even to aim!

Change began in the line-up of Aberdeen's cinema halls when, in September 1920, James Donald's lease on the West End expired and he was immediately followed as proprietor by Aberdeen Picture Palaces. Among the latter's early bookings for the West End was D.W. Griffiths' *Broken Blossoms*, starring Lillian Gish. An important example of its producer's work, *Broken Blossoms* is now recognised as a screen classic, despite the initial doubts of some of Griffiths' own staff who dubbed it *Busted Posies*! A further piece of business had been concluded by APP just before it took over the West End—the purchase of the entire Union Club building at No.42 Union Terrace, and with it the Picturedrome, on which Henry Phillips' lease had only a few months to run. (The land records state that the property was officially made over on 17 August.) The sequel to this we shall presently see.

1920 also brought a brief professional reunion, after several years' working separately, of 'the other Walkers' of the first decade of this century. Since 1912, G.W. Walker had done little or no cinematography, preferring to concentrate on stage and impresario work. In 1911, at the suggestion of Harry Lauder, a Scottish concert party called 'The Caledonian Four' had been formed, consisting of Walker, Jeannie Hendry the dancer, James Scott Skinner, and Jeannie Middleton, soprano and accompanist. The team fulfilled some very important engagements, among them the opening of the London Palladium, where they scored a great success, but George Walker fell ill and the party broke up. In 1912 Walker formed another concert party, with which he toured South Africa.

British tours followed, and in 1914 the party left for a return visit to South Africa, but the disruptions of war prevented it from reaching its destination. The war years were spent working in Australia (where the team arrived in 1915), and in New Zealand. The wonder of radio was exploited sooner in Australia than in this country, and Walker and a member of his troupe, Jessie Bunting, sang in Melbourne's very first broadcast. In 1918, the party reached South Africa at last, now in the company of Harry Lauder, for whom George Walker acted as personal representative. After the tour's completion, Walker continued his concert activities as before, never happier than when out on his travels.

George Walker junior, meanwhile, had remained in the employ of Henry Phillips at the Picturedrome and the Kings, from the pay box of which he had kept an eye on the queues outside the short-lived Lyceum in nearby John Street. In late 1920 his father, back in London from yet another spell in South Africa, chanced to see a showing of the French director Abel Gance's *I Accuse* (*J'Accuse*), a war story which concluded with a striking montage of the dead of the Somme, Flanders and elsewhere marching towards the camera from above their graves. Impressed, he immediately secured a renting of the film, and wired his son to make an evening's booking of the Music Hall. *I Accuse* was such a sell-out that the Walkers went on to give a series of Saturday night shows under the name 'Pioneer Picture Company'. Once again Burwood Nicholls was in charge of the music, and each programme included variety acts, among them the 79-year-old Scott Skinner—surely an occasion of much reminiscing about the 'old days'.

Typical of the films on those Saturday nights were Griffiths' *The End Of The Road*, and *The Wonder Man* starring boxer-turned-actor George Carpentier. Occasionally there were week-night films of a different nature—*The Dangers Of Ignorance*, for instance, outspokenly sought to illustrate the dangers of venereal disease, an increase in which had been one of the war's more insidious by-products.

G.W. Walker's touring continued all through the 1920s, to the eventual detriment of his health, but not even the chronic bronchitis with which he returned from a trip to Australia in 1930 was allowed to get in his way. After only a month's recuperation he was off again, touring the north of Scotland. Such an assault on his rapidly failing constitution proved too great, and in November 1930, still 'on the road', he died in the Fife Arms Hotel, Dufftown.

In late March and early April 1921, the leases on the Picturedrome and Coliseum expired. On 22 March, a benefit concert was held for the 'Coliseum Entertainers', Nellie Dean and Will Elliot. Like most benefits, it contained no films; instead it consisted of contributions from stage artistes appearing at the Casino and other halls, plus a turn by the Palladium's Jack Francis. Four days later, the old 'Colly' showed its last film *The Arlington Mystery*, and D. Brown McGill returned to music teaching. In 1923 he opened a commission agent's office at 46 Bon Accord Street, but after 1927 the business is shown as being in his wife's name. By 1934 the premises had become McGill's Hotel, the name that it still bears.

On 25 March 1921 the Picturedrome's popular manager Hermann Cohn also received a benefit, on the bill of which was G.W. Walker. Phillips' last show at the Picturedrome took place on 9 April, when the main films were *Who Has The Better Time?*, *Fame And Fortune* starring Tom Mix, and an episode of the serial *Daredevil Jack*, starring boxer Jack Dempsey.

Aberdeen Picture Palaces, meanwhile, was about to put into operation an ambitious scheme for the reconstruction and enlargement of the West End. Perhaps it was with an eye to this that Bert Gates and his colleagues had purchased the Picturedrome the previous summer, securing a replacement hall for the period during which the West End would be out of action. Perhaps, again, the Picturedrome was snapped up by APP before the company knew whether or not it would actually obtain the lease on the West End. That would have made sure that APP had one hall or the other—and of course there was always the fine large office building on Union Terrace as an additional investment. Whatever the background intricacies, the West End closed on Saturday, 2 April with a film entitled *Should A Husband Forgive?*, and APP continued business at the 'Drome, which reopened on 18 April with *The River's End*, one of several bookings lying over from its previous tenant. Once these previous bookings had been used up, APP's own programmes went in and the number of seat reservations (always a popular facility) increased dramatically. One notable feature brought to the 'new' Picture-drome, with its admission prices of 5*d.*, 8*d.* and 1*s.*, was Mary Pickford's *Pollyanna*, one of the first releases from United Artists, a new film company formed by the shrewd Mary, her husband Douglas Fairbanks, Charlie Chaplin, and D.W. Griffith.

On quitting the Picturedrome, Henry Phillips moved to the Coliseum, which recommenced on Monday, 11 April 1921 under the name NEW KINEMA. The building was open all that afternoon so that the public could inspect the new seating and other improvements, and all proceeds from the evening's performance were donated to the Earl Haig Fund. Admission was a now tax-free 8*d.* and 1*s.*, and films included *I Accuse* and more of the *Daredevil Jack* series. As at the Picturedrome of old, Balcony seats were bookable in advance.

Torry gained a cinema of its own once again with the opening, on Monday, 2 May 1921, of the TORRY PICTURE HOUSE. At the ceremony, Lord Provost Sir

31   The Trades Hall, Belmont Street, as the New Kinema, 1935 (ADC, Dept of Planning)

James Taggart recalled the day when the area's population was little more than 20, as compared with the 20,000 or so that lived there by this time. He also commented on how welcome the development was, considering the neglect of entertainment in Torry over the years.

Promoters of the enterprise were the same group of businessmen that had operated the old Torry Rink before the war, and who now formed Torry Pictures Ltd (later Torry Cinemas). The Torry's first main feature was *The Life Of Christopher Columbus* ('the most sensational event in your life would be a mere incident in this man's career'), and admission prices were 5*d.*, 9*d.*, 1*s.* 3*d.* and 1*s.* 6*d.*—quite expensive for the better seats. Manager was Mr J.H. Forrester, and musical director was Mr Harold Pollard, of whom the earliest mention so far found is in an *Evening Express* cinema column of November 1919 when he was working at the Picturedrome as pianist in a new orchestra under the leadership of a Mr Fyfe, cellist. After that he had been musical director for James Donald at the West End. Playing in picture houses was only one part of Mr Pollard's activities; he also had a music shop in the New Market (later in Guild Street).

The Torry cinema was, like the Casino, designed by Messrs Sutherland and George. Two sets of plans for it were approved—one drawn up in July 1919 and a later (undated) one lodged with the authorities in January 1920. The second plan was a more elaborate version of the first, showing a balcony where previously there was merely a raised area at the back, the addition of a stage tower to allow the 'flying' of scenery for cine-variety shows, and some revision of the frontage. Attractive glass-domed kiosks were shown in the foyer. What came to be built lay somewhere between the two plans. The balcony was provided, but not the stage tower. The harled frontage followed the 1920 drawings, but with some of their (very handsome) detailing simplified or omitted. The frontage's basic concept did not, however, alter between the two drafts. The Casino's low square tower and semi-circular window devices were borrowed, but with the centre of the frontage culminating in a simple pediment, following the line of the pitched roof. Above the semi-circular central window was a smaller circular space or *oculus*, and on either side were ordinary square windows. The composition was a satisfying one, but it had to be altered at a late stage by the insertion of small upper windows to light the operating box. This gave the frontage a slightly quaint appearance, resembling from some angles a cartoon face—not at all what the architect intended! The 1920 plan shows the proscenium with some kind of Eastern 'pavilion' on either side, adding a little exotic touch to an otherwise fairly conventional building, but whether this design was actually carried out it is now too late to say.

By no means a first-run hall, the Torry nevertheless drew full houses for its Westerns, popular romances and detective films, all of which changed at the half-week. Bookings were available for the higher priced seats.

Across town at the Casino, J.P. Kilgour's son Ormonde L. Kilgour (1896-1945) had taken over as proprietor on the death of his father, and had also inherited the waste business next door. Ormonde Kilgour was a well-educated man for whom dealing in rags held no great attraction, and within only a

32 Torry Picture House, later Torry Cinema, Crombie Road, 1935. All exterior detailing and most windows replaced by harling in the 1950s

33   Ormonde L. Kilgour, 1944

year or so the Waste Factory had gone. Local cinema-trade lore has it that he was quite a stickler for his appointments book, running it perhaps a little more strictly than might have been to his advantage. Even renters' representatives on their usual fairly informal rounds had to arrange in advance to visit the Casino, and while no doubt Mr Kilgour had good reason for this, it was considered a strange regime in a business that depended so much on contacts.

No such restrictions were to be found on trade visits to James Donald during the 1920s. Such occasions were always most convivial, with all comforts attended to and some kind of entertainment always on the agenda. Usually this took the form of an evening at the Ballroom where the guest would be treated to a delicious meal, usually consisting of a particularly tasty make of meat pies, which quickly became renowned among 'reps' for their excellence!

'Energy—Enterprise—Success' tooted an advert for La Scala in May 1921. 'Up to the present we have been dependent on the town for gas to drive our powerful electric plant, but we are now independent and use no gas, no town

34   Playhouse Advertisement (*EE* 14 Nov. 1922)

electricity and no coal, but we have electric light'. Petrol was not used either, and the means by which this feat was accomplished at 'The House Of Enterprise' is shrouded in the mists of antiquity!

That same month, La Scala, which had carried Fatty Arbuckle's first Aberdeen billing, carried his last. An old Keystone re-issue appropriately entitled *The Village Scandal*, the film was described as 'not a morality play, but Fatty Arbuckle, the Human Mountain of Fun'. Just then its star was headed for a mountain of anything but fun. Later in the year he fell abruptly from grace in a grimy little scandal of his own, centring on the death, in very questionable circumstances, of a starlet named Virginia Rappe, at whom Arbuckle had apparently set his cap after a rather well 'bootlegged' Hollywood party. Although Fatty was cleared of the ensuing murder charge, his career was finished. People who could not wait to pin something on what they were convinced was the terrible sin-land of Hollywood had a banquet handed to them, and the public—or at least certain vocal sections of it—went up in arms. In the States, objects were thrown at the screen if an Arbuckle film was shown. New Arbuckle features ready for release had to be scrapped at the cost of thousands of dollars, and in Britain he disappeared overnight. He subsequently secured some work as a producer, but was never again seen in pictures.

The great Dempsey/Carpentier fight of July 1921 was proudly announced by the Casino as being due on its screen on the very day of the film's release. Unfortunately the New Kinema slipped in with the same film on the same day, and the Casino's fire was stolen!

Typical among the 'problem' films that were then in fashion (another symptom of the post-war climate) was one entitled *Unmarried*, shown at the Casino in May under the auspices of the recently-formed National Council For The Unmarried Mother. Every day for a whole week queues stretched right down Wales Street, and only by visiting or phoning the Casino in advance (number 1081) to book a seat could admittance be guaranteed. However constructive the aims of *Unmarried*, the Casino's advertising material was quite something else:

> ...this human story concerns the tragic
> experience of two young girls—one rich, the
> other poor, both of whom have
> LOVED NOT WISELY, BUT TOO WELL !!
> They love their children, passionately, almost
> fiercely, do these
> MOTHERS WHO HAVE NO MARRIAGE BONDS !!
> Yet what a problem—what a drama they arouse.
> You must see the Children's Palace crowded with
> happy erstwhile
> ---- UNWANTED CHILDREN !! ----
> It is the climax in 'Unmarried'.

In keeping with the new craze for jazz, La Scala, towards the middle of the year, introduced special Friday Jazz Nights, at which Mr Lox Willar with his Champion Jazz Band would, it was reported, be seen to 'beat the band—and himself', whatever that meant. Not to be outdone, the Palladium brought in Jazz Nights that June, with a band led by Little Jackie, 'the youngest conductor in Vaudeville'.

By the end of the summer, the former West End had been transformed into the 1,000-seater PICTURE PLAYHOUSE, opened on 14 September 1921 by Bert Gates in the presence of his fellow company directors. Also present were the cinema's architects George Sutherland and Clement George, and a variety of other local VIPs. The Picture Playhouse (generally known as simply the PLAYHOUSE) had not been finished quite in time to take its intended opening programme, but a worthy replacement had been found in *A Yankee At The Court Of King Arthur*, supported by a comedy *Jerry On The Spot*, a Pathé Gazette and a 'short' about the structure of the human ear! Aberdeen Picture Palaces was now the proud possessor of a large, well-situated 'flagship' house, and Union Street now sported a fine up-to-date cinema.

Messrs Sutherland and George's design for the Playhouse adhered strictly to 'classical' lines, in accordance with the cinema's west-end status. The Union Street entrances were surrounded by white Sicilian marble facings on a black marble base, owing much, it was reported, to Greek influence. Above that, the original upper front was retained. The central paybox was oval in plan, with one end in the vestibule and the other end in the front foyer, a large area decorated in plaster mouldings, cornices, and Austrian oak panelling. In the vestibule was a mural frieze, with a painting of Aberdeen Picture Palaces' own 'coat of arms' above the doors.

After the paybox and inner doors, a carpeted marble stairway 12 feet wide led upwards through the Union Street part of the building to the first-floor main foyer. Off the foyer were the usual cloakrooms, etc, and to the left a precipitous stairway led above the manager's office to the new balcony. Beyond the manager's office was the wood and glass partitioning of the Ingleneuk, a very well-conducted little cafe where 'the daintiest teas in town' were served between 10 a.m. and 6 p.m. At the end of the foyer were the doors to the auditorium's Back Stalls.

The auditorium walls were decorated in plaster panelling and mouldings, and the curved ceiling, which rose in a sharp step over the balcony, was textured in small gilt squares. The stage was shallow, with a gilt proscenium arch 25 feet across (2 feet less than the Casino's). At the upper corners of the proscenium, which cleverly followed the line of the ceiling, were gilt plaster reliefs of lions' heads—a nice touch. Dark wooden panelling angled inwards to frame the slightly translucent curtains, through which, with the curtains closed, the screen could be rather mysteriously glimpsed under pink lighting. The front of the stage was cut away to give space for the orchestra.

The auditorium floor had the usual rake towards the back, but, in line with latest practice, started to slope gently upwards again at the half-way mark, minimising cricks in the neck for Front-Stallites! The velvet upholstery matched the thick crimson carpeting, and each seat was spring-padded for comfort. The secondary lighting system, which extended throughout the building, took the form of beautiful copper gas fittings with opaque white shades, while the electric light fittings in the stairways and foyer had conical cut-glass shades with edge reliefs that showed the beginnings of Art Deco influence.

The outward appearance of the building was highly distinctive, its roofline descending in three stepped levels, the highest above the balcony and operating box, the next reaching approximately half way down the auditorium, and the third and longest stretching back to Justice Mill Lane. Only the first step was apparent from inside the hall. Each roof section was steeply pitched and slated, the slates extending down the vertical end faces of the first two levels.

Associated with the technical side of the Playhouse was Joe Gray, who arrived via the Casino. Leon Pokorny, back in circulation, led the small orchestra, while in the manager's office was Bert Gates himself. A few years later Gates handed over managerial responsibility to William Pirie, who had first joined APP as elocutionist (in company with Mrs Pirie) at the Star while Gates was away on war service, and who up until this promotion had been in charge of the Globe.

The Picture House, doubtless feeling the heat from its new Union Street rival, was quick to reply with a combination of coffee and orchestral music in the restaurant and sensationalism on the screen. The latter was exemplified during the week of 24 October, by a well-advertised showing of *The God Of Luck*, the last film of Gaby Deslys, who, while making the final scene, was said to have received a premonition of her own subsequent death from cancer. The film's scenario had, of course, been changed to reveal this presentiment.

The element of tragedy could indeed be profitable; the next week, the New Kinema did well with *The Spite Bride* starring Olive Thomas (Mary Pickford's sister-in-law, who died in 1920 of accidental poisoning), and *A Twilight Baby*, the last film of Virginia Rappe to whom attention had come only now that Arbuckle was bound for court over her death.

After an eventful year, 1922 was ushered in at the Torry cinema with special matinee programmes and varieties, most notable among the latter being 'L'Ada—the original master mind', presented in 'a gorgeous electric throne setting'. 'Is it Spiritualism? Is it a trick? Is it wireless? Is it a code? Bring a photograph and test L'Ada for yourself!'

Jackie Coogan, fresh from his success with Chaplin in *The Kid*, so packed the New Kinema in *Peck's Bad Boy* that a re-run was promptly booked for March. The Playhouse had Mary Pickford in her latest feature *Suds*, while Norma and Constance Talmadge, Bebe Daniels, Snub Pollard, Corrinne Griffith, cowboy star Hoot Gibson, Ramon Novarro, Virginia Valli, Constance

Bennett, Marie Prevost, John Gilbert, Leatrice Joy, Rod LaRoque, Ben Lyon and Adophe Menjou were just some of the screen personalities that would become increasingly familiar to the film-going public as the year went on.

At the Music Hall, James Donald presented a series of special New Year picture shows, top attraction at which was the famous ten-reeler *Over The Hill*, starring Mary Carr. On Monday, 3 April 1922 this film formed the centre-piece to Mr Donald's return to full-time cinema work in what had been Allan's Stores at 286 George Street, now converted to become the GRAND CENTRAL. In addition to *Over The Hill* there was a 'topical budget', a documentary *The Wonder Sights Of London*, and a succession of 'shorts' of the usual kinds, including the almost inevitable Mutt And Jeff. A chief operator, it was reported, had been brought in from the south, and Harold Pollard returned to Mr Donald's employ as musical director, playing for the Music Hall shows and taking charge of the Grand Central's 4-piece orchestra until the end of 1922 when he left to go to the Electric. He was succeeded by a well-known ex-theatre musician, Burton Denham, who remained for some time.

The Grand Central was in those days very small—only one storey high—and quite plain. The chief decorative feature of the little auditorium was a series of mock ceiling beams supported on pilasters at intervals along the walls. The seats were in crimson plush, and the floor, designed on the same principle as that of the Playhouse, was covered with durable cork linoleum and carpets. The foyer was entered through three sets of double doors, with the centrally-placed pay-box ahead and the auditorium doors to either side. Stairs from either side of the foyer led upwards to a small balcony and projection box. In the event of an emergency, the house could be cleared in seconds, the opening of the emergency doors bringing on lights in the narrow lane behind the building. A large extractor fan kept the hall well ventilated, and this cosy new outpost of filmland in the north-east quarter of the city centre soon became known for its comfort as well as for good entertainment.

Films were still being shown in other buildings besides cinemas. The YMCA continued its Saturday night pictures as before, and from the beginning of May 1922 the Palace Theatre, now equipped with a 'Gardiner Velvet Gold Fibre Screen', ran a cine-variety season, beginning with a production entitled *Caught By The Mormons*. If ever a film had a novel advertising stunt, this was it. One day, passers-by in Union Street were amazed to see two men get out of a taxi, approach two girls who were apparently innocently walking along the pavement, grab them and bundle them into the car, which drove off at speed amid general commotion. The incident looked like a real kidnapping until cards 'plugging' the picture were thrown from inside the car to the bewildered crowd! At the end of the season, the Palace went back to the dramas, pantomimes and revues which were by this time its staple fare. Pictures remained as 'fill-ins' when business was quiet—which, thanks to competition from cinemas, was now all too often the case.

In rural areas, the day of the travelling picture show was by no means over. Williams' Movies ('reliable and delightful') toured places that had no cinema, as did the Super Film Company (recorded as bringing *The End Of The Road* to Inverurie Railway Institute Hall in the spring of 1922), and the

Highland Cinema Company. Until the coming of the talkies, with their more complicated techniques, there would still be plenty of business to be done 'on the move'.

Associated Provincial Picture Houses, proprietors of the Picture House, had by now become integrated with the larger Provincial Cinematograph Theatres company, with which it had been associated and had shared directors. PCT's departments employed between them a vast concentration of talent, and somebody in one of those departments came up with an original publicity idea for Derby Day, Wednesday, 31 May. The race would be filmed and the negative flown in a De Havilland plane from Epsom to the Kinema Company's plant at Barnet to be processed and printed straight away. Six De Havilland Swifts would then carry prints along the main air routes to Aberdeen, Glasgow, Peterborough, Liverpool, Portsmouth and Bristol, parachuting copies down for immediate showing at major PCT houses on the way. Aberdeen, at the very tip of the long circuit, would be the farthest north that a London newsreel had ever been shown on the day of the event. Also, the De Havilland company's chief pilot, the famous Allan J. Cobham, hoped to break existing records by covering 500 miles at an average of 100 miles per hour, slowing down only to make his deliveries at York, Newcastle and Edinburgh.

The race was run at 3 o'clock that afternoon, filming went smoothly, and although printing took a little longer than expected, the Aberdeen plane was in the air by 5.30 pm. By 10 o'clock, Castlehill and every other vantage point was crowded as thousands turned out to scan the sky over the Tullos Hill area where the drop was to take place. Presently, the sound of an engine was heard on the calm evening air, and the plane came into view. As the plane circled Torry Hill Mr T.K. Kirkby of PCT threw the bag out, but its little parachute tangled in the plane's rudder wires and was torn off. A crowd of boys watching from a lane between Crombie Road and Victoria Road saw the package plummet over their heads and into the back yard of No.161 Victoria Road. First in the general scramble was 16 year-old Alexander Russell, who grabbed the bag, jumped on a tram in company with two of his friends, and was soon at the door of the Picture House where the manager, Mr Jennings, was handed the precious prize. The boys were suitably rewarded, and at 10.50 p.m. the audience was able to cheer the winner, Captain Cuttle, in a race that took place that very afternoon at the other end of the country. The 'airmail' package also contained pictures taken specially for the Aberdeen *Daily Journal*, whose readers the next day saw the North-East's quickest-ever printing of press-photos from London.

On Monday, 25 September 1922, Provincial Cinematograph Theatres gave a 2-hour cinema show for the Royal Family at Balmoral, replacing the annual Gillies' Ball which had been cancelled because of the mourning for the late Duchess of Albany. An audience of 300, made up of Royals, guests and tenantry, saw a programme that included Robert Flaherty's renowned *Nanook Of The North*, filmed at Hudson's Bay over a whole decade, and Cecil Hepworth's *Through Three Reigns*, an historical documentary tracing events from the later years of Queen Victoria and containing early footage that was even then said to be unique. Among the special effects brought in for *Nanook* was a wind-machine for the blizzard scene, and there were even Eskimo folk-songs sung by a Mr Foley from London— surely the eminent baritone Tom Foley. The musicians, drawn from London and Glasgow, were directed by Louis Levy, head of PCT's music department, and in the audience was Cecil Hepworth himself.

By August, Henry Phillips' lease had run out on the King's Cinema, which then became part of Aberdeen Picture Palaces' growing circuit. For a short while the MUSIC HALL CINEMA flourished under the management of a Mr Billy Steven, with a series of 'super-productions'. It began in October 1922 but lasted only a few weeks. The Palace Theatre had cine-variety for its winter season, while over the latter part of the year the Playhouse presented a series of operatic films, accompanied by music from the operas themselves.

The Playhouse was visited that September by the Wanderwell Motor Party, a team of ladies and gentlemen who had been travelling the road for no less than three years, and who 'dropped in' with their leader, Captain Wanderwell, to talk of their many and varied experiences. One of the Playhouse's many big film attractions of this time was *Rob Roy*, the first Scottish 'epic'. Shot in the shadow of Ben Lomond and based entirely on history rather than on the romanticised tales of Sir Walter Scott, *Rob Roy* had a cast of 2,000 including more than 400 troops from Stirling as extras. The film was reported as having been so popular in the Edinburgh halls that it had been re-booked by them immediately!

The Queen's, in early October, began supplementing its films with live 'stage scenarios' after the manner of the top American and London halls, while down at the Casino 'the man with a thousand faces', make-up wizard Lon Chaney, received his first Aberdeen picture billing in *The Heart Of A Wolf* (not the original title—many American features of the silent era were issued in Britain under changed names). Community singing was firmly entrenched at the Picture House with its Friday 'Kinema Khorus Nights', and on stage the Original Hawaiian Orchestra regaled audiences with native songs and melodies. The Picture House was also the first Aberdeen cinema (late in 1922) to bill a little cartoon character whose name is still well remembered although the original film series has long since disappeared—Felix The Cat. Completely indestructible whatever anybody tried to do to him, Felix, in the words of the little song that was written about him, 'just kept walking on'!

Aberdeen's oldest cinema, the Palladium, had continued on its unspectacular way under the management of a certain Mr Robert Pennycook, former owner of La Scala, Falkirk and the Picture House, Camelon. An *Evening Express* headline 'Aberdeen Cinema Manager in Court for Fraud' (*Express* 8 January 1922) announced that Mr Pennycook's business in Falkirk was not quite finished. He was obliged to make a return visit to give an account of his financial methods there, having been declared bankrupt, but he was well enough thought of at the Palladium to merit a monster benefit night when he left in May 1922. In later years he was to become a proprietor again, with several cinemas of his own in the south of Scotland.

Alterations were put in hand over the summer of 1922 to improve the entranceways to the Palladium's Stalls and Circle. In January 1923 its ownership changed once again, passing this time to a Buckie lawyer, Mr James Archibald, and it re-opened that June with cine-variety, regular Sunday night gospel meetings organised by one of the local Evangelical groups, and the most popular addition of all—a heating system! The Palladium underwent some more refurbishment in the course of 1923, but although described by the younger George Walker, from his brief experience of it under Henry Phillips, as 'quite pleasant', there still seems to have been little to put it in the luxury class.

In April 1923 the full force of Rudolph Valentino-mania hit Aberdeen with the showing, to a constantly thronged Picture House, of *The Sheik*, co-starring Agnes Ayres. This rather unlikely tale of 'a lover with a heart hot as the desert sands' ('when an Arab sees a woman he wants, he takes her') was adapted from an E. Mayne Hull novel that would probably be laughed at now but in those days was considered decidedly torrid. It firmly established Valentino as the greatest male sex-symbol of his day, and enriched the popular vocabulary by the addition of the term 'sheik' to describe the 'ladies' man' of the time. The word was also applicable as a verb for the act of sweeping tent-wards one's very own Agnes Ayres, and any young chap able to cultivate the 'Latin lover' image could find life quite interesting. Such a special 'Photoplay of Passionate Love' called for its own special music; this was supplied with the film and played by the Picture House orchestra under its new conductor Noel de Beer.

Those seeking further Valentino epics in the course of the year could find them at the Playhouse, where *The Four Horsemen Of The Apcalypse* was given three showings each day for a fortnight in July, with augmented orchestra, sound effects, singer Maggie Inverarity, a stage prologue, and the Prophecy of St John delivered by Bert Gates himself. *Blood And Sand* (a tale about bull-fighting) and *The Conquering Power* also brought Valentino fans out in their hundreds. Second helpings were available at the Electric, where Valentino re-runs did a roaring trade.

Actor/director Erich von Stroheim, already earning a reputation for extravagance in the films on which he worked, had his first local mention as a star in *Foolish Wives* at the Electric in January 1923, while in February Bebe Daniels and Gloria Swanson had the same in *The Boundary* at La Scala and *The Great Moment* at the Picture House respectively.

Favourite film subjects for the Aberdonian of the time were comedies of the 'domestic misunderstanding' variety (*Scrambled Wives*, *The Woman In His House*, *Through The Toils*, etc), sharing pride of place with the usual romances.

Anything with a Scottish flavour was also assured of popularity, and *The Little Minister*, based on the J.M. Barrie book, was a smash-hit at the Picture House in June. Its tone was firmly set in the 'picturesque' Scots of its advertising material:

> If ye've read the buik ye'll ken hoo guid th' pictur' maun be, if ye havna it disna maitter, the writer's name's eneuch. O' a' th' couthie hameower stories written aboot oorsel's there's nivver an ee in a' Scotia (or oot o't) tae beat this Barrie maister-piece. Its hameliness charms; its roguishness brings th' lauch tae th' lip; its pathos catches at th' hert-strings an' fills th' een wi' tears. If ye miss seein' this pictur' ye'll nivver richtly ken ye'r brither Scot, his honesty an' simpleecity— his releegius fervour an' pawky humour—an' a' thing else that's made his name a byeword amang th' nations. That's a'.

The choice of music can hardly have been a difficult one, and if Mr De Beer was not thoroughly conversant with the Scottish idiom on the Monday morning he certainly would have been by the Saturday night!

In general, programmes were becoming more of the A- and B-feature type, with fewer 'shorts'. There were even a few experiments with double A-feature bills, beginning at the Playhouse that August with a showing of *Lorna Doone* paired with *A Debt Of Honour*.

At La Scala, a violinist and pianist provided music in the tearoom over the summer, while down at the Queen's there was a jazz band. Some local newsreel production was evidently still going on, as La Scala had a special film of the students' Gala Week stunts that year.

Of all the extra events and attractions in Aberdeen's cinemas over the early 1920s, the most significant took place at La Scala on the evening of 5 May 1923—a demonstration of the very latest marvel, radio. This came about after three weeks of research by experts from London and Glasgow, assisted by a group of local men that included Mr C. Bruce Miller, founder of the long-established firm of dealers in all things musical, and Mr William Robertson of Aberdeen Radio. Concert programmes from London, Manchester, Newcastle and Glasgow were brought loud and clear to La Scala's auditorium and tearooms, and the reception of the signal was the best yet obtained in the city centre. Still greater things were to come. On Wednesday, 10 October the first broadcast went out from Aberdeen's very own BBC studio in Belmont Street (code sign 2BD), and radio truly arrived in the city.

With picture pioneer William Walker and his family now back in Aberdeen after several years in Newcastle, where part of their trade had been in radio equipment, we might well make assumptions as to the ownership of 'Walker's Wireless' which occupied a large shop on the corner of Broad Street and Queen Street from 1923, and outside which a crowd listened to that first broadcast from 2BD. It seems entirely appropriate that the man who introduced the cinematograph to Aberdeen should have been among the city's earliest dealers in equipment for the second great new mode of communication to develop in the twentieth century. No evidence exists as to any other commercial activity on the part of Walker (if William Walker it be) and he may well have retired when the shop closed in 1925 or 1926. He died about 1937.

Cinema bosses were not so thrilled at the coming of radio. Many had visions of a mass desertion of picture-going, as had already occurred in the States. In the USA, however, there were dozens of commercial radio stations to contend with, a situation not encountered in Britain, where the cinema remained as popular as ever. In Aberdeen, only a week or so after the first Belmont Street broadcast, the Picture House's manager Mr Mailler had loudspeakers installed in the cinema vestibule to relay music over the air to the regular (and quite undiminished) queues.

There was just one desertion from the local cinema world to that of radio. Harold Pollard, joined 'them' as 2BD's regular pianist, in which capacity he remained for several years before going into dance band work.

In September 1923 the Playhouse's second anniversary was marked by a special Jazz Night in addition to the usual Tuesday Chorus Night. During the week of 22 October, La Scala took part in an unusual screen experiment—a special showing of the Operatic Film Company's production of Mozart's *The Marriage Of Figaro*. The aim of this Scottish project was to combine film and music by the introduction of a cast of six from the Carla Rosa Opera Company, plus another two London artistes, to perform extracts from the original opera at appropriate places in the story. At these points the film would be stopped and slides inserted. An augmented orchestra under Miss Nan King accompanied the three-hour work, and the producer, Mr Buckland, was present to acknowledge the warm applause. For the still fairly reasonable prices of 9d., 1s. 3d. or 2s. 4d., culture of this kind might have been expected to gain popularity, but the picture audiences of the day were not in quite that frame of mind, and nothing further is recorded of the venture.

That December, Picture House patrons were relayed the General Election results direct by wireless, together with dance music by the Savoy Orpheans. This broadcast musical treat was apparently much enjoyed, as radio programmes by the Savoy Orpheans and Savoy Havana Band (the illustrious house bands of London's exclusive Savoy Hotel) were played in the Picture House for some months thereafter.

The old Woodside Electric was in as much of a financial mess as ever, having just ruined its latest lessee, Albert Whittaker. In order to pay some urgent bills the unfortunate Mr Whittaker had sold off some of the building's fittings—a fan and an electric motor—and as a result ended up in court in December. The 'Rinkie' may already have closed as a cinema. It became a garage, then for many years a warehouse for the Hay lemonade company, and it still exists as industrial premises.

Chapter 8

The Great Silent Years 1924—1928

During the second half of the 1920s the silent film reached its full flowering both as entertainment and as art form. In the USA, large promoters countered the challenge of radio by building super-colossal movie palaces in which to present spectacular cine-variety shows. Under this stimulus, American cinema design evolved in two distinct schools: the 'hard-top', which took classical styles to undreamt-of heights of splendour, and the 'atmospheric' which turned movie-palace interiors into romantic Spanish courtyards, Chinese temples, fabulous Eastern palaces—anything, in fact, that didn't look like a cinema. The fantasy realm of the silent film was thereby given its ideal setting, with everything larger than life as rival movie house architects let their fertile imaginations run riot.

A few UK companies responded by building their own 2,000-3,000 seater 'giants', beginning in 1924 with the large Pavilion, Shepherd's Bush, London, the first cinema considered important enough to merit an award from the Royal Institute of British Architects. Other outstanding examples of the early British-owned 'super' were the immense 4,000-seater Green's Playouse, Glasgow (1927-28), the Davis Theatre, Croydon (1928), the Regal, Marble Arch, London (1928), and the Playhouse, Edinburgh (1929).

By the end of the 1920s the huge American movie companies Metro-Goldwyn-Mayer (MGM) and Paramount were opening even more lavish transatlantic-style picture palaces in major British cities, but developments of such size were comparatively rare. The average capacity of the British 'super' of the 1930s was to settle at closer to 2,000 than 3,000.

On the Continent, and particularly in Germany, enthusiastic young architects and interior designers were striving to evolve a new style that would stand on its own as a proclamation of the cinema building's function. Elaborate decoration was seen as a gimcrack futility. Instead, new building techniques and materials were utilised to realise modernistic concepts which strongly influenced British cinema design in the 1930s. For the present, however, most of this country's picture exhibitors, blissfully innocent of such aspirations, were content to provide 'tasteful' halls of a far more traditional sort.

The question of rival architectural methods for cinemas was purely an academic one in Aberdeen over most of the 1920s—between 1922 and 1929 not one new cinema opened in the city. The great period of investment had yet to come, but local cinema companies did develop in size and influence through takeover of rival concerns.

On 1 January 1924, Aberdeen Picture Palaces assumed control of the Torry Picture House by purchasing a majority share in Torry Cinemas, Ltd. New programmes were put in, and business improved. Suggestions were invited for a new name for the cinema, but no change ever took place; evidently Torry folk were quite happy with things as they were!

Up until APP's arrival, the Torry had been managed by Frank Walker, who will be remembered from the Picturedrome's early days. After the take-over, William Pirie was brought in from the Globe as temporary replacement until 26 February when a new permanent manager arrived—Mr James Noble, formerly of the Maxwell Picture House, Pollokshaws, Glasgow. An able musician and singer, Mr Noble made certain that there were plenty of good musical entertainments during his spell in charge.

Aberdeen Picture Palaces seems never to have been really interested in the Picturedrome, and in 1923 the former Union Club block was sold to the Loyal Order Of Ancient Shepherds, which continued the cinema for a while under its own auspices. In May 1924, however, an agreement was signed with a new lessee—James Donald. On Monday, 11 August the old Picturedrome, restored and improved, came back into operation as the CINEMA HOUSE. Films that day were *The Woman Who Obeyed* and *The Shadow Of Death*. The small orchestra was led by R.A. Chatterton, Tuesday nights were Chorus Nights, and unless the main feature was a really important one the programme changed at half-week. Initially James Donald held the premises on a 20-year lease, but eventually they were bought outright.

With jazz and dance music firmly established in the public ear through radio and records, cinema musical directors found themselves having to move with the times. Pops of the day were just as much in demand as the light classics and decorous drawing-room intermezzos that had been staple fare for so long, and Drdla's 'Souvenir' now had to share the music stand with 'My Sweetie Went Away' and 'The Sheik of Araby'. At the very beginning of 1924, La Scala's manager Mr Patterson took the step of having the orchestra (still at that time under R.A. Chatterton) moved from its old place at one side of the stage to a new central position, in full view of the audience. A new orchestra platform was built, with a backdrop of ultramarine framed by trellis-work, and lit by spotlights in blue and green.

For some of its Friday 'Music Nights' the Playhouse brought in the band from Madame Isobel Murray's Dancing School to play numbers popularised by the Savoy Orpheans. Playhouse 'Chorus Nights' were still held on Tuesdays, and until July the orchestra was led by Alexander Nicol. After that, Mr Nicol was replaced by a Mr Hyndman from the King's, Dundee.

In the Picture House orchestra was a Londoner, Mr Maurice Bromburgh, who since his arrival at the beginning of the year had been delighting audiences with the delicacy of his violin playing in both solo and concerted items.

35   The Cinema House, Skene Terrace, 1935

The New Kinema's Tuesday Chorus Nights, meanwhile, took place with an augmented orchestra which was prominently advertised as containing *a saxophone!* No-one could call the New Kinema behind the times.

At La Scala, Wednesday Chorus Nights, led by well known local tenor Walter Schaschke, were part of an enthusiastic musical policy pursued by new manager Frank McGuggan, who came to Aberdeen from Rutherglen that May. One of Mr McGuggan's first projects was a general freshening-up and repainting of the hall. All seats were cleaned, floors were recarpeted, and old worn Stalls carpeting was replaced with easily-cleaned lino. Among the several popular novelties that Mr McGuggan introduced was the 'Game Of The Sunspot', in which a spotlight was flickered over the audience, halting when the music stopped. The person under the 'sunspot' was then presented with a gift such as a box of chocolates, or, at Christmas, even a turkey.

In or around the spring of 1924, the Electric came into the Aberdeen Picture Palaces orbit, its owner Bruce MacKenzie joining APP's board of directors. Behind the amalgamation was an idea of Bert Gates' to repeat the success of his Playhouse project by replacing the Electric with an even larger flagship theatre on this very favourable site. Until such time as this plan could be put into effect, the Electric's appeal was increased through the introduction, on Monday, 27 October 1924, of the 20-piece Steadman's Symphony Orchestra, giving Aberdonians their first taste of the big-city picture hall.

The orchestra, under its pianist-leader George Steadman, played interludes, provided accompaniments for the live stage prologues that became a regular feature from then on, and, most importantly, accompanied films in the 'close-fitted' manner that was by then expected in the best halls, although it must be said that in the latter Steadman, like many of his peers, took short-cuts. The best film accompaniments were those 'tailor-made' by the cinema's musical director from suitable musical themes of all kinds, specially chosen to complement the moods of each individual picture. Others, like those of Steadman, were played from music cards printed with ready-made themes for 'Love Scene 1, 2, 3' etc, requiring only a decision as to which theme to use.

Steadman (a Mancunian) is reputed to have been at times a somewhat difficult fellow to deal with. A little hard of hearing in one ear (and, some murmured, conveniently so in the other when it suited him), his constant exhortations to 'play louder' caused considerable annoyance among his players—particularly to his Dutch cellist who one day, finally pushed beyond endurance, cried back in his strong Netherlands accent, 'If you do not stop it, Mr Steadman, I will break this *$*#!! cello over your head!'

The orchestra's debut was, none the less, a revelation for Aberdeen, and it must have been every bit as fascinating to watch the musicians at work as to watch the film. From April 1925 the BBC had a microphone in the Electric's pit, relaying live programmes between 6.30 p.m. and 7 p.m. each Friday night and at other times during the week as well. Prominent in the orchestra were two brothers Wiseman, one of whom, Ernest, specialised in xylophone and glockenspiel solos, and turns on flute and piccolo. Also popular were Mr A. Metcalfe, violinist, and Mr W. Fogg, cellist.

Towards the end of 1924, the New Kinema orchestra was enlarged and put under the leadership of another violinist from London, Richard D. Garioch. When La Scala's chorus vocalist Walter Schaschke went off to London for further voice training, his place was taken by Mr Frank Auld, billed as 'The Vocalist With The Voice'. In January 1925 the Playhouse orchestra was expanded to eight players under a new musical director, pianist R.E. Cahill, whose association with the Playhouse was to be a long one, taking him eventually from orchestra pit to manager's office. It seems likely that his musical background was that of a bandsman, as he always retained a love for military and brass band music, and it has been said that a breezy march tempo pervaded much of the Playhouse's orchestral work!

Across town at the Grand Central, J.M. Taylor spent some time as musical director before being succeeded by Marjorie Littlejohn, Harold Pollard's immediate successor at the Electric. By November, orchestral music had spread as far as the tiny King's, where musical director was a Mr William LeRoy. Frank Auld, regular participant in what La Scala called its 'Jazz Upheavals', was also booked at the King's to launch Chorus Nights. For a while his services were divided between the two houses, but before very long he had a full-time engagement with APP, moving around their various cinemas.

By the end of 1925 orchestral music was billed large as an important part of the entertainment at almost every Aberdeen cinema, the only exception being the apparently struggling Queen's, where no orchestra is mentioned at all. Musical stage acts came thick and fast, especially at the APP East-end halls and at those traditional strongholds of cine-variety, the Casino and the Palladium (by this time known as the NEW PALLADIUM).

Joe Gray had joined the staff of the Electric, which, thanks to him, was able to provide its own exclusive coverage of the Royal opening of Aberdeen's Cowdray Hall, War Memorial and Art Gallery on 29 September 1925. From farther afield came newsreels of the opening of Wembley Stadium in May and the aftermath of a blaze that destroyed Glasgow's Kelvin Hall on 10 July. During the week of the Cowdray Hall film, a demonstration was given at 8.15 every night of a new musical instrument called the 'Electrolele', invented by a member of the Electric's orchestra (no doubt one of the Wiseman brothers). The exact nature of this feat of 'Originality!! The Hallmark of Genius' is not clear, but the instrument's title suggests some kind of ukulele, perhaps amplified. What would those musicians of 1925 have thought of the 'Electroleles' that our pop groups play now?

At New Year 1926, Mr Edward Bell commenced a long period as manager of the Torry Picture House. Mr Bell was a wartime Sapper with a special line in dramatic recitations of the old school—no quarter asked or given—and was a great showman in a 'military' kind of way. Weekly programmes were decked out with a wide variety of novelties, stage acts, and special presentations. The naval battle thriller *Zeebrugge* was given with effects and elocutions; similar treatment was accorded to *Ypres* and *Hill 60*, the latter having 'special music, organ and actual effects' plus special prologue written and recited by Mr Bell. That week's advertising line, 'Britain Expects You To Visit The Torry Picture House', left no doubt at all as to the nature of the occasion!

Revitalisation of the King's ('On A Throne—All Alone') continued over 1926, when as a setting for the 'Right Royal, Refreshing Entertainment' ('Kome In Krowds!') the redecorated stage was fitted with a new 'Eastern' back-drop. It also acquired a surround of multi-coloured glass panels for 'orchestra lighting effects', apparently somewhat after the manner of La Scala. Frank Auld appeared in the King's many musical presentations, which consisted mainly of popular material but also included old favourites such as Amy Woodforde-Finden's 'Indian Love Lyrics', sung by Mr Auld in full costume. The orchestra, claimed as the best in the east-end, was enlarged that January by the addition of an unusual instrument for the time—a piano-accordion. This occasioned a strong and most untypical reaction from the Globe, where, apparently quite forgetful of fraternal ties, the Bijou Orchestra under Bert Glennie was advertised soon after as:

> Already the best combination of musical instruments in the East End: An attraction without noisy or new-fangled instruments!

At the Picture House, Friday chorus nights were, by early 1926, being led by Mr J. Frame, baritone. The Electric had 'The Popular Broadcasting Baritone' R.E. Anderson, La Scala had tenor James Smith, but the Globe had, instead of a singer, the song 'Cartunes' of the Max Fleisher studio (makers, in the 1930s, of the popular Betty Boop and Popeye talkie cartoons).

In 'Cartunes', a funny little clown character called Koko pointed out the words of songs in rhythm for the audience to sing, the orchestra accompanying in time to his actions. Koko first appeared at the Globe's Big Band chorus nights in late January 1926, and several rival variants of the idea quickly followed at other halls. This would surely have delighted the Community Singers' Association, whose representative, Mr Gibson Young, visited the Picture House that July to meet members of the audience and to generally champion this healthy vocal pastime, promoted by the Association as ideal for virtually any occasion!

The Palace Theatre, long a venue for pantomimes and revues, had recently 'gone legit' for the first time in its history, having been leased in early September 1925 to Mr Arthur Hinton as a base for his professional drama company. At the close of Hinton's first season, the theatre hosted some ambitious film presentations by Henry Phillips, starting on 25 January 1926 with a Western, *North Of '36*. The mood of this picture was set by a full stage prologue in which two cowboys and a cowgirl, Buck, Chick and Tex, from 101 Ranch, USA, gave an exciting display of skill with lariats and stock-whip. Of the pictures that Phillips brought to the Palace, several were Scottish premieres, among them Charlie Chaplin's *The Gold Rush*.

On Monday, 1 February a 'novelty broadcast' was transmitted from La Scala, with James Smith singing the latest popular songs, 'Sally Come Back' and 'Yes Sir, That's My Baby'. In June, Playhouse patrons were entertained by the 20-piece Aberdeen Banjo, Mandoline and Guitar Orchestra in half-hour 'musical melanges', while occasional attractions at Torry included the Hiawatha Japanese Band (!), Carnegie and MacDonald's Torry Jazz Band, Binky Morris And His Jazz Band, a female impersonator, a gipsy band, and other novelty ensembles. The orchestra at Torry was now led by Mr Colin Nicol, and included among its members Mr James Murray, accordionist.

Back in November 1925, Aberdeen had gained its first public dance hall, the Palais de Danse in Diamond Street, converted from the extensive former premises of cab-hirers Charles Campbell and Cay. The hall's proprietor was a

Londoner named Ernest Bromberg, who was also an avid cinema enthusiast. In February 1926, he held at the Palais the first of many cinema-orientated events—an Aberdeen Cinema Ball, at which prizes were awarded for the best and most original costumes, and for the best likenesses to screen stars. Judging the costumes was Miss Ursula Hughes of the company currently giving the musical show *The Street Singer* at His Majesty's Theatre, and Mrs A.D. Hay of Aberdeen Picture Palaces was on hand to present the prizes to the lucky young Rudolph Valentinos, Marion Davises, Gloria Swansons and John Barrymores.

That summer, the Picture House's music came under the directorship of Mr George Harkins, a first class violinist who had worked his way to the top from ordinary membership of the orchestra. In October the Grand Central sported a new seven-piece orchestra under Marjorie Littlejohn, while that November Mr Ernest Gautier, formerly of the Altringham Picture House, Birmingham, took over as leader of the Cinema House Orchestra, J.M. Taylor moving to the New Kinema. The New Palladium had a Bijou Orchestra, and music at the Casino was under the direction of a Mr T. Clayton. Chorus vocalists and 'jazz nights' were everywhere.

From 4 May until 13 May 1926, the General Strike brought Britain to a standstill, but Aberdeen's cinema managements were not caught out again. By one means or another they managed to carry on much as usual, with the Electric giving a return week of Mary Pickford's *Little Annie Roonie*, the Casino showing Harold Lloyd in *College Days* (plus full variety programme) and, at Torry, Richard Talmadge in *Youth and Adventure*. Along with Talmadge and his Fairbanks-style stunts ('with all the spice of life') came a film of that year's Aberdeen Student Gala, and for the second half of the week the main feature was Jackie Coogan in *The Ragman*.

La Scala's advertisements demanded: 'Why Is La Scala Tyred?—Because it is going to take you to *California Straight Ahead* with Reginald Denny at the wheel'. Those not satisfied with this 'rubber-tyred riot of rollicking romance and racing cars', featuring the sunny situation comedy of one of the highest-paid Englishmen in Hollywood, could visit the New Kinema for Dorothy Revier in *Remorseless Love*, the Picture House for *Sealed Lips* and (later in the week) Tom Mix in *The Best Bad Man*, or the Playhouse for the latest Griffith opus *Hearts Of The World*. If none of these appealed, there was always the Beach Pavilion where Harry Gordon's Entertainers made light of a bleak situation.

> Music has come to play a big part in local entertainment. Strange though it may seem, it is nevertheless true. Aberdeen cinema-goers who visit a kinema ostensibly to see films will applaud vociferously during musical interludes in the picture programme, and no exhibitor can afford to ignore the public's demand for music.

Thus spoke the *Evening Express* of 19 October 1926—and if the reader is beginning to suspect the author of orchestras-on-the-brain, there is the defence. Nowhere can the demand for music have been better fulfilled than at La Scala between 1926 and 1928. During the height of the General Strike, musical director David Sutherland left to go to the King's, and was replaced by a newcomer, Mr Meyer Kalson, whose magic touch soon made the orchestra a greater attraction than the films.

Born in Grimsby, Mr Kalson showed proficiency as a violinist long before he left school at the age of $13\frac{1}{2}$. 'Sitting in' with his instructor's orchestra at the local cinema was part of his musical training, and it soon became clear that the lad had a flair for this type of work. After the Great War he spent several years in intensive study of the art of cinema musical direction, working a passage to America as ship's stoker in order to see at first hand the methods employed in the best movie houses at the very heart of the film world.

On returning to Britain, he spent a while freelancing for various agents, then in 1924 auditioned for a place in the orchestra at the Pavilion, Shepherd's Bush. In the course of the audition, a film was shown of Prince George's journey to Australia. At the point where the scene moved aboard ship, musical director Louis Levy suddenly stopped the orchestra and instructed the young Meyer Kalson, who was sitting with the second violins, to carry on with something suitable. This he did with the Sailor's Hornpipe— an answer which, he later commented, may not have been original, but was still good enough to give him a place in one of the finest cinema orchestras in the country.

At the end of that engagement he freelanced again, this time for a Glasgow agent, and was just completing a 6-month engagement as leader of Louis Freeman's orchestra at the Picture House, Greenock, when the agent offered him the La Scala post. After a quick phone call to Aberdeen to confirm his acceptance, Mr Kalson was on his way, reaching his destination on time despite the strike. His first action was to hire an entirely new orchestra— only a quartet, but consisting of the best musicians available. In order to ensure their continuing services he arranged for them to be paid the generous sum of £5 per week instead of the usual £2 or so. All music was specially selected from Mr Kalson's library, the catalogue of which he held in his own memory. Each theme was individually timed and fitted to the action on the screen, a time-consuming operation that required much patience but was fully justified by the results.

Music sensitively chosen, fitted and played could add immeasurably to a silent picture, reinforcing its moods and making the characters seem to talk with no need of dialogue. An advance synopsis of each film was sent around by its renters; further information could be gathered by reading press notices and by looking at still photographs, so that when a general impression of the picture had been built up, suitable music could be prepared without the need of a preview. Final details could be attended to on the Monday—no trouble at all for the M.D. with ability and experience.

Naturally, the success of all this hinged on a steady rate of film projection. Cinema managers in those days had a habit of hurrying things along in order to squeeze in extra showings on busy days, and if La Scala's manager, Charlie Williams, decided to do this, up would go the speed of the projectors and

36   Myer Kalson, 1920s

nothing would fit any more. Protests by musical directors were to no avail!

The high quality of Meyer Kalson's work soon came to the public's attention, and La Scala's attendances increased, but suddenly, after only a few weeks, it looked as if trouble was brewing. Mr Kalson was just leaving the orchestra platform at the end of the show one night, when he saw the manager beckoning to him from the side aisle. The circuit's proprietor, George Green, had telephoned during the performance, insisting on a personal interview with his new M.D. over the cost of the orchestra, which, in Mr Williams' estimation, stood a very good chance of being dismissed, director and all!

The ensuing journey to Green's office in Glasgow was a tense one, and Mr Kalson's apprehension was in no way alleviated by his employer's opening remark that for the sort of money he was paying for La Scala's music he could just about have run another couple of cinemas! But to the musician's great relief and delight, Mr Green went on to say that if he was going to spend so much on an orchestra he may as well have the largest and best in the circuit. La Scala could now, therefore, have eleven players on a nine-month contract, and Mr Kalson could have a free hand in their organisation. At the end of the contract period the orchestra's forces would revert to four.

No time was lost in engaging the requisite number of first-rate players (some at higher salaries than Mr Kalson himself), and from then on all of their director's spare time went into the task of preparing musical arrangements for coming films. A composer colleague was on hand to write any necessary additional material—linking passages, for instance, to join themes together smoothly—and with such a musical establishment La Scala enjoyed a heyday. All tastes were catered for in style, as can be seen from an interlude listing from September 1926: Selection from Verdi's *Il Trovatore*, some 'jazz' items, and a 'Rhythmic Fantasia' of the kind then popular, on Wagner's *Tannhauser*!

In November 1926 the Torry Picture House presented special demonstrations, both live and on screen, of the Charleston, fashionable in the UK although it had been superseded in America. Its energetic steps did not suit everybody, and a less athletic derivative, the Flat Charleston, was shown at the Picture House by Madame Isobel Murray, but the original was still quite the rage in late-1926 Aberdeen. Winners of the Charleston competitions which followed the demonstrations at Torry received prizes of 10s. and 15s.

It was also in 1926 that James Donald's son Richard, after gaining some experience at the Cinema House, was promoted to charge of the Grand Central—at 15, surely the city's youngest-ever cinema manager. Cinema work was not the only string to his bow. Long before leaving school he had been perpetuating his father's sporting abilities through a great aptitude for football, although such activities often had to take second place to giving dancing instruction at the Gondolier School—another inherited talent. This, as Mr Donald once commented, resulted in the very probable forfeiture of a schoolboy football cap! By the age of 17 he was playing professionally for Aberdeen Football Club, remaining in the team until 1939. Football has always been his consuming interest, and since 1968 he has been the Club's Chairman.

His brother Herbert M. Donald did not at this stage take such a direct part in the cinema trade. Choosing the profession of optician, he opened his first shop in 1924 at No.7 Market Street, moving in 1931 to more extensive premises in Back Wynd, just behind the Queen's Cinema. There the shop was marked by a large red neon sign that gave more than a hint of the family's other line of business!

As 1927 arrived, James Donald gave a New Year Holiday show in the Music Hall with, as main film, *The Admirable Crichton*, starring Gloria Swanson. There was a supporting programme of comedies, and at the organ was Mr Alexander Fyfe. At Torry, Jack Gordon, brother of the better-known Harry, appeared 'in song and story', and other acts included bands and the Flashlight Concert Party. The Globe's 'Big Band Melodious Nights' were a popular attraction on Tuesdays, and the YMCA was as active as ever with its usual Saturday night film shows.

This period was not a very happy one for the New Kinema. By the middle of 1926 Henry Phillips had run into financial difficulty and, in order to reduce costs, had given his long- serving manager Hermann Cohn the choice between a salary cut or a fortnight's notice. Mr Cohn had no working contract with Phillips and was consequently at a severe disadvantage when, unenamoured of this 'offer', he went to the Sheriff Court, claiming three months' salary in lieu of the longer notice which he felt was due him after so many years in Phillips' employ. At the hearing in February 1927, Phillips held that a fortnight's notice was all that he (Phillips) had ever been accustomed to as employer or employee. Aberdeen Picture Palaces' lawyer James Clapperton and the Casino's Ormonde Kilgour, who had been called in as advisers, agreed with the Sheriff that a month's notice would have been far more appropriate, but Mr Cohn was in such a weak legal position that all he could be awarded was a month's salary (£30) plus 15 guineas expenses.

Henry Phillips' mother, Rebecca Phillips, who was by this time the real power behind the running of the New Kinema, had now decided to rescue the business herself, installing her son as manager, and so the original alternative of retention at a lower salary was withdrawn. A sadder and wiser Mr Cohn therefore disappears from Aberdeen and from this narrative.

In the event, the affair did the Phillips no good. Only a short time later they decided to move back to London, offering the company (with five years of the lease still remaining on the building) to their assistant manager, George Walker jnr. Mr Walker was assured by Phillips that he was the only party to whom sale would be considered, but there was then a very long wait for details of price. Eventually the subject was broached again to see if Mrs Phillips had made up her mind; she had, and the price was £800. Mr Walker then buttonholed his brother-in-law, trawl-owner James Brebner, with the idea of a partnership in the cinema business. Mr Brebner was interested, and when Phillips departed George Walker became not only manager but also a director of the New Kinema. Phillips, meanwhile, had vanished entirely. While in London some time later, George Walker went to look up his old employer at the forwarding address that he had been left; there was no sign of Phillips there and no-one had ever heard of him!

The Queen's was the next Aberdeen cinema to see change. In 1923 the auction house of its founder, Robert J. MacKenzie, closed and he and his son ceased to be registered at their address, Braehead, Bridge Of Don, which suggests that either Mr MacKenzie had died or had perhaps retired and moved away. The Queen's Rooms Cinema Syndicate continued to trade, but from the sporadic and low-key nature of its advertising, and from the paucity of important films, it seems clear that all was not well. In the spring of 1927, James Donald made an offer for a majority share interest in the company, the offer was accepted, and on Monday, 24 July a reseated and redecorated Queen's opened under his control with the film *Dreams Of Monte Carlo.*

Music was in the fair hands (all six) of Miss Bessie Singleton's Trio from the Opera House, Dublin. In between films, patrons could buy ice cream freshly made in the kitchen that still survived from the building's former days as a restaurant. Although the new film programmes were still rarely 'first-runs', they were a great improvement on the old, and the Queen's, with its prominent Union Street position, became a popular house once again.

Interestingly, on 8 March 1928, in the course of alterations, the building's foundation stone was discovered. In it was a bottle containing copies of the local papers, the London Times and the Edinburgh Courant for 1836, together with a selection of coins ranging from a five shilling piece to a farthing. Cemented to the stone was a brass plate testifying to its having been placed there 'in the presence of many members of the Society of Advocates' by the president of the time, Henry Lumsden of Tilquhilly. The articles were handed over to the Society, in whose possession they remain.

Hawaiian and Gypsy bands were still favourites at the APP East-end halls, and when in September 1927 the New Palladium reopened after cleaning and decoration, (it had by then taken to closing over summers—since what year is not known), it did so with an orchestra of no less than twelve, and with Walter Schaschke as vocalist.

The Casino came into the news that October when an application was submitted for a drinks licence—theoretically grantable for buildings which, like cine-variety halls, were licensed for music-hall entertainments. There was a storm of protest, with objections from the nearby St Clement's U.F. and Albion Street Congregational Churches, Aberdeen U.F. College, Gordon and Shuttle Lane Missions, and from many local residents. Counter-petitions from Casino patrons as far afield as Woodside, Ferryhill and Rosemount were of no effect; the application was turned down on the grounds that the Casino was more of a cinema than a music hall—and, of course, because there would certainly have been a flood of other applications had this one been allowed! It was also, perhaps rightly, pointed out that the area already had plenty of bars and that one in the Casino would simply encourage an unacceptable degree of coming-and-going during performances.

Pausing for a glance at some of the films showing in the city during late 1927 and early 1928, we find, during the week of 31 October 1927, the Picture House with the first run of *Ben Hur*, a spectacular success for Ramon Novarro and Francis X Bushman. Its high spot was a great chariot race that made it picture of the year when first released in the States in 1926. During the week of 14 November 1927 La Scala made a break with its usual run of popular material by putting on the remarkable *Metropolis*, made in Germany under the distinguished director Fritz Lang, who was soon to be bound for Hollywood.

A grim look into a future of mechanised slavery, *Metropolis*, based on a story about revolt against opression, was notable not for its plot or its acting but for its amazing range of ingenious special effects. By means of clever trick-photography and manipulation of printing processes, the studio technicians managed to make mysterious encircling bands of energy bring a 'robot-woman' to life, and (prophetically) to replace telephones with video screens. The film's fantastic, geometrical background sets and strange, inhuman atmo-

37 Queuing to see *Ben Hur* at The Picture House (*EE* 5 Nov. 1927)

sphere created such an impression that at least one city minister, the Rev Leslie Belton of the Unitarian Church, made it the subject of a sermon the very next Sunday.

During the week of 16 January, La Scala had one of Aberdeen's greatest film hits of the time—*It*, starring Clara Bow and named after the term coined by its authoress, the influential and controversial Elinor Glyn, to define 'that magnetic sex-appeal which is irresistible'. The vivacious Clara, whose films were avidly watched by any flapper worthy of the name, was accorded the title of the 'It-girl' and was one of the great youth symbols of her day. *College*, starring 'Stone-Face' Buster Keaton, and *The Perfect Sap* with Ben Lyon were also big attractions, as was comedian W.C. Fields in one of his early successes, *So's Your Old Man*, shown at the Playhouse.

There was also a straw in the wind. John Barrymore's *Don Juan*, shown at the Grand Central during the week of 16 January, was, on its release in the States, the first commercially-produced film with a recorded soundtrack. Sound films were, however, so new even in America that the vast majority of its showings there were as silent as its UK ones.

All down the years since 1823 when the earliest parts of the Music Hall were built to designs by the famous architect Archibald Simpson, the premises had been owned and administered by a private company, but since the Great War income from the halls had fallen steadily, and in February 1928 the Music Hall Company was forced into liquidation. The building was offered for sale, and an agreement was arrived at for its purchase by the Town Council at the reasonable price of £27,250. This companionable arrangement was suddenly upset when the Music Hall Company received offers of £32,250 and £33,250 from two cinema promoters (unidentified in reports), a pattern of events not unfamiliar in other parts of the country when public halls ran into trouble.

At a rather sparsely attended meeting, the Music Hall shareholders made a resolution calling on the Council to raise its bid to the lower of the two rival sums, otherwise the building would be sold for £33,000. This action, coming after a grateful eulogy from Councillor Beaton on the Music Hall Company's public-spiritedness, caused quite a furore. A correspondent in the Aberdeen *Press and Journal* suggested that instead of bidding against 'the ubiquitous cinema concern', the Council should turn its attention towards acquiring and adapting Simpson's fine Royal Infirmary building in Woolmanhill, then being vacated as its departments moved out to the new hospital at Forresterhill. However, a further meeting of the shareholders produced a firm sale offer to the Council—for £34,000! This time the transaction was completed, and the Music Hall has remained in local authority ownership ever since.

One of the last major functions held in the Music Hall under its original proprietors was a grand Cinema Ball in aid of Lord Provost Lewis's Joint Hospital Fund on Tuesday, 7 February 1928. Prizes were awarded for the best costumes, judged by Provost and Lady Lewis and Mrs A.D. Hay. The opening remarks were made by Bert Gates, who also introduced the Lady Provost, and at the end of the evening the vote of thanks was proposed by James Donald. Bouquets were presented to the lady judges by youngsters Betty and Mamie McGuggan, whose father was now working for APP, managing the King's. A grand time was had by all, and £100 went to the Fund.

The Music Hall was still, in 1928, the occasional venue for large-scale film presentations, and in August of that year APP showed the last and perhaps the greatest of all silent Biblical epics, Cecil B. de Mille's *The King Of Kings*. H.B. Warner was Jesus, Joseph Schildkraut was Judas, Victor Varconi was Pilate, and William Boyd (Hopalong Cassidy of the talkie years) played the part of Simon. Inevitably, *King Of Kings* sparked off some controversy, but it also had immense impact. In his book *A Pictorial History Of The Silent Screen* (first published in 1953), Daniel Blum reported that over half a billion people had seen it. No less than 600 copies were at one time available during Lent, with subtitles in twenty-three different languages. Paulist Fathers in the remotest corners of the world had shown it to peoples that had never seen a film before in their lives, and missionaries had taken it with them as they canoed up the farthest reaches of the Ganges and the Congo.

What was the reaction to it in Aberdeen? In the *Evening Express* of 27 August 1928, an unnamed columnist wrote:

> In the view of all but the extremists, the question is not so much whether it should have been filmed as whether the story is handled with the care and reverence appropriate to the most sacred biography in the world.
>
> The simplest scenes are the most impressive; when the screening becomes flamboyant or seems to stray from the best taste we are aware of it at once and what has been effected by the better work is lost.
>
> The opening is a mistake. There was no need to give a Hollywood version of Magdalene's house and its evil; that part might have been left out altogether.
>
> The introduction states that the film is 'a story of Jesus of Nazareth', not 'the story'. That is evident. There are all sorts of incidents and dramas brought in that belong to the scenario writer's imagination, which is not exactly on the level with the Gospel truth. The miracles in the film are no more than a series of something very like conjuring tricks.
>
> But taking 'The King Of Kings' as a film simply, it is an exceedingly good piece of spectacular work. The crowd scenes, especially those of the Temple, are finely done, and there are thrills in the earthquake and storm scene at the time of the Crucifixion.
>
> Here and there the quieter scenes achieve much impressiveness, but when men begin to light their cigarettes one realises that the grip has been lost. The acting is, on the whole, good. The part of Christ is played with a quiet dignity, and Judas and Peter are well portrayed. Nothing is better than the portrayal of Caiaphas, the High Priest. The trial scene is spoiled because Pilate looks like an American in fancy dress.

The orchestra was directed by R.E. Cahill, and Burwood Nicholls returned to the Music Hall organ for the last time before his death only a month or two later.

In addition to the well-known orchestras of George Harkins at the Picture-house, Meyer Kalson at La Scala, R.E. Cahill at the Playhouse and George Steadman at the Electric, the picture-going public of 1928 could find F.J. Archer's orchestra at the Grand Central, James Skene and his Ideal Orchestra at the New Kinema, Bert Seal's Orchestra at the Queen's, and a resident Viennese band that played on Wednesday and Thursday nights as a stage act at the Star.

Some of the larger film productions of these last silent years had their own 'theme songs', specially written for playing or singing at appropriate points in the story. Certain of these were big hits and can still be heard today—'Jeannine', written for the Colleen Moore/Gary Cooper feature *Lilac Time*, 'Ramona' from the film of the same name starring Dolores Del Rio, 'Charmaine' from *What Price Glory* starring Dolores Del Rio and Victor McLaglen, and 'Diane' from *Seventh Heaven*, the film that established Janet Gaynor and Charles Farrell as favourite young screen couple of the late 1920s.

Seventh Heaven arrived at the Picture House in March 1928 and was accompanied by the 'special vocals' of a Miss C. Bruce; at the Electric that September *The Golden Clown* ('a drama of life behind a mask of gaiety') was prologued by Mr W. Carnegie singing the first part of 'I Pagliacci'.

Gloria Swanson's celebrated *Sadie Thompson* (at the Picture House in November) rounded off a year in which the film industry was becoming increasingly overshadowed by the great unknown—talkies. These, cinema managements opined, would do one of two things—either die a natural death or cause a very expensive upheaval. If they caught on, all new halls would have to be built with them in mind, and all exhibitors would have to buy costly equipment—as if there were not enough problems already. Over the past couple of years, there had been observed both in Britain and in the States a worrying swing away from picture-going. A feeling was growing in the trade that the silent film had been taken as far as it could, and that people might at last be tiring of it—hence the introduction of theme songs and other gimmicks to keep audiences interested. And even if talkies did become general, what guarantee was there that the craze would last?

In such an atmosphere of uncertainty it is hardly surprising that Aberdeen Picture Palaces postponed action on a plan which had been drawn up by Clement George in December 1927 (and approved in January 1928) for a brand-new Electric, expanding westwards on an adjoining piece of ground to give a seating capacity of 2,130 as against the old 1,060. Instead, the interior decorating team of Alexander Copland descended upon the existing Electric, which, at a grand reopening on Monday, 26 March 1928, the public found 'changed as if by a magic hand'. American ideas had been borrowed to transform the auditorium into a show of Chinese lacquer-work and mural decorations, with new fittings and lighting, painted lattice-work where previously there had been only plain ceiling-beams, and a Chinese story in pictures running right round the walls. All that week, the big film was *Wreck* featuring Shirley Mason, and each performance commenced with a special Chinese song scene devised by George Steadman and sung by Miss Dorothy

Forrest and a Mr Cruickshank of the Lyric Opera Company, in keeping with the theme of 'Britain's First Atmospheric Cinema'.

The term 'atmospheric' as applied to the Electric was, of course, strictly a comparative one. British first or not, an old interior tricked out with Oriental decoration could hardly have been classed as on a par with the real 'atmospherics' that were then opening in bewildering variety on the other side of the Atlantic, and were just finding their first echoes in the UK. The rejuvenated Electric was nonetheless an advance for an Aberdeen that was shortly to go cinema-mad as it experienced the great talkie boom of the 1930s.

Chapter 9

The Talkies   1929—1930

Since the cinematograph's birth, inventors had cherished ambitions of making pictures talk as well as move. 'Singing pictures' had explored the medium as best they could, but while a reasonable degree of synchronisation between film and record was achievable with patience, satisfactory means of amplification was lacking. It was not until the time of the First World War that advances in radio and allied techniques made possible the building of an amplification system that would give the required clarity and quality of sound.

Much important radio research work was carried out by one Dr Lee De Forest, a British-based American scientist who, in 1906, had invented the amplifying valve. After the war, De Forest was one of a number of people working on the photographic engraving of sound patterns on ordinary film stock, a principle which had existed in rudimentary form since the nineteenth century. By feeding a sound signal through electro-magnets attached to a small shutter, fluctuating patterns of light can be made to fall upon moving, unexposed negative film. When the film is developed, those patterns show up as light and dark bandings. A positive print is made, and when it is run between a continuous light source and a photoelectric cell, the light code is translated back into sound. Placing light patterns in a strip along the side of a film gives it a built-in soundtrack.

De Forest patented his own sound-on-film system, and by 1923 his first commercial 'Phonofilms' (mainly single-reelers) were ready. They generated considerable interest, pushing as far north as Edinburgh in 1925. De Forest even managed to insinuate sound equipment into a few theatres in the States, and although play-back quality tended to be a little muddy, it looked as if his Phonofilms would do well.

But he reckoned without the Hollywood establishment. Yes, there was some concern about flagging attendances, but weren't silent films a way of life? Wouldn't the re-equipping and even complete rebuilding of studios mean colossal outlay? Who was going to jeopardise their huge investment in established stars for the sake of something that might just fade out? Hollywood mogul William Fox, who had been trying out De Forest equipment in a few of his extensive chain of theatres, decreed that the experiment must end, and that, as far as he was concerned, was the end of the matter.

But it was not the end of the matter, as by that time (about 1925) others were in on the act. Developments in electrics and early electronics had been legion since the early 1920s, and in 1926 the enterprising Western Electric company was able to put on the market a reliable talkie system. The quality of De Forest's photo-electric soundtracks had not impressed Western Electric's engineers enough for them to want to employ his principle. Instead, they opted for the already-established technique of electrical recording on disc, using a 16-inch record that played from the centre on a special turntable linked to the projector. The optimum playing speed settled upon was $33\frac{1}{3}$ r.p.m., which suited the projector gearing and gave adequate playing time while still allowing satisfactory sound quality. The LP record, therefore, had a common origin with the talkie film!

A couple of Lee De Forest's one-time associates, gentlemen by the name of Theodore Case and Earl Sponable, had meanwhile been working on their own much more sophisticated system of sound-on-film recording. A prototype was ready by 1926, but still the movie magnates did not wish to know. In Germany the story was the same—an ingenious system called 'Tri-Ergon' was sold by its inventors to the giant UFA film company, which did nothing with it.

Finally, one smallish American film studio broke the impasse—Warner Brothers, which signed with Western Electric for the use of its patent sound-on-disc system, to be given the house-name 'Vitaphone'. Warner's aim was to provide first-rate recorded musical accompaniments, complete with sound-effects (but not dialogue), so that even the smallest movie house could afford the best of presentations with full symphony orchestra. After a little shoal of experimental Vitaphone 'shorts', Warner's first full-length sound film was *Don Juan*. Its musical sound-track, played by the New York Philharmonic Orchestra, was liberally garnished with sword-clashes, etc, and so enthusiastic was the film's reception at its premiere in the Warner Theatre, New York on 6 August 1926 that William Fox began to have second thoughts, and Messrs Case and Sponable found themselves with a customer.

'Fox Movietone' was not in commercial production until 1927, but the wait was worth-while. Far more flexible than the unwieldy Vitaphone, Movietone's relative portability made it particularly suitable for newsreel work. Sound footage was immediately taken of Mussolini and of aviator Charles Lindbergh, and by the end of 1927 Fox Movietone News was born.

Compared with Movietone, Vitaphone (and its assortment of cheaper rivals) was fraught with problems. Its playback stylus had to be put down precisely at a central arrow-mark, and the film wound through the projector until it reached a marked frame. When the projector and turntable were started and the sound was switched on, film and disc would be synchronised, but if the stylus jumped a groove or was jogged, the audience would be treated to a succession of peculiar effects for the rest of the reel. If anything happened to the film itself—if, for instance, it tore—that exact length had to be replaced in black celluloid, resulting in a chorus of catcalls when the screen suddenly went dark half way through a scene!

Disc recording allowed no editing, and there were as yet no facilities for superimposition of sound (which would have been very difficult on discs anyway) so life was not easy for the studio. Renters had all the trouble of sending out the large, heavy records with the reels of film, and making sure that each record was taken back for replacement after a certain number of playings. The sound-on-disc system was so inconvenient and its playback quality so quickly overtaken by sound-on-film that in 1930 Warner's switched to a Vitaphone photoelectric system, manufactured by Western Electric, who also happened to make Fox Movietone equipment!

In the interests of sound quality, the old projection speed of 16 to 20 frames per second was increased to a constant 24, which made talkie films shorter in duration than silents, but no-one seems to have been unduly put out. The need for a steady projection rate, however, did not go down so well with managements who had previously liked to speed up the machines and cram in extra showings!

The follow-up to *Don Juan* was a while in coming, but when it did arrive it made an even greater contribution to film history. Called *The Jazz Singer*, it starred Al Jolson, an irrepressible character whose larger-than-life stage charisma could hold an audience spell-bound for hours. And when, in the middle of a soundtrack originally intended to consist only of music and songs, 'Jolie' began to *speak*, Hollywood listened.

Silent films in preparation quickly received the addition of song sequences or dialogue, sometimes in just one reel, so that over 1928 and 1929 a rash of rather unsatisfactory 'part-talkies' went the rounds, with cinema orchestras expected to accompany the silent parts as usual. The phrase '100 Per Cent Talking, Singing and Dancing' was coined in order to distinguish the genuine talkie from its rather crudely improvised predecessor, but in those early days novelty alone was enough to guarantee crowds for any film whose sound came from the screen rather than from the orchestra pit.

The first talkies reached Britain in 1928 when *The Jazz Singer* played London's Piccadilly Theatre, and Warner's first full-dialogue talkie *Lights Of New York* came to the Regal, Marble Arch. The response was good, and as talkie features became more plentiful and hire purchase schemes were set up for the expensive equipment required (it was initially desirable to have both play-back systems available in the operating box), more and more cinemas throughout the country wired for sound.

1929 saw a clean sweep of most cinema orchestra pits in America and 1930 the same in Britain, but talkies did not gain wholehearted acceptance overnight from the trade or from the public. Silent films, although punctuated by titles which broke up the action, allowed far more use of the imagination than did talkies, which to many must have seemed very unsubtle. Also, early talkie sound quality was rather tiresome, often muddy in the lower and middle frequencies while shrill at the top. As both picture and sound had to be recorded at the same time, and silent cameras had not yet been invented, the camera had to work inside a silencing box, which meant its complete immobility.

The actors could hardly move either. Before somebody ignored the experts and slung up the first boom microphone, all dialogue had to take place next to microphones strategically concealed in vases of flowers, behind stage props or even about the persons of other members of the cast. For that reason, virtually the only actions possible during dialogue (which meant most of the time) were those of standing up and sitting down. Enthusiasm for talkies waned somewhat when this stultifying effect upon movement became realised, but once the practical problems had been resolved there was no stemming the tide. Soon silent films and the majority of their most illustrious stars were gone, little mourned.

In Aberdeen, early 1929 found business continuing much as usual. Stanley Copeland and his orchestra were resident at the Queen's, the Cinema House orchestra was being led by Myer Moss (an excellent musician), while at the Playhouse R.E. Cahill and his players emulated Steadman in broadcasting once or twice each week on 2BD. These transmissions went out during afternoon shows, no doubt complete with audience laughter and other noises-off, but no-one seems to have minded!

Mary Garden was not the only native of the Granite City to find her way on to celluloid. Sixty-year old Margaret Mann was born in Aberdeen but lived in South Africa up until 1918, when she went to Hollywood as an 'extra'. She had since become a star through portraying the kindly old mother in the Francis Bushman feature *Three Sons*, a domestic melodrama about a German family. In January 1929, at the end of a six-week return visit to Aberdeen, she was asked by the *Evening Express* to give her impressions. About local cinemas she was not at all complimentary. Accustomed to American picture halls in which smoking was confined to lounges set apart for the purpose and the wearing of hats was politely discouraged, Miss Mann voiced a particular dislike of watching films through a smoke-screen, whose presence she held to constitute disrespect to the film-maker's art. It had been hoped that a copy of *Three Sons* could be brought north for a charity showing to coincide with her visit, but this proved impossible and Miss Mann left Aberdeen quietly. Returning to Hollywood, she continued her career as screen 'mother' until her retiral in 1939. She died in 1941.

Manager of the Picture House since 1926 was a man named Bert Darley, who lived with his family in the flat at the top of the building. One dark night in January 1929, Mrs Darley awoke to see the face of an intruder peering round the door of the bedroom where she and her husband were sleeping. Pluckily, she sprang out of bed, and the miscreant and an accomplice took to their heels. The police were called, and the ensuing chase ended on the cinema roof where the pair were arrested. The two men, who were in a rather advanced state of intoxication, had managed to find their way into the building through a lavatory window. They had made a beeline for the office, which they ransacked, damaging hats and coats kept there and attempting (fortunately unsuccessfully) to make a bonfire of letters and papers. They 'found their way inside' all right—for three and for six months each.

In avoidance of fires, not every cinema was so lucky. On Sunday, 3 February (only five days after the Picture House incident) Inverurie Public Hall, then in use for pictures, burned down. A few weeks after that, a disastrous fire completely destroyed the £120,000 Palladium at Southport. Later in 1929 a blaze damaged the Regent, Brighton, and one Sunday in October Green's Playhouse, Ayr went up in smoke, taking with it £4,000 worth of talkie equipment that was waiting to come into use the next day. Making the brave announcement that the latter cinema would be rebuilt forthwith was its manager Fred Davies—could this have been the Fred Davies/Cruickshank that we have already encountered in connection with the Electric and La Scala? The cinema trade never did need too much reminding of the high risk to its buildings, which were usually insured to the hilt.

At the Electric, Ernest Wiseman of Steadman's Symphony Orchestra was still popular with his novelty solos on such instruments as xylophone and Swannee whistle. At La Scala, baritone R.E. Anderson continued to entertain. Back in 1928, Meyer Kalson had been called away from La Scala to supervise the musical arrangements and to lead the orchestra for the first few months of Green's Playhouse, Glasgow. This was a very prestigious post, with an orchestra numbering no less than thirty, but in April 1929 Green's Playhouse entered the talkie market and Mr Kalson returned to La Scala. During his temporary absence, his place had been filled by pianist S.O. Goldsmith, formerly of the Picture House and now, according to the local press, a 'well known organist from the Shepherds Bush Pavilion'. The same report credits him as bringing from London a 'specially constructed organ of which he is an expert player'—presumably some kind of harmonium, but as the report refers to Meyer Kalson as 'La Scala's new musical director Mr Kalsam', anything is possible!

Initially, Mr Kalson wanted full charge or nothing, but George Green did not want to lose or demote Goldsmith, and Mr Kalson agreed to come back to La Scala on the assurance that he and Goldsmith would get along quite well as co-directors. Goldsmith was a perfectly good musician and the two men did get on well enough, but somehow Mr Kalson did not feel at ease. After a while he took the surprising step of moving to Steadman's Symphony Orchestra as a rank-and-file member.

This was not on account of any sudden fancy for the Steadman set-up. The reason lay in the presence there of a very fine violinist named Theodore Crozier, whose playing Mr Kalson very much admired, and under whom he eagerly took further study during his brief sojourn at the Electric. Next he answered an advertisement for the post of musical director at the Torry Picture House and was quickly accepted, but music counted for little at this noisy hall. After only a fortnight he left to take up a post as orchestra leader at a large cine-variety house in the north of England. Once again talkies made him redundant, and this time he came back to Aberdeen to stay. For many years he led his own string quartet (the only regular ensemble of its kind in the city) and was also leader of the University Symphony Orchestra. For some time he ran a small theatre in Montrose as a side-line. Up until his retirement he had interests in the fur trade, but music remained his great passion up to his death in September 1977 at the age of 82.

Shortly after Meyer Kalson's return to La Scala in 1929, a new manager arrived—Mr William Muir, a native of Edinburgh and a 'veteran' of 17 years in the Navy before joining what was then the young cinema industry as cameraman and operator. Having worked his way up to the post of manager of a picture hall in Brighton, he had returned to the Navy during the war. On demob, he went to the Palladium, Mile-End, London, where the charity shows that he organised were very much appreciated. From there he moved to the Picturedrome, Bridgeton, Glasgow, before coming north. La Scala was by this time past its best; rather back-dated and down-at-heel, it was losing ground so quickly to competitors that Mr Muir obtained permission from Green's to replace some of its usual run of film programmes with less commercial material to attract the growing number of film connoisseurs, for whom the Union Street house soon became a welcome haven.

38   John R. (Jack) Poole, 1930s

At the Palace Theatre, Arthur Hinton's drama group had been torn apart by disputes and tensions between its members, and in March 1929 the theatre's doors closed for the last time on full-time stage entertainment. Already in January the building had been sold for between £15,000 and £20,000 to John R. Poole, third generation of the family with whose Dioramas, Myrioramas and early cinematograph we are already familiar. The Poole company had now an extensive chain of cinemas, with houses at Gloucester (its base), Stourbridge, Oxford, Ipswich, Cheltenham, Portsmouth and Edinburgh, to which latter city Mr Poole had gone to establish his own branch of the family concern. Setting up a cinema and office at the Synod Hall, Castle Terrace, where his family had been active with films as far back as 1906, he eventually came to assume administrative control of the entire widely-flung circuit—no mean organisational feat.

Sensing possibilities in Aberdeen, he bought the Palace, which re-opened on Monday, 8th April 1929 with what was described in a complimentary booklet as 'Continuous Pictures and Vaudeville Entertainers'—and with a drinks licence, although that may not have lasted for long! The main opening feature was *Sons Of The Sea*, starring Esther Ralston, Charles Farrell, Wallace Beery and George Bancroft. There was a supporting comedy *Has Anybody Here Seen Kelly*, and on stage were comedians Rosa Loader and Tom Laney, playing concertina, accordion and piano in a burlesque entitled 'Musical Absurdities'.

From experience at the Synod Hall (and no doubt also having heard about Steadman's success at the Electric) Mr Poole knew that a good orchestra would be required for the Palace. He therefore brought from London an able musician, Jack Frere, to lead the nine-piece Poole's Symphonic Orchestra (the only cinema orchestra in town with two pianos, a Mustel organ and a third piano on stage) in the accompaniment of films and live acts, and in its own regular stage 'turns'.

39   Jack Frere and Poole's Symphonic Orchestra at the Palace (*BA* 3 Aug. 1929)

Harmony Nights were on Thursdays and Fridays, and admission prices were 6*d*. for Circle and Stalls and 3*d*. for the Gallery until 4 p.m., when Centre Circle became 1*s*. 6*d*., Side Circle 1*s*., Stalls 9*d*. and Gallery 4*d*. On Saturdays prices changed again, with Circle at 1*s*. 6*d*., Stalls at 9*d*. and Gallery 4*d*. Children were admitted for 9*d*., 5*d*. and 4*d*. up to 4 p.m.

No doubt in an attempt to increase the appeal of conventional cinema entertainment on the eve of talkies, several of the city's picture orchestras attempted to update their style by becoming more like dance bands. There was James Skene's Syncopated Five at the New Kinema, for instance, or the Casino's 'Cinema Orchestra with the Dance Band Rhythm' under W.R. Smith, but the collapse of their world began on Monday, 17 June 1929 when, after a repertoire week to use up silent bookings, the Playhouse's screen squawked to life with the first permanent talkie installation north of Edinburgh. The main film was one of the last of the great silents, *Wings*, which starred Clara Bow, Gary Cooper, Buddy Rogers and Richard Arlen, and won the first-ever Oscar award. No amount of spectacular stunt flying, however, could match the interest aroused by the Vitaphone shorts that made up the rest of the show. Curious Aberdonians came along in such numbers that the programme was specially held over for the first half of the following week. Only one of that first set of shorts was named in press reports—it was of the J.C. Squire Celeste Octet playing popular numbers—but a second set, shown from the Thursday of the second week (after *Wings* had finished its run) is noted as including songs by comedian Leslie Sarony and music by the Lido Dance Band.

Full-length talkies arrived the following Monday, 1 July, when at four separate daily houses (to avoid the comings-and-goings inherent in continuous programmes) a jam-packed Playhouse saw and heard George Jessel in *Lucky Boy*, which arrived in Aberdeen only four weeks after its British premiere at the Regal, Marble Arch. By the end of the first day the public was being recommended to come to the early showings to avoid disappointment. Although scarcely a screen masterpiece, the film enjoyed great popularity on this and subsequent runs, and although it was soon superseded and forgotten, one sentimental song from it, 'My Mother's Eyes', is still occasionally heard today.

It was not the music or the singing in *Lucky Boy* that made the most immediate impression in Aberdeen—it was the strong American accent, about as intelligible to the average Aberdonian of 1929 as a fuzzy recording of an Aberdonian to a New Yorker. The *Evening Express* of 1 July 1929 remarked:

> Undoubtedly the talkies are a novelty and therefore an attraction, but silent films can hope to hold their own if 'Lucky Boy', shown at the Picture Playhouse this week, is typical of them all.
>
> There is no doubt that George Jessel, the star, is an actor with outstanding talent, but his voice is unmistakably American, or at least that part of it which

can be understood, for the chief defects in the film, not only of George Jessel, but of his supporting cast, are faulty intonation and enunciation.

Notwithstanding this, there are moments of really enjoyable entertainment, and those who do not object to losing part of a joke or words here and there will certainly enjoy 'Lucky Boy'.

Most certainly the film's recording quality was poor. Just as importantly, though, Bert Gates, like many of his fellow exhibitors, took a very cautious attitude towards the entire talkie question, and the play-back equipment that he brought in for what was essentially an experiment to gauge public opinion was not of full-price Western Electric type but one of its cheaper competitors. The exact make of the installation is not known, but, further hampered by the Playhouse's acoustics, which were never intended for talkies, it proved to have serious shortcomings. It was therefore not entirely the fault of the film's cast and makers that *Lucky Boy* failed to occasion overbrimming critical enthusiasm!

However much apprehension may have been felt by local cinema managements as the wave of change approached, they wore an impassive face and carried on as before. On the stage of the New Kinema, Carlette the illusionist conjured up live rabbits to give away to patrons as pets. Varieties were as integral a part of things as ever at the Casino, and the Electric had Stordy's Serenaders and Davina the Jazz Singer. But in an unmistakable atmosphere of 'pulling out all stops' to meet the new challenge, live musical turns were arriving in abundance. 'Repertoire Weeks', using up a film booking each day, could be found on the APP and Donald circuits, and 'Watch For The Talkies' became an advertising catch-phrase for the Cinema House, although it was to be some little time before talkies became an actuality there.

Over a second week's run at the Playhouse, *Lucky Boy* played as support feature to *The Divine Woman*, in which Greta Garbo was billed (with obvious thankfulness) as 'Seductive, Satisfying and Silent!' For the next fortnight, top feature was the Scottish premiere of *The Donovan Affair*. This '100 Per Cent Sound' opus starring Jack Holt and Agnes Ayres no doubt justified its billing of 'At Last—The Real Goods', but after it the Playhouse reverted to silents.

Aberdeen's first full-time talkie house was Poole's Palace, where, after some weeks of preparation, a £6,000 General Electric-built RCA sound system was unveiled on 12 August with the Lola Lane film *Speakeasy*. The rest of the programme consisted of a comedy, shorts of George Bernard Shaw giving *An Intimate Talk* and of Gertrude Lawrence singing the song 'I Don't Know', and Aberdeen's first sight of British Movietone News. The Palace's talkie installation, capable of coping with both sound-on-disc and sound-on-film, was hailed as a great success, but it did not hold its monopoly for long. Exactly a fortnight later the first Western Electric system in the city was inaugurated at the 'acoustically perfect' Picture House with Jolson's follow-up to *The Jazz Singer*, *The Singing Fool*.

The Singing Fool (whose theme song, 'Sonny Boy', is still for richer or poorer with us today) was a smash-hit with talkie-hungry Aberdonians. It was held for a full three weeks—a record for the Picture House, but quite a common occurrence in other places where it was shown. The *Evening Express* enthused:

40   Talkie speakers are installed at the Picture House, August 1929. *The Singing Fool* is on its way! (*BA* 24 Aug. 1929)

Occasionally there flashes across the film firmament a particularly bright comet in the form of such pictures as 'The Ten Commandments', 'Vaudeville' and 'Seventh Heaven'. None has been brighter or aroused so much interest than 'The Singing Fool', which is being shown at the Picture House all this week.

The thousands who queued up yesterday afternoon and evening were rewarded by seeing and hearing a talkie that is a triumph of up-to-the-minute motion picture art. Not but what the picture has its faults. The pronunciation of the feminine stars does not, for instance, please, while many might consider that too much sentimentality is introduced. But, after all, the pathos never descends to bathos, and these are minor blemishes on a big canvas.

Altogether, 'The Singing Fool' is a wonderful entertainment, and the man who makes it is, of course, Al Jolson.

He pours out his heart in the exaggerated, jazzy, conquering way that makes him irresistible, and displays, all through, his exceptional powers of emotional expression and his genius for moving us all to tears or laughs. Jolson's singing of 'Sonny Boy' was a memorable thing.

Next at the Picture House was *Coquette*, Mary Pickford's first talkie, of which the *Evening Express* also approved, crediting her with a perfect screen voice, all the adorable qualities that had earned her the title of 'The World's Sweetheart', and a superb piece of acting. Gone, however, was the 'little girl'. Curls had given way to bobbed hair as Mary portrayed a Southern Miss tangled up between a clandestine lover and a domineering father. *Coquette* was the first talkie to be adapted from a stage play and was also the first to win an Oscar. Its critical acclaim should have made it a sure-fire success, but Mary was the original victim of type-casting, and somehow she never quite rallied her public again. In 1933 she retired altogether from the screen.

An anecdote of the time concerns the removal of the Picture House's original screen in preparation for the fitting of sound equipment. The old screen was no ordinary canvas one—it was a huge cement slab attached to the back wall of the small stage, and it had to go in order to make way for the large talkie loudspeakers and a new porous screen through which the sound could penetrate. Its demolition turned out to be quite a task. Together, the cinema's operating staff and the sound technicians from London heaved and hauled at the solid mass, which refused to budge until a concerted effort finally sent it crashing into the orchestra pit in a shower of debris. Unfortunately, the erstwhile orchestral percussionist, sharing the expectation of many of his colleagues that talkies would last for about a fortnight and that he would soon be sent for, had been misguided enough to leave his big kettle-drums in the pit, directly in the way...

La Scala's management had delayed the introduction of talkies until some of their early problems had been resolved, but at the end of September 1929 the cinema closed for a few days to allow the setting up of sound equipment. It reopened on 2 October with a week of silents followed by full talkie programmes that began with *The Doctor's Secret*, starring Ruth Chatterton. The

41   William Muir (left) receives the Green's Cup from Mr William Hutcheon, Aberdeen, for greatest progress on the circuit over the past season. (*BA* 26 April 1930)

auditorium's shape gave rise to some apprehension as to its acoustical properties, but, to the delight of all concerned, the results were admirable. With
its prices of 1*s*. and 1. 3*d*. for Stalls, and 1*s*. 6*d*. and 2*s*. 6*d*. for Balcony (not
extravagant for talkies, which were more expensive to produce than silents),
La Scala took its place among the more successful of the city's older talkie
houses.

Myer Moss's Musicians at the Cinema House, F.J. Archer's seven-piece
orchestra at the Queen's and Jack Robinson's orchestra at the Grand Central
still accompanied James Donald's silent programmes, which at one point
included the non-talkie version of *The Jazz Singer*. Shown at the Grand Central
over the same week that Poole's introduced sound, its silence was made up
for with a big presentation that included 'special vocals' by Mr Jack Mac-
Lachlan, 'The Scottish Al Jolson'!

Walt Disney's Mickey Mouse first spoke in *Steamboat Willie*, which came to
Aberdeen as part of a Poole's Palace programme that September. *Movietone
Follies of 1929*, which came to the Picture House towards the end of the year,
was the first in the city of a stream of musicals churned out by the Hollywood
studios as they rushed to take full advantage of the new opportunities in

combining sight with sound. Starring Sue Carol, it contained a catchy little dance number called 'The Breakaway' plus a colour sequence, 'Under The Sea', which attracted great interest.

Who prefers Silent Pictures and A Good Orchestra? If you do—visit the Playhouse. The public have the last word in choosing their entertainment, 'Talkies' or 'Silent'. Give a lead by patronising the fare you prefer.

Nothing, it seems, could quite convince Bert Gates about talkies, not even a week's run of *Moulin Rouge* (the Playhouse's 'first great synchronised film') which opened on 2 September 1929. The public did give a lead, though. The above advertisement was run in the *Evening Express* during the week of 14 October 1929; by the end of the month a new Discus sound system was in place for the showing of the '100 Per Cent All Talking, All Singing, All Dancing' extravaganza *Broadway Melody*. The film's excellent musical score included the songs 'Broadway Melody', 'You Were Meant For Me' and 'The Wedding Of The Painted Doll'; the latter was the basis of a sequence made in a two-tone colour process which, although rudimentary, was nevertheless considered essential for any talkie spectacle. Established stars Bessie Love and Anita Page acquitted themselves well, while baritone Charles King was the first of many Broadway stage stars to be co-opted into films on the strength of a fine singing voice.

That same week, Poole's Palace rivalled *Broadway Melody* with a film called *Syncopation*, 'jazz' being no longer quite the in-word. Shortly after that, the Picture House had *Mother's Boy*, featuring one of the first crooners, 'golden voiced tenor' Morton Downey. Big-name presentations continued through the remainder of the year, most notably *This Is Heaven*, in which Vilma Banky's unexpectedly strong Hungarian accent rather taxed the ears of Picture House patrons, *Bright Eyes*, the talkie debut of vivacious British star Betty Balfour (Playhouse), *Bulldog Drummond* with Ronald Colman (Picture House), and *Lucky Star* with Janet Gaynor and Charles Farrell (Poole's).

The Picture House orchestra had by this time been reduced to a trio consisting of violinist George Harkins, his pianist brother, and cellist Maurice Bromburgh. Its only function now was to play short interludes between films, and presumably to be present in case of breakdown in the talkie system—a fairly common occurrence, which compelled cinemas still to employ stand-by pianists. The orchestras of La Scala, the Playhouse and Poole's Palace had vanished along with all stage varieties, and as players became redundant, musical directors at the remaining silent houses were able to have their pick of them. The Torry Picture House, for instance, now boasted a twelve-piece orchestra under Mr Herbert Jennings, formerly of the Queen's Hall Cinema, Newcastle.

Grandness had not so far been the most conspicuous attribute of James Donald's somewhat diminutive Grand Central in George Street, but with

42 The Grand Central from Craigie Street, 1935 (ADC, Dept of Planning)

expansion as his aim Mr Donald had managed to acquire first the properties next door to the north and then an old hall to the rear. In 1927, plans for an enlarged (although still fairly plain) Grand Central had been drawn up by Aberdeen architect George Watt but, like APP's scheme for the Electric, shelved. In the autumn of 1929 Mr Donald finally gave the go-ahead, and preparatory work started behind partitions in the old auditorium. It was not until Saturday, 16 November, after the last showing of *The Bond Man*, that the cinema finally closed to allow the scheme's completion. Dividing walls were demolished, new outer ones built and an extra storey added, all in record time—a matter of considerable pride to Mr Donald, who personally supervised the work. The Grand Central's capacity was increased from its original 730 to 1,640—a good 400 more than any other hall in town.

The reopening ceremony took place on 30 December 1929, with Provost Rust officiating. Even as eager crowds gathered outside the doors that night, plasterers and decorators worked frantically to add the finishing touches to an interior that differed markedly from its very conservative wood-panelled first draft of 1927. The *Evening Express* described it as 'a fairyland of waving trees, stately pillars and smiling skies of blue', in which:

> The beauty of the artist's brush is enhanced by the shaded lights, rich and varied in colouring, which hang suspended from the roof and nestle in the corners of the walls. It is a landscape hall, or to use the parlance of the cinema world, an atmospheric theatre.

On either side of the stage was an alcove containing a seven-feet high platform. One alcove held decorations (presumably of an 'atmospheric' shrubs-and-trees variety), while in the other was the orchestra, Myer Moss and his Ten Talented Musicians. First film was *The Three Rings*, and on stage was a Welsh Miners' Quartet, making its first Scottish appearance after an engagement in London. Mr Peter Donald was manager of what the new sign above the entrance could now justifiably proclaim as the 'Grand Central Super Picture House'.

No photographs of the Grand Central's 1929 decor have so far come to light, but its 'atmospherics' were certainly mingled with traditional features—curved ceiling, plaster swags, mouldings, etc—which survived subsequent alterations to the interior. In size, the 'Grandie' was not quite on a par with the very large 'supers' that would soon arrive in the city, but it was an important pointer towards things to come.

Vandalism may not be as much the preserve of present day society as some suppose. In 1929 Aberdeen's east-end had a gang of youths who derived amusement from starting fires behind the open doors of dwelling houses, and who one day turned their attention to James Donald's store in Albion Street, using spare padded seats as fuel. The smoke was spotted in time to save the building's contents of furniture and fittings, but the damage was considerable.

Fourteen windows were smashed, and it seems reasonable to suspect that little was done for Mr Donald's faith in the younger generation.

By the beginning of 1930, Hollywood was concentrating almost entirely on talkie production, much to the discomfiture of smaller exhibitors whose cinemas still showed silents and who had good grounds for feeling that they were being passed by. Not only did they fear that their supply of films might suddenly dry up before they could obtain talkie equipment; they also saw a threat in the poor quality of the material reaching them—principally talkies edited and served up minus their soundtracks. The aggrieved exhibitors would certainly have wholeheartedly endorsed the remarks made by the *Evening Express* current film critic, Lewis Hawes, in the *Express* of 12 May 1930:

> Of the 4,000 cinemas in this country, about 1,700 are now wired for talkies. This means that considerably more than half the cinema-going population has still to be content with silent films, and the truth is that there are hardly any silent films now being released that are worth seeing.
>
> So-called silent versions of talking films are usually not worth seeing because they are merely a makeshift for the real thing. Produced as talkies, and dramatically constructed solely with the talkie aim in mind, they are bound to suffer when adapted as silents. The quality of the purely silent output of the film companies, that is to say films made only as silents, is now so contemptible that it is a wonder the majority of the nation's cinema-goers who still have to put up with them do not rise in their wrath and refuse to go to the silent cinemas at all.
>
> Film profits nowadays, of course, are all with the talkies, and the producers cannot be blamed for concentrating their energies where the big money lies. But in almost entirely neglecting the great number of cinemas that are still not in a position to show talkies, and the vast public that still has to be content with the wretched silent films they offer for want of anything better, the producers are certainly not playing the game.
>
> Now that cinemas can produce talkie equipment on the hire-purchase system there will doubtless be a rapid increase in the number of theatres wired, but even so, at least another year must elapse before the unwired houses are reduced to a small minority. What are they going to do in the meantime? If they try to keep going for a year on the type of silent film they are now showing there is a distinct danger that their patrons will become so disgusted that they will lose the cinema-going habit altogether before the talkies arrive.
>
> If that stage is reached, the producers who should now be nursing this potential talkie market with good silent pictures will be sorry they neglected it.

When talkies first came on the scene, the issuing of silent films had stopped altogether, and it was only through pressure from the trade that they had become available once again. Some proprietors of 'silent' halls also advanced the theory that in treating them so badly Hollywood was cutting its own throat as well as theirs, but as the year passed it was proved that throat-cutting was entirely the province of those who did not, or could not, show talkies. For the rest of the industry, talkies turned out to be precisely the tonic that had been required, and as for Hollywood, all overheads were still being cleared on US first-runs leaving the income from British showings as pure profit!

The more that talkies improved, the more the Aberdeen public took to them. Queues for *The Desert Song*, which arrived at the Picture House in January 1930, began at the Palace Hotel on the other side of Bridge Street and stretched all the way around the block. *The Desert Song* starred handsome John Boles as Red Shadow in the first screen adaptation of the well-known operetta, and was a guaranteed house-filler for anyone who showed it in the city thereafter. With more local re-runs than any other film of the time, it must rank as Aberdeen's most popular screen feature of the early part of the decade.

Sunny Side Up starred Janet Gaynor and Charles Farrell, and contained the topical number 'If I Had A Talking Picture Of You'. *Innocents Of Paris* gave La Scala patrons Aberdeen's first sight of the young Maurice Chevalier, playing the role of a nobody from the streets of Paris who, against all odds, rose to fame on the stage and (more importantly) won the hand of his girl. 'Louise' was Chevalier's big song in this film.

As the flow of musicals reached flood proportion, both public and critics were captivated—for a while. In the *Evening Express* of 3 March 1930, Lewis Hawes wrote:

> Musical comedy is riding back to favour on the crest of the talkie wave. The tuneful and often graceful blend of pre-war days, until it was killed by jazz and raucous revue, is rising Phoenix-like from its ashes in the new medium of audible screen entertainment. Hollywood is now producing talkie musical comedies as fast as it can turn them out, and it is pleasing to note that there is a distinct endeavour to raise this form of attraction to something approaching genuine artistic level. The scenario writers are doing their best to evolve stories with some claims to plot, and they are succeeding to a quite surprising degree, while the composers are writing scores that are musically more meritorious than anything heard during the height of the jazz era...
>
> ...We have often been told that jazz is dying, but the truth of the matter is that jazz is already dead. It took to its death-bed several months ago when the musical possibilities of the talking screen began to be exploited. The development of the theme song put the first big nail in the jazz coffin, and the peaceful invasion of the talking screen by melody as opposed to syncopated noise has completed its demise. Syncopation, of course, will never die, for used moderately, syncopation is a legitimate and attractive feature of worthwhile music. The syncopation we are getting now in the latest musical talkies is nearly all of the subdued kind to which even the highest-brow could not take exception.

More than that, recording technique was advancing so quickly that in some films the sound quality could actually be heard to improve from reel to reel. In that same column Lewis Hawes was able to report:

In the last two or three musical pictures I have experienced the keen delight of being able to pick out the distinct tone colours of the various constituents, strings, woodwind and brass. In the early days of the talkies this was quite impossible, the canned music simply coming through in a confused blur like a bad gramophone record...

...The screen medium enables the film makers to present musical comedy with a wealth of spectacle and gorgeousness of colouring beyond the wildest dreams of the theatre stage—and the limitations of theatre finance. They can give us huge choruses, enormous ballets, vast scenes of dazzling riches; and they are doing so now in every new musical picture that comes over from Hollywood.

There seems to be a contest proceeding between the great producing concerns to see who can stage the most elaborate spectacle, for each new musical show that comes over is, if anything, more sumptuous than its predecessor. Where the race will end is problematical, but end it must somewhere, for presumably even Hollywood finance is not unlimited.

End it did, but not by reason of finance; the market in musicals became so glutted that finally the public became tired of them. Knowledgeable and perceptive though he was, Lewis Hawes did not quite hit the mark in referring to the 'demise' of jazz, which was undergoing change at that time, but in respect of high-quality score and song writing he was well on target. Perhaps one of the most positive features of the 1930s was its wealth of excellent popular songs, many of them written for the motion picture.

The week starting Saturday, January 18 1930 saw the last commercial use of the Music Hall for cinema purposes. Main feature was the Dolores Del Rio silent *The Trail Of '98*, given (possibly by James Donald) with the usual matinees and trimmings, but for the public it was talkies all the way, and the day of the Music Hall 'carnival' was over.

Back at the Playhouse, it seems that the sound equipment was still not quite satisfactory. Programmes were part-silent until the end of February 1930 when Bert Gates finally suspended talkies for the installation of a full Western Electric system. Inaugurated on Monday, 31 March with *Footlights And Fools* (one of the last films of one-time silent screen favourite Colleen Moore), it signalled the end for the Playhouse orchestra, which dispersed, mainly to other cinemas. Richard Garioch went to lead the orchestra at the still-silent King's, but R.E. Cahill was promoted to the post of manager and stayed on as a familiar figure at the Playhouse for the remainder of his career.

That April, La Scala's showing of a film called *The Cocoanuts* was heralded by a press report that spoke of:

A large beach hotel containing four mad jesters exchanging snappy dialogue and quick fire fun—an adorable heroine and a handsome hero...

Literally 'The Cocoanuts' is bubbling in irresistible humour; fooling that is like nothing ever witnessed here; music, song and dancing; Oscar Shaw and Mary Eaton making love; a whirl of chorus beauties; gorgeous settings. All that and more in this bright talkie.

43   Bert Gates (left) and staff, pictured outside The Playhouse during the early years of the Talkies (courtesy of Aberdeen Picture Palaces)

The report omitted to say that the fooling was that of the Marx Brothers, making their first sally into screen territory after a successful career on stage. *The Cocoanuts* was indeed unlike anything ever witnessed in Aberdeen. Just how comprehensible the Brothers' zany, very American, quick-fire patter would have been in the Aberdeen of nearly 60 years ago is a matter for conjecture, but the conspicuous absence of the team's early productions from the major picture halls of the city may furnish a clue!

Wait! Why worry about the talkies. All the best talking pictures will be shown at the Grand Central Picture House and the Cinema House. Only the best is good enough for us. Even though these installations will cost us thousands of pounds, our prices will remain the same. Now, don't worry.

So James Donald's patrons were reassured in the columns of the *Evening Express* of 12 April 1930, preparatory to the equipping of the two cinemas with sound as of Monday, 21 April. The Cinema House began talkies with *The Perfect Alibi* and the Grand Central with *Bulldog Drummond*. Sound films were now plentiful enough for exhibitors to be able to offer two re-runs a week as in silent days, and soon, one by one, Aberdeen's smaller cinemas made the change. On 5 May *The Singing Fool* made redundant W.R. Smith's orchestra at the Casino. On 28 July the New Kinema brought in talkies with *The Rainbow Man*, starring Charles King and Bessie Love, and on 6 August the Queen's became 'The Finest and Clearest Talkie House in Town' with *So This Is College*.

Bert Gates had never any intention of installing talkies at the Electric. With Steadman's Symphony Orchestra now numbering twelve after the addition of several 'new captures', he strove to perpetuate the old order of things. 'Is your ear drugged?', he enquired in the *Evening Express* amusement column during the week of 12 May. 'Have you forgotten the true tone of violin, cello, brass, drums, etc? Keep your tonal critical faculty awake. We have still Steadman's Symphony Orchestra. Take a course of ear exercises with us.'

The public did not want 'ear exercises'. Neither did it share Mr Gates' enthusiasm for 'pictures free from scratch, ground noise, lisps, adenoids, hum, crackle, over-modulation, echo, reverberation or distortion—because they're silent!' APP bowed to the inevitable, and on Saturday, 30 August the Electric closed temporarily after showing its last silent films *The Naughty Duchess* and *The Man In Hobbles*. In went a Western Electric sound system, and out went Steadman, lock, stock and Swanee whistle. The Electric reopened on Monday, 8 September with *The Rainbow Man*.

The Torry Picture House capitulated on Monday, September 15 with *The Trial Of Mary Dugan*, starring Norma Shearer, and the Kings followed suit on 29 September with *Mother's Boy* and *Elstree Calling*. On Monday, 13 October, *King Of The Khyber Rifles* marked the start of talkies at the Star. Silent programmes returned to the New Kinema, but only to allow the installation of a new 'super talkie system' which came into use on 27 October. When, that same day, *Happy Days* introduced talkies at the Globe, Aberdeen's last cinema orchestras (apart possibly from the Harkins trio at the Picture House) packed their bags. The increasing reliabilty of sound equipment soon made stand-by musicians unnecessary, and before long the lid of the old cinema piano closed for good. Musicians joined the growing ranks of the unemployed, and the number of street-buskers in Britain's cities rose sharply.

There was just one Aberdeen picture hall that did not follow the rest into the talkie age. In 1929-30 the New Palladium was the subject of detailed plans for enlargement to a seating capacity of well over 1,000. Two successive plans were commissioned in the name of the manager, Mr Arthur L. Purchase, from architects D. & J.R. McMillan of Crown Street. The first, drawn up in May 1929, was for a refurbishment of the old hall with the intention of future expansion on the site of tenements to the south-west of the building. The second, dating from exactly a year later, provided for the pushing out of the building's truncated south-west corner over the neighbouring site. The interior would then have been opened out to make a new, large auditorium. (Above the stage were to be fire-escape windows which, endearingly, opened automatically in the event of a blaze!) In both plans the floor above the cinema was to be converted into a large billiard room with a separate entrance in the adjacent Shiprow building to the south, added to the complex in 1920 in order to make the Balcony and Stalls entrances, which would have been retained in the new plans. On the very top floor was to be staff accommodation, and in the 1930 plan there was a 'tea lounge' in the large waiting hall area above the original entranceway. Existing frontages were to be retained. For reasons that are not clear the scheme was abandoned and in the summer of 1930 Dove Paterson's old Gaiety, where 'it all began', became a shuttered, empty reminder of days bygone.

During the early hours of 28 August 1930, William Muir of La Scala was asleep in his Crown Street flat when he was awakened by the light of a pocket torch in the room. Standing there was a policeman with an urgent message— La Scala was on fire! A vigilant member of the Force, out patrolling his beat, had spotted smoke coming through the roof and had at once called the Fire Brigade.

Another surprise awaited Mr Muir as he hurried towards La Scala with the policeman. Arrangements for carrying electricity below the streets of Aberdeen were not quite of the standard that they are now, and overheatings and explosions in mains cables and junction boxes were not unusual. A direct short-circuit could produce spectacular results, as Mr Muir discovered just as he and the policeman approached the corner of Crown Street. All of a sudden, a mighty detonation resounded through the city's quiet thoroughfares and a 20-foot jet of flame shot from a manhole in the pavement directly ahead. With it went the manhole cover and the junction box, both of which, luckily, flew in the opposite direction. The noise, which brought a crowd of alarmed, partly-dressed citizens tumbling into the street, was heard by the firemen at

La Scala. No-one had ever been injured in such an incident, but it was generally agreed that the consequences might have been serious had this one occurred by day.

On arriving at the cinema, Mr Muir found that despite thick smoke and fumes, the firemen had managed to contain the outbreak before it could gain a firm hold. Probably started by a dropped cigarette-end in the back stalls, the fire had destroyed several seats, scorched the adjacent right-hand wall, destroyed an emergency fire-box and burned through the floor into the joists below. If not detected, it would certainly have spread up the lathing of the wall and into the balcony, resulting in a major blaze. Part of the auditorium wall had to be chopped out in order to tackle the flames below, but there was relatively little water damage, and a rather smoke-stained (and probably malodorous) La Scala was able to open for business as usual the next day.

Crowd control in cinemas was a highly sensitive matter just at that time. A tragic incident had occurred in Paisley at New Year 1930 when, during a special Hogmany matinee, a reel of film started to burn in the operating box of a small cinema packed with children. The trouble was quickly dealt with, but the sight of smoke escaping into the auditorium caused blind panic among the young audience, leaving 69 dead, 150 injured (37 of these severely) and the manager facing a charge of culpable homicide. In the wake of this, local authorities began to look very closely at conditions in cinemas under their jurisdiction, and to rigorously tighten safety regulations.

The practice, previously tolerated, of allowing overflow audience to stand at the back of some Aberdeen halls on busy nights was quickly outlawed. Quite a ripple was caused among local exhibitors by the imposition of a £15 fine on James Donald's company, Aberdeen Cinemas Ltd., for allowing patrons to queue single-file on the Grand Central's wide balcony stairs, for allowing them to stand at the back of the balcony (even though they were well clear of the exits) and for permitting the use of a corner of the foyer and a waiting-room stair at the Queen's as waiting areas. The Grand Central's queues had in fact been moved inside after neighbouring shopkeepers had complained about obstruction of their doorways—to the same authorities that were now making sure that the queues went outside again! The pressure was on, and for some time afterwards cinema advertising in the city carried lines urging attendance at queue-free early houses.

Trickling in from Germany were reports of a man called Adolf Hitler who, to the wild applause of his followers, announced his ambitions of using Britain as a stepping stone in conquering the world. Little reaction was caused in this country; minds were on matters closer to hand, such as the onset of the Depression, which had begun with the collapse of the American economy in October 1929, and which would shortly bring hard times to many.

44   Queue for The Picture House—with Talkies (*BA* 14 Nov. 1930)

Over a Christmas season fraught with apprehension, cinemas offered such spangled attractions as *What Price Melody*, *The New Movietone Follies Of 1930*, *Puttin' On The Ritz* (a film that spawned a new in-phrase with its title as well as containing a hit theme song), and *The Vagabond King* starring Jeanette MacDonald and Dennis King. With the silent era and all its works now but a memory, the day of the super talkie-house was dawning as 1931 approached.

Chapter 10

The 'Super' Arrives 1931—1935

By the time that 1931 was out, Britain felt the full force of the recession. Wages and benefits were cut, companies collapsed, and unemployment rose to peaks previously unheard of. The only real growth industry was the cinema as investors rallied to provide just what would suit the taste of a population under duress. The great years of picture house building, now finished in the States, were just beginning in the United Kingdom, and immense strides were being made in cinema construction and design as exhibitors went out of their way to give even the poorest patron the experience of stepping into a splendid palace of fantasy in which the outside world could be forgotten, however temporarily.

The Modernist option in architecture was now being widely explored, its way paved by the Paris 'Exposition Internationale des Arts Décoratifs' of 1925, from which came the term 'art deco'. Art deco took elements of Ancient Egyptian art (all the rage after the Tutankhamen expeditions of the early 1920s), added a touch of Aztec art, and combined these with modern elements to produce an influential and distinctive idiom that more or less epitomises its period. Lending itself well to new techniques that were emerging in the use of steel, glass and concrete, it was avidly assimilated by designers in their continuing quest for a new kind of architectural expression. There is a saying that 'just about everything built in the 1930s looks like a garage or a cinema'. And why not? Both were unashamed symbols of their age and of a sleek brand of consumerism that flourished between the Depression and the outbreak of war in 1939.

Aberdeen's first wave of all-talking all-singing mania had subsided by 1931, and what musicals there were were of a more sophisticated nature. First of this new generation was *Song Of The Flame*, which reached the Picture House early in the year. Another, which arrived a little later, was *Hit The Deck*, starring Jack Oakie and Polly Walker, and using the excellent Vincent Youmans score from the original stage show. Of Polly Walker two biographical backgrounds have been recorded—one that she was born in Alford of a stage and circus family, emigrating to America when very young, and the other that she was born in Chicago of an Aberdonian father; in either case she had a strong link with North-East Scotland. Later she was to add a British stage career to her achievements as popular screen and recording artiste.

In connection with a Picture House run of *Whoopee* (first feature film starring comedian Eddie Cantor) the Palais De Danse held a 'Whoopee Jamboree', with dancing to the new resident band, Vincent Norman and his London Band. Competition prizes were contributed by the Picture House, the Palais, and Messrs Francis, Day & Hunter of London, publishers of the songs in the film—in those days it was not sales of records but of sheet music that registered a hit!

Among a succession of local premieres given at the Grand Central in the early part of 1931 was *Romance* starring Greta Garbo, and *The Unholy Three*, first and only talkie by the great master of disguise, Lon Chaney. Other popular

45   A turn-out of the Gordon Highlanders to The Playhouse, March 1931.
Note Cinema's signboards and original fascia. (*EE* 10 Mar. 1931)

films of the year included the classic *All Quiet On The Western Front*, adapted from the Erich Remarque novel of the Great War, and *Just Imagine*, starring Maureen O'Sullivan and El Brendel. *Just Imagine* was set in the year 1980, by which time, supposedly, everyone was known entirely by numbers, all things to do with love and marriage were under State control, cities were made up of great sky-scrapers with landing-pads for airliners (directed by flying traffic cops!), and all food and drink was in tablet form. Nearly right!

The King Of Jazz, one of the most important productions of the previous year, featured the famous Paul Whiteman Orchestra with its vocal trio 'The Rhythm Boys', a member of which was the young Bing Crosby. Shot in colour, it starred Laura La Plante and John Boles. It incorporated some outstanding dance sequences, several memorable songs, of which 'It Happened In Monterey' and 'A Bench In the Park' have become 'standards', and its high-spot was the first filmed performance of Gershwin's 'Rhapsody In Blue'.

At La Scala, *Paramount On Parade* consisted of 'party pieces' by no less than thirty Hollywood stars, ending with Chevalier 'Up On Top Of A Rainbow (Sweeping The Clouds Away)'. This catchy little song is seldom heard nowadays, but it was quite typical of the 'take it on the chin and grin' kind of number that was popular during the Depression years.

That June, La Scala gave the first Aberdeen showing of a film co-starring the much-acclaimed German actor Emil Jannings and a remarkable unknown girl who played the part of *femme fatale* to devastating effect. The film was *The Blue Angel*, and the girl was Marlene Dietrich. Elsewhere, Bela Lugosi starred in *Dracula*, while Howard Hughes' war spectacular *Hell's Angels* featured Ben Lyon and brought to notice another screen newcomer, platinum blonde Jean Harlow.

In November 1931, the Sub-Committee of the Aberdeen Juvenile Organisers' Committee published the conclusions of a survey that it had been conducting into the Board Of Trade's grading of films. This survey was modelled on a Birmingham prototype, and was carried out by sending representatives to various Aberdeen cinemas each week for two months to report on how suitably the films, amounting to 190 or so main features in all, had been classified.

Of those 190 films, 25 had an 'A' certificate for adult exhibition only and 118 a 'U' for general exhibition. The remaining 47 displayed no Board certificate at all, but this was not what troubled the Committee. The problem, according to the report, was that some of the 'U' certificate material did not belong in that category at all, while some that was classed as 'A' hardly seemed to warrant such a grading. The report also spoke of 'A' features being shown at children's matinees, and of cinemas where children were admitted regardless of what film was on. The showing of 'A' category films to children was condemned on the grounds that it caused alarm in the more violent scenes, spread fear and 'unhealthy excitement', gave incentive to crime, murder, suicide, gang and prison life, fighting, drunkenness, gambling and night-club life, sex, indecency and 'unhealthy humour', and portrayed as attractive deceit, vice and immorality. It was further alleged that some east-end halls were admitting children-in-arms to an atmosphere that was 'very

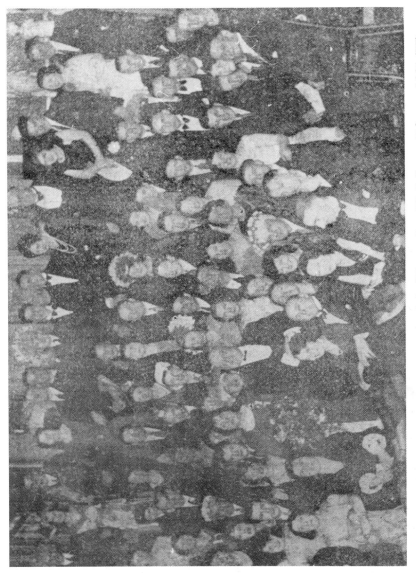

46 James F. Donald (Aberdeen Cinemas) Ltd. Staff Dance, Donald's Ballroom, February 1931 (*EE*)

47 Foyer Display for *Hell's Angels* at the Picture House, September 1931

heated and often vile', and that the children were present right until the end of the house at 10.45 p.m.

The reactions of children to the films that they saw were also tested, 200 five to fourteen year olds being given questionnaires to complete on the subject. From the answers supplied, it was gathered that the majority visited the cinema once a week, chiefly to see war and adventure pictures. Too much violence was not liked, but neither was too much love! Generally speaking, no firm evidence was found of the children's being much influenced or disturbed by what they watched. Some agreed that films might show them how to steal, but others thought that the good deeds portrayed would have the greater influence on them. Stuffiness in cinemas, however, was widely commented upon, and some youngsters considered that smoking ought to banned there (even in 1931!). Shortage of seating and lack of waiting room accommodation for the long daily queues were also mentioned, as was lack of supervision by attendants.

The report's concluding recommendation was that the city should adopt the Home Office's published Model Conditions for cinema licensing, which stipulated that no film could be shown that was likely to be 'injurious to morality, incite crime, or be offensive to public opinion'. Stressing (as ever) the cinema's educational aspect, the Sub-Committee called upon Aberdeen's magistrates to explore the legal situation regarding the Conditions' enforcement. The major stumbling block in lobbying for local censorship powers along the lines of those held in the South was always the fact that under Scots Law, licensing authorities' jurisdiction over cinemas and theatres went only as far as ensuring public safety. Changing this would be a very difficult business, involving Act of Parliament, so instead Aberdeen's Corporation Order Confirmation Act of 1911 was pointed to, containing as it did sections on hall licensing and the imposition of penalties for infringement of regulations.

As was the custom when matters such as these came into the news, the *Evening Express* interviewed 'a cinema manager', whose answer was published in the issue for 25 November 1931. The manager agreed with the report's general tone and confirmed the accuracy of some of its findings, but aired the view that by definition, 'A' and 'U' gradings were so wide in scope (viz the differences of opinion between the Official Censor and the Committee) that hard and fast rules were a practical impossibility. On the subject of children-in-arms (a matter which, curiously, did not come in for specific discussion when the question of children in cinemas was raised in 1913), he stated that at first he had steadfastly refused them admission, but when other halls did not follow suit he had been more or less forced to give in. Even so, young children brought in by parents (who would not otherwise have been able to come to the cinema at all) generally slept. He held that young children did not follow dialogue in the way that they had been able to follow the scenes in silent pictures. The status quo in Aberdeen he described as quite fair to both public and exhibitor, a view supported by all other cinema managers that the paper's reporter spoke to thereafter.

Not everyone's response was quite so placid. In *Bon-Accord* of 13 November,

William Muir called the report 'a false representation of the true facts' about the feelings and desires of those in the trade.

> ... These good people who are delegated to visit the cinemas must have surely had their souls purged for daring to risk the danger of moral corruption if their opinion is true in word and fact.
>
> The writer has had experience of the work of such committees in the past and while not desirous of doubting the sincerity of their desire to improve the morale of the people in their city I feel justified in giving some analysis on the point of the usual characteristics of the work of such committees.
>
> Firstly, these people often attach too much importance to what suits their side of the question in which they are interested, and magnify the importance of what they feel is the backbone of their pet scheme.
>
> Enquiries conducted by people of strong views are usually unsatisfactory. Predilections and prejudices are fatal to sound judgement. For example, some two years ago two women were appointed to enquire into the state of the drink traffic in a certain London district—Mrs A, a pussyfoot, with an ardent desire to interfere in other people's habits; and Mrs B, a believer in moderate drinking and a strong advocate of individual freedom. Mrs A reports that the inhabitants are being ruined by drink and that nothing short of prohibition can save the district.
>
> Mrs B reports that there is very little drunkenness, and that all is for the best in the best of all possible worlds. Both parties are quite honest but neither description is accurate. Usually scientific investigators are not prone to letting their personal views interfere with their judgement. But sometimes these investigators are so convinced that their pet theory is right that they marshal facts in such a way as to give it the maximum support, and so possibly it is with this committee, who, though quite honest in their endeavour are, nevertheless, over-ridden by prejudice.
>
> The tone of the report reminds me of the ideas of the early Victorian days in which these good people are still living. In this advanced year of 1931, one would ridicule the attitude of our forefathers in view of the evolution of man and his ways. To The Pure All Is Pure.

Like its predecessor of nearly twenty years before, the report was of little effect, but it stands as a fair example of the kind of missile that the cinema industry still received from time to time.

The problem set by the presence of young children in cinemas was indeed a serious one, but it must be seen against the squalid, depressing, cold and overcrowded conditions in which a significant proportion of this country's urban populations lived in those days. Cinema-going constituted the only easy (or affordable) means of escape, and there were no such things as baby-sitters to help out when friends or other members of the family were not available to take care of children.

Finally, the note of exasperation discernible in Mr Muir's broadside may not have surprised those who saw a rather crusty letter from La Scala in an August 1931 issue of *Bon-Accord*. Headed 'A Magnanimous Offer', it read:

> If the person who is in the habit of removing the pictures from the frames outside the theatre will call on the Monday at the conclusion of the run of each picture, we shall be pleased to present him with any picture he desires, so saving him the

bother of nocturnal expeditions with a screwdriver, and perhaps at the same time saving him from embarkation upon a criminal career.

Whether or not the culprit had the good taste to read *Bon-Accord* we shall probably never know, but what does seem clear is that in one way or another Mr Muir was being sent his share of things to try him!

Jack Poole's estimation of the Palace's potential as a cinema had been a shrewd one. Although, as a building, it was far from ideal for its new purpose, it had been a great success with the public. Just one aspect of the enterprise had disappointed him—lack of capital to effect a complete rebuilding and modernisation of the premises. Mr Poole therefore contacted a couple of influential colleagues at the Southern end of the company—R. Sutton Dawes of London, who had contacts in 20th Century Fox, and Bradford lawyer and financier William Firth. Mr Poole put to them a proposal to form a new subsidiary company, Aberdeen Palace Theatre Ltd, through which the work that he so much desired could be carried out. Mr Poole must have had quite a way with people, for he managed to 'sell' to Messrs Dawes and Firth not only his ideas on the Palace but also another highly ambitious project that had been taking shape in his mind—the construction of an entirely new sister cinema in another area of the city, to show second-runs from the Palace.

Plans drawn up and formalities completed, the Palace's last week before 'the transformation' was that of 2 March 1931. 'Take A Last Look At The Old Theatre—And Then The New', said the adverts; those who did come for a last look at the old Palace saw as feature films Richard Cooper in *Lord Richard In the Pantry* and Grant Williams in *Dancing Sweethearts*.

As downtaking progressed over spring and early summer, two old cottages on the Crown Terrace side of the building were cleared away and other sites which had been acquired to the west were prepared for a 4,800 square-feet extension containing entranceways, foyers and ancillary accommodation. Of the old structure, nothing was kept but the walls. Its entire area was given over to form the new auditorium, seating capacity of which (2,000) was only a slight increase on the old (1,714), but now the old Circle and Mezzanine were replaced by a large modern Balcony.

A huge new steel frame was erected to support the building's weight, and the foundations were reinforced with 150 tons of cement. Close on another 50 tons of cement went into the manufacture of 800 or so Ferrocrete units, pre-cast at the Gray Street yard of contractor W.J. Anderson. These units were used to make up such features as doorways; only the stairs were made on site, and the interval between casting and setting in place was only about ten days—quite exceptional for 1931. All work on the new cinema was carried out by local firms using locally-supplied materials. The frontage to the extension was in Rubislaw granite, with corners, windows and margins in harder Sclattie granite. Within, all decoration-work was carried out by

48   The Palace, Bridge Place, showing 1931 extension

49   Interior of The Palace before 1931 rebuilding

50   Interior of The Palace after rebuilding (*EE* 27 Nov. 1931)

Messrs Bruce MacKenzie, and all carpeting (two miles of it) was supplied and laid by Messrs J. & A. Ogilvie.

The new main foyer was painted in shades of blue and green, and was floored in the synthetic 'terazzo' work that was becoming very popular for buildings of this kind. The auditorium's colour scheme, described as combining 'a sunshine effect with autumnal tints', blended upwards from tawny brown through orange and yellow to a ceiling in blue and yellow with gold reliefs. Set behind a bronze and gold-painted proscenium arch of simple, almost severe lines was the screen, which measured 36 feet square as against the standard 24 feet, and was claimed as the first of its kind in the country. In front of it were two sets of curtains, the outer set made of sumptuous green velour and decorated with appliqué floral work. These decorations were designed by Mrs Jack Poole and carried out by Mr A.C. Rogers, art director to the Poole company since the days of Dioramas.

All seating was silent in movement, and the centre stalls area was dipped by some ten inches to aid sight-lining. The house lighting system in red, blue and amber could be controlled from the manager's office as well as from the spacious new operating box which replaced a cramped and badly-sited predecessor in the former theatre limelight booth. Never built with projection in mind, the booth's height above the back of the auditorium had meant a very steep working angle for the projectors, with consequent loss of picture quality. Due to the shape of the building, the new box could not be set quite as low, or the balcony as far back in relation to the screen as was strictly desirable, but neverthless the improvement was immense.

Designed nominally by Newcastle architects Marshall & Tweedie, the 'new' Palace was actually the work of a Yorkshire man named Watson. The Poole family had strong Yorkshire connections, and Watson (who had recently become associated with the Newcastle firm) was something of a favourite when it came to the placing of commissions for new halls. The scheme's initial budget was £40,000 but during construction it was found that far more steelwork was required than had been expected. It was therefore a much more costly project that came to fruition on Saturday, 28 November at 8 p.m., when the Palace, described as having been 'dedicated with pride to the amusement-loving public of Aberdeen and the Highlands, and visitors to the Granite City the world o'er', was opened before an audience of guests and general public. The central attraction of this 'the event of 1931' was the Charlie Chaplin film City Lights, and the occasion was made even more special by the holding of a special Charlie Chaplin Carnival at the Palais De Danse, masterminded by Ernest Bromberg in association with Poole's.

The search for a suitable site for Poole's second Aberdeen house had not been long in progress when word was received of a possible find in the city's west end. Jack Poole came to reconnoitre, and went away delighted; soon everything was signed and sealed, and when, in July 1931, the Palace scheme was approved by the city's Planning Committee, plans were also passed for its brand-new companion, the REGENT.

The sites of both buildings possessed long historic associations. Bridge Place, on which the Palace stands, is part of a ridge that extends from Holburn Street to Crown Terrace. There it slopes steeply downwards towards the harbour, forming a natural amphitheatre which was used in mediaeval times for the presentation of entertainments, notably the ancient morality play *Halyblude*. Along the ridge were fought the bitter battles of the Craibstane, the Langstane and the Justice Mills as the citizenry of Aberdeen defended itself from invasion during the course of Scotland's troubles in the distant past.

The place acquired for the Regent was the site of the Upper Justice Mill, at the Holburn Street end of the ridge. Situated at the farthest limit of the ancient Borough boundary, the Justice Mills are thought to have taken their name

51   The Justice Mills—Upper Mill top centre, Lower Mill to the right foreground
(*PJ* 1931)

from their customary use centuries ago as a meeting point for town officials and travelling 'justiciars' or judges. The Upper Justice Mill stood behind Justice Mill Lane just as it rounds the corner into Holburn Street, while down the brae, in Union Glen, stood the Lower Justice Mill, its mill-pond midway between the two buildings. 'Justice Mills' of some sort had been in existence as early as 1320 when they became the property of the Borough of Aberdeen; they assumed their final form in the nineteenth century, and for decades were tenanted by the same families—the Frasers at the Upper Mill and the Alexanders at the Lower.

By the 1920s they were the last water-mills left in operation in the city, but had evidently been in decline for some time—early this century it had been proposed to reuse the site to house a Council refuse destructor! By 1931 the Lower Mill was empty, and although the 74 year-old Alfred B. Fraser was still in business at the Upper Mill (assisted by his son William), it was now more as a grain merchant than as a miller. The Council had long wished to see the area cleaned up, but the site's 30-foot slope had so far made it of no interest for building. Poole's appearance was therefore welcome, a fact recognised by the Council in its handing over to the company of part of the ground at no more than feu value.

The Frasers moved to the Lower Mill, which from then on became purely a store. The Upper Mill's displenishment sale was held on Tuesday, 26 May 1931, and demolition was soon under way—not the easiest of tasks on solid walls two feet thick. The Lower Mill pond was drained and filled, the three lades (the main one of which still runs under the site) were diverted and covered, and the site was levelled by excavating it back towards Justice Mill Lane. Opportunity was taken by the Council of widening and improving the Lane (a project that continued throughout the early 1930s), and a little path that ran from the Upper Mill to the Lower was widened and extended to make a new thoroughfare into Union Glen. The cinema cut across the eastern end of where the Upper Mill had been; the western part of the mill site, vacant for many years, is now occupied by the McClymont Halls of Holburn Central Church plus a miscellany of business premises and car parks.

If the cinema industry was buoyant in 1931, other forms of entertainment were taking the recession hard. Theatres all over the country were in the doldrums as never before, and in Aberdeen the fortunes of His Majesty's Theatre reached such a low ebb that in October the building was advertised for sale at an auction to be held in the Palace Hotel on Tuesday, 10 November. With cinema-trade eyes known to be looking in its direction, the theatre was in imminent danger of being lost as a 'live' house. It was for that reason that, with considerable urgency, the Aberdeen *Press & Journal* instituted a scheme for the floating of a publicly-subscribed limited company to purchase the premises from its owners Robert Arthur Theatres Ltd, (a subsidiary of Howard & Wyndham), if no other theatre concern made a successful bid. Anyone interested in partcipating in this 'rescue' was invited to contact the paper, stating how much he or she would be prepared to give for a share in the company. The response was encouraging; no acceptable alternative bid was lodged, and so a prospectus was issued, a managing body was formed, and the plan went ahead. Instead of outright purchase as had at first been envisaged, a long lease was secured on the building, and although the next couple of years were scarcely to be the most brilliant in its history, its continuance was, for the time being, assured.

Solace of some kind may well have been on the minds of many that bleak year, and one wonders what effect the deepening Depression may have had on the numbers attending Aberdeen Evangelistic Association's Sunday night meetings, held at the Playhouse over winters throughout the 1920s and 1930s. One might also speculate as to how many were able to do anything more than admire the latest consumer goods on display at that December's Radio Exhibition in the Music Hall. Just one thing did come free at the Exhibition—the music of the Bullturn Phantom Orchestra under its leader, a certain Mr George Steadman.

By 1932 the craze for Hollywood musicals had given way to one for gangster thrillers. Dialogue in some 'adult' pictures had become quite racy even by today's standards, adding fuel to a renewed 'clean up Hollywood' campaign. Worried by the 'sin city' image peddled by the popular press, the continual campaign being waged against it by some religious groups, and by the widely-publicised scandals that had plagued it for years, the Hollywood establishment brought in its 'Public Relations Officer', Will H. Hays, to pour oil upon troubled waters. Hays persuaded the moguls to tighten up an existing (and largely ignored) code of practice to form a set of 'do's and don'ts' designed to cut out anything that might cause an unhealthy stir. By the end of 1934 a whole list of taboos was in force, ranging from spicy dialogue to overexposure of the human frame. Even such acts as the blowing of raspberries were firmly proscribed!

Some saw this as a victory for decency, while others loudly condemned it as a capitulation to the Mrs Grundys. In an *Evening Express* article of February 1932, Lewis Hawes added his voice to the controversy, deploring the early horror pictures like those of Bela Lugosi, and the spread of so-called 'sophistication' on the screen. The latter he described as:

> Too much mental undressing of already half-dressed women, too many scarcely-veiled sex allusions and innuendos crammed into would-be smart dialogue spoken in 'speakeasies', unventilated bedrooms and night clubs reeking with cigarette smoke and liquor fumes.

It may be easy for us to dismiss Hawes (with his admitted relief at the resurgence of the wholesome Western) as a provincial prude, but what, even nowadays, might one make of the titles of some films reaching Aberdeen in 1931 and 1932, however innocuous their actual content—*Ladies Love Brutes,*

Hot Curves, Call Of The Flesh, Soldiers And Women, Compromising Daphne or *Anybody's Woman?* No wonder that the YMCA's Saturday night shows were still silent.

Work on the ancient Justice Mill site's very twentieth century Regent Cinema progressed at such a rate that people would make a point of dropping in each day just to watch, hardly able to believe their eyes. The steel girder-and-truss frame positively snaked up, allowing the outer shell to be speedily built around it in concrete—a construction method said to be entirely new to Aberdeen. Credit for the efficiency of the operation must go in the main to Bruce MacKenzie, who, in addition to holding the commission for interior decoration, acted as general co-ordinator.

As usual, virtually all materials and labour came from local sources. The 7-feet deep, 86-feet long cantilever girder that supported the balcony was the largest of its kind so far made in the city. The frontage was finished not in the faience or brick so beloved of cinema designers in other parts of the country, but in the sparkling Rubislaw granite-work of masons Edgar Gauld of Gilcomston Terrace. Wood for the joinery work came from Sweden and Finland, and all wooden edgings, etc, were in Oregon pine.

The Regent was of importance in other respects than constructional advance. It was the city's first all-new cinema since the Torry Picture House a decade before, and it constituted the first step into practical picture hall design for its architect, Mr Thomas Scott Sutherland. A sound designer of (and an astute dealer in) houses, Sutherland was perhaps best known at that time for the dozens of pleasant little granite bungalows on the Broomhill estate. Houses certainly seem to have played a large part in his life, as over the years he owned a succession of Aberdeen's most palatial. He would explain that due to his refusal to kow-tow to the upper classes this was the only way that he was ever going to see the interiors of such premises!

It was not, however, with a plan for a house but for a super-cinema that he had gained his architectural diploma in 1922, and although the Regent was his first actual cinema commission, he displayed great awareness in knowing what was required. The exact circumstances surrounding the choice of Sutherland as architect when Poole's Yorkshire connection was so strong remain obscure, but it is known that his fee was a very reasonable one—considerably less than Poole's were used to paying. Perhaps, indeed, as a man of some influence he may have suggested or helped to secure the site.

Jack Poole, then, had every reason to be pleased with his handsome modern cinema, built so efficiently and at such an attractive price. The Regent was proudly opened at 3 o'clock on the afternoon of Saturday 27 February 1932, with an audience predominantly of guests, as at the Palace a few months before. The main feature film was *Over The Hill*, a remake of the successful early 1920s 'silent'. Starring James Dunn, Sally Eilers and Mae Marsh (stalwart of Biograph days) it was described by Lewis Hawes as a 'sob picture of the first order'. It told of the mother who works her fingers to the bone bringing up a family, only to have them all turn against her as she gets older, with the exception of a son who has been jailed for a crime that he did not commit. On release her son finds a job and sends money to his brother to support the old lady, but rascally brother pockets the money and puts dear old mother in the workhouse from where she is eventually rescued by faithful son and his blushing bride—all good melodramatic stuff. Second on the programme was Gordon Harker in *The Professional Guest*.

The *Evening Express*'s coverage of the opening day was most enthusiastic:

> As [the Regent] neared completion and the singular beauty of the design began to be apparent, large crowds of citizens began to pay visits to the site and experience the aesthetic delight its appearance provided.
>
> Even though Aberdeen has many magnificent edifices, there is nothing quite so distinctive as the modern design of the front of the new Regent. Fine use has been made of straight lines and curves placed in sharp contrast, and the face that looks through the entrance to Justice Mill Lane on to Holburn Street has an imposing dignity about it and yet an elusive note of gaiety in its composition. It is built of grey granite decorated with bands of red terracotta, and a polished black granite base.
>
> When under the intense illumination of the neon lights and flood-lighting of the powerful projectors surmounting the canopy its full grandeur will be realised.

Far from presenting problems in the Regent's construction, the contours of the site actually worked to its advantage. Excavation of the top of the Justice Mill slope allowed the auditorium floor to be placed below street level, necessitating only short flights of stairs to connect the balcony to the foyer— quite the antithesis of the dizzy heights involved at the Playhouse nearby. The structure was set on a thick concrete base which, in combination with the sunken uprights of the steel frame, gave a solid, stable foundation to support the great weight above it.

The light, airy foyer was panelled in light Austrian oak with decorations picked out in silver. The warm beige of the auditorium was set off by bands of blues, red and brown, with details in gold and silver. 'Jazz-patterned' carpets in soft browns, blues and reds, old-gold moquette seats, and a four- colour lighting system extending all the way around the ceiling cornice and pro-scenium arch completed the scheme. The proscenium was made extra-wide to take the latest large Magnascopic screen, while, to allow for the future presentation of cine-variety if demand arose, stage and dressing room facilities were provided.

The metal components of the handrails and balustrades, and the half-ton ornamental iron screen that dominated the balcony entrance, were assembled using new welding techniques instead of the conventional nuts and bolts. The auditorium walls were specially treated to stop the unwanted echo that caused such a nuisance in older halls. To ensure safety there were seven exit points from the stalls and four from the balcony. All equipment was (naturally) of the newest, safest design, and the cleaning staff's job was made easier by the installation of Aberdeen's first central vacuuming plant, necessitating only the plugging of suction hoses and brushes into junctions strategically placed in the floor.

The frontage was floodlit by night, and was outlined by the city's first neon display, while on a gantry above was the large neon 'Regent' sign—altogether an effective piece of 'night architecture'. The verticality of the central windows, giving the impression of height, became something of a Sutherland trade-mark and was used to great effect in subsequent cinema designs. Interestingly, this was the only cinema in which Sutherland used terracotta tiling to outline window margins and to implant other details. It was soon to be proved that even in picture palaces of the 1930s Aberdeen's native building material looked perfectly well on its own.

For all its novelty and advancement, the Regent was still fairly conservative in interior design and detail. The foyer panelling was of conventional type, the auditorium ceiling was the curved affair long beloved of cinema architects, and there was relatively little of the art deco styling that had already become closely identified with picture palaces. The building's general treatment, however, was remarkably skilful, making an impression without intruding on the townscape. Only from a distance did (or, for that matter, does) the size of the auditorium behind the entrance block become fully apparent, making the latter look just a little 'tacked on'.

52   Bert Darley (left) and J.K.S. Poole at the time of the opening of the Regent
(*BA* 26 Feb. 1932)

General manager of 'Aberdeen's Super Two' (as the Regent and the Palace were advertised) was Bert Darley. In April 1929 he had given up his post at the Picture House to become the very first manager of the Beach Dance Hall and Restaurant (now known as the Beach Ballroom), where the music was under the supervision of his old colleague from the Picture House, George Harkins. In December of that same year, Mr Darley had 'returned to the fold', succeeding Mr Albert C. Duncan as manager of the Palace. Executive manager of the Regent was Jack Poole's son John K. Stafford Poole, assisted by Mr Wilfred Pryor, while the Palace's day-to-day affairs were under the charge of Captain S. Gordon Wingfield.

Aged only 21 when the Regent opened, J.K.S. Poole was one of the city's youngest cinema managers. He was soon receiving mention in the trade press for the originality of his displays, one of which incorporated a small motor car sitting invitingly in the foyer. More typical, perhaps, was a promotion that he carried out for a film entitled *Moonlight And Melody*. Sutherland's ornamental iron screen at the balcony entrance proved invaluable as a frame to support three large cut-out art figures of glamour girls from the film, superimposed on cardboard 'moons'. Below these, a line of smaller cardboard chorus-girls 'hoofed' their way across from one balcony stair to the other. Careful lighting heightened the effect, and the cinema trade paper *Universal Weekly* described the display as one of the picture's most attractive advertising campaigns.

Advertising stunts devised by J.K.S. Poole were part and parcel of life at the Regent. One such intended stunt entailed the smallest usherette walking down Union Street with a huge St Bernard dog to publicise the film *Call Of The Wild*. Everyone thought the idea splendid except the dog, which refused point blank to set a paw beyond the cinema's front steps!

Often, the military would be invited along to see action films (Westerns included), and at the end of a performance it was quite common to see the house lights come up on one hundred Gordon Highlanders in full regalia, ready to acknowledge the treat by marching, pipes a-skirl, through the cinema stalls and foyer, out through the doors and back along Union Street to barracks. On at least one occasion the stalls were decked out in sandbags and the foyer dressed up as a war-time trench to add authenticity to the spectacle. During the show, weapons would be left in the foyer, which resembled an armoury!

So well did the public take to the Regent, with its small army of ushers in snappy uniforms and its usherettes in charming 'Scottish' outfits with little cock's-feather bonnets, that, much to Jack Poole's surprise and delight, it soon began to outstrip the Palace in popularity. Before long it had ceased to be a 'second-fiddle' house and was showing many first-runs of its own as people trekked from far and wide just to come to the big new cinema.

All in all, it may be said that the arrival of Poole's in Aberdeen rather set the cat among the pigeons for other exhibitors. This was thought to be the root cause of a gentle but persistent trickle of rumours concerning the new Palace. These began more or less as soon as the place opened, and alleged (depending upon which particular set of whispers one listened to), that struc-

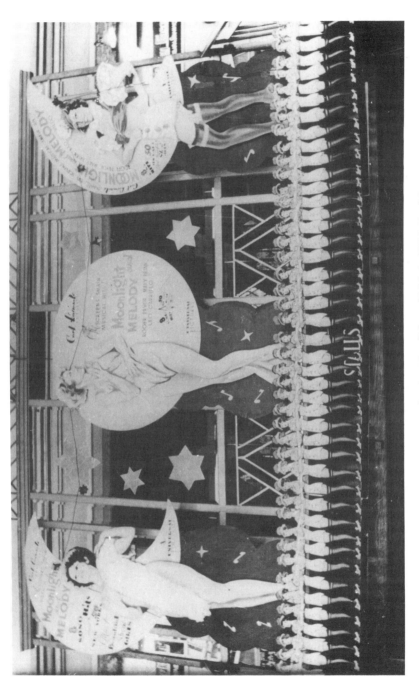

53   Regent Foyer Display for *Moonlight and Melody* (J.K.S. Poole)

54   Regent Foyer Display for *Tarzan the Fearless* (J.K.S. Poole)

55   Regent staff, 1932 (J.K.S. Poole)

56 Regent staff, 1932 (J.K.S. Poole)

tural defects had brought about cracks in the ceiling or roof, or had made the balcony unstable, or had made the foundations subside. Perhaps these rumours gained spurious authority from the fact that the building had been found to require extra strengthening at the construction stage, but after a well-publicised visit and a favourable report by the City Engineers in March 1932 the tongue-wagging was finally stilled and peace reigned once more.

On screen over 1932, Gracie Fields starred in her first feature film *Sally In Our Alley*, premiered for Aberdeen at the Palace. *Monte Carlo* starred Jack Buchanan and Jeanette MacDonald, who sang the film's big number 'Beyond The Blue Horizon', Edward G. Robinson made his reputation as a screen crook in *Little Caesar*, Chevalier was the *Playboy Of Paris*, Joan Crawford was in *Laughing Sinners*, Dietrich in *Dishonoured*, and Gloria Swanson in *Indiscreet*. Low-comedy team Wheeler & Woolsey were in such offerings as *Caught Plastered*, Sybil Thorndike starred in the influential British production *Hindle Wakes*, and Boris Karloff was in the original *Frankenstein*.

The worldly-wise gold-digging blonde made her presence felt in films like *Platinum Blonde* with Jean Harlow and *The Greeks Had A Word For Them*, in which Ina Claire, Madge Evans and cheeky Joan Blondell played 'a little syndicate of prospectors into men's pockets'. *Out Of The Blue*, at La Scala that August, was Jessie Matthews' first screen appearance, while the following month Poole's brought to the Palace the first provincial showing, straight from the Empire, Leicester Square, of *Scarface*, a Howard Hawkes gangster thriller that went out of its way to be the ultimate of its type. Considered to be the most violent of a number of pretty tough gangster subjects made before the Hays Code, it even attracted the attention of the most legendary hoodlum of all, Al Capone, who, from the jail cell into which he had at last been thrown, made it clear that he was not at all happy about films that showed gangsters in a poor light. Hawkes, for his part, was quite convinced that Capone money was behind a campaign mounted by some pressure groups against this picture and others of its kind.

Scarface (the name by which Capone was sometimes known— in his absence) was claimed to portray an actual event in American police annals, and to have been made with the intention of stirring public opinion towards the banning of firearms in the States. Public-spirited folk on both sides of the Atlantic turned out by the thousand to witness Paul Muni smashing acres of plate glass and shooting up entire fleets of cars (at a reputed total cost of £250,000) as he gunned his way to the top. Even with much of the really rough stuff edited out by the censors it caused quite a sensation, and Lewis Hawes, in his *Evening Express* column, was very quick to comment upon what seemed to him a tide of films of this nature. One example that he cited was *While Paris Sleeps*, featuring towering tough-guy Victor McLaglen and containing a scene in which a gang, engaged in battle, takes refuge in a bakehouse, and a member of the opposition gets thrown into one of the ovens!

The bulk of the Regent's early screen fare came from 20th Century Fox through the agency of R.S. Dawes. Also, with an eye to the weekly returns sheet, Dawes obtained from British International Pictures (forerunner of ABC's film-making department) cheap rentings for holiday times when cinemas were guaranted to be busy. Offered at flat rate as opposed to the more usual percentage-of-takings arrangement, the only thing to commend that particular species of film was its favourable hire price. J.K.S. Poole was by this time developing a keen interest in the booking side of the business, and, seeing Aberdeen Picture Palaces with a local monopoly of Metro Goldwyn Mayer product (expensive to hire but very profitable for the exhibitor), he began pressuring his father to approach MGM for a share of their new releases.

An average weekly return of between £700 and £900, minus renters' fees of about thirty per cent, was considered quite satisfactory for the Regent, but by making (in his own words) a thorough nuisance of himself Mr Poole managed to persuade his father that the extra outlay would be worthwhile. A telephone call from Head Office duly informed him that the company had secured a guaranteed thirty per cent of MGM's new features, the first of which could be expected soon. Thus, after an intensive campaign of foyer and canopy advertising, Johnny Weissmuller's original *Tarzan The Ape Man* opened on Monday 17 October 1932. Such was its financial success even at a booking fee of fifty per cent that when the week's returns were submitted, an anxious phone call came from Head Office, enquiring whether the figures were correct! From then on there was no quibbling about costs, and the number of top films at the Regent increased dramatically.

Sunday charity film shows reappeared at Aberdeen's cinemas in the course of 1932. Cine-variety had undergone some resurgence nationally as certain managements responded to the reduction in their public's spending money by embellishing programmes. Variety acts reappeared at weekends at Torry, and on an occasional basis at their old home the Casino, where they were accompanied by an orchestra under the direction of Fred Archer, one-time musical director for James Donald.

At the Picture House that September, manager George J. Pain gave place to Mr Thomas A.K. Lunn, whose father had been BB Pictures' touring manager before 1910. Needless to say, Mr Lunn had been connected with pictures all his life; born in Yorkshire, he had first come to Scotland as a youngster, 'for' (as he put it) 'a piece of haggis and a sprig of white heather'. Before moving to Aberdeen he had worked with PCT and its successor, Gaumont-British, in Edinburgh, Darlington, Sunderland and Leeds. In 1934 he left to become a cinema proprietor in his own right in Edinburgh.

As soon as news of the impending Poole developments leaked out, Aberdeen Picture Palaces had been quick to revive its long-held ambition for a new super-cinema on the site of the Electric. Clement George was requested to revise and up-date his 1927 designs, and he brought this commission with him when, in May 1931, he entered into partnership with one of Aberdeen's architectural 'lions', his one-time mentor Dr A. Marshall MacKenzie. MacKenzie's father and uncle had both been distinguished architects, and as a whole the family had been responsible for many of Scotland's finest and most prestigious buildings. Marshall MacKenzie's son Alexander G.R. Mac-Kenzie was the third generation in the profession, and was by that time effectively in charge of the practice.

Clement George's 'new' plans came before the authorities at the same time as those for the Regent and Palace. They received approval, but were not immediately put into effect. Some revision was apparently still going on, and perhaps also the work on the Poole cinemas was 'tying up' key contractors. It may be, furthermore, that Clement George was in failing health and unable to co-ordinate the operation, as on 23 February 1932 he died in an Aberdeen nursing home at the age of 52.

The rebuilding project had to go into temporary abeyance as A.G.R. MacKenzie picked up the threads, but site clearance still went ahead, and on Saturday 16 April 1932 the Electric showed its last film, which starred Anne Grey, Benita Hume and George Barraud and was appropriately entitled *The Happy Ending*. A few weeks later, the old building had gone. It seems hardly, in fact, to have required much demolition—some of its interior walls consisted of nothing more than a few courses of brick surmounted by thin partitioning, requiring only a good push by three workmen to knock them over! So far, the planned replacement cinema still retained the working title 'Electric', but within a few months it had been given a new name—the very American one of CAPITOL.

On Sunday 6 November 1932, Aberdeen Picture Palaces suddenly came within an ace of suffering an unexpected and premature reduction in the size of its circuit. Early that morning, a sawmiller by the name of James Mackie, walking along Park Street, noticed a cloud of smoke pouring from the Star's side ventilators in South Constitution Street. He immediately raised the alarm, and very soon two fire engines were on the scene. Already, the glow of flames could be seen through the building's shuttered windows. Inside, the firemen found a corner of the balcony ablaze, the adjacent wall burned through and the rafters alight. Before a hole could be cut in the ceiling to admit hoses, fire burst through the roof and the situation looked bad, but after two hours' hard work the outbreak (the cause of which, like that at La Scala a couple of years previously, was attributed to a dropped cigarette) was extinguished. The operating box, being fireproof, remained intact, and although the structure and wiring of what *Bon-Accord* pithily described as 'a blazing Star' had sustained considerable damage, the cinema was put out of action for only a fortnight.

Even as the Capitol's impressive steel structure reached skywards over the latter part of 1932, A.G.R. MacKenzie was still adding the final touches to this the most modern project so far tackled by his firm. Although the commission had passed to him more or less by chance, Aberdeen Picture Palaces could hardly have found anyone more suitable to bring it to fruition. Heavily influenced by Modernism, MacKenzie possessed a unique talent for combining its idioms with the strong sense of form and quality that he had inherited from his forebears. He subjected Clement George's plans to a bold reworking, painstakingly refining and restyling them along such distinguished and up-to-date lines that the Capitol instantly became one of the wonders of its day. Bert Gates and his partners had embarked upon the scheme with a determination to have a cinema that would rival any of its size in the country; what they received exceeded all their expectations.

Clement George's plans, dated September 1931 and slightly revised just prior to his death, were, as already mentioned, a modernisation of those which he had drawn up several years before. They retained the original Union Street building, remodelling the ground-floor cinema entranceway and flanking shops (which either belonged to or were about to belong to APP, and which were included in the site plan), with much use of diamond-patterned leaded glass—once very popular, but for a 1930s 'super' decidedly *passé*. On the first floor above the entrance and shops were flats, the area of which would be used to make a high-class restaurant, with manager's flat adjoining.

It is clear that much work and thought went into George's scheme, but its style, when compared with others of its time (and certainly with what actually came to be built) was of a previous generation. George's architectural language was a very personal one, possessing great charm, but it was highly traditional in outlook—a world away from the art deco of the modern movement—and his use of new idioms at the Capitol was rather uneasy. He had also, of course, been working within the confines of an already-agreed upon set of ideas which it took MacKenzie, the 'new broom', to materially alter. One may therefore, without casting any aspersions upon Clement George's professional skill or merit, speculate as to the Capitol's success had his plans been used in the form in which he left them.

The most profound change brought to the scheme by A.G.R. MacKenzie was the sweeping away of the old Union Street building in favour of a sparkling new dressed granite frontage, pleasantly asymmetrical in layout without being obviously so. The shop spaces on either side of the wide, bright entranceway were retained as a source of rent from the otherwise redundant front ground floor. Above the entranceway were three tall windows, each surmounted by a carved panel. Above the left shop were two shorter divided windows, and above the slightly wider right shop were three of the same, the extra window lighting not a flat but the restaurant kitchen. The frontage continued upwards in a plain but elegant pediment that added immeasurably to the effect while also hiding from street view the high, steeply-pitched auditorium roof. (The roof line as built was considerably lower than that which had at first been contemplated, the original intention having been to terminate the auditorium in a tall harled gable.)

The entrance foyers were revised in layout, and the entire decorative scheme was redesigned to drawings by interior designer David Stokes, son of a well-known London architect. In Clement George's plan, the auditorium (described as boat-shaped) was dominated by a large double lighting dome in the ceiling, another smaller dome under the balcony, and a large sound-reflector board in the shape of a sunburst over the proscenium (intended, presumably, to carry a gold or silver finish). Perhaps considering all this a little overpowering, Messrs MacKenzie and Stokes simplified the sounding board to a plain surface with an elegantly curved ribbon of silver running round its outer edge. The broad, fluted proscenium arch that merged into the original sounding-board was slimmed down, its surface ribbed to catch the light, and its inner margin decorated in overlapping V-shaped art deco motifs.

Conventionally patterned glass light bowls were exchanged for the back stalls lighting domes, and the main auditorium ceiling was given two transverse lighting troughs, one of which ran just forward of the balcony, following its contour. The other ran above the sounding board, and both were constructed in the form of miniature galleries, accessible for maintenance, and housing one of the new six-colour lighting systems manufactured by the Holophane Company of London. This lighting system was also applied around the proscenium and grilles and (a feature not shown in Clement George's plan) in 'tubs' around the back balcony and back stalls, making the Capitol the very first British cinema to fully utilise the Continental principle of painting-with-light. According to the Holophane Company, twenty-eight different blends of colour were possible every week for four years without repeating.

In the side walls below and immediately in front of the balcony were little alcoves in which stem-and-leaf sculptures in coloured polished aluminium glittered under concealed lighting. The grilles on either side of the proscenium, shown in Clement George's plan as rather ordinary-looking clean-cut oblongs filled with fretwork, were transformed into a pair of exuberantly fanciful theatrical ornaments, their upper reaches overhung by fibrous plaster 'draperies', and their recessed central areas containing light-catching corrugated vertical members. The composition was framed by round, slender columns surmounted by fantastic plaster sculptures suggestive of pineapple leaves, or perhaps of the more adventurous headgear creations worn by Carmen Miranda during the following decade!

To A.G.R. MacKenzie and David Stokes must go the credit for making the Capitol so remarkable. In any extensive application of the Holophane system the Capitol was preceded only by a namesake in the Didsbury area of Manchester, which opened in 1931 and had some Holophane lighting. After only a year or so of operation a fire destroyed the auditorium, and in the rebuilding a full Holophane system was installed. The Aberdeen Capitol, however, opened several months ahead of its resurgent English rival, and, furthermore, has survived, whereas the Didsbury house ended up as a television studio during the 1950s and is now an annex to a local school or college, with not a scrap left of its old interior.

The cost of the Capitol (exclusive of the price of some small properties in Justice Mill Lane) was estimated at between £60,000 and £70,000, with about £40,000 of that (equivalent to the full cost of the Regent) spent on interiors alone. To finance this, APP was obliged to issue a good many additional shares.

As usual, most of the contracts for construction and fitting were given to local firms, and several well-known names crop up yet again—Edgar Gauld for granitework, George Bisset for steelwork, A.B. Robertson for plumbing and electrics, and Bruce MacKenzie for painting. S.B. Russel of Affleck Street built the Capitol's outer shell, using a million and three-quarter bricks—a more conventional construction method than the Regent's revolutionary cast concrete work. Calder & Henderson of Oldmill Road held the contract for woodwork, and the Union Grove firm of Charles Maitland & Son (which had roofed La Scala twenty years previously) supplied and fixed in place the 40,000 slates and the 5,400 feet of roofing felt, using a hundredweight of tacks and six hundredweight of slate nails. A new record for the North-East of Scotland was set by the size of the 38-ton balcony cantilever, and so extraordinary was the nature of the project that as the building grew it became a regular visiting-place for parties of architectural students, shown around by the consulting engineer, the eminent Alexander 'Crooky' Cruickshank.

Choice of seating for the Capitol was made by the public itself at a plebiscite held in the foyer of the Playhouse. Each company tendering for the contract set up an example of its wares for trying out and taking a vote upon; winner on all points of appearance, comfort and price was the local product of Messrs J. & A. Ogilvie, who thereby became the North's largest suppliers of theatre seating and fittings. Work was provided for one hundred employees (many of them specially taken on for the contract) at Ogilvie's Union Street and Willowbank Road works, while the casting of the seats' iron frames made welcome business for the Torry Foundry.

The Capitol was opened at 3 p.m. on Saturday, 4 February 1933, when Mrs A.D. Hay officially unlocked the main doors with a gold key bearing a sprig of lucky white heather, presented to her by one of APP's directors, G.A. Wilson. Once the many guests and those of the public fortunate enough to gain admission were seated, a formal stage ceremony was conducted by APP's directors together with Baillie Watt, who deputised for an indisposed Provost Alexander. Concluding the speeches, Bert Gates expressed the directors' thanks and conveyed a message to any who might question the launching of such an enterprise in these straitened times. Borrowing Bismarck's line, 'In time of peace, prepare for war', he adapted it to read, 'In times of depression, prepare for prosperity', and then went on to say:

> It is a long lane that has no turning. We have built the Capitol not for today but for the generations of Aberdeen people to come. The Company has dedicated the Capitol to the people of Aberdeen, their children and their children's children in the hope that in generations to come they may appreciate what has been given them.

The people of Aberdeen were by no means slow to come and see just what *had* been given them. Passing the shop of the Canadian Fur Company on the

57   The first night of the Capitol, 4 Feb. 1933 (*BA*)

left of the entrance, or Bonici's Washington Soda Fountain (long a neighbour of the Electric) on the right, they walked under a canopy trimmed in Staybrite stainless steel, which echoed the upper outline of the frontage above. Round the canopy's outer edge, current film titles were displayed in bright red movable letters.

The mood of the Capitol was set directly at its outer doors, with their modish stainless steel semicircular hand-plates which formed full circles when the doors were closed. Next was a vestibule with electric heater panels in its walls, a floor in characteristic circle-and-bar design terrazzo-work, and an unusual figure-of-eight fluorescent light fitting that grew out of a 'flying saucer' suspended from the ceiling. Tucked into the far corners of the vestibule, by the inner doors, were the payboxes (said to have been hastily added at the last minute when someone realised that they had been overlooked!), while straight ahead was the wide carpeted stairway to the Balcony Foyer. Stallites proceeded down terrazzo-work steps to their own foyer, which was oval in shape and relatively plainly decorated, but had striking art deco-patterned Korkoid flooring in shades of grey, red, blue, cinnamon and terracotta (replaced in later years due to wear).

The similarly shaped balcony foyer was luxuriously carpeted and its walls embellished with fluted columns. At ceiling level were scalloped wood and plaster friezes, while flanking the stairs to the back balcony and operating box were beautiful mirrors of blush-coloured engraved glass. On a horseshoe-shaped landing above the stair-well, enclosed by attractive wrought-iron and chrome banisters and hand-rails, was a tea-terrace beyond which was the café. There, 120 patrons could sit on gold wicker-work chairs and partake of tea and dainties at little tables. Placed among the tables were small aspidistras in wooden stands, the stem of each plant appearing neatly through a polished copper cover made in two parts, each part carrying half of a copper tube. The plush curtains of the Union Street windows were surmounted by large pelmets of singular design, continuing the 'drapes' motif, and the café's general decor was in purple and gold.

Beneath the restaurant's black and gold carpet was a polished oak dance floor (not actually used because the noise travelled to the hall). In a side recess, the decorative valance of which recalled the outline of two further blush-glass mirrors on the opposite wall, was a dais for a small band. Usually, a pianist played background music while the Capitol's own team of uniformed 'Nippies', modelled on those of Lyons' Corner Shops, served at the tables. Restaurant manageress was a Miss Skein, and catering was by the nearby Bonici's Washington Soda Fountain.

The auditorium's Holophane illuminations were the talk of Aberdeen and the North. As their delicate colours blended from one to another, winking from the silvered proscenium arch, grilles and other decorative details (in which much use had been made of real silver leaf) they brought the plain biscuit-coloured walls and ceilings enchantingly alive, turning the interior into a bowl of ever-changing light. The large stage, equipped for live acts as well as for cinema use, also had lighting by Holophane. To the rear, it had a large concave Cyclorama screen on which could be projected such back-

58   A Capitol 'Nippy' (*EE* 2 Feb. 1933)

grounds as 'sky', 'dawn', 'flames', 'rain', etc, and the smooth plaster surface of this solid structure fulfilled a valuable function as a sound reflector. There were 26 different scenery settings and six sets of tableau curtains, all of which, together with the large Magnascopic screen and the talkie speakers, could be hoisted away out of sight in the Capitol's 80-feet high stage fly-tower. The main stage curtains were in deep sea-green, and it was said that this colouring together with the auditorium's silver decorations represented Aberdeen's title of 'Silver City By The Sea'.

The provision of a full stage was made possible by the acquisition of a block of small shops and houses at numbers 8 to 14 Justice Mill Lane, part of a miscellany of former Damhead Croft sites adjacent to the old Electric, which APP had bought at least as early as May 1927. At that time numbers 10A and 11 Justice Mill Lane were still tenanted, so that the projected new building could not yet cover the whole site, and only a shallow stage was shown in the 1927 plans. By 1931-2 this difficulty had been resolved and the building is shown as extending all the way back to Justice Mill Lane, but still, for some reason, with only a shallow platform instead of a stage. An empty space, intended for a future stage extension, was left between the rear wall of the platform and that of the building itself, while the dressing rooms were also labelled for construction at a later date—perhaps because of uncertainty as to the continuing popularity of cine-variety. Only in the final drafts of August 1932 onwards do full stage facilities appear. The refinement of a fly-tower appears to have been introduced as late as November 1932, previous plans showing a flat stage roof with a deep downward step about one third of the way back.

In the operating box were the latest type of Ernemann projectors, equipped even at this late date for sound-on-disc as well as for sound-on-film, although discs were long out of use. (The facility for playing them was soon dispensed with.) Connected to the sound system were Ardente hand-phones for the hard-of-hearing—a service soon adopted by other cinemas in the city. An ingenious double projector called a Brennograph superimposed slides and coloured backgrounds on the screen, Cyclorama or curtains, and in addition to the main spotlight in the 'box' two smaller Holophane arc spots shone downwards to the stage from a little room in the centre of the ceiling light well, connected with the operating box by a catwalk in the roof void. The Holophane house lighting system's main control panel was in the 'box', with certain circuits also controllable from the stage lighting switchboard.

Aberdeen's 'Cinema In Excelsis' had yet another trick up its sleeve— something that proclaimed 'super' status for any cinema during the 1930s. At each performance, (usually just before the main film) the house lights would dim and a spotlight would pick out the silvered art deco console of the North of Scotland's first theatre pipe organ as, to the strains of the organist's signature tune, it and its player rose majestically on an electric lift from the centre of the flower-filled orchestra pit. At its keys was Mr Edward O'Henry (formerly organist of Madame Tussaud's Cinema, London) specially engaged to devise and play interludes of between ten and twenty minutes' duration as an entertaining and diverting part of each programme over the Capitol's first six weeks. Installed at the cost of approximately £2,500 by the John Compton Organ Company of London, Britain's most prolific manufacturer of cinema organs, this wonderful instrument came complete with real drums, bells, xylophone, vibraphone and sound-effects, all sounded from the console's keyboards and controls. Of moderate size, but speaking out loud and clear from behind the right-hand set of ornamental grilles, it ranked as a typical and effective example of its kind.

Information has come to light suggesting that Aberdeen might nearly have gained a cinema organ (although not of the Capitol type) long before 1933. There is a tradition at the Laigh Kirk, Kilmarnock that a pipe organ installed there in 1921 by the Aberdeen organ builder E.H. Lawton was originally intended for an Aberdeen cinema. If this is true, the cinema in question must surely have been the very high-class Playhouse. The Torry, although only a little smaller, seems a far less likely candidate. It is difficult to imagine where a bulky instrument of the church type (popular in cinemas further South for bolstering up or replacing orchestras during the silent era) might have fitted in the Playhouse's auditorium, but if, for example, a late change was made to the interior plans so that there was no longer any room for the organ, this could explain the cancellation of the order.

Could the idea of putting an organ in the Capitol have sprung from memories of an earlier, abortive scheme? Space was provided for it in Clement George's 1931 plan, so its installation was no afterthought. When the matter was discussed in detail in 1932, APP's directors took a trip to the Regal, Glasgow, to see and hear its large Compton organ in the hands of 'The Broadcasting Organist', Bobby Pagan. Although Bobby had to come from his sickbed for the demonstration, he clearly made an impression, for they bought!

Cinema organs were often to be heard on the radio in those days, but few Aberdonians had ever seen one 'live'. Audiences came to the Capitol as much to hear the organ as to see the films, and week by week for 24 years the Compton formed an integral and extremely popular part of entertainments.

Manager of the Capitol was Mr Jack Wright. A native of Alloa, Mr Wright had begun in the cinema business as a member of Paramount Pictures' publicity staff, coming to Aberdeen from the Playhouse, Edinburgh, where he had been assistant manager. Chief electrician was Mr Edward Crombie, whose entry into the trade had been at the Star, where he spent 14 years before moving to the Electric. Cinema work seems to have run in his family, as his younger brother Charles was an operator at the Playhouse, and another (late) brother had also been in the trade. It is interesting to note that on Mr Crombie's death in July 1935 at the early age of 42, he was reported to have been the oldest cinema operator of chief rank in the city.

Edward Crombie's main responsibility would have been the operation and maintenance of the stage and lighting equipment. Chief film operator was Bert Ewen who, after gaining experience of talkies at the Picture House, had accepted an attractive offer to return to APP as 'chief' at the Electric, where he supervised the installation of sound in 1930. Now, still only in his early twenties, he had been promoted to a high position at the Electric's glittering successor.

59 Capitol, lower foyer with poster for *Dames*, photographed during the week of 28 Jan. 1935 (courtesy of Aberdeen Picture Palaces)

60 Capitol restaurant, *c.*1933 (courtesy of Aberdeen Picture Palaces)

61   Capitol ladies room, *c.*1933 (courtesy of Aberdeen Picture Palaces)

62   Capitol operating box, *c.*1933. Note sound-on-disc playing equipment
attached to projectors (courtesy of Aberdeen Picture Palaces)

The three-hour cine-variety programme given on the Capitol's opening night
and during its first week featured Joan Crawford and Robert Montgomery in
Letty Lynton. On stage was a presentation by the Henrietta Fuller Dancing
Troupe. During the second week the big film was *Grand Hotel*, the cast of
which included Garbo, Crawford, Wallace Beery and Lionel Barrymore; the
stage act was Ralphono the juggler. Further film attractions during the
Capitol's first two months or so included Maurice Chevalier and Jeanette
MacDonald in *One Hour With You*, Laurel and Hardy in *Pack Up Your Troubles*,
Edward G. Robinson in *Tiger Shark*, Tallulah Bankhead, Charles Laughton
and Gary Cooper in *The Devil And The Deep*, and Marlene Dietrich in *Blonde
Venus*.

Edward O'Henry's organ interludes, *The Gay Nineties, Memories Of
Beethoven, Cavalcade, A Trip Round the World, Carmen*, and *Memories Of Harry
Lauder*, evoked so much interest that on Wednesday, 22 February at 11 am
a special concert was held for local organists and other parties curious to see
and hear the instrument. On Saturday, 27 April Edward O'Henry's short term
of office came to an end, and on the following Monday he was succeeded by
the Capitol's first resident organist, Harold Coombs. A 'wonder boy pianist'
on the theatre stages of his native Sheffield while still in his teens, Harold
Coombs became a church organist at the age of 14. His entry into the world
of the cinema was as organist and musical director at the Abbeydale Picture
House, Sheffield, where he spent 11 years before coming to Aberdeen. The
Capitol was his first appointment at a modern cinema organ, but he quickly
proved himself a very able and popular performer.

In addition to interlude work, the organ was used to accompany the stage
acts which continued to form part of the Capitol's programmes from time to
time during its first few months. It played an integral role in the Albyn
Entertainers' potpourri presentation that May; thereafter, however, use of the
stage became more sporadic, dying out altogether in the later 1930s.

Further films that Aberdonians saw over 1933 were *Looking On The Bright
Side* starring Gracie Fields, *Say It With Flowers* featuring Jack Payne and his
band, *The Big Broadcast Of 1932* starring Bing Crosby and a host of other
stage and screen personalities, and *The Kid From Spain*, starring Eddie Cantor.
'Hear Mae West sing the songs that made New York blush', exhorted the
Palace's billings for *She Done Him Wrong*, second screen vehicle for the lady
who seemed to be able to inflame the censorship lobbies just by being present.
The Regent gave Aberdeen its first taste of a new kind of Hollywood musical
that August with *42nd Street*, starring Ruby Keeler, Bebe Daniels, tenor Dick
Powell, Warner Baxter, wisecrackin' blondes Ginger Rogers and Una Merkel,
and, perhaps most of all, the stunningly-photographed sequences of dance
director Busby Berkeley. This was followed the next week by *King Kong*,
starring Fay Wray and the best loved of all movie monsters. As an advertising
stunt, a costumed human 'ape' disported itself on the cinema frontage! The
Capitol's September presentation of Clark Gable and Helen Hayes' *The White*

63   A classic Regent stunt—a human 'ape' advertises *King Kong*, August 1933
(*EE*)

Sister began with a stage prologue in which a quartet from Hall Russell's Male Voice Choir, decked out in monks' habits, sang to the accompaniment of the organ.

In June 1933 the Palace was used as a local centre for a Paramount Pictures talent hunt that was claimed to take in every English-speaking country. The competition's purpose was to select fifty men and fifty women from whom a short leet of sixty candidates would be drawn up to form the 'beauty chorus' in a forthcoming production entitled *The Search For Beauty*, starring Larry 'Buster' Crabbe, Ida Lupino, Robert Armstrong and James Gleason. A lucky ten would be selected for silent screen tests, by means of which just one would be singled out for sound tests in London and a possible screen career.

The Search For Beauty was to be made in Hollywood under the direction of Lloyd Sheldon, whose film *Love Me Tonight* had been a big success in 1932. Each of the chosen few would (providing that they made good) be given a suite at a top hotel for the five weeks of filming, plus a salary of £12 per week—most folk in 1933 were doing well if they made £2! From such things could come fame and fortune, and as a result of this campaign Paramount's Hollywood offices were besieged by thousands of young hopefuls looking for a break. Paramount paid a fortune in fares home.

By the autumn of 1932, the caretaker management at His Majesty's Theatre was approaching the end of its allotted span, and once again the finding of a new proprietor had become a matter of pressing urgency. It came as a great relief when the news broke in October that a local man was to acquire the premises. That local man was James Donald, who officially took over on 4 June 1933. His first action was to embark on a comprehensive renovation and refitting of the theatre, which thereby gained the (then) only revolving stage in Scotland. All draperies, lighting and seating were renewed, the back balcony was raised slightly to improve sightlining, a new operating box was constructed at the back of the circle, and all parts of the auditorium were made accessible from the main entrance. Talkie equipment and new 'riser' microphones, which appeared automatically from just behind the footlights, were installed in preparation for the part-time presentation of cine-variety as the theatre's financial bread-and-butter.

By night, the fine granite frontage was illuminated by the largest theatre neon lighting system in Scotland. The name and the two central decorative columns were picked out in red, while above was a blue arch 20 feet high by 15 feet wide, surmounted at either side by a huge red torch. The scheme was completed by further ornamental work in green.

Decorator Alexander Copland's men used the latest paint-spraying techiques in applying the auditorium's new rose and ivory decor. Messrs Ogilvie's excellent work at the Capitol made them the choice over all rivals as suppliers of the 1,430 red velvet seats, the iron frames for which were made at Henderson's Kings Works in King Street.

64   James F. Donald, 1930s

To provide music for the wide range of shows planned for His Majesty's Theatre, a new resident 14-piece orchestra was formed under the direction of Mr Lambert Wilson. Until 1939, its leader was George Harkins, who, after a spell in the RAF during the Second World War, moved to the Tivoli where he remained up until his retirement. He died in 1950.

Interim manager W.W. Lothian gave place to J.F. Donald's son Peter, who supervised the grand reopening on Monday, 14 August 1933. This took the form of a sparkling evening's entertainment by Mrs Jack Hylton (stage personality Ennis Parkes) and her band. Her impresario/band leader husband had himself visited the theatre with his famous dance orchestra the year before. Hopes of star drama presentations and off-season musicals were seldom if ever realised during the Depression, but that was a mere detail. With a regimen of twice-nightly variety over summer seasons and cine-variety during slacker periods, the difficult times ahead could be faced with confidence.

At about this time, La Scala's owners, the Glasgow firm of George Green (now under the control of Mr Fred Green) was laying ambitious long-term plans for a chain of splendid super-cinemas extending throughout Scotland and northern England—a project eventually thwarted by the outbreak of war. Presumably as an early step towards this goal, and certainly as a response to the coming of the Capitol, Green's announced their intention of reconstructing La Scala as a 3,000-seater—more than double its existing size.

By 'reconstructing', Green's meant in effect completely replacing the old premises, utilising next-door sites which the company had been buying up since 1930. A prominent feature of the new building was to be an extensive granite frontage with current programmes displayed upon it in large neon letters. *Bon-Accord*'s report on the scheme (printed in the issue of 1 September 1933) describes the new frontage as measuring 'close on 200 feet', which is surely a misprint, as the total length of the site along Union Street was only 80 feet! Car park, medical facilities, public telephones and all sorts of other trimmings were to be provided, but although the drawings (the work of Glasgow architect John Fairweather, designer of the Playhouse, Edinburgh, and later of the huge Green's Playhouse, Dundee) were passed by the authorities, that was as far as the idea went. Such a frontage would have quite changed the look of the west end of Union Street, and the Capitol would undoubtedly have had a very strong competitor, but instead the history of the site was to take another direction—as we shall see later.

If 1933 was a notable year for Aberdeen's cinema-goers in general, it was nearly an even more notable one for the New Kinema, where the cleaner arrived on the morning of Sunday, 9 July to find a charred back stalls seat with the floorboards under it smouldering. Luckily the maple floor (a legacy from rink days) did not catch fire easily, and relatively little damage resulted, but a hole two feet across was burned in the floor and the fire brigade had to be called to drench the smoking timbers!

For Aberdeen, 1934 was the year of the celebrated Jeannie Donald murder case, which began with the finding of a little girl's body in the corridor cupboard of a tenement in Urquhart Road. (Slides had been flashed on the screens of all cinemas, appealing for information from anyone who had seen the missing child.) The new Dyce Airport experienced its first accident—the crashing in flames of the ten-seater plane 'Aberdon', from which the passengers and crew were lucky to escape with their lives. In the national headlines was the Gresford colliery disaster, the worst of its kind in twenty years. In aid of the relief fund for the dependents of one hundred miners who died, J.K.S. Poole quickly arranged a special showing of *Cavalcade* at the Regent, raising the highly creditable sum of £106. Abroad, nothing seemed to be able to stop Hitler as, amid ominous rumours and mysterious assassinations, he elevated himself to Presidency as well as Chancellorship of Germany.

On Sunday 4 March 1934, James Donald, seriously ill for several months, passed away at his North Silver Street home, aged 64. A hard-headed businessman who had built up his company from nothing, he had also been one of the city's most active charity fund-raisers, running special cinema shows for causes that ranged from war-time reliefs to the Willing Shilling

and Poor Coal Funds of the Depression, with hospitals also as frequent ben-
eficiaries. There were few that did not know 'Jimmy' Donald, for many years
a city councillor, and on the day of his funeral literally thousands of people
lined the streets as the 800-strong, mile-long cortège made its way to St
Peter's Cemetery. Even after the burial service mourners were still filing
through the gates to pay their last respects. Leadership of James F. Donald
(Aberdeen Cinemas) Ltd. passed to Messrs James R. Donald, Peter J.P. Donald,
Richard M. Donald and Herbert M. Donald, who, with the able help of
their mother, would shortly make the family firm a major force in local
entertainment circles.

Lewis Hawes of the *Evening Express* began the year by noting, in his column
of 1 January 1934, a rise in the general quality of films over the previous
twelve months. He also remarked upon how the public, short of cash for
entertainments, was becoming increasingly discriminating in its choice of
films. The pictures that were doing business were the ones considered to give
value for money.

This must surely have meant a full Capitol for *Gold Diggers of 1933*, starring
Ruby Keeler, Joan Blondell, Dick Powell and Ginger Rogers, and showcasing
once again Busby Berkeley's dance sequences. Other popular features shown
in Aberdeen over 1934 included Gracie Fields in *This Year Of Grace*, Marie
Dressler and Wallace Beery in *Tugboat Annie*, and Conrad Veidt in *The Wan-
dering Jew*. Veteran actor George Arliss played one of his celebrated historical
roles as *Voltaire*, while box-office was brisk for Charles Laughton in *The Private
Lives Of Henry VIII* and Mae West in *I'm No Angel* and *Belle Of the Nineties*.
There was more Berkeley magic in *Footlight Parade*, in which a 'hoofing'
James Cagney was added to the Keeler/Powell/Blondell team, Laurel And
Hardy were in their customary mess in *Fraternally Yours*, and Jean Harlow
was the *Blonde Bombshell*—a screen species that soon fell foul of the Hays
Office. Jessie Matthews starred in *Evergreen*, and in November Regent audi-
ences were given Aberdeen's first sighting of Shirley Temple in *Girl In Pawn*.

In the hands of the enterprising Poole family, the time-honoured cinema
novelty was still very much alive. When the latest Busby Berkeley spectacular
Fashions Of 1934 came to the Palace that June, each performance began with
a special stage prologue featuring local singer Miss Nancy Young. Later that
same month *On the Air*, which brought to the screen Roy Fox's band, comedy
duo Clapham and Dwyer, xylophonist Teddy Brown, and many others, was
prologued at the Regent with a piano 'spot' by Ruby Duncan, wife of the well-
known broadcaster Moultrie Kelsall. At the Palace during the week of 30
June, all ladies named Nellie were invited free of charge (on production of
their birth certificates) to come and see Paul Muni's *Hi, Nellie*. Some while
later, Cecil B. De Mille's *Cleopatra* (also shown at the Palace) was the basis of
a competition in which ladies were invited to submit reviews of the film for
judging by the editor of the *Evening Express*. Two of these critiques were
selected each day during the film's run, and their writers treated to a free

Eugene permanent wave at the hairdressing shop of J.F. Neave! Not every Poole's stunt came off, though. In advance of the arrival of Al Jolson's *Wonder Bar* at the Palace in October 1934, a license was requested for the dispensing of free drinks at the cinema's very own 'wonder bar'. The reaction of the magistrates need hardly be described.

In Harold Coombs' daily organ interludes the Capitol possessed an endless supply of musical novelties to suit all occasions. Some interludes took the form of sing-alongs, some consisted of cleverly-devised stories centred around well-known melodies, with narration by means of slides, while others were simply musical presentations heightened and complemented by the Capitol's wealth of lighting effects. Hits of the day and more serious items were delivered with equal finesse by the hard-working Mr Coombs, who spent every morning in practice, beginning with an hour of basic keyboard exercises. The gusto with which he put over his livelier numbers earned him the affectionate title of 'Bouncing Harold' among his Capitol colleagues (although perhaps not to his face!), and his first-rate playing and friendly manner, together with his choice of the Scott Skinner melody 'The Bonny Lass O' Bon Accord' as signature tune during his stay in Aberdeen, brought him great public popularity. A Scott Skinner memorial interlude in August 1934 was particularly well received by Capitol patrons, who fairly lapped up the melodies of 'The Strathspey King', rendered upon the most modern of musical instruments.

The first official hint of another super-cinema for Aberdeen appeared in the *Evening Express* of 17 March 1934, in the form of a brief announcement detailing an application for a feu, for entertainment purposes, of an unspecified piece of land at Kittybrewster. The Town Council's Finance Committee had recommended that the feu be sold at public auction, subject to the condition that the site be used for the stated purpose. Whether there were any other contenders for the site is not known, but the applicants obtained the land for £100 per year with the customary entrance on Whit Sunday—another example of development being encouraged by the transference of land at a favourable rate. That the development was to be of some importance was evident from talk of car parks, shops, etc, and it was not long before the news emerged that part of the old Central Park, just north of Kittybrewster Auction Marts, was to have upon it the city's latest wonder picture palace, the ASTORIA.

Back in 1920, proposals to build on Central Park (a favourite recreation area) had provoked a public outcry, but this time there was no such protest, and on Monday 28 May a small group of people met on the site to cut the first turf. Performing the ceremony was the project's chief protagonist Bert Darley, who had quit Poole's to form a new company, Aberdeen Astoria Cinema Ltd. Mr Darley's initial brief as General Manager was to plan and supervise the equipping of the building in co-operation with its architect, T. Scott Sutherland, also present that day. Other members of the party were the company's directors and financial backers A.B. Robertson (chairman), Reginald S. Bisset, Councillor (later Provost) Thomas Mitchell, advocates

Alfred E. Milne and William D. Reid, and James Scott, builder, plus House Manager A.I. 'Sandy' Matthews, who in 1932 had exchanged a journalistic career in Fife and Angus for a sub-managerial post at the Regent, and who now also joined the new company from Poole's.

With the expanding catchment areas of Kittybrewster, Powis, Woodside and Hilton so close to hand, and with no near-by competition, prospects seemed good for a first-rate modern cinema on this prominent main-road site. By the beginning of July construction work on the £45,000 building's framework was well advanced, and soon the granite frontage was taking shape on Clifton Road. Behind that, the long concrete slab of the auditorium, surmounted by a line of five of A.B. Robertson's large patent cylindrical ventilator drums, became a prominent feature of the vista from George Street and Powis Terrace.

The Astoria was inaugurated on Saturday 8 December 1934 with the Paul Lukas film *I Give My Love*. Admission prices ranged from 7*d*. for the Front Stalls to 1*s*.6*d*. for the Front Balcony, and a total of 2,060 patrons could be accommodated in the comfort of well-padded seats, the only extra luxury in the more expensive parts being the provision of padded arm rests as opposed to the ordinary wooden ones. If the Capitol was Aberdeen's 'cathedral of the motion picture', then the Astoria was most certainly its foremost 'parish church', albeit of later and very different design. The Capitol's theme was one of artistry and sumptuousness, whereas the Astoria's declared emphasis was on spaciousness, relying upon simplicity of form to create a pleasing impression of clean-lined functionality. Into its planning and construction went all the experience gained in the Regent project of three years before, and use was made of the same advanced concrete techniques. Concrete-work, steelwork, electrics and plumbing were 'home jobs' for Robertsons, Bissets and Scotts, while woodwork was by John Bisset of Hilton (a relative of George Bisset). Plaster and terazzo-work were by Roger & Baxter of Summer Street, and once again the ubiquitous Bruce MacKenzie turns up as decorator.

The absence of surrounding buildings gave Sutherland the opportunity to increase the scale of the Astoria's excellently-massed frontage beyond that of the Regent, and to develop some of the ideas already tried there. Once again the basic concept was used of a tall central section containing three narrow vertical window spaces, flanked by somewhat lower side portions. At the Astoria, the upper halves of these side portions were deeply recessed, suggesting two pairs of large balanced cubes. Not only did this appear satisfying geometrically, but it also made good use of light and shade. As at the Capitol, the wide central entrance had shop spaces to either side. Its large neon-lit canopy was the first in Scotland to have illuminations continuing all the way into the vestibule. Neon tubing also picked out the frontage in red, green and amber.

In the entrance hallway, the stalls doors and payboxes were built into a handsome single unit finished in walnut panelling and Staybrite steel bands. Above were large saucer-shaped glass light bowls, variants of those in the auditorium; all of these light fittings were specially made for the Astoria. To either side of the payboxes were stairs leading to a spacious balcony foyer

65   The Astoria's steel framework near completion, August 1934 (*BA*)

66   The Astoria, Kittybrewster, 1960s (courtesy of Aberdeen Picture Palaces)

with an attractive domed ceiling, thick Wilton carpets, and illuminated display cases around the walls, available for local businesses to rent for advertising purposes. Also on that level were the offices.

The auditorium was decorated in shades of warm rose set off by bands of brown, silver and gold, and the ribbed proscenium arch reflected the lights behind and around it to striking effect. Into the seating (made by Ogilvie's) went about 30 tons of iron castings and about a mile of moquette. The balcony steps were illuminated in accordance with recently-introduced regulations, and a buzzer system between balcony and pay-box instantly conveyed whatever information was required on seating space.

The Astoria's stage, measuring 22 feet in depth, had a main curtain of green artificial damask, chosen for its pleasant draping qualities. The screen tabs were in silver Roman satin, usable for Cyclorama effects, and the screen itself was claimed as the largest in Aberdeen at 28 feet by $22\frac{1}{2}$ feet. Behind it were the multiple speakers of the RCA talkie system, the first of its kind in Scotland. Always the best cinema for sound quality in the city, the Astoria owed much of this success to the scientific acoustical treatment of the auditorium, in which selected wall surfaces were sprayed with an inch-thick coating of asbestos fibre in order to damp out echo—a process which would now be totally forbidden! The projectors were of the RCA Simplex type, and all sound and electrical equipment was duplicated in case of failure. A special sound room was provided for monitoring purposes and for the making of announcements by microphone. The projection box was manned by a staff of three under chief operator Mr Victor Trapnell.

Although technically and acoustically one of the best cinemas in the whole of Scotland, the Astoria never possessed very extensive stage facilities. It did, however, have one of the very latest Compton theatre organs, installed at the prompting of an acquaintance of an otherwise undecided Bert Darley. A natural stream ran directly under the solid bed of concrete on which the building rested, so that there was no possibility of sinking a lift-well. Organist and console were therefore made to slide out as decorously as possible from stage right on a special little metal railway designed by Mr Darley, coming to rest centre stage in front of the curtains.

The organ itself spoke from behind attractively patterned grilles to the left of the stage. It was of similar size to the Capitol's, but incorporated a few extra refinements, among them a large glass console surround in which coloured lights were blended from shade to shade by means of a small dimmer system. Musical moods could be reinforced by suitable colours at the discretion of the organist, or the dimmers set to keep the colours constantly changing in the course of an interlude. This piece of showmanship, which added a whole new dimension to presentations, was by now a feature of many modern cinema organs. Indeed, some cinemas farther south even made their auditorium lighting controllable from the organ console. A claim was made to the Astoria's possessing the first illuminated theatre organ in Scotland, but in fact that honour had just gone to ABC's new Regal in Paisley!

The ingenious John Compton had also developed a device called a Solo Cello, consisting of a single steel string stretched in a frame and set in vibration

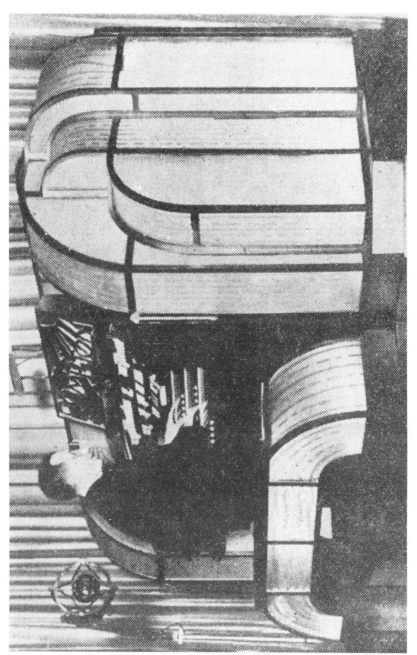

67   Harold Titherington at the organ of the Astoria (*BA* 23 July 1937)

by a circular resined 'bow'. A set of electro-pneumatically actuated 'fingers' produced the notes by pressing on the string at the appropriate places, and the sound was picked up by a microphone and amplified. A Solo Cello was provided at the Astoria, but in common with most of its peers, was not a success. Difficult to keep in order, it was removed early on; Compton soon dropped the idea and concentrated on something much more historically important—one of the earliest electronic organs. Selected from, reportedly, a list of 150 applicants for the post of Astoria organist was Harold Titherington, who came to Aberdeen from the Rialto, Blackburn, Lancashire, and remained until 1939.

That turf-cutting ceremony in March was witnessed by an additional, unofficial spectator, an elderly gent by the name of Robert Gibb. Throughout most of his 72 years, Mr Gibb had pursued a highly absorbing hobby—the watching of buildings under construction. Starting as a youngster with a simple hen coop, he had progressed to ever greater things, often cutting short lunch-breaks at work in order to go and offer assistance to the workmen on his latest pet project. The Astoria was his supervisory *tour-de-force*, and the daily journey that he made there from his home in Cattofield Terrace caught the fancy of the *Evening Express*, which, on the eve of the cinema's opening, immortalised him thus:

> Now that the last of the 30,000 screws is flush with the wood, the pensioner strides about the vestibule, his thumbs slung in his waistcoat—a man proud of his work well done....
> ... Mr Gibb has his complex, and it is the role of spectating building operations. He knows the why and wherefore of every nut and bolt in the Astoria. Many people have hobbies which they pursue so keenly to the exclusion of everything else that they become a mania with them. The average person is half interested in a number of subjects, but takes most things for granted.
> That's a pity. What people don't know they don't appreciate. It is impossible to know something about everything, but if people made it a hobby to learn a little about the everyday things their life could be made a lot happier.

The Astoria's management also acknowledged Mr Gibb's keen interest—at the opening ceremony he was made guest of honour!

1935. Italy invaded Abyssinia as Germany busily rearmed itself in the face of all peace agreements. Even amid the Coronation Silver Jubilee celebrations there was speculation about future war. In Aberdeen, a desperate shortage of housing brought about the billeting of some 200 council tenants in the former Jute Works at Froghall. Others finished up in the hastily-converted Torry Battery as new council housing developments slowly worked their way through the drawing-board stage.

Some degree of national economic recovery had been accomplished, and such items as domestic refrigerators made their first appearance in Aberdeen at the *Press & Journal* Exhibition in the Music Hall that year, following on the first mildly encouraging budget since 1930. Entertainments Tax was reduced, and home amusements and hobbies came more within general reach—some of these hobbies very expensive ones, as exemplified by the popular (and highly dangerous) do-it-yourself mini-plane, the 'Flying Flea', one of which buzzed around the Aberdeenshire countryside that summer.

On Jubilee Day, 6 May 1935, Aberdonians joined the rest of the country in festooning their streets with flags and buntings for a long-awaited opportunity to 'let their hair down'. A flag-bedecked Capitol showed a film documentary of the King's reign. Processions filled Union Street, and a great festival service was held in St Nicholas' Church. On Brimmond Hill just outside the city, Britain's largest bonfire flamed into the night sky, and from it could be seen no less than thirty other bonfires on hills in the area.

Dames, starring the Powell/Keeler/Blondell team, had its Aberdeen premiere at the Capitol, complete with pictorial interlude by Harold Coombs. At the Picture House, the much-acclaimed British production *Jew Suss*, starring Conrad Veidt, told a portentous story of anti-semitism in eighteenth century Germany. The queues outside the small Picture House waited their usual half-hour to see Maurice Chevalier and Jeanette MacDonald in *The Merry Widow*. At the Palace, Bing Crosby was partnered by songbird Kitty Carlisle in *Here Is My Heart*, in which were heard the popular hits 'It's June In January' and 'Love Is Just Around the Corner'. Charles Laughton's *The Barrets Of Wimpole Street* showed at a newly- redecorated Playhouse, where admission prices had been considerably reduced after the opening of the Capitol. In close rivalry with Poole's 'Aberdeen's Super Two', the Capitol and Playhouse were at this time being advertised as 'Aberdeen's Premier Pair'!

At His Majesty's Theatre that April, the highly popular Roy Fox and his band (currently appearing at the Beach Ballroom) played a celebrity guest spot each evening during a week's run of the film *The Party's Over*. To advertise Gary Cooper's *The Lives Of A Bengal Lancer* (at the Capitol the week after the Jubilee) two 'real' Bengal Lancers rode on horseback up and down Union Street. On Wednesday, 29 May a horse was 'mailed' from Queen's Cross Post Office to the Picture House, where it was treated as guest of honour at a special preview of the next week's film *Strictly Confidential*, a horse-racing story which, it was reported, the animal seemed to quite enjoy!

Sunday charity concerts were still a prominent part of the local cinemagoing scene, and Jack Poole himself intended to be present to address the audience at a big Willing Shilling show in the Palace on 13 January. Unfortunately, business commitments kept him in Edinburgh, and in a telephone conversation with the Palace's new General Manager, Captain Wingfield, he ruefully remarked that the only thing for it would be to somehow connect the Palace's telephone to the talkie system. An idea glimmered at the Aberdeen end, and a short while later Mr Poole received a return call enquiring as to whether he would care to participate in a little experiment. The operators had indeed found a way to link the telephone with the amplifiers, and the

68   The horse that was posted to The Picture House, May 1935. The picture
on the screen is a clever insert by the *Evening Express* photographic staff (*EE*
29 May 1935)

audience sitting in the Palace that night was able to hear Mr Poole loud
and clear from his home, 'Four Ways', Gillespie Road, Colinton, in distant
Edinburgh—a stunt believed to be unique in British cinema history.

For years the New Kinema in Belmont Street had run quietly and unspec-
tacularly under the proprietorship of James Brebner and George Walker. No

69 The Picture House, now with neon sign, 1935. The Gordon Highlanders were guests at a showing of George Arliss's *The Iron Duke* (*BA* 19 April 1935)

claims whatever were made to 'super' status, but the custom was there, and one day Mr Brebner voiced the opinion that the company ought to be branching out with a large new cinema, perhaps redeveloping a site somewhere in the city centre. The preferred course of action was to buy over an existing cinema, obviating the delay involved in changing the use of sites. Prime candidate for purchase was La Scala, which Mr Walker described as 'an awful place'. Although popular with those who enjoyed the foreign connoisseur films and the less 'commercial' features in which it specialised from time to time according to availability, it was, as a building, completely out of date, with its balcony far too close to the screen for modern requirements. It was also, by 1935, in the sort of state whereby no-one could be quite confident of being able to sit down in a seat without falling through it. Perhaps more importantly, nothing had come of Green's great rebuilding plan of 1933, but the company still held the adjoining sites to the west on Union Street and to the east on Union Row.

Through the agency of William Mann (formerly of APP, and by this time managing Green's Playhouse, Glasgow) discreet enquiries were made by Messrs Walker and Brebner as to Green's attitude towards selling their entire Aberdeen holdings. The response was favourable, and immediately negotiations began. A new public company named Caledonian Theatres was floated to finance the operation. Managing Director was James Brebner, while Chairman (and presumably major shareholder) was Lt-Col Henry J. Kinghorn, a veteran volunteer soldier and one of Aberdeen's most popular Territorial officers up until his retirement in 1923. The company's other directors were Mr Alexander Davidson of Cults and Mr John D. Paton of the family that has owned the Grandholm estate at Woodside since the seventeenth century.

Next step was to engage an architect, and who better than Councillor T. Scott Sutherland. Told of the option that Brebner had secured on the relatively small La Scala, Sutherland was less than enthusiastic, but when it was explained that other properties were to be included in the deal, that was different. The outcome of the meeting was a place among Caledonian Theatres' directors for Sutherland, who immediately commenced what he considered to be his most ambitious and advanced project, a 2,600-seater to be named the MAJESTIC. The purchase of the site was concluded, and La Scala closed on Saturday 18 May 1935. Its manager, William Muir, who in the course of 27 years in the picture industry had worked as cameraman, operator, consulting engineer 'on the road', technician, traveller, director of a cinema company—in fact, everything except pianist—remained with Green's, moving back to Glasgow, where he had been manager of the Bridgeton Picturedrome before coming to Aberdeen.

Improvements were carried out at the New Kinema, which closed on Saturday 8 June 1935 for renovation and the renewal of its heating plant, lighting and sound equipment. On Monday, 24 June the old Trades Hall reopened under yet another new name—the BELMONT. Main feature film was *The Radio Star*, starring Ray Walker, and on the small stage was the Embassy Band in an interlude of current hits—the first of many such engagements for the band.

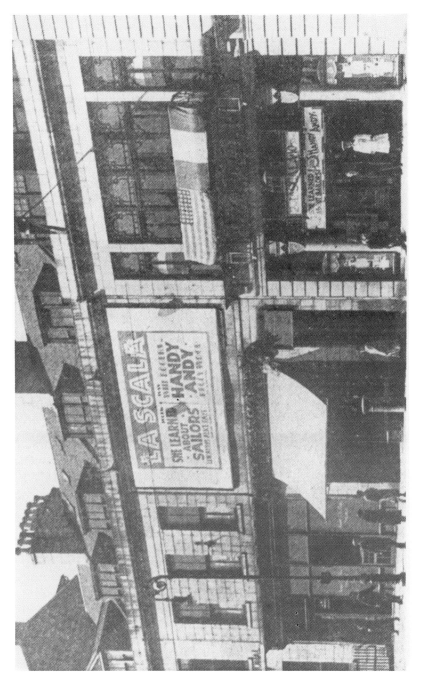

70 La Scala pictured shortly before its closure (*BA* 19 April 1935)

Completion of the Majestic was to be more than a year away, and for now 'Tommy' Sutherland was busy with two further cinema designs, the VICTORIA, Inverurie (see chapter 14) and a third city 'super', this time on a site to the west of George Street, where clearance of old houses had begun by January 1935. With the latter scheme, preliminary plans for which had been drawn up in December 1933, Aberdeen Picture Palaces was moving into a market thus far untapped in the east-end, replacing the venerable King's with a large modern hall that could offer luxury at very reasonable prices. By September, the completed shell of the CITY CINEMA was towering over the surrounding backland buildings, and on Monday, 4 November there came into use the latest 2,500 additions to Aberdeen's rapidly-swelling total of picture hall seats. That afternoon, Mrs A.D. Hay ceremonially opened the front door, admitting guests and public to hear the usual speeches and to watch Warner Baxter in *Pampas Moon*.

Tucked away behind the houses and shops of George Street, with tenement windows above its entrance canopy, the City possessed a rather nondescript outer prospect, belied by a very attractive and unusual interior. From the entranceway (in former shop spaces) a long, wide foyer led to the auditorium which, due to the shape of the site, was unusually short and wide. At 110 feet across, it was one of the widest cinema auditoria in Scotland, and a great challenge was set in ensuring the proper visibility of the screen from all seats. Taking full advantage of the possibilities inherent in the shallower-than-usual auditorium space, however, Sutherland evolved a clever design wherein no seat was more than 100 feet away from the screen. Great trouble was taken over acoustic treatment, and what could easily have been a disaster was turned into a roaring success.

Most of the auditorium decor was in the warm but fairly neutral shades of rose that were popular for such places, with a dado of bright red and with groups of particularly handsome black and gold decorative sidewall columns enclosing illuminated 'organ grilles', although the City Cinema never boasted any such instrument. The proscenium arch was pleasantly clean-lined and neat, its deep recess concealing lights that gave the effect of a continuous band of illumination around the stage. Special lighting troughs carried varying colours across the ceiling, while from up in the operating box a Brennograph projected further effects on to the screen or curtains. The City's manager was Frank McGuggan, who, it will be remembered, first came to Aberdeen as manager of La Scala. Moving on to this fine new hall after several years at the King's, Mr McGuggan, an affable man, was to remain a kenspeckle figure in the Aberdeen cinema trade for a further three decades.

Construction work on the building was carried out by the usual firms of Bisset, Robertson, and MacKenzie, with James Archibald & Sons supplying the carpets, etc. While the firm of James Nicol & Sons was working on the steel framing, there occurred a tragic accident which cast a shadow over the project, and which may perhaps account for the somewhat muted tone of the opening ceremony as compared with other occasions of that nature.

Then as now, failure to check lashings on building materials being hoisted into place could have disastrous consequences. One day a girder, which had

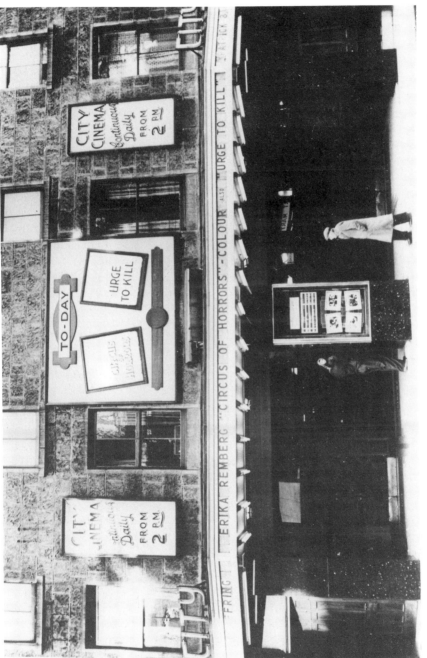

71 City Cinema, George Street, 1960s (courtesy of Aberdeen Picture Palaces)

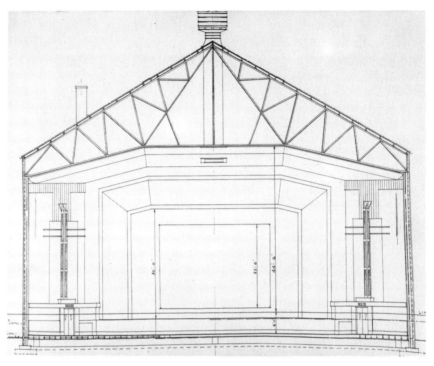

72   City Cinema—T. Scott Sutherland's modernistic original draft of the front
auditorium, December 1933 (altered after April 1935) (ADC, Dept of Planning)

73   City Cinema auditorium as built (*EE* 2 Oct. 1935)

not been properly secured at one end, fell and dragged over the whole crane—
itself none too firmly anchored. The thick wire rope flew, hitting and killing
a workman, Mr John Sharp. After an inquiry and court case, the Glasgow
firm carrying out the work (presumably under sub-contract) was found guilty
of negligence, but, for lack of firm proof, only on a technicality. All that could
be awarded to the unfortunate man's family was court expenses—£3.

Up until post-war times the City's stock-in-trade lay in duplications of
up-town programmes, notably the second-runs and lesser features of the
Playhouse. Fussy as Aberdonians were in choosing their screen entertainment, those who could afford it turned out to the cinema two or three
times per week. Another important source of custom was the crowds of
holidaymakers that arrived in Aberdeen during the sunny but unpredictable
summers of the 1930s. Exhibitors responded to this demand by building more
and more halls, and it is indicative of the popularity of picture-going in
Aberdeen that, even though the prospect of over-provision of cinema accommodation was beginning to cause some concern, such large houses as the
City were built with an exclusive policy of second-runs in mind.

74   The corner of John Street and George Street with the King's Cinema on
the left, 1935 (ADC, Dept of Planning)

Something equally remarkable, and no doubt thoroughly mystifying to Aberdeen Picture Palaces, was the resistance with which the City met from the very public that it was built to attract. Those used to the old 'Globie' or King's should in all conscience have been delighted to come to such a comfortable, well-appointed cinema. Surely people didn't *still* want to go and sit in the cramped, smoky, ill-ventilated King's, did they...? They did, and through public demand APP was obliged to keep the King's open.

APP was not the only Scottish cinema company to encounter this strange anomaly. About three years later, Jack Poole, deciding to open an up-market companion to his popular but ancient Synod Hall in Edinburgh, built at great expense the elegant and beautifully lit Roxy in the working-class district of Gorgie. Local folk stayed away, but nobody would say why. Eventually it turned out that, although the people liked the Roxy well enough, it felt cold, formal and unwelcoming after the friendly neighbourhood atmosphere of the smaller, humbler houses—widely but not necessarily derogatorily referred to as 'flea-pits'. It took Messrs Poole a long time to establish the Roxy as a popular house, and parallels might well be drawn between it and the City.

Among Aberdeen's screen attractions of late 1935 were the latest Shirley Temple offering, *Bright Eyes*, and the great *David Copperfield*, in which W.C. Fields stole the show as Mr Micawber. 'The Picture That Is Too Big For One Theatre', it filled both the Capitol and the Playhouse that August, and a special competition was held in which entrants were invited to read the Dickens novel and to make up star casts of their own. The best entry won a free six-month season ticket to the Capitol.

There was melody in Gracie Fields' *Look Up and Laugh*, Fred Astaire and Ginger Rogers' *Roberta*, *Sanders Of the River*, featuring the deep, rich voice of Paul Robeson, and in *The Big Broadcast Of 1936*, which contained stars galore, but perhaps the pick of the musical crop was the splendid *Gold Diggers Of 1935*, last and finest of the big-budget Busby Berkeley extravaganzas. Combining mind-boggling camera angles, ranks of dancers, and the song-writing talents of 'maestros' Al Dubin and Harry Warren, *Gold Diggers* was brought to Aberdeen by Donald's, who first showed it at His Majesty's Theatre that November.

Suspense abounded with Cagney in *G–Men* and with Robert Donat (co-starring with Madeleine Carroll) in *The 39 Steps*. *The 39 Steps* was chosen for showing to a party of one hundred blind people at the Picture House on 3 December, under the auspices of the Aberdeen Town And County Association For The Teaching Of The Blind In Their Homes. This somewhat unorthodox cinema audience was able to enjoy the show through the medium of a commentator who gave an introductory explanation of the plot and described the action during the silent parts. Sponsored by Gaumont-British, the experiment was very much appreciated, and was followed by further performances of the same kind.

A rainy Christmas kept cinema crowds down somewhat, but those ven-

75   Times past—billboards near Frederick Street advertising cinema attractions, 1935 (ADC, Dept of Planning)

76   ... and at the corner of George Street/Hutcheon Street (ADC, Dept of Planning)

turing out could find (among many other popular films) Will Fyffe in *Rolling Home*, Laurel & Hardy in their classic *Bonny Scotland*, and Bill Boyd in his best-remembered role as *Hopalong Cassidy*. The Astoria's Christmas Eve showing of *The Gay Lady* concluded with Harold Titherington playing Handel's 'Hallelujah Chorus' on the organ. Well may the carol singing have gone with a swing now that, after half a decade of economic disaster, things were at last beginning to look up.

Chapter 11

Peak Years 1936—1939

The silver screen's invasion of Aberdeen was all but complete by 1936, even down to the introduction of sound films as part of Sunday worship at Bon Accord Congregational Church (now the Buffaloes' Institute), Bon-Accord Street. A couple of winters previously, with the aim of cultivating interest in church-going, the minister, Rev A.J. Parker, had installed above the pulpit a 12 by 14 feet screen on which could be projected the words of hymns, anthems, etc, and even the Benediction. The idea proved as popular in Aberdeen as in the other cities where it had been tried, and in February 1936 talkie equipment was installed, enabling the congregation to see (on safety stock, of course) the Religious Film Society's dramatisations of stories from the Bible, incorporating scenic footage specially taken in Palestine.

It was not the subject of talkies in church, however, that was causing the greatest excitement in local cinema circles at this time. Neither was it the Casino's 20th birthday celebrations on 4 February, when, to some publicity, the cake was ceremonially cut by Ormonde Kilgour and one of his oldest patrons, a Mrs Stewart. Nor was it a widely-advertised cabaret appearance at the Palais De Danse by Mildred Harris, Charlie Chaplin's teenage bride of 1919. The main talking-point was a communication that had come through the letter boxes of APP, Astoria and Caledonian Theatres in late November 1935, offering a mass takeover by the rapidly-growing London-based company Union Cinemas.

At approximately the same time, Poole's Aberdeen holdings had been the subject of a substantial takeover bid from ABC. These bids constituted more than just a couple of speculative attempts by outside concerns to gain a foothold in the city; they were a symptom of the fierceness of competition between the ever-expanding national exhibitors, headed by the ABC circuit of the Scot, John Maxwell, and the huge Gaumont-British company.

It had always been the case that the larger a circuit grew, the greater became its influence and booking-power. At one point a merger had actually been negotiated between the rival ABC and GB giants, but the amalgamation process was mysteriously halted. It has been suggested that the ultimate explanation for this may lie on the other side of the Atlantic, where powerful interests would have been threatened by such a British alliance.

Union was out to attain maximum influence in the minimum time, and its expansion programme was, to say the least, vigorous. During the first week of January 1936, the Aberdeen papers carried a statement from Union, claiming that a £3,000,000 contract had been signed with the three local companies approached. This statement was also published in the cinema trade press, apparently signifying a *fait accompli*.

Control of APP, Astoria and Caledonian would at that time have been the closest that anyone could come to a monopoly of Aberdeen's cinema industry, given the situation with the Poole houses and discounting the impregnable GB and Donald interests. Union had great faith in this 'blanketing' policy, which served the purpose of keeping down film rental costs through mass booking and repeated showing, while cutting out as much competition as possible. Its intention was to combine the three Aberdeen companies under the name of Aberdeen Cinema Holdings. Caledonian, by reason of the favourable placing of the as yet unbuilt Majestic, appeared ready to sell between 18,000 and 20,000 (51 per cent) of its £1 shares at a generous 5s. bonus, while Astoria would sell a similar percentage of its 30,000 shares at a 1s. bonus, the remainder becoming five per cent preference shares. Shares in the new group were to be guaranteed for 25 years. Bert Darley and Mr Fred Bernhard (head of Union Cinemas) were to be its joint Managing Directors, while two out of the five Astoria directors were to give place to Union representatives. No doubt a similar agreement would have been made with Caledonian.

That triumphant (and premature) claim to supremacy was not only a good example of Union's aggressive style, but may also, to read between the lines a little, have constituted a serious blunder. By 31 January 1936 Aberdeen Picture Palaces had decided that the offer was unsatisfactory, and had withdrawn from the negotiations. Might Bert Gates and his partners have been mistrustful of this apparent railroading? Perhaps, perhaps not, but next the Astoria company began to express misgivings about the offer's terms. Blaming the resulting delay, Union, after (to quote the company) 'pressure from its solicitors', withdrew, and by 7 February the matter was closed.

Perhaps even at that time all was not well with Union. Its claims regarding size and importance were every bit as extravagant as its expenditure policies on new buildings and on the 'blanketing' of towns where it tried to crowd out competitors. The enterprise was a bold one and grew to very large proportions in only a couple of years, but it did so at the expense of its own financial and organisational strength. Before long Union was in serious trouble, and although attempts were made to right the situation, the death of financial director David Bernhard (Fred Bernhard's father) in September 1937 finally toppled the delicately-balanced house of cards. By the end of that year Union had become a subsidiary of ABC. What would have happened had the Aberdeen deals gone through and the company then failed is an interesting, indeed sobering, subject for conjecture.

ABC's bid for the Poole cinemas was also unsuccessful, but this was not to be the end of the story for amalgamations and takeovers at the Astoria, the Regent, and the Palace. Business at the Astoria had not been as good as was hoped. A fine building was all very well, but booking power for top films was of vital importance in an increasingly competitive world, and the Astoria company was not large enough to wield that power. For residents of the area, the pick of the city's film programmes was only a short tram journey away; meanwhile the Astoria's location was too remote from the general path of the holidaymakers that might have sustained it over summers.

One might, with hindsight, wonder why these potential problems had not been foreseen, but be that as it may, the Astoria's directors, somewhat concerned at the disappointing trading figures for the first year, were more of a mind than ever to effect a link-up with a larger company. So it was that, on 20 March 1936, Aberdeen Astoria Cinema shareholders were advised to accept a premium offer from Messrs Donald for 16,000 of the company's share stock—the usual controlling 51 per cent. A week later, on the 27th of the month, the deal was concluded. The shareholders made a five per cent profit on each share sold, control of the Astoria remained in local hands, Messrs Donald gained their first large 'super', and it was agreed by all parties that even if the desired extra impetus to business did not materialise, no-one would be any the worse off.

Not included in the bargain were the services of Bert Darley, whose contract, with three-and-a-half years still to run, was bought out for £1,750. Replaced as manager by Richard Donald, he returned to London in early April. Just prior to his departure, he gave a press interview (printed in the *Evening Express* of 4 April 1936), in which he estimated that Aberdeen must to date have spent more on entertainments than any comparably-sized centre in Britain. He also credited Aberdonians with considerable film sense. Thanks to the vast amount of film literature available, some members of the public were more knowledgeable than people in the trade, and while local tastes were less predictable than they had been during the previous decade, he was well able to confirm what any picture house manager or proprietor already knew: that no amount of advertising would make box office out of a poor film.

Of Mr Darley's subsequent career, little or nothing is known. When, years later, J.K.S. Poole made casual enquiries as to his whereabouts, it was reported that he was working for ABC under the name of Fletcher. That may seem a trifle odd, but he was known to have had a career as a film actor and producer before going into the cinema trade. It was also thought that he had some kind of theatrical background and was used to working under assumed names, but there the trail ends.

Even as Bert Darley bade farewell to Aberdeen, his old employers at the Regent and Palace were making ready to do the same. An attractive offer had been received from another southern company, County Cinemas, for Poole's houses in Devonport, Derby and Plymouth, Poole's Regent being among the latter city's best cinemas. County Cinemas, whose activities centred upon the south of England, had initially no intention of moving into Scotland, but somehow Aberdeen's Regent and Palace had been slipped into the package, and in order to secure the remainder County was obliged to accept. The deal was announced on 16 July; very soon after that the Poole's logo disappeared from

Regent and Palace advertisements, and the two halls began showing mainly the same programmes. Staffing, however, remained unchanged, the only departure being that of J.K.S. Poole, who went to assist in the running of the Synod Hall, Edinburgh, and the family's remaining houses at Dundee, Gloucester, Ipswich and Rickmansworth.

Once again, through some strange coincidence, as a new Union Street cinema (this time the Majestic) was going up, an old-established house elsewhere in town went up too—in flames. On Thursday 4 June the staff of the newly-redecorated Queen's took their usual 12 o'clock lunch break, leaving everything apparently in order. Less than half an hour later, the Queen's was on fire.

According to press reports, the outbreak began in a fuse-box at the top of the entrance stairs; another account has it that a faulty extractor fan was to blame. The flames quickly spread up the old dry lathes of the wall, and soon the ceiling was well alight. In Gillespie's fruit shop below the cinema, a customer, Mr David Kyd, noticed smoke and summoned a policeman. The men dashed upstairs to find wall and ceiling ablaze and the whole floor level full of thick, choking smoke. After expending eight fire extinguishers on the flames the two could stay in the building no longer, but by that time the fire brigade had been sent for. Two fire engines and a turntable ladder were soon in action, watched by a crowd that filled Union Street, and hoses were run in at every conceivable point, including the ground-floor furniture shop of Messrs Allan, where redecoration had just been completed and where it would now have to be done all over again. A cloud of black smoke hung over the building, and even as the firemen set to, flames erupted from the roof. Things looked far worse than they had at the Star in 1932, but after a great struggle the fire was brought under control and at last extinguished. Once the building was safe to enter, an *Evening Express* reporter went in to record the aftermath:

> Inside was a scene of desolation. The back section of the hall was scarcely touched apart from water. But the lower part, where the cheaper seats were situated, was a constantly rising heap of debris. Charred beams came hurtling down, still smoking and glowing. In a short time the whole area was completely under a mass of embers. Practically the whole of the roof was gone and firemen could be seen precariously perched on walls directing the hose on the parts that were still alight.
>
> Water came rushing through into the shops below. In Mr J. Lizars' shop, which is directly under the cinema, the water was pouring in like a rainstorm, and as quickly as it was swept out with brooms the floor was again covered up.
>
> There was a similar scene in the shop of Mr K. Gillespie, fruiterer. Water also filled the windows, and wreaths and flowers were destroyed.
>
> Down the long stairway, foaming and dancing like a waterfall, came a torrent of water which rushed across the pavement.

After the danger from fire came danger from water, the weight of which might, it was feared, send the entire upper floor crashing into the shops below. One shopkeeper was informed that a hole might have to be cut in his ceiling to allow the flood to escape, but in the event the emergency passed and the lower storey was left wet but structurally intact. It was, however, a sorry sight that met the eyes of Messrs Peter and James R. Donald, who arrived from Stonehaven just as the firemen were completing operations.

The fire was a costly one. Water damage to scientific instruments, lighting system and wooden panellings at Lizars, and to stock and interiors at Allan's and Gillespie's. Upstairs, the complete destruction of the roof dome and the ruination of the once-splendid rooms below it. Any remaining roof spars had already been pulled down, and the rest of the roof was so waterlogged that it too would have to go. The rubber screen had somehow escaped intact, but much seating had been destroyed and the areas that had escaped the flames were seriously damaged by smoke and water. The total bill was expected to run to between £12,000 and £15,000, and just to add insult to injury the fire occurred the day after the renewal of the cinema's exhibition licence!

Before the last of the debris had been cleared away, architects George Watt & Stewart of Union Street (designers of the enlarged Grand Central in 1929) were engaged to draw up a replacement for that which had been lost. Soon workmen were busily demolishing what remained of the old interior to make way for a new Queen's Cinema, the granite outer shell of which would be all that it held in common with its predecessor.

Behind the glitter of the cinema world as its public saw it, not all was glamour and romance. Staff hours in cinemas were long by present-day standards, while rates of remuneration were relatively small. A union did exist—the National Union Of Theatrical Workers—but by no means all cinema employees in the city were members of it. Cinema employers, meanwhile, had their own organisation, the Cinematograph Exhibitors' Association, the Aberdeen contingent of which was headed by Bert Gates. For all the close rivalry of its members, the Aberdeen CEA was firmly united in one respect— a strong disinclination to have any truck with unions. This appears to have stemmed as much from set ways as from a simple dislike of organised labour. Nothing was considered to be wrong with existing grievance procedures; the general feeling was 'My office door is always open'.

Back in 1930, a narrowly-averted cinemas strike had been the first public indication of discontent among some staffs over salaries and conditions. The great surge of super cinema-building since 1931 had greatly increased the membership of the NUTW's Aberdeen branch, and by the spring of 1936 the union felt strong enough to start applying pressure for recognition by the CEA. On Thursday, 14 May a sandwich-board demonstration was held outside the Grand Central, with leaflets distributed urging patrons and passers-by to 'refrain from entering any picture house until the employers recognise the employees' trade union wages and conditions of service'. Lack of numbers precluded simultaneous demonstrations at other cinemas, but talks were entered into with the Scottish Trade Unions Council with a view to extension of activities.

Approval of these actions was not unanimous among those that the union sought to recruit. After a meeting of Donald circuit staffs on 16 May, a statement was issued (signed by Mr John Conlon, chief operator of the Cinema House, and by Mr Charles Rea, his counterpart at the Queen's) affirming contentment with a fifty-hour working week for a box staff of chief operator, second and third operators and apprentice, the latter being the lowest paid at 30s. per week, sometimes less. Attendants and usherettes also received about 30s. per week, with hours usually similar to those of the box staff, and many of these also signified contentment with the status quo. The statement was published in the *Evening Express* that night alongside an assurance from 'an exhibitor' that no complaints had been received from employees, but if they had been dissatisfied 'things would have to be looked into'.

The Donald organisation looked after its staff and in return received great loyalty, but if some were happy with their lot, the tone of a meeting held in the Trades Council building on 17 May was not so conciliatory. In some Aberdeen cinemas employees were working as many as sixty hours per week (a ten-hour day) for only 35s., a situation described by Mr Thomas O'Brien of the union's London headquarters as 'among the most appalling in the country'. It was made clear by Mr R.A. Fraser, chairman of the Trades and Labour Council, that the demonstration three days previously was not to be the last of the matter. After warnings were issued against any attempts at intimidation, temporary calm returned as plans were laid for the campaign's resumption after the summer. Dialogue continued between the Aberdeen TUC and the Scottish TUC, which sent an official letter that July pledging full support. Action was expected to start again with a general preliminary meeting in August, but before July was out the entire question of labour relations within Aberdeen's cinema industry had been pushed unexpectedly and decisively into the open.

On Friday, 25 July, nine girl employees at the Palace were, according to the union, unfairly dismissed by their manager, Gordon Wingfield, when they made an approach for the restitution of a once-customary fortnightly half-holiday. A call by Patrick Jeffrey (secretary of APP and of the Aberdeen CEA) for a meeting between the two sides went unheeded; instead, a mass union meeting was held in the Trades Hall building between 10.30 p.m. and 1 a.m., with TUC and NUTW officials in direct telephone contact with Thomas O'Brien in London.

Appraised of this, Captain Wingfield gave his side of the story—how, on the day in question, the girls had asked for assurance of a half day off during the next week, an arrangement that was not provided for under their employment conditions, but which was implemented whenever possible. As it was the holiday period and Charlie Chaplin's *Modern Times* was showing, the past week had been a particularly busy one. The girls had been told to go off to their work and to make an approach through their foreman, but instead of doing so they had walked out without completing the hours for which they had been paid the previous evening.

Now claiming seventy per cent membership among full-time Aberdeen cinema staffs, the NUTW began to speak of a possible strike by about 200 employees. The CEA played its cards close, declaring that no action would be taken by its members until a stoppage came into effect. Events moved quickly,

77   The Queen's Cinema, Union Street, 1935

78 ... and ablaze, 1936 (*EE* 4 June 1936)

and on 29 July a deputation from the NUTW arrived at the London offices of County Cinemas. Central to the union's case was a statement, signed and sworn to by all the girls from the Palace, that their half days had been suspended even though the management had made it clear that one half day would be allowed per fortnight. Approached to reconsider, the manager had flared up and told them to get out—in effect, dismissing them. This was in direct contradiction to Captain Wingfield's published statements, and it posed an important question: were they sacked or did they leave? The longer the argument dragged on, the longer the girls would have to wait for benefit if wrongful dismissal were proved. If it were not proved, they would receive nothing.

Feelings ran high, and a strike on 31 July looked likely. At a large union meeting at Belmont Street late that night a vote of support for the girls numbered 73 in favour to only seven against. Membership of the NUTW rose by a further 15, and a communication from the TUC National Executive conveyed encouragement. A wrongful dismissal claim was lodged with the NUTW's lawyers, and at the same time a group of demonstrators (including the usherettes and cash girls with whom the dispute had begun) took up position outside the Palace.

The next day, 30 July, brought claims of progress by the union, prompt denials from the other side, and a trump card from Mr William Brown, local secretary of the TUC, in the form of a statement by Gaumont-British expressing willingness to give the union the recognition that it sought. Even then, the Picture House management claimed that the statement applied to London only. What no-one could deny or counterclaim, however, was a rumour that the union's representatives, still in London, had spoken in person to County Cinemas' managing director Reginald Bromhead. Although Captain Wing-field did his best to play down this unconfirmed report, a mass union meeting heard it that same day along with GB's statement. Also, it became known that the National President of the CEA had been in contact with Mr William Fraser of the Trades and Labour Council, deprecating the intransigence of the Association's Aberdeen branch.

In an interview with the *Evening Express*, Mr Fraser described GB's action as a 'fine and friendly one', and aired the opinion that other cinema companies would now follow its example. Also interviewed were Patrick Jeffrey, who simply reiterated the CEA's stance on the matter, and Captain Wingfield, who complained of catcalls being shouted at him and of approaches being made to patrons during the previous night's demonstration. Denying once again that he had sacked the girls, he maintained that they had been given three opportunities to go back and complete their week's work.

Friday 31 July came with peace seeming no closer, except that the intended strike, due that day, had been postponed pending dialogue with County. The NUTW claimed that five out of the nine usherettes taken on to replace those at the heart of the affair had been persuaded to support the union and 'black' their jobs. Managements, meanwhile, remained confident that their staffs would not come out, and that even if some did they would easily be replaced—a viewpoint not shared by the union, which was equally sure that as by law a complete and qualified staff had to be on duty during opening hours, even a partial stoppage would paralyse cinemas in the city.

Still Gaumont-British seemed to be acting inconsistently. The NUTW had at its London headquarters a letter from GB's Chief Divisional Superintendent, Mr Lundy, clearly indicating that union recognition was forthcoming, and that the Aberdeen CEA had been informed of this. But when the *Express* asked GB's Divisional Superintendent for Scotland, Mr Ritson Bennell (a relative of J.J. Bennell) about the letter, Bennell denied all knowledge of it. He wanted no part in the dispute; speaking for himself, he would have been happy enough to see the union recognised, but, as he had explained on a special visit to the Picture House the evening before, GB was a member of the local CEA, so things were not that simple.

Stalemate. The union continued its picketing, claiming great success. Dark hints were dropped of more action to come, and it looked as if a confrontation might be on the the way, but at 8 o'clock on the evening of 31 July William Brown arrived unexpectedly at the Palace to call off the demonstration. The meeting that followed at Belmont Street was the largest yet, and although no-one would say more than that settlement talks were in progress over the dismissals, the situation at last looked hopeful. The demonstrations had worked, noticeably reducing the Palace's takings for *Modern Times*. This had led to questions being asked, and to the company directors themselves taking up both of the matters at issue.

The talks with County Cinemas were officially announced on Saturday, 1 August, and by the Monday an agreement had been reached. The Palace girls went back to work, and at a further meeting with County a couple of days later the question of union recognition received a sympathetic hearing. Gaumont-British's London office issued a clear statement of recognition, and finally, after some further negotiations, the Aberdeen CEA relented, taking cognisance of the union as of March 1937.

Discussions began on the subject of wages and conditions, and eventually an agreement was worked out setting the maximum number of working hours per week at 55 for male staff and 48 for female staff. This may still seem rather a long week to us nowadays, but with the new arrangement came regular payment of time-and-a-half on Sundays and double-time on one recognised Scottish holiday each year. Accord was also reached on general leave procedures, and a conciliation board was set up as mediator in case of any further dispute.

The Aberdeen NUTW gained fifty new members, and William Brown was accorded honorary membership in appreciation of his efforts. The employers, still operating from a strong position as a closely-knit group in the city's business community, can hardly have lost by the deal. Indeed, regularisation of working relations must surely, in the long run, have been to everyone's advantage.

During that same summer, Messrs Donald were busy on a project for the replacement of the antiquated Queen's, Stonehaven, built in 1913 as a companion house to the Aberdeen Queen's. Mid-May saw the closure of the old Allardyce Street premises, followed by their rapid demolition. Just three and a half months later, on 4 August, the inaugural film *Jack Of All Trades* was shown at the new 1,000-seat Stonehaven PICTURE HOUSE. The opening ceremony was chaired by the town's Provost Thomson in the presence of James R. Donald, architect Leslie R. Rollo, and Captain D. Polson Hall, partner in Rollo's firm. Stonehaven was now well served for cinema entertainment, a fact much appreciated by the summer visitors that flocked there each year.

Promoted to the post of manager at Stonehaven from second-in-charge at the Astoria was 'Sandy' Matthews, who left for Edinburgh in 1941 to resume journalism. A talented artist, he had two paintings exhibited by the Society of Scottish Artists, one being subsequently selected as part of a travelling educational display. Great was the shock when, in June 1943, the news came that he had died suddenly at the age of 35 while on holiday in Doune, Perthshire.

At 6.30 p.m. on Saturday, 5 September 1936, Aberdeen gained only the second example in Scotland of a NEWS CINEMA. Intended specifically to provide diversion for those with limited time to while away, programmes lasted approximately an hour and were made up entirely of comedy and local interest shorts, newsreels, cartoons, etc. News Cinemas were already part of daily life in centres further south. They were ideal for travellers awaiting transport connections, and London's Victoria Station had a News Cinema of its own.

Aberdeen's News Cinema belonged to Ernest Bromberg, and was situated next door to the Palais in Diamond Street, just off Union Street and not too far from the railway station. A conversion of a former stable building which Bromberg had owned since 1931, it consisted of little more than a long narrow room terminating in a 10 feet by 13 feet screen. Its interior decor, which survived until the late 1950s, was in a durable green plastic paint with maroon bandings, and its atmosphere of cosiness and intimacy was much enhanced by such small touches as dim amber floor-lights in the aisles and similarly coloured filters in the attendants' hand-torches. The acoustics and the RCA talkie system were excellent, and all in all the little cinema more than made up in comfort and quality for what it lacked in size.

Construction work on the Majestic, set back during the discussions with Union, was by now well advanced. At the time when negotiations began, building operations were at an early stage, and it was suggested—presumably by Union—that the plans should be revised to give a smaller but more luxurious auditorium. This was done, and on failure of the takeover it was decided that the scheme would proceed using the new drawings.

In the original layout, the screen was to have been placed at the Union Street end of the auditorium, an arrangement that would surely have made the planning of entranceways and corridors somewhat difficult. In any case, the city authorities considered accommodation for such things as toilets to be inadequate, so changes would sooner or later have been required. Under the revisions, the auditorium's orientation was reversed, with access from Union Street via the conventional vestibule and foyer. Some walls that had already been built had to come down again, but very soon the Majestic, with its new seating capacity of 1,800, was rising grandly among the buildings on the north side of Union Street.

In his 1950s autobiography *Life On One Leg*, Sutherland states that the Majestic was his finest design, on which he had allowed his imagination to run riot, and that its success exceeded his dreams. Its square Kemnay granite frontage (a development of a style that might without too much facetiousness be described as 'Sutherland Perpendicular') stood a good 15 feet above the gracious 1913 Clydesdale Bank building to the east, quite dwarfing Sutherland's own Amicable House (opened in 1935) to the west, and breaking up the hitherto continuous sightlining of the block. Not everyone liked the structure—some called it prison-like—but it effectively demonstrated Sutherland's talent for using granite in simple shapes to produce something that was unmistakably of its time, yet possessing a distinctive local flavour.

Departing from the exact formula used for the Regent and Astoria frontages, Sutherland's characteristic window columns were set in side panels, with a vertical decorative neon strip between each column. At the top of the frontage, and in the centre, was the red neon 'Majestic' sign, while below that was a large oblong space filled with rows of movable aluminium squares set with translucent red plastic letters. These were illuminated from behind to advertise programmes by night as well as by day.

The entrance was flanked by shops with fine bronze fronts, while on the Union Row side of the building were more shops. Five sets of double outer doors, with a pay-box on the right, led to a rather shallow foyer, reduced in depth because of space limitations in the revised design. Between the two sets of inner doors that opened into the stalls was the confectionery kiosk. On either side were flights of stairs leading upwards to the spacious first-floor balcony foyer and café, in which the latest craze was catered for by the incorporation of a milk-and-soda bar.

In the auditorium, Holophane colours outlined a shining silver proscenium arch of 'beaded' pattern. The Holophane system also traversed the ceiling in a series of troughs which extended into coves at the tops of the walls so that the effect was of a tunnel of light focusing upon the pale fawn silk velour tab curtains. Another distinctive feature of the Majestic was an abundance of little amber lamps in the ceiling under the balcony, giving a particularly pleasant feeling of cosiness when the house lights were down. The walls were painted in cream tones, the deep luxurious carpeting was in green, rose and light brown, the stalls seating in green and rose, and the balcony seating in gold. The fair-sized stage was able to cope with the usual run of variety acts, in preparation for which the screen and speakers could be hoisted out of sight. The dressing rooms were above the Union Row shops. Space was left under the stage for an organ, although one was never installed.

As always, Aberdeen tradesmen were involved in most of the building and fitting—Bruce MacKenzie, Calder & Henderson, Ogilvie's for flooring, A.B.

79   Majestic, March 1973 (M. Thomson)

Robertson, Galloway & Sykes for curtains, Roger & Baxter for plasterwork, and Alexander Masson for granite-work. The seating was made by Kalee of London, from Birmingham came the fascia lettering, and from the Newalls Acoustic Insulation Company of Glasgow came a new type of acoustic treatment for the auditorium. The projection equipment was of the very popular Simplex Super De Luxe make, and the sound system was by Western Electric.

The Majestic opened to the public on Thursday 10 December 1936 with the main feature film *Eliza Comes To Stay*. National history was in the making that day; during the programme a special bulletin was flashed on screen bearing the announcement of King Edward VIII's abdication.

Manager of the Majestic during its early years was Stanley R. McPherson, an enthusiastic young man who had started at the New Kinema at the age of 14 in the humble capacity of chocolate-seller, crying his wares over the music and chatter of a so-called 'silent' film show. Since then, his career had progressed rapidly. After a short while as relief pianist at the Torry Picture House, he had returned to the New Kinema as assistant manager, putting up such an impressive performance that at the age of only 22 he was now in charge of Aberdeen's latest Union Street 'super'. Very soon he had established himself as a popular and go-ahead figure, the flair that he showed in publicity stunts for the Majestic standing him in good stead for his other consuming

80 Stanley McPherson and staff at Dress Rehearsal for the opening of the
Majestic, December 1936 (*BA*)

interest—politics. It seems, indeed, that he was almost as well known for the
promotion of local election candidates as he was for that of films.

In early August 1938 he left for Calcutta, having been selected from a short
leet of six to take up the post of manager at the New Empire there. One
of India's most luxurious cinemas, the New Empire belonged to Humayan
Associated Theatres Ltd., a very extensive concern in what was then Bengal.
Typically, he was soon promoted to general managership of the whole circuit.
On the outbreak of war in 1939 he was made entertainments advisor to the
RAF in India, and on demob a post awaited him as a European member of
the Bengal Legislature. All his energy went into his vocation, and his political
activities flourished. While home on leave in 1945 he even found time to act
as agent for Central Aberdeenshire election candidate Sq. Leader D. Sinclair
Hay, but all of this was tragically cut short when, in August 1946, he had
to return home seriously ill. He died on 3 October of that year, aged 32.

Aberdeen cinema-goers of 1936 found a wide variety of film fare. Greta Garbo
was in *Anna Karenina*, Will Hay in *Boys Will Be Boys*, the Jack Hylton orchestra
in *She Shall Have Music*, and the young Hughie Green in *Midshipman Easy*.
Hollywood's unique interpretation of the Shakespeare play *A Midsummer
Night's Dream* was given by the once-in-a-lifetime cast of James Cagney, Dick
Powell, Olivia De Havilland, Joe E. Brown and Mickey Rooney. The latest
Astaire/Rogers musical was *Follow The Fleet*, shown simultaneously at the
Astoria (with organ interludes by Harold Titherington) and at His Majesty's
Theatre (with a stage act by 'Lambert Wilson and his Hillbillies'). Charles
Laughton and Clark Gable starred with Franchot Tone in *Mutiny On The
Bounty*, and the Marx Brothers clowned in *A Night At The Opera*. At the Palace,
a 20-piece boys' harmonica band played on stage as support act to *Sunshine
Ahead*, featuring the Jack Payne band; Jeanette MacDonald and Nelson Eddy

sang in *Rose Marie*, W.C. Fields was his inimitable self in *Poppy*, Al Jolson appeared with the Cab Calloway band in *The Singing Kid*, and Jean Harlow starred in *Riffraff, China Seas* and *Suzy*. The Capitol's Christmas treat was *The White Angel*, starring Kay Francis as Florence Nightingale. On stage was a big dancing and novelty presentation entitled 'A Dream of Christmas', in which Harold Coombs appeared at the organ as Santa Claus and all patrons received gifts.

By the end of January 1937, building work at the Queen's had reached the girder stage, and on Thursday 27 May the completed cinema opened with *Rainbow River*, featuring the now-forgotten child star Bobby Breen. The auditorium now took up virtually all available space, and the building's outward appearance was altered by the filling in of most of the windows, leaving those of the office and other facilities. The interior structure was now supported by a heavy steel frame, with a balcony and a strong new floor. The stage was at the Union Street end of the auditorium, and on to the back of the building was skilfully grafted a granite extension to accommodate the new operating box.

Seating 550 (as compared with the original 430), the new Queen's was a cheerful little place. The auditorium was decorated in warm rose tones, with bands of colours around the walls and proscenium. The wall dadoes were of walnut panelling (then becoming very popular as a decorative material), and the walls and stage grillework had the usual coloured lighting arrangements, setting off the silver and flame-coloured curtains.

The front and back stalls were separated by a wide passageway—an arrangement unique in the city. The old marble stairway from the street now ended at a small foyer, on the left of which was the paybox and two doors which led into the side of the auditorium. On the right were stairs to the small balcony, which was also entered from the side, via a little connecting platform high above the stalls. At the Union Street end of the foyer lay the manager's office, the cloakroom, and a ladies' room with mirrors and make-up tables. As before, the Queen's was very popular with those who wished to catch up on missed first runs, to see favourite films again, or simply to take advantage of its very reasonable prices.

The Queen's had not yet reopened when Messrs Donald began preliminary work on still another cinema development, this time a very large one. On 1 April 1937 the Town council put up for auction the feu on a sizeable piece of land in Frederick Street (the site of Aberdeen's original fire station). In the expectation of keen competion among interested parties, a reserve price had been put on it of £120 per annum. Potential bidders acted coolly, with no-one displaying any great anxiety to have the site. If this heightened the Council's hopes of attracting large offers, there was a shock on the way. The gathering in the Town House was duly opened, the starting price called, the Aberdeen Cinemas bid made, and then—nothing. To the amazement of the Council, the anticipated rivals sat back as if watching a show. Again and again an advance was called for, but still there was no response. Down came the hammer on the upset price, and Messrs Donald went their way rejoicing. Alongside the *Evening Express* report of the day's events (in the issue of 7 May

81   The boarded-up Palladium, 1937 (*EE*)

1937), it was made public that Messrs Donald had already acquired a piece of ground adjoining the one in question—an astute move of which the other would-be developers must certainly have been aware. The site secured, planning could now start for the KINGSWAY.

The building of the Kingsway was to be some time away, so for the present we may turn our attention to the old Gaiety/Palladium, which had lain shuttered for close on seven years. Still owned by James Archibald, it was advertised for sale in early 1937 along with the surrounding St Katherine's Court properties. Immediately, Aberdeen Picture Palaces contacted Mr Archibald and arranged a three-month option on the whole site. Bert Gates then announced plans for his company's all-time largest cinema—a 3,000 seater with its main entrance on Union Street, retaining the original St Katherine's Hall as a waiting area capable of accommodating a further 1,000.

It was anticipated that extra shares would be issued to finance the project, which was expected to cost approximately £80,000 to £90,000, plus £20,000 for the land, and that the new cinema, intended as a sister house to the City, would open at about Easter 1938. So confident was Bert Gates of being able to proceed that he went to the length of commissioning for submission to the authorities no less than five different sets of plans, of which only one set came from a local architect.

Even with its intended capacity later reduced to 2,500, this would have been a very large cinema, and it was expected to bring Aberdeen's picture hall accommodation to saturation point. In their report for the year ending 31 May 1936, the City Engineers calculated that the city possessed enough picture houses and theatres for 425,310 people to be able to see a different entertainment each week—or for every person in the city to see five different performances in a fortnight! At about the same time, *Bon-Accord* estimated Aberdeen's total cinema capacity to be in the region of 24,000 seats for a population of 175,600, giving a ratio of one seat per seven persons—more than double that of London, with its one seat per fifteen. It was clear that cinema construction in Aberdeen could not continue at such a pace for much longer, and it is understandable that the cities' two rival circuits should have wanted to make the most of whatever opportunities were left.

Had Bert Gates succeeded in securing the old Gaiety site, Aberdeen Picture Palaces would have become a major power indeed, but suddenly the company found its ambitions thwarted. On 21 August 1937 came an announcement that another offer had been made for the property—by ABC, now even larger and more powerful after having taken over Union. Of this approach Mr Archibald would initially say nothing, but on 24 August APP received the bad news that it had been outbid. 'This is a surprise and a blow to us', Bert Gates told the *Evening Express* that night, and when asked if he would be looking elsewhere, his sole response was 'Aberdeen will be over-seated now as far as picture houses are concerned.'

The coronation of King George VI on 12 May 1937 was celebrated with a morale-boosting patriotic jamboree (particularly welcome in those worrying

82 The Capitol, decorated to celebrate the Coronation, 1937 (courtesy of
Aberdeen Picture Palaces)

times as the likelihood of war with Hitler's Germany grew), and Coronation fever was as much to the fore in Aberdeen as anywhere. At a flag-bedecked Capitol, the week's feature film, *Mama Steps Out* was quite incidental to a full newsreel of the coronation ceremony (sent by air that same evening) and to the Capitol's largest-yet stage presentation, a bumper production entitled 'Dancing Through The Reigns'. Devised jointly by organist Harold Coombs and dancing teacher Babs Wilson, 'Dancing Through The Reigns' ran the full gamut from minuets and polkas, through reels, waltzes and jazz, to eccentric dancing and mime, all in lavish costumes ranging from Victorian to the very latest fashions.

The new King's coronation speech was relayed to all cinemas and theatres, and at the News Cinema coronation films were shown every half hour. A great fireworks display at the Links the next evening marked the end of Aberdeen's official celebrations, but films of the entire Westminster Abbey ceremony could be seen during the whole of the following week, particularly at the Capitol, where the Royal procession was shown in the new Cromex colour process.

Among the Majestic's live acts in April 1937 was a visit by the Aberdeen Students' Gala Week Concert Party. Harold Titherington's Astoria organ interludes often included contributions by special guests, notably Aneurin Lewis, 'The Singing Accordionist', and at the Majestic that October the Evening Express Scott Skinner Strathspey and Reel Contest was won by a young man called William Hardie, now recognised as one of the foremost Scots fiddlers.

At a special gala performance in the Regent on 6 September, a copy of Gaumont British News' Coronation edition was presented to the Lord Provost as a gift to the city, in whose archives it remains. On stage that night and all week was the large Theatre Orchestra of Haydn P. Halstead (one-time Musical Director at the Tivoli), playing selections of 'good theatre music'. That same month, Capitol organist Harold Coombs, who by that time had broadcast more than fifty times over home and foreign wavelengths, became a radio personality outwith the world of music. As compère of an unusual programme from Aberdeen entitled *Unaccustomed As We Are*, he joined such well known local BBC personalities as Willie Kemp, John Mearns and pianist Marie Sutherland in roles quite unfamiliar to the listening public.

Harold Coombs' contract expired in November 1937, and his last Capitol broadcast was transmitted on Thursday, 25 November at 11.45 am, with his farewell performance following that Saturday. His conscientiousness in making a success of his appointment at the Capitol, his gentlemanly disposition and the readiness with which he gave his services as organist or pianist in local musical events had earned him great popularity and respect, and Aberdonians were very sorry to see him go. His next post was at the new Westover Cinema, Bournemouth, and the major part of his subsequent career was spent as musical supervisor for the Westover's proprietors, ABC. In later years he became Bournemouth's Borough Organist, remaining in that capacity until his death in 1964.

On Coombs' departure from the Capitol the organ fell silent for a while, apart from occasional airings by visiting players. First of these, appearing for a week from 27 December 1937, was Jack Scott. Scots-born and trained in America, he was a member first of Union Cinemas' and then of ABC's team of organists. He went over well, the *Evening Express* hailing him as 'a corker'!

Among the many top films of the earlier part of 1937 was the annual *Big Broadcast* (this time featuring Jack Benny, Benny Goodman and Leopold Stokowski's Symphony Orchestra), *Keep Your Seats Please* starring George Formby, *Swing Time* with Fred Astaire and Ginger Rogers, Charles Laughton in *Rembrandt*, and William Powell and Myrna Loy in *The Great Ziegfeld*. A new production of *Showboat* featured the stage show's original star Paul Robeson, Bing Crosby crooned his way through *Pennies From Heaven*, and suave Jack Buchanan entertained in *This'll Make You Whistle*. In August, a Playhouse 'B' feature *The Old Corral* was the Aberdeen screen debut of cowboy hero and singer Tex Ritter. Sonja Henje demonstrated her virtuoso skating skills in *One In A Million*, and the Marx Brothers displayed their very own brand of humour in *A Day At The Races*. First seen in Aberdeen at the Capitol in September, *A Day At The Races* was chosen for a special showing to the Royal Family at Balmoral. The response was an immediate request for a repeat performance! In November the Majestic carried a huge front display of illuminated banners for Ronald Colman's *Lost Horizon*, a 'Chinese' Paul Muni and Luise Rayner won great acclaim in *The Good Earth*, and at Christmas the Capitol's main feature was *Saratoga*, Jean Harlow's last film, unfinished at her tragic death and completed using 'doubles'.

Over much of 1937, the Majestic supplemented its film programmes with double variety bills, beginning in March with Teddy Ball and his Swing Band from the Palais, and Helen St Just and Johnnie Porter in speciality songs and dances. The acts changed each week, but usually one was a dance band and the other a contrasting turn of some kind. Often bands would play on stage at the Belmont as well.

One Saturday morning in December, the Scottish Educational Film Association took over the Majestic and Astoria to give the first of an intended series of instructive picture shows for Aberdeen children. The programme consisted of documentaries on such subjects as coal-mining, the London waterfront, etc, and was liberally laced with cartoons. So many youngsters packed the two cinemas that the Association regretted not having booked a third!

Obtaining an audience in this way was easy, but by the end of 1937 smaller exhibitors throughout the country were finding it increasingly difficult to attract the public. The only way to do so was by showing the right films, but there were now far too many cinemas in Britain for the number of important releases available. As pressure on smaller concerns grew, many sold out to larger firms. The more powerful the larger firms became, the worse the squeeze on the smaller ones that remained.

83   The Majestic promoting *Lost Horizon*, 1937 (*BA*. 15 Nov. 1937)

Seeking (belatedly) to safeguard the United Kingdom's film-making industry, the Government had introduced legislation requiring a certain percentage
of the films shown in this country to be British-made, but far from boosting
investment this produced an influx of cheap and inferior 'quota quickies',
thrown together as makeweights. There could hardly have been a better way
of reaffirming Hollywood's supremacy. American films were what British
cinema-goers wanted to see, and with demand for new, good-quality features
greatly exceeding supply, competition among exhibitors was intense. Symp-
tomatically, by the beginning of 1938 there was noticeable in Aberdeen's
cinema advertising (particularly that of the independents) a new and urgent
element of hard-sell.

84   Messrs Donald discuss the Kingsway scheme with architect Leslie Rollo
(seated), 1938. Left to right, Richard Donald, Herbert Donald, James Donald,
Peter Donald

The directors of Caledonian Theatres had as much cause as any to feel
anxious. The Majestic's trading figures for 1937 constituted proof positive
that no amount of advertising and promotion could make up for lack of
booking power. An approach made by Gaumont-British in October 1937 for
control of the company might, had it succeeded, have dramatically changed
the structure of the cinema trade in Aberdeen, but it was not with GB that
Caledonian finally effected a link. Towards the end of the year Messrs Donald
made an offer for 18,500 of Caledonian's 35,000 £1 shares at a twenty-five
per cent profit to their holders, plus dividends to come later in 1938. This
met with approval at Caledonian's Annual General Meeting shortly after, and
on Tuesday, 4 January 1938 it was announced that James F. Donald (Aberdeen Cinemas) Ltd was now in control of the Majestic and the Belmont.

If signs of the times were present in the cinema world, they were also very much so in international affairs. At the beginning of February 1938, Hitler closed Germany's borders and weeded out 'unsympathetic' army officers preparatory to seizing power in Austria. That same week the News Cinema had a special film and lecture, entitled *War Is Hell*. Britain was devising Air Raid Precaution policies and black-out procedures, and vigorous recruiting campaigns were being put in motion for volunteer army organisations. Searchlights in the playgrounds of Aberdeen's Hardgate and Middle Schools were demonstrated to the public as part of the defences that it was hoped would never have to be used.

The Capitol's succession of interim organists continued with a week's engagement, from 7 March 1938, of Gaumont-British's Edward Harold. Next, in April, came a special week of interludes by student Roderick C. MacLean, organist of South St Nicholas Church, Belmont Street and composer of the music for that year's student show *Beating Time*, from which his programme included a selection. Then came Douglas Walker of ABC to play during the first fortnight of June, but finally, on Monday, 27 June, with a presentation entitled 'Holiday Reminiscences', broadcasting and recording organist F. Rowland Tims FRCO began a residency that was to last for twelve years.

Frederick Rowland Tims commenced his musical training at the Cathedral of his native town, Truro, and was for many years a church organist. In 1923, he accepted an engagement to tour variety theatres with a concert party that centred around a large transportable pipe organ. On this organ he played all kinds of music to all kinds of audiences, making easy a step into the cinema world. Between 1925 and 1934 he held the post of organist at another Capitol Cinema, that in London's Haymarket. Since that time he had played in a succession of cinemas, his last port of call having been the Odeon, Guernsey. From Guernsey he made a long journey by aeroplane to appear in Aberdeen the very same day—a first-rate publicity stunt for 1938!

He immediately set to work reinstating the organ as an important part of the Capitol's daily programme. Like his predecessor, he took part as organist and pianist in many of the city's musical performances, and before long he became organist of the nearby Gilcomston South Church. For most of their time in Aberdeen, he and his wife Violet lived in an upstairs flat at 407 Union Street, so close to the Capitol that a short-cut via operating-box, fire-escape and a few outside ledges made possible a quick and easy journey from the cinema to his own back window! The signature tune that he had always used, the Prelude to Act 3 of Wagner's *Lohengrin*, was first heard on the air from Aberdeen on Thursday, 10 November 1938 at 6 o'clock, and remained familiar through many subsequent broadcasts.

Aberdeen University students' 'Canit' Citizens Concert Party visited the Majestic for that year's Gala Week. Douglas Walker, during his brief stay at the Capitol, played the organ along with Tommy James and his Band as part of a special presentation for the early underwater adventure *Submarine D1*, while at the Astoria Harold Titherington's interludes included duets with pianist Jimmy Loughlin. In August, the Palais De Danse presented a Film Favourite Dance, at which prizes were awarded for the nearest natural resemblances to Joan Crawford and Spencer Tracy, who were starring in *Mannequin* that week at the Capitol.

That October, ARP staff were made special guests at a Picture House showing of Tyrone Power and Alice Faye's *In Old Chicago*—all about the 1906 fire! Feature films to cheer a gloomy, foreboding Christmas and New Year were in short supply, and just to further dampen any festive spirit, Christmas Day, usually the time for a family outing, fell on a cinema-less Sunday!

Great excitement surrounded a visit by Anna Neagle to the Regent on Monday 30 January 1939, in connection with the Aberdeen premiere of *Sixty Glorious Years*, a follow-up to her immensely successful 1937 historical feature *Victoria The Great*. Crowds had turned out to welcome her as she passed through the city on her way back from filming *Victoria* at Balmoral; this time Aberdonians were given the opportunity to really make a fuss of her as the city's official guest of honour. Camera shutters clicked as she posed in the very room in the Palace Hotel that Queen Victoria had used as a sitting-room on Royal visits. As part of a special tour of Aberdeen she officially set the *Evening Express* presses rolling for the edition that carried the report of the occasion.

Miss Neagle arrived at the Regent to find such a throng awaiting her that she had to stand on a chair in the cinema's entranceway in order to be seen by those at the back of the crowd, which extended almost as far as Holburn Street. Attired in a black velvet gown and small white ermine coat, she made her way, spotlit and heralded by pipes and drums, down the Regent's aisle to the stage, where she was introduced to the audience by Gordon Wingfield.

In a short speech she told of how the prospect of portraying a Queen held in such respect and affection (especially in Aberdeen with its Deeside connections) had at first made her think twice. After the success of *Victoria The Great*, however, it had occurred to her and to her director Herbert Wilcox (who she was later to marry) that there was a great deal of Victoria's life not yet touched upon, and so they had gone on to make this film. By way of a footnote, the *Evening Express* pointed out a remarkable coincidence—the showing, just twenty-five years ago that week, of *Sixty Years A Queen* at Henry Phillips' old Picturedome!

Other special cinematic events in the city during this period included another Scottish Educational Films Association show, this time at the Capitol, City and Playhouse, where over 5,000 children saw *The Last Of The Mohicans*. It was also just about the last of the occasion's organisers, who spent all morning dashing about from cinema to cinema with successive reels of their one copy of the film!

Although Messrs Donald had secured the Kingsway's site in 1937, it had been March 1938 before plans were submitted and passed. It was another full year before the building was finished, but at long last, at 3 p.m. on 1 March 1939, the Kingsway opened to the public with a programme consisting of Edward Ellis and Anne Shirley in *A Man To Remember* (described as 'a vivid drama of a fighting family doctor'), and Hugh Williams and June Clyde in *His Lordship Goes to Press*. The next day and for the rest of the week the main feature was Richard Dix in *Sky Giant*. In a speech at the opening ceremony, Baillie W.P. Milne, an old colleague of James F. Donald, spoke of their association, of how James Donald had been so proud to see his sons made Burgesses of Guild, and of how the firm had been built up from such very humble beginnings.

Designed by Leslie Rollo, the Kingsway was functional but comfortable, in accordance with its purpose of rivalling the City as large-scale provider of film entertainment at attractive prices. Above its attractive modern entranceway was a cream-coloured canopy on which large red fascia letters slid into place to advertise programmes. The elegant wood and glass outer doors gave on to a large semi-circular vestibule, built into a former shop-space on the corner of King Street and Frederick Street. Beyond that was the main waiting area, panelled in walnut, floored in light-coloured terrazzo-work, and lit entirely from concealed sources.

The 2,380-seater auditorium on Frederick Street was lit by an extensive Holophane system, the colours of which reflected from distinctive large silver flutings that took the place of grilles on either side of the proscenium. Lighting 'tubs' in the curved ceiling were integrated with and encircled by ventilation louvres. The stage curtains were in silver, the seats in the less expensive parts were in brown moquette, the balcony seats in orange velvet, and there was, as always, plenty of nice thick carpeting. Prices ranged from 4d. for the Front Stalls to 1s. for the Front Balcony.

Interestingly, on the sites of both the Kingsway and the Majestic were discovered old wells, thought to have been part of Aberdeen's domestic water supply up to and during the eighteenth century. The one at the Kingsway was found to consist of a brick-lined shaft 35 feet deep with about five feet of water in the bottom, and it still exists, covered over, beneath the auditorium.

At one point, correspondence was entered into with Compton's on the subject of an organ for the Kingsway. The type of instrument under discussion was smaller than Aberdeen's existing two and was modelled along the lines of what was currently being supplied to major circuits in the south. An organ would certainly have given the Kingsway the edge on any other cinema in that part of town, but in the event the scheme was, like many of its time, abandoned.

On 2 May 1939, Astoria patrons heard their last organ interlude by Harold Titherington, who for a while left the musical world, taking up employment at Davidson's paper mills, Woodside before moving south again. His successor at the Astoria a couple of weeks later was Charles Saxby ARCM, an excellent cinema, church and concert organist, a fine all-round musician, and a colourful, outspoken character into the bargain. Previously associated with the Paramount circuit, and well known through broadcasting and recording, he very soon found himself much in demand for autographs. The musical taste of the average Astoria audience tended towards tunes-of-the-day, but Saxby (like the Capitol's F. Rowland Tims) came of a classical background, and there was always something a little more substantial available on demand. His signature tune 'Charlie Is My Darling' always heralded a first-rate presentation.

Cinema building may have been coming to a close in Aberdeen proper, but there were still the suburbs. Large housing developments had just been opened in the Powis area, stretching out towards Woodside, which had had no cinema since the days of the old 'Rinkie'. Despite the comparative closeness of the Astoria, both Aberdeen Cinemas and Aberdeen Picture Palaces obtained sites in the extreme north-east of the city, APP's on Great Northern Road, just by the Woodside fountain, and Messrs Donald's at the other end of Marquis Road, not far away. Approval was granted in June 1939 for both companies' building proposals but neither cinema was ever built. No drawings survive of either, but it would appear from reports that APP was contemplating a 1,600-seater with no balcony, costing some £25,000. This does not suggest anything very elaborate; possibly it was to have been on the 'stadium' plan, with a raised area at the back—just like the old Queen's in 1912!

Given that Aberdeen's cinema accommodation was about to become saturated, it seems natural that promoters should have begun looking towards diversification into other entertainments. One pastime for which no facilities as yet existed in the city was indoor ice-skating. In 1937 a company called the Aberdeen Ice Rink Ltd had commissioned plans from T. Scott Sutherland (who may have been connected with the concern) for a giant ice stadium on the site of the old C. & D. Morton's preserves factory in South Mount Street, latterly the second-hand goods warehouse of 'Cocky' Hunter before being destroyed in a spectacular fire. This rink would have been Scotland's largest, accommodating in luxury the then very fashionable sport of ice-hockey, but the scheme came to nothing, and instead the site was used for an award-winning block of flats.

Donald's Ice Rink in Spring Garden (close by the Grand Central) was therefore Aberdeen's sole venture of its kind when it opened on Friday 16 June 1939 at 3 p.m. No ceremony was held—instead, to the strains of 'The Skaters Waltz' and then 'The Blue Danube', between thirty and forty participants took to the ice. Rhodesian-born instructresses Betty and Nancy Seear, who had recently taken part in a very popular ice show at His Majesty's Theatre, inspired eager learners with a virtuoso display of precision skating. Donald's Rink was not of the proportions contemplated for the Aberdeen Ice

Rink Company's building, but it could hold as many as 800 skaters at one time. Immensely popular, it held its position as the city's one and only ice rink throughout its 40-year lifespan.

The Aberdeen Ice Rink Company did attempt another large stadium, this time at the foot of Anderson Drive. The building's exterior was completed, but the outbreak of war halted any further operations. Damaged in a celebrated incident when a German fighter plane was shot down and crashed on to it in the course of a raid, it never opened as a rink. It served a variety of uses until its site was redeveloped for housing in the early 1980s.

The Torry Picture House, controlled by APP through a majority share interest since 1924, was bought over entirely in early 1939. That July it closed to have its entrances doubled in width, a neon-lit canopy added, its foyer re-organised with new pay boxes on either side, a new waiting area made, offices and operating box refitted, and AC electric supply installed. Along with a new Mirrophonic sound system came a new larger screen and new curtains. New light fittings were provided, and the auditorium was repainted in panels of pale pink. Also at this time or perhaps a little later, the none-too-flattering vertical 'Torry Cinema' sign was removed from the frontage. Permission was sought to erect a large new billboard immediately adjacent to the east side of the cinema front, but this was not allowed. By the end of August, work on the building was complete and a new film policy had been arranged, advancing the Torry's place in the circuit through the introduction of parallel programmes with the City. Everything was ready for the reopening, but the occasion had to be postponed—and for a very good reason...

Chapter 12

At War Again   1939—1945

On Friday 1 September 1939 Germany invaded Poland, and two days later Britain declared war. Immediately, Government contingency plans swung into action. As an elementary defence against night bombing, a total black-out was imposed and all exterior lights had to go out. All cinemas and theatres were closed, with no provision made for their reopening until some experience had been gained of conditions under air attack. Only then would some halls in areas not too badly affected be allowed to resume at the discretion of local authorities.

The cinema trade lodged a strong protest, and the Government was persuaded to change its mind. Taking into account the possible effects of prolonged closure on morale and on the well-being of the cinema industry, not to mention on sorely-needed tax revenue, it was decided to allow some London outer-ring cinemas to reopen on Saturday 9 September. Consideration of other areas was to follow, and among the first to be cleared was Aberdeen. The city's Chief Constable McConnach, with whom the local decision rested, initially took a cautious line, announcing that the situation would be reviewed in the course of the following week, but Aberdeen's cinemas were permitted to resume business on Monday 11 September, well ahead of the general sanction four days later. Full black-out regulations were, of course, in operation, and a national 10 o'clock curfew meant that audiences had to be in their seats by 7 pm to see the whole programme.

As soon the Regent and Palace reopened, Captain Wingfield (soon to be moved to a new post in the County Cinemas circuit) arranged a series of first-aid lectures for all cinema and theatre staffs. These were given by a recognized practitioner, and were illustrated with live demonstrations.

For some time, each cinema manager had possessed his own little mountain of ARP posters, propaganda material and Government literature on war-time do's, dont's, blackout drill, fire precautions, etc. Now, ARP films and slides were a regular part of cinema shows, and no-one was left in any doubt as to what to do in the event of an air-raid. Directly the warning went up, the manager would stop the show and go on stage to calm the audience. No-one was compelled to stay; those who wished to make for their own homes or shelters were quite free to do so, but the advice was always 'Keep Your Heads—And Your Seats'. All cinemas had been made splinterproof, and could very quickly be emptied in the normal way if necessary. On no account were gas-masks, which city dwellers were expected to carry at all times in case of chemical attack, to be put down on the floor where they could be damaged or left behind, or where injury could be caused by tripping over them.

With the opening of the Kingsway, the number of cinemas in Aberdeen reached an all-time peak of nineteen (twenty including His Majesty's Theatre, which showed films), but soon after the outbreak of war Aberdeen Picture Palaces decided to close its three oldest and least profitable halls. The area surrounding the Star was becoming depopulated as old housing in Hanover Street and Albion Street was cleared to make way for the new Beach Boulevard. Work on the Boulevard had been halted, but Bert Gates had ideas for times ahead. On 23 November 1939 he bought out Ormonde Kilgour's remaining stake in the Casino with the intention of converting the Casino and the Star almost directly behind it into a single large cinema fronting on the important new thoroughfare. Business was concentrated at the Casino, and towards the end of November the ancient 'Starrie' put its shutters up. Over New Year 1939/40 the building housed an indoor fun-fair, then for the remainder of the war years it served as the Boulevard Ballroom, where dancers had the interesting experience of trying to fox-trot up and down its raked floor!

At the beginning of 1940 the 'Globie' was also given over to the forces, as an instructional and training centre. The 'Kingie's' closed its doors at around this time and was re-let by the Northern Friendly Society as the City Ballroom, renamed Maxime's in October 1941. In November 1944, after the installation of a large new refreshment area in its former balcony, it became the Locarno, lasting in that form until January 1955 when it closed as a public hall. The building's George Street frontage was modernised in 1957 and all trace of its previous history removed. The hall remained a forgotten relic, used as workshops by an electrical firm, until about 1979 when it finally gave place to car parking space.

What films did people queue to see during these early months of the war? There was Gracie Fields in *Shipyard Sally*, Dick Powell and Ronald Reagan in *Going Places*, with its big hit song 'Jeepers Creepers', Gary Cooper's *Beau Geste*, and Cary Grant in *Only Angels Have Wings*. *I Was A Captive Of Nazi Germany* told of the experiences of an American journalist there, and Edward G. Robinson starred in *Confessions Of A Nazi Spy*. Basil Rathbone's *Hound Of The Baskervilles* was at the Picture House, while at the Regent and Palace Aberdonians had their first sight of Lupino Lane singing and dancing one of the great hits of the day—*The Lambeth Walk*.

The year 1940 saw the end of the quiet Phoney War period and the start of German air-raids on military and civilian targets. With this came a greater sense of purpose and cameraderie among the population. Grumbles about black-outs, ARP wardens and shortages lessened. The instant cataclysm dreaded by many had not materialised, and morale was much heightened by the bulldog determination of the new Prime Minister, Winston Churchill. Everywhere were posters with war-time slogans, and in cinema foyers film publicity sheets (now strictly rationed) had to a great extent been replaced by such messages as the Land Army's 'Dig For Victory' or the celebrated 'If You've Got Secret Information—Keep It Dark'. Other propaganda urged cinemagoers to help the war effort in various ways, such as saving food and materials in order to beat Germany's blockade of Britain.

As in the First World War, Aberdeen cinema proprietors were very quick to put themselves about in the matter of charity shows, sending £700 to the War Comforts Fund during the first few months of 1940 alone. A typical example of the Sunday cine-variety concerts that raised this money was one given at the Capitol and Astoria in March, with turns by the organists, a team of singers, a comedian, a hand-bell soloist, a conjuror, and pianist Lena Dunn. At both cinemas the show was rounded off with a liberal helping of cheerful community singing!

The phenomenally successful *The Wizard Of Oz*, starring young Judy Garland, received its Aberdeen premiere at the Astoria and H.M. Theatre on Monday 15 April 1940. In the *Evening Express'* cinema advertisements of Monday 29 April the line 'Garbo Gets Tight—At The Capitol' heralded the arrival of *Ninotchka*, its star's first attempt at comedy. Strangely enough, this gem of tasteful wording is absent from the next issue of the *Express* onwards. As summer approached, further attractions included Basil Rathbone and Nigel Bruce in *Sherlock Holmes*, Gary Cooper and newcomer David Niven in *The Real Glory*, Marlene Dietrich and James Stewart in *Destry Rides Again*, and Leslie Howard and Ingrid Bergman in *Escape To Happiness*. The Fleischer studio tried its hand at full-length cartoon-making in *Gulliver's Travels*, but Walt Disney soon proved his supremacy with *Pinocchio*, which spent a whole three weeks at the Picture House that September.

Monday 16 September brought the gala opening, at the Capitol, of *Gone With The Wind*. Its booking fee was so high that admission prices had to be doubled to 3s. 6d. and 6s. for reserved seats, and 2s. for unreserved. This caused Bert Gates some apprehension, but it proved groundless. *Gone With The Wind* was among the greatest-ever box-office hits, and it set a record for the Capitol with a run that lasted for four weeks.

By the end of the year, Pétain's capitulation had brought about Vichy France, London was experiencing the blitz in all its fury, and over the whole of Britain there hung the grim threat of invasion. The street railings with which Aberdeen had bristled since the nineteenth century were vanishing as all non-essential metalwork that could legally be removed was salvaged for munitions. Strict regulations were on the way to prohibit wastage of food, and ration cards had long been accepted as part of everyday life, as had their inseparable companion the black market.

Cinemas, as busy public buildings, came to occupy a position of their own in the front line as enemy action on cities intensified. Aberdeen had its share of bombing and strafing raids, but although some apprehension may have been felt at the Astoria, just across the road from the Kittybrewster railway yards, no serious incident occurred involving any of the city's picture houses. Each major cinema (and possibly some of the smaller ones as well) had firewatchers who looked after the building and kept an eye on the surrounding ones. Should incendiaries be dropped, it was vital to guard the space above the auditorium ceiling, where those nasty lumps of burning chemical would be likely to lodge if they pierced the roof. If caught in time they could be smothered with the large buckets of sand that came along with the standard war-time kit of hoses, stirrup pumps, sandbags and anti-splinter window tape, but they became far more of a menace when the Germans started equipping them with explosive charges!

In particular, the Majestic's flat roof required vigilance. It also afforded an excellent vantage point over the city, and for these reasons the Majestic was made an ARP post, with teams of volunteers more or less living in the building. It had the edge on the Astoria, higher up but much farther away, in the superb panoramic view that it commanded of the harbour and of the periodic attacks on the shipyards and departing ocean convoys. At such times bombs and tracer would light up the night sky with an aerial display almost unreal in its magnificence, and 'dog-fights' would be plainly visible far out over the sea. The Majestic also had an air-raid siren, perched high above the corner of Union Street and Union Row, in close proximity to the operating box. This siren could if necessary be activated from the box, but for most if not all of the time it was remote-controlled, making the post of operator at the Majestic rather unsuitable for those of a nervous disposition.

When the sirens signalled a raid, some of Aberdeen's cinema audiences would leave for the shelters, but the majority, determined not to be done out of their entertainment by those blasted Jerries, stayed stolidly put. This attitude was not confined to Aberdonians. There is a true story about one London cinema which took no less than twelve incendiaries on its roof, but yet the audience would not leave until forcibly ejected by the Fire Brigade, amid sparks and plaster! In fact, a solid steel and concrete structure like a cinema afforded ideal protection from strafing and provided excellent shelter from any bombing short of a direct hit. Even then, when a large high-explosive bomb landed right on one of the Granada circuit's London houses during a performance, the casualty list among an audience of several hundred was remarkably small.

Just on the eve of war in 1939, the Regent had entered upon a new phase in its existence, following a merger between County Cinemas and the large Odeon circuit. Again its staffing remained unchanged, but at the end of July 1940 the 'Regent' sign came down to be replaced by one that read ODEON, the cinema's official designation as of the 29th of that month. The former Poole's Regent could now rival even the Picture House for major features, and while Scottish premieres still came the way of local independents, the balance was tipping in favour of the large national companies.

Astoria organist Charles Saxby's engagement ended in June 1940, and the only time that the organ was heard between then and October was when a player by the name of Jack Lawson paid a short visit at the end of September. As of Monday 21 October, however, the Astoria had a new resident organist—'The Broadcasting Organist' Bobby Pagan.

A native of Cupar, Fife, Bobby was originally expected to enter his family's legal firm, but music beckoned and in 1926 he became a full-time cinema organist. After several cinema appointments he had ended up at the Trocadero, Elephant And Castle, London, playing the largest Wurlitzer organ in Britain. During his stay there he appeared as guest at the Palladium, Copenhagen, which also sported a Wurlitzer.

Shortly after Bobby's return from Copenhagen came news that the Trocadero organ was to be closed down 'for the duration'. Hearing, via Compton's, of the Astoria vacancy, he made enquiries and very soon was on his way, together with his wife and three small sons, to Aberdeen. The author, on inquiring of Bobby about his Astoria days, received such a full, courteous and interesting reply that, for the flavour of the times as much as for the peripheral subject of Aberdeen's cinema organs and organists, there can be no-one better to tell this part of the story than Bobby himself:

The Astoria made a tremendous impression on me from various points of view. I had recently returned (reluctantly) from Copenhagen, and the Kittybrewster cinema had much to induce nostalgia with its uniforms so similar and the spotless appearance of the theatre, looking as if it might have been opened the day before. I was later to learn a Naval expression about a clean ship—'you could eat your scran off the deck'. That could be said of all the Donald cinemas.

It was something of a novelty to slide out on rails playing the signature tune against the sometimes violent jerks of the handle, cranked on occasions by a small breathless boy. On that first night I remember playing as an encore 'The Breeze And I' (sometimes known as 'Andalusia'), and going off to tremendous applause, having arranged with the handle-cranker to take it slowly so I could do the train noises. Off to a good start!

The Astoria audiences by this time were predominantly female with so many men already in the Services, but there were many visitors from the RAF at Dyce. One of the advantages was that there was no nearby property to disturb, and the presence of fire-watchers made it possible to be in the building and rehearse far into the night. This proved to be invaluable when one recalls that the film programme changed on Thursdays and the general policy was a fifteen minute recital and a Sing-Along on Saturdays, the first of which in the early afternoon was slanted for the children (Roy Rogers, Trigger, Gabby Hayes, Blondie ... Ah yes, I remember it well!)

Then of course there was the additional business of playing for at least twenty minutes at 'Doors Open', so it will be seen that the week expended a great deal of material.

In that context, I recall that Aberdeen could frequently be isolated by wintry conditions, whereby 'Film Transport' could be completely defeated and there would be no film on a Monday. On one such day I went to the organ at 1.25, and some forty-five minutes later I was still playing. This was after I had started appearing in the kilt, and by this time that wee bit of skin between the back of the knee and the stocking was getting well and truly scorched by the decorative coloured lighting which was even in the surround of the stool. I turned round and said 'I'm sure you will understand if I turn off the lighting ... I wonder how many of you have ever sat on a thing like this for three quarters of an hour in a kilt?' Time went on and I was just about running out of material, and said so. A lady in the stalls who I remember gratefully to this day said 'What about The Desert Song?' Bless her; you can spin that one out for at least twenty minutes. During that 'life-saver' I got the signal that a stand-by film had come in!

Bobby Pagan's arrival at the Astoria coincided with Trafalgar Day; also significant for him was the anniversary, in the Spring of 1941, of the Battle of Jutland—it was the day on which he received his call-up to the Navy! During his periods of leave he returned to make appearances in uniform (always assured of a good round of applause), and to broadcast as the last item in the Sunday night Forces Programme. This, as Bobby relates, resulted in his name being mentioned in very high places:

> The then Alan Herbert, in the House of Commons, was campaigning vigorously for some let-up in the restrictions on Sunday entertainments. He took the House through the Sunday Radio Times, concluding with the words 'and finally we close down with Bobby Pagan at the cinema organ'. Sticklers for accuracy are welcome to check with Hansard, but I believe, subject to correction, that Sandy [MacPherson] and I are the only cinema organists to have been mentioned in the House!

On Monday 7 October 1940, increased Entertainments Tax reduced the number of cheap cinema seats and finished altogether the 'penny' (or, at least, the cut-price) matinee. That same day, new regulations were introduced in Aberdeen, easing pressure on sparse train and bus services by staggering cinema closing hours so that only one house at a time was allowed to empty in each part of town. This measure, which had the additional effect of alleviating pressure on shelter accommodation during raids, involved the city's division into three areas, closing at 10.00, 10.15 and 10.30 respectively, and alternating with one another on a rota.

As in the First World War, convalescent servicemen received VIP treatment in cinemas, and that Christmas the Co-ordinated Scheme Of War Comforts gave a special seasonal treat at the Capitol for wounded sailors. By the end of the year, Messrs Donald were in process of setting up regular monthly Sunday war charity film shows, under a committee consisting of the Lord Provost, Sheriff Laing, Messrs Herbert, Richard and James R. Donald, Frank McGuggan, and Wilson H. Smith.

By 1941, forces' entertainments were well organised. On Sunday 12 January a Garrison Theatre (with Bert Gates as a member of its governing committee) was inaugurated at the Music Hall by popular actor Jack Warner. It was an

DONALD'S and ASSOCIATED CINEMAS

PRESENT A

SUNDAY CONCERT

AT THE

KINGSWAY CINEMA

On SUNDAY, 3rd MAY, 1942

At 7-30 p.m.

IN AID OF WAR CHARITIES.

   STALLS, 1/-

85   Ticket to a Donald Bros war charities concert, 1942 (courtesy of Coral
Social Club, Kingsway)

instant success, and on Sunday 9 March it moved to the Capitol, where
visiting acts, local entertainers and troops appeared in more commodious
surroundings.

Between December 1940 and March 1941 the Casino hosted a series of
troop-orientated stage variety shows and revues, the casts of which included
servicemen. The season began with 'New Year Revels'. This was performed
entirely by visitors, but in its successors 'Sparkles' (a revuette), 'Scotch Follies
Of 1941' (presented by comedian Harry Harper), 'The Talk Of The Town'
(variety) and 'Gossips And Grumbles' a large part was played by local people.

There next took place two events which are of great importance to our story.
First of these was the purchase by Messrs Donald of a controlling interest in
their long-time rival, Aberdeen Picture Palaces. In June 1936 A.D. Hay,
senior partner in APP, had died, followed in April 1937 by his brother W.D.
Hay and then by his wife only three weeks after that. Finally, in April 1938,
Mr Hay's youngest son Arthur G.T. Hay, returning from a day in the country,
complained of head pains. Hours later he too was dead. The Hay family's
connection with Aberdeen Picture Palaces was severed, and much of the

86   Aberdeen Picture Palaces Directors. Left to right, Mrs A.D. Hay, Mr and Mrs A. Johnston Hay, Mr and Mrs Bruce Mackenzie, Mr and Mrs J.M. Clapperton, Mr and Mrs B.H. Gates and Mr A.D. Hay (*BA* 21 Feb. 1936)

driving force went out of the company. On the death in 1939 of accountant Patrick Jeffrey, Bert Gates and the rest of his directors, all advancing in years, were left to face the pressures of a changing world.

Odeon was in town, and ABC was on its way. The war was affecting attendances (only a small decrease may have been required to close the three old cinemas), and of APP's remaining halls only the City and Capitol were doing really good business. Should either of these have been put out of action, the company would have been in difficulties. It was therefore felt that the time had come to arrange a takeover. Feelers were put out, attracting a very substantial offer from Gaumont-British, and dialogue was entered into with other cinema concerns as well. There is a story that one of the Donald brothers, meeting Bert Gates on the steps of James Clapperton's office one day, was hailed with an inquiry as to how he would like to 'buy the Capitol'. This anecdote may or may not have substance, but, adhering to the facts, an offer from Messrs Donald for a majority interest in Aberdeen Picture Palaces was submitted and accepted, and the transaction's conclusion was announced on Friday 23 May 1941.

Of APP's £1 share issue, the normal fifty-one per cent changed hands,

while the remainder was converted into half-and-half 10s. Ordinary and
Cumulative Preference shares, with interest on the first part at 6 per cent,
and on the second part at twelve per cent. The price of each share was 25s.,
the same as for Caledonian's in 1938, and it was agreed that should the
company be wound up, a 10s. premium would be paid on all Preference
holdings. Of APP's directors, Bruce MacKenzie and James Hill retired in favour
of the Donald brothers, but Bert Gates stayed on, retaining a close interest in
the firm until his death in 1952. Bruce MacKenzie died in the mid-1950s,
and James Hill in 1946, aged 89. The Eastern Star bar, on the corner of East
North Street and Park Street, was still known as 'Jimmy Hill's' when progress
caught up with it about 1970, leaving in its place a corner of the present
traffic roundabout at the top of the Beach Boulevard.

87   During the Second World War women returned to cinema operating
boxes. Mrs Helen Morrison at the Picture House projectors in February 1942
(BA)

The second important event of 1941 was the arrival upon the national cinema scene of a man by the name of J. Arthur Rank. Rank, who had made his fortune as a miller, was a devout Methodist. During the 1930s he bought studios and began the production of short religious films, only to meet with a lukewarm response from the exhibition trade. Deciding to enter into cinema ownership on his own account, he did so in style by purchasing control of not one but two of this country's largest circuits. First of these was Odeon, on the death of its founder and major shareholder Oscar Deutsch. Only months later came Gaumont-British when its chairman Isidore Ostrer sold his shares. Combined as the Circuit Managements Association, this conglomerate was powerful in the extreme, succeeding in buying back a large American holding in Gaumont-British. Apprehensive of monopolies, the Government insisted that considerable autonomy be given to the erstwhile rival companies, but for administrative purposes the two were more or less merged.

J. Arthur Rank's own influence was enormous. One of his first acts on becoming a cinema proprietor was to put into practice his personal dictum that children should see 'the right films in the right atmosphere'. His extensive studios were soon busily turning out features and shorts specifically designed for showing to youngsters at Saturday morning Mickey Mouse Clubs. Initiated in the mid-1930s by Gaumont-British and a few independents, these clubs were built by Rank into a national institution; come better times they would be introduced at all three of his Aberdeen cinemas.

Donald's and their subsidiary cinemas' war charity scheme was inaugurated one Sunday in July 1941 by Lord Provost Mitchell and Sheriff Laing with a showing, at the Majestic, of the feature film *She Shall Have Music*. Further attractions of the time were *The Road To Zanzibar* with Bing Crosby, Bob Hope and Dorothy Lamour, *Penny Serenade* with Cary Grant, and the Aberdeen premiere (at the Picture House that October) of Walt Disney's renowned *Fantasia*. Anton Walbrook was in *Dangerous Moonlight*, from which came the oft-heard 'Warsaw Concerto'. 'Big-hearted Arthur' Askey (of 'Bandwaggon' fame) starred in *I Thank You*, named after his well-known catch-phrase. When *Target For Tonight* (an extremely popular production about British bomber crews) reached the Odeon in September, invalid airmen paraded to a special matinee premiere. At the end of that evening's performance, Flying Officer Whiteside gave a special address in which he described the film as a 'striking impression' of the RAF's bravery, and urged young men to come forward and volunteer.

The News Cinema was still making its own local newsreels, and on the night of Friday 31 October the cameramen captured on film a unique document of the tragic fire that completely destroyed the upper part of the Palace Hotel, claiming six lives. Official war-time newsreels were popular for more than just information or propaganda value; many patrons watched them avidly in the hopes of catching a glimpse of a husband, friend or relative among the hundreds of troops that passed in front of the camera. At the Odeon in October 1940, a lady thought she spotted her Signaller brother, who had been reported missing at the time of Dunkirk. The Odeon's manager of the time, Mr Eric Robyns, arranged to have the film run for her in slow motion the next morning, and while the lady could not positively identify her brother, she left in a hopeful frame of mind. Awaiting her at home was the news that he was safe!

An old army 'regular' and First World War Captain, Mr Robyns came to Aberdeen as replacement for Gordon Wingfield. In mid 1941 he was transferred to the Palace, his place at the Odeon being taken by Mr Wilfred Pryor, one of the original Poole's staff. Soon Mr Pryor was called to the RAF, and for the rest of the year the Odeon was supervised by Mr Alexander Webster from the Pavilion, Airdrie. At one time, Mr Webster had been a well known London concert and oratorio tenor, and had subsequently appeared in variety halls with his wife as 'Alberta, Brilliant Violinist, and Her Tenor', the two reaching the Tivoli, Aberdeen during their travels.

Down in the Shiprow nothing stirred. ABC had not received official approval for its new cinema until March 1939, and scarcely had building operations begun before war was declared. Work had continued at a very slow pace, but in 1941 the project fell foul of a Government priorities regulation halting all further construction of this class of building unless roofing had begun. As the roofing stage had not yet been reached, all that could be finished was the outer shell. The new Union Street entranceway was boarded up, and the scene remained one of near-desolation for more than a decade.

Russia's entry into the war was accompanied by a wave of pro-Soviet propaganda, typified by the Ministry of Information film *Salute To The Soviet*, of which a special showing was given at the Grand Central on Sunday 7 December, 1941 (the day of the Japanese bombing of Pearl Harbour). Among the screen attractions of 1942 could be found *Ziegfeld Girl*, starring Judy Garland and James Cagney, *A Yank In The RAF* with Tyrone Power and Betty Grable, and a film version of the radio show *Hi, Gang*, featuring Bebe Daniels (her first screen appearance in years), Ben Lyon and Vic Oliver. Sonja Henje was equal attraction to the Glenn Miller Orchestra in *Sun Valley Serenade* at the Capitol in March, while that same week the Majestic had Orson Welles' celebrated (and controversial) *Citizen Kane*. Favourites later in the year included Will Hay in *The Goose Steps Out*, and Alan Ladd and Veronica Lake in *The Glass Key*.

It had long been common for Aberdeen cinema proprietors to show the same film programme simultaneously in different parts of town. County Cinemas began this practice at the Regent and Palace in 1936, APP's 'second-run' houses took it up after the opening of the City in 1935, and Messrs Donald also adopted it as the size of their circuit grew. Now, after the joining of the APP and Donald circuits, the Kingsway was added to the usual combination of Majestic (now sometimes the Capitol instead) and Astoria for particularly important features. Under this system were presented Greer Gar-

son and Walter Pidgeon's *Mrs Miniver*, Bogart in *The Maltese Falcon*, Phil
Silvers' and Jimmy 'Schnozzle' Durante's *You're In The Army Now*, and the
world premiere of Vera Lynn's *We'll Meet Again*.

Throughout the war, cinema organists gave yeoman service in aiding morale.
At the Capitol, F. Rowland Tims ran a scheme whereby servicemen abroad
were invited to send in requests for their folk at home. The dedicatees were
then made special guests to hear the number played just for them—a personal
touch which meant a lot. BBC staff organist Sandy MacPherson was presenting, on the foreign wavelengths, a regular series of programmes entitled
'Sandy Calling', in which friends, wives and relatives of troops overseas read
out their own messages on the air and Sandy played a request for each. These
broadcasts were transmitted live from organ-equipped cinemas all over Britain
(although the possibility of air attack made it impossible to publish locations
in advance), and Aberdeen's turn came on 1 May, 1942. Between 6.30 and
7.30 that night, musical greetings went out from the Capitol to the other side
of the world, compered by Sandy, the first organist to become a national radio
personality in his own right.

Amid the seemingly countless re-runs of *Gone With The Wind*, the Aberdeen
filmgoer of early 1943 could find a wide choice of other material. Titles like
Counter Espionage and *Nazi Agent* (the latter film starring Conrad Veidt, himself
a refugee from Hitler's regime) were still current, but there was now a
noticeable shift of emphasis from war adventures to musicals and sophisticated comedies and dramas. At the Capitol, Kingsway and Astoria over
the week of 17 May 1943, Aberdonians first saw *Casablanca*, one of the best-
remembered films of the war years and surely the most quoted-from of all.
Later in 1943, Anton Walbrook and Deborah Kerr played the lead roles in
The Life And Death Of Colonel Blimp, Flanagan & Allen were in *Theatre Royal*,
and Laurel & Hardy played a pair of comic air-raid wardens in *Jitterbugs*.

Although the authorities turned down applications from the national cinema trade for Forces' special Sunday shows to be opened to the public, the
public was quick enough to applaud the presence of wounded and convalescent servicemen at normal shows. Repatriated P.O.W.s also came in
for attention; Aberdeen soldier Alex Clunes returned from captivity that
November to find himself quite a celebrity, with a guest singing 'spot' at the
Capitol as part of the festivities!

Newspapers of this time carry reports of a hitherto unheard-of phenomenon
which manifested itself all over Britain and from which Aberdeen was not
immune—a sudden and unexplained plague of seat-ripping. For no apparent

reason, seats in cinemas, on buses and in other public places were being attacked with knives, scissors, or any other sharp article that came to hand. These senseless actions gave rise to great concern, coming as they did at a time of such shortages in man-power and materials. The persons responsible would have had more to think about had they been sitting in the cinemas of Germany or occupied Europe, where Nazi propaganda was pumped out non-stop under the eyes of armed guards. In 1941, members of the audience in a Berlin picture house were shot by the SS for repeatedly shouting 'We want no war' during a particularly gruesome Nazi film. The Dutch author Jan de Hartog, on escaping to Britain in September 1943, wrote in the national press of how the large cinemas in Amsterdam, Rotterdam and other cities in his native country had more or less become centres of resistance against the invaders. One night a whole audience suddenly took a violent fit of sneezing each time a German uniform was seen in one of the newsreels, and shouted 'One-Two-One-Two' when the hated Gauleiter Seyss-Inquhart appeared on the screen. Silence was restored only when the lights went up and German revolvers were pointed from all corners of the house.

In the course of an anti-black-market propaganda film in Amsterdam, there came into the picture a ship with the word 'Orange' (the name of the Dutch Royal Family) on its bow. Immediately, up went the Dutch National Anthem. The houselights came on and the manager begged silence, but when the film resumed the operator had rewound to the same scene, and exactly the same thing happened. This time a large uniformed Dutch Nazi jumped up on the stage shouting 'Who began this riot?' An entire houseful yelled back 'The Jews'—a calculated insult, as the Germans' first act on occupation had been to ban all Jews from cinemas. That got the place closed for a week, but no doubt there were plenty of further opportunities for the people of Amsterdam to continue their own brand of warfare.

Never mind what Lord Haw-Haw said, by 1944 the course of the conflict was turning decisively against Germany. Hitler, in desperation at the failure of his 'lightning war', was trying to smash London and the strategic South Coast ports with his new V-1 rocket (and later the V-2, or 'doodlebug'), but the worst of the bombing was over. Even in Britain's most heavily blitzed areas cinema attendances were improving, much to the relief of proprietors and managers.

A return visit to the Capitol by Sandy MacPherson in March 1944—this time for a Forces programme, 'Sandy's Half Hour'— came in happier times as the Nazis were slowly but surely beaten back in Europe. September 1944 brought the liberation of Paris and Brussels; Allied offensives gained momentum, and by April 1945 invasion forces were swarming over Germany. (The Capitol's main feature just at that time was You Can't Do That To Me!) On 2 May, 1945 Hitler committed suicide, and five days later Germany surrendered.

At last, the long-awaited ending of the black-out was announced, although

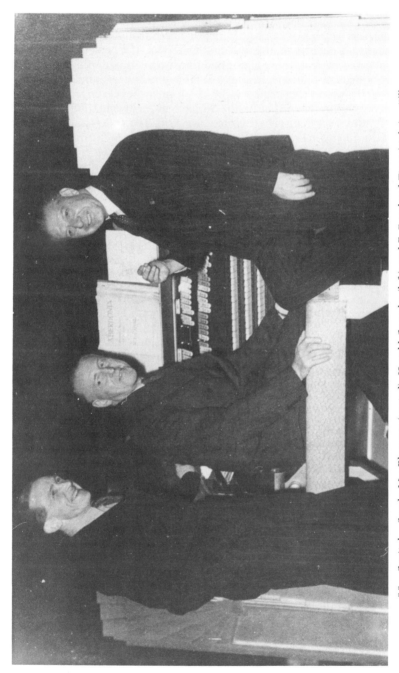

88 Capitol—Sandy MacPherson (seated), Harold Coombs (left) and F. Rowland Tims (right)—'I'll Play To You' Broadcast, 28 August 1945. On the music stand is a copy of 'Aberdonia' by R.E. Cahill

(*BA*)

it would be a full five years before power restrictions were eased enough to allow use of all the exterior light fittings that had been receiving anticipatory overhaul since the end of 1944. Bonfires blazed on Tullos and Broad Hills, and pre-war size queues waited to see such films as *He Snoops To Conquer*, starring doyen of troop entertainers George Formby, *Arsenic And Old Lace* with Cary Grant, *Dodsworth* with David Niven and Mary Astor, and Latin American extravaganzas *Down Argentine Way* with Don Ameche and Carmen Miranda, and *Brazil* with Virginia Bruce.

After the nuclear bombings of Hiroshima and Nagasaki, Japan formally surrendered and the war was over. Official news of this reached Aberdeen in a special edition of the *Press & Journal* distributed in the first few minutes of V-Day, Wednesday 15 August. Straight away, the accumulated tension of six years of war, plus all the worry and uncertainty that preceeded it, erupted in a great surge of high-spirits. By the 29th the resulting demand for celebratory drinks had soaked up most of the city's limited beer supply, leading to a virtually pub-less week-end, but the cinemas were ready with plenty of fun that carried the advantage of having no unpleasant after-effects.

On 28 August 1945, Sandy MacPherson made his third and final visit to the Capitol for an edition of his long-running programme 'I'll Play To You'. This was a bumper affair with singers, pianist Ruby Duncan, F. Rowland Tims and a special guest appearance by Harold Coombs, who had been invited back to make the occasion even more memorable.

With many old friends in the North, Harold Coombs never forgot Aberdeen. One day in the early 1960s, quite out of the blue, the Capitol's manager Jack Wright received a telephone call from him. He was just wondering if the old place was still there. Mr Wright was able to assure him that indeed it was!

Chapter 13

Before The Flood   1946—1955

Once again, the politicians' 'New Britain' started somewhat inauspiciously, with high unemployment as men were demobbed from the Forces. The years 1946 to 1950 were an austere period, with fuel and commodities remaining scarce and food still subject to rationing as, for the second time, Britain's shattered economy rebuilt itself after war. Once again, with few other amusements affordable or available, cinema-going boomed, although this time the boom period was brief. Unlike during the First World War, the British film industry had flourished between 1939 and 1945, and was now in an unaccustomedly healthy condition. Top feature films, while in shorter supply than during the war years, were by no means scarce.

Still prominent among Aberdeen's 'bright spots' was Donald's Ballroom, North Silver Street, where at New Year 1945-46 one of the North-East's first Hammond organs was introduced, providing music for dancing while the resident band, David Main And His Music, had its breaks. Organist was Bobby Pagan, who had resumed his duties at the Astoria on demob in November 1945; during Bobby's holidays F. Rowland Tims took over as deputy. Unfortunately, Bobby was lost to Aberdeen when, in September 1946, someone in the depths of BBC Glasgow decided that cinema organs, even when played in Scotland by a Scot, were not Scottish enough to be retained on Northern schedules. Off went the Astoria from the air, and off went Bobby back to London, leaving F. Rowland Tims at the ballroom organ for the time being.

In May 1947 live music returned to the Astoria with a year's engagement of Norman Whitehead, 'The Rhythm Organist'. Taking over duties at the ballroom, he also deputised at the Capitol when Mr and Mrs Rowland Tims went on holiday to the Mediterranean that August. Coming so soon after the war, and bearing in mind the economic circumstances of the time, the couple's journey was remarkable enough for the *Evening Express* of 8 September, 1947 to carry a substantial piece on it, written by F. Rowland Tims himself and describing their travels around the Riviera and the Côte d'Azure. Trips nearer home were also very much to their liking, and motoring through Aberdeenshire and up into the Deeside hills was a recreation of which they never tired.

1947 is generally held to have brought some of the coldest spells of winter weather ever, made worse by fuel restrictions and threats of power cuts if

89   Bobby Pagan at the organ of the Astoria, 1940s

voluntary saving of electricity was not effective. February broke a 100-year record for frost, and March topped that when Aberdeen harbour froze solid.

Cinemas were always nice and warm, although the choice of films for the public to go and see in them continued to be a little narrow, and would become more so. In a misguided bid to stem the drain of dollars from Britain, the Government slapped a punitive 75 per cent tax on the revenue going to

America from UK releases—based not on what was being earned, but on what the Government thought would be earned in the future! The movie moguls of Hollywood retaliated by stopping all further exports of films to Britain, so that when the stockpile of new features ran out at the end of 1947, all that was left was a pile of reissues. Britain's film studios, which were geared to producing only a tenth of the number of films shown in the nation's cinemas each year, were unable to fill the gaps. Negotiations for the export of British films to America were wrecked, and soon the British cinema exhibition industry was heading for serious trouble. The measure was repealed in 1948.

Typical of the films of 1948 were Charlie Chaplin's sophisticated *Monsieur Verdoux*, Betty Grable in *Song Of The Islands*, Bogart and Bacall in *Dark Passage*, William Graham and Garry Marsh in *Just William's Luck*, and Alan Ladd and Veronica Lake in *Saigon*. *Blythe Spirit* starred Rex Harrison, and the young Richard Attenborough portrayed a villain in *Brighton Rock*.

Saturday morning children's shows at the Odeon, Palace and Picture House had, since their reintroduction in 1947, more than lived up to their good name, but still not everybody was happy. In a lecture given to the YMCA in December 1948, calling for a national open-air recreation drive, the Children's Hour film critic, Mr Eric Gillett, made a well-publicised assertion that in his opinion children would be far happier out-of-doors than sitting in cinemas. Had he put his statement to the test he would have found himself over-whelmingly outvoted. In those days the cinema held boundless fascination for the young mind, and all the greater was its addictiveness when along with it came the sense of fun and 'club spirit' so effectively fostered by Arthur Rank. Saturday mornings at the pictures remained unassailably the high spot of the week for countless youngsters, not just in Aberdeen but throughout Britain.

Over the Christmas season, the Rank houses, with the enthusiastic participation of their patrons, perpetuated Aberdeen's charitable tradition by placing in their foyers Christmas trees hung with gifts for children in care and in hospitals. Just before New Year, Messrs Donald (who had raised £15,000 for charities between the outbreak of war and 1946) resumed their special Sunday shows, this time in aid of a Christmas party fund for children in care, and with that pleasant thought we turn to 1949.

The Royal Command film of 1949 was John Mills in *Scott Of The Antarctic*; also popular was a new series of *Huggets* features, based on the long-running radio series and featuring Jack Warner and Kathleen Harrison. Laurence Olivier's screen interpretation of *Hamlet* was shown at the Odeon's first-ever long season that February, *Floodtide* was the first film to headline Gordon Jackson, and the cast of *A Boy, A Girl And A Bike* included the young Honor Blackman. Bogart and Bacall brought the crowds out again to see *Key Largo*, and the celebrated *Whiskey Galore* spent a fortnight at the Picture House on its first run that August.

One of the great controversial issues that year, on which endless impassioned argument raged, was the Labour Government's commitment to nationalisation of key industries. Nowhere were mistrust and apprehension more acutely felt than in the film studios, where the very thought of ending up under the control of politicians was enough to conjure up all the dire visions contained in George Orwell's recently-published novel *1984*. The open championing by certain trade unions of state ownership in the film industry did nothing to alleviate fears, although it was pointed out that the film medium was able to relay more than just one colour of propaganda!

The threat of nationalisation turned out to be the least of the trade's worries. The cinema's surge of popularity during and just after demob was expending itself. Both Rank and ABC still made films, but their commitment was now turning increasingly towards the financially safer exhibition side of the business. The British public was becoming less inclined to go to the pictures as a matter of habit and more minded towards choosing specific films that caught its fancy—a trend which caused considerable dismay nationally, but was not unheard of in Aberdeen! Probably more directly damaging was the Government's refusal to reduce Entertainment Tax, increased on three occasions during the war and now standing at a little over 40 per cent of the industry's gross annual takings of £109 million. The UK cinema trade had already entered upon a slow decline.

In 1950 came the welcome de-rationing of sweets and petrol. Shoppers at the New Year sales found the greatest-yet reductions in prices since the war. The world was brought firmly into the nuclear age when news leaked out that Russia had built its own H-bombs, while at the General Election that year a 'warmonger' campaign against Churchill was partly instrumental in putting the Labour Party back in office—the defeated candidate for North Angus and Mearns being the well-known film and radio personality James Robertson Justice.

The Rank group began 1950 with the first of what were to be many rationalisation moves, reshuffling the names of its cinemas so that most of the mixed bag of Picture Houses, Regents, New Victorias, etc, that had been inherited from Gaumont-British, PCT before it, and through other takeovers, became standardised as Gaumonts if no cinema of that name already existed in the town. Odeons generally remained unchanged. Under this policy, Aberdeen's Picture House was rechristened the GAUMONT on Monday 22 March, with a large new vertical neon sign on the front of the building—a luxury made possible by the relaxation of power restrictions only a few months before.

Films of 1950 included Orson Welles and Joseph Cotten in *The Third Man*, Jack Warner, Jimmy Hanley and Dirk Bogarde in *The Blue Lamp*, and Gregory Peck's *12 O'Clock High*. The celebrated *Treasure Island*, starring Bobby Driscoll and Robert Newton, arrived in August, while on 20 November *Annie Get Your Gun*, starring Betty Hutton and Howard Keel, began a two-week run which created the Capitol's all-time box-office record.

90   George Blackmore at the organ of the Astoria, 1954

On 20 March 1950, the Astoria organ's illuminated console slid out on to the stage with a new resident player at its keys—George Blackmore, formerly of the Gaumont, Birmingham. Born in Rochester, George underwent his early musical training at the Cathedral there. Seeing the theatre organ's great possibilities, he soon mastered its intricacies and became organist at Rochester's Majestic Cinema, from where he soon began broadcasting. After war service in the RAF he toured Scotland as director of a small RAF dance band, and while visiting Aberdeen met his future wife, London-born singer Joyce Hampton. The Blackmores enjoyed great popularity as a musical team, appearing frequently at the Astoria and elsewhere.

In the Summer of 1950, F. Rowland Tims retired from the cinema world to concentrate on his other musical activities, which by that time included the post of organist at West St Andrew's Church (nowadays Langstane Kirk), Union Street, and conductorship of Hall Russell's Male Voice Choir. In these capacities he continued until his death in December 1955 at the age of 69. In the absence of an immediate successor to Rowland Tims, George Blackmore's duties were, as of January 1951, divided between the Capitol and the Astoria. With George at the helm, the Capitol organ went back on the air, the BBC having temporarily decided that it did not like the Astoria instrument!

George held the post of organist at St John's Episcopal church, was in demand as pianist at the BBC's Beechgrove studios, and played the Hammond organ at Donald's Ballroom. All in all he was a busy man, and it must have come as something of a relief when, over March and April 1951, there appeared a potential new resident organist for the Capitol—Donald Thorne, a popular broadcaster, formerly of Granada Theatres. However, a residency never came about, and once again George Blackmore divided his time between the Capitol and the Astoria, depending on the importance of the features showing. Finally, Monday 7 December 1951 saw the arrival at the Capitol of Howard Jennings, who stayed for two years, sharing duties with George at the ballroom.

Early 1951 brought a new development at the Gaumont, where the manager of the time, Mr R.E. Miller, hit on the idea of using the former restaurant space (empty since 1928) to make a small art gallery. Ideal for the likes of photographic exhibitions, the Gaumont Gallery was a popular innovation. It remained a popular forum for camera enthusiasts until well into the following decade, and was, as far as the author can ascertain, unique in a Scottish cinema.

The Beach Pavilion, now long without its old attraction Harry Gordon, had since the war been run by its owners, the Town Council, as a summer-time variety venture, presenting many top artistes of the day. After the 1950 season, though, the Council abandoned the promotion of its own shows and leased the building to Messrs Donald, under whom it reopened on 18 June 1951 with a variety bill headed by lanky comedian Dave Willis. 'Residents' were the Pavilion Girls, singer Joyce Hampton and compere George Gee. From the Ballroom came the Hammond organ, and from the Astoria came George Blackmore as musical director. Over the next four summer seasons guest performers included Ronald Chesney and his harmonica, vocal group The Kordites, Julie Andrews, pianist and singer Kay Cavendish, and even Peter Sellers.

During the early 1950s Aberdeen Town Council was making plans for its first major restoration project on an historic building—the ancient Provost Ross's House in the Shiprow. The house's previous owners, ABC, had intended to restore it as a staff residence for the new cinema, and as such it would have been unique, but the outbreak of war put an end to this imaginative scheme. The old house remained empty, and by 1945 fire damage caused by squatters had left it in an all-but ruinous state. In 1948, a demolition proposal was put to the authorities and was rejected. ABC then took the generous and forward-looking step of donating to the city not only the building but also £6,500 towards its rehabilitation. Fortunately the attitudes of those who would sooner have had it flattened than see a halfpenny of public money spent on it did not prevail, and, handsomely restored some time later, it stands to this day as one of Aberdeen's last remaining ancient residences, its fortuitous brush with the city's cinema history little known.

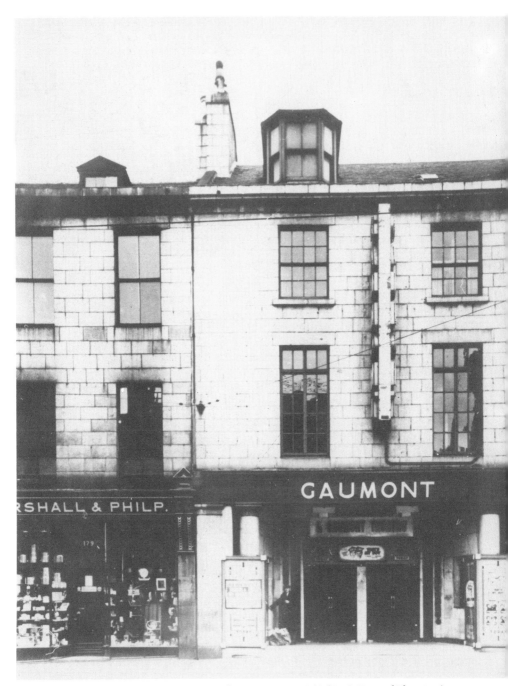

91   The Picture House as the Gaumont, 1951 (ADC, Dept of Planning)

92   The Belmont, formerly Coliseum and New Kinema (*EE* 18 Feb. 1952)

In 1952, a major link with the past was broken by the closure of the Belmont, which had been under threat since 1946 when the Ship Constructors & Shipwrights Association, holders of a bond on the Trades Hall complex (presumably in return for some financial assistance), decided to offer the whole building for sale. Contesting the Association's right to sell, the Trades Council had taken the matter as far as an appeal to the House Of Lords in 1949, but to no avail. Equally unsuccessful was a bid by Messrs Donald, through their Majestic Holdings company, to buy the premises outright. The property was sold to the NAAFI that February for conversion to new headquarters, and on Saturday 29 March the Belmont—a period-piece, with wooden seating in the front stalls, gas emergency lighting, and its operating box reached via the Gents—showed its last film, Robert Hutton in *The Steel Helmet*.

When, in April, work began on adapting the building to its new function, there was discovered an old boarded-up stairway leading from the main hall. Stowed there, amid an assortment of old wooden forms and other rubbish, were eight silken Trades banners. All of these were returned to the Trades Council, but only one was found to be salvageable after having lain there since, probably, the days of William Walker!

In the Belmont's latter years, amusement was derived by some from tagging it as 'flechy', but in fact members of George Walker's family had always been very industrious in cleaning and in keeping the wooden floor well scrubbed. Mr Walker, who remained manager of the Belmont right up until the end, had a short and simple answer for those who thought it clever to call his cinema flea-ridden—'Well, you shouldna ha' brought them in, should you?'

After the cinema's closure Mr Walker became manager of the Tivoli Theatre, and retired four years later. Thereafter he was familiar as a morning 'regular' in the Majestic café until age and failing health curtailed his mobility. He died in 1976, in his mid-eighties.

Feature films were plentiful once again by 1952, and among the popular attractions of the year were Anna Neagle's *Lady With A Lamp*, Gene Kelly and Oscar Levant in *An American In Paris*, and (a new name in films) Frankie Laine, heart-throb of a whole generation of 'Bobby Soxers', in *Sunny Side Of The Street* and *Rainbow 'Round My Shoulder*. Amongst the more conservative fare could be found Cecil B. De Mille's circus extravaganza *The Greatest Show On Earth*, starring Betty Hutton, and the Vivien Leigh and Marlon Brando screen version of Tennessee Williams' play *A Streetcar Named Desire*. Mitzi Gaynor was hailed as successor to Grable in *Golden Girl*, Gary Cooper was in *High Noon*, and Howard Keel sang the songs of Jerome Kern in *Lovely To Look At*. Coming to the fore were Dean Martin, Jerry Lewis and Marilyn Monroe, who made her full dramatic debut with Richard Widmark in *Don't Bother To Knock*.

Aberdeen had its first sight of a new generation of science-fiction fantasies in *The Thing From Another World*, the Scottish premiere of which was given at the Majestic. At the Odeon, Sea Cadets proudly hoisted a White Ensign on stage on the opening night of Trevor Howard and Richard Attenborough's *Gift Horse*, all about the attacking of occupied St Nazaire during the war.

The Coronation, on 2 June 1953, was an occasion of great national rejoicing, on which the makers of newsreels truly 'went to town'. All the following week, a full length colour film of the parade and ceremony (with musical background played by the London Philharmonic Orchestra) was shown exclusively at the Capitol, supported by a programme of cartoons, short subjects, and sing-songs with the organ. Special matinees were given for children. Rank's celebratory offering *A Queen Is Crowned* spent a fortnight at the Gaumont, and News Cinema programmes seemed to contain nothing but Coronation films.

It was also on Coronation day that the BBC made its very first outside television broadcast, relaying the Westminster Abbey ceremony directly to those fortunate enough to possess TV sets. TV dealers did a roaring trade during the weeks leading up to the ceremony, and set owners found themselves much in demand among friends and neighbours on the day itself. The Coronation was an important landmark not just in the advancement of television broadcasting technique, but also in the stimulus that it gave to the spread of the cinema's arch-enemy.

In America, cinema attendances had already been badly affected by television, and the studios were searching for something new to bolster their flagging fortunes. First, experiments were tried in three-dimensional projection, towards which tentative steps had been taken by MGM as far back as 1935. To obtain a three-dimensional effect, it was necessary to watch the screen through special glasses containing either polarised lenses or (the older system) one red and one green filter. Despite its inconvenience, 3-D was all the rage in America for a while, and it was introduced to the UK at the Festival Of Britain in 1951.

By 1953 it was on the British cinema circuits, arriving in Aberdeen at the Capitol on Monday 15 June 1953 in the form of a twenty-minute MGM novelty entitled *Metroscopix*, shown as support feature to Lana Turner's *The Bad And The Beautiful*. Next came the full-length *Sangaree* (at the Gaumont from 17 August), in which the 3-D process was employed for action scenes. The following week, with Vincent Price's *House Of Wax*, the Majestic became 3-D's premier showplace in the city. Follow-ups came in November with George Montgomery's *Fort T* (the first 3-D outdoor epic), and in December with *It came From Outer Space*, in which the alien objects that seemed to hurtle in full colour from the screen caused some members of the audience to involuntarily duck their heads, just as the first generation of film-goers had ducked to 'escape' the oncoming trains and falling bricks that flickered across the canvas before them!

As of Monday 4 January 1954 the Majestic's advertisements and front canopy carried a new legend 'See It On The Giant Panoramic Screen', and a week later 3-D viewing resumed with *The Charge At Feather River*. Next was *The Maze* in May, and John Wayne's *Hondo* in June, but by the time that Vincent Price's *The Mad Magician* arrived in September, 3-D production had been discontinued because of its high cost and cumbersomeness of operation. It relied on the simultaneous showing of two separate film prints, each carrying a different part of the colour spectrum, and with the drive mechanisms of the two projectors linked together by a metal rod to ensure synchronisation. This made instant change-overs impossible in the standard operating box with only two or three machines, and so extra-large spools and retaining cans were employed to minimise the number of intervals required for reloading. The reels' size and weight put a strain on the clutch device that turned the projector's take-up spool, and constant regulation was required. The repair of breaks or tears in film prints was very tricky indeed.

Patrons who already wore spectacles were severely disadvantaged by the necessity of using special glasses. Furthermore, while red-and-green glasses were cheap enough to be sold at 1s. a pair, those with polarised lenses had to be imported from America and were quite expensive. Intended for return at the end of each performance, many of the latter simply disappeared. Then on one occasion a Majestic patron complained bitterly to the management that the latest 3-D offering was no good at all—not worth the money. A little tactful enquiry established that he had been given his viewing glasses as usual and had put them away safely in his pocket, where, slipping his memory, they had remained throughout the performance!

The film studios soon found simpler alternatives to 3-D that would give an enhanced viewing effect without the disadvantages. By the beginning of 1954, 20th Century Fox's epic *The Robe*, photographed and shown in Cinemascope, was on release through Rank, filling Aberdeen's Odeon daily for three weeks from 8 March.

Cinemascope is a process whereby a wide-angle picture is squeezed on to a standard 35 mm film frame by means of a special lens. A corresponding lens on the projector turns the strange compressed image back into a normal picture, which is thrown on to a wide, slightly curved screen. The wider the screen the better the effect, and when used to its full extent the system could produce spectacular results. The usual commercial proportions for a full Cinemascope screen were 2.35 units of breadth to 1 unit of height, as opposed to the old standard screen size of 1.33 to 1. There was also available a popular and easy to fit 'large screen' measuring 1.70 units of breadth to 1 of height; this was the type installed at the Majestic and at hundreds of other British cinemas where nothing wider could be fitted in without either extensive structural alteration or disruption of sightlining through the necessity of bringing the screen forward of the proscenium.

Early wide screens had the irritating disadvantage of masking off the top and bottom areas of conventionally-projected pictures, so that film makers had to keep all important action to the middle of the frame. Man's ingenuity triumphed, however, and soon screens with movable masking sections were available, instantly alterable to whichever shape was required!

Cinemascope found great favour, and might have been universally adopted if 20th Century Fox had not tried to pressure exhibitors into buying expensive stereophonic sound equipment to go with it. Rank jibbed at this, and, after *The Robe*, switched to Paramount's rival system, Vistavision, which required no special projection equipment at all, only a simple masking plate in front of the projector lens to give the appropriate picture shape. All action was kept to the middle of the frame, and any loss of definition resulting from the extra magnification involved was compensated for by the use of high-quality 70 mm negatives in making the (normal-sized) prints. The results, when at their best, were very like Cinemascope, but far cheaper.

Thus the field was opened for independents to step in with Cinemascope where Rank would not, and from June 1954 the Capitol sported a new wide screen for the showing of *Flight Of The Heron* and *King Of The Khyber Rifles*. Stereophonic sound was spread by speakers all around the auditorium, making the voices seem to come from different locations on the screen as the characters moved. On 6 December, the Astoria and Kingsway (their programmes still usually linked) came in with *King Of The Khyber Rifles* and Robert Wagner's *Beneath The Ten Mile Reef*. Soon, alterations were in hand to adapt the Grand Central and the Torry Cinema for Cinemascope. Up until this time, the Grand Central's original stage area had survived unaltered, right down to its little orchestra platform, which since the coming of talkies had been filled with curtains and decorative lighting. Now all this was replaced by a new low stage and oblong proscenium arch decorated in gold stars on a dark background—a favourite design of the day. A similar arrangement was introduced at Torry, and both auditoria were slightly shortened by the new forward placing of the screens.

Royal Command film of 1954 was *Rob Roy*, starring Richard Todd and Glynis Johns. James Stewart and June Allyson starred in *The Glenn Miller Story*, and the blondes that gentlemen preferred that year were Jane Russell and Marilyn Monroe. Paul Douglas came from Hollywood to play a rich American in *The Maggie*, and Doris Day and Howard Keel scored a big hit in *Calamity Jane*. *Doctor In The House* starred Dirk Bogarde and broke all records with a five week run at the Gaumont in May and June, while *Three Coins In The Fountain* was a big draw at the Capitol over the three weeks that it showed there in September. Two local boys, five year old Vincent Wilder (a pupil at Walker Road School, Torry), and eight year old Jon Whitely of Monymusk, starred along with Duncan Macrae in *The Kidnappers*. The *Evening Express* of 2 February 1954 hailed young Vincent as 'the biggest discovery in child stars since Shirley Temple', and the film enjoyed much popularity in Aberdeen.

On Monday 26 July 1954, the new REGAL in the Shiprow opened at last, after a decade and a half's delay. Campaigning had begun in the Autumn of 1952 (and possibly earlier) for permission to finish the building, and in July 1953 the matter had been taken up by the MP Hector Hughes. ABC's case for a relaxation of the still-strict Government regulations was considerably strengthened by the fact that most of the work involved in the £38,000 completion project was of a specialised nature, requiring relatively little of the materials and manpower that were so much at a premium for housing.

Interestingly, Mr Hughes declared that Aberdeen was now *short* of cinemas for the peak tourist seasons. This, in the light of worsening trade conditions and bearing in mind local exhibitors' pre-war worries, seems a trifle odd, but Aberdeen was at that time experiencing something of a tourist boom, and Mr Hughes had statistics to back him up. According to his figures, the city had slipped from its former ratio of one seat per seven of population to one seat per eight—22,660 seats in all for 182,714 potential customers. The example with which this was compared was Blackburn, Lancashire, which possessed one seat per six. Following on improvements in the supply of materials, and with the approach of winter when more labour would be available, the Government finally gave its consent, and on 28 October 1953 ABC announced that work on the Regal was to recommence.

First the long-abandoned outer shell had to be cleared of a deep accumulation of debris, flora and fauna. Soon the roof was on, and by the Spring of 1954 the building was more or less complete. As the date of the gala opening approached, advertisements were placed for staff and a beauty contest was announced to select Aberdeen's twelve prettiest girls as programme sellers on the night. The winners were also given the opportunity of meeting guests of honour Richard Todd and Anne Crawford—stars, along with Ava Gardner, in the inaugural film *Knights Of The Round Table*.

The plans for the Regal's interior were recast along up-to-date lines by the circuit's new architect C.J. Foster, a former associate of his late predecessor William R. Glen. This task entailed striking a compromise between modern requirements and the dictates of what had already been built. A slight cut in seating capacity (from the originally-intended 2,000 to exactly 1,914) was made necessary by the bringing forward of the proscenium line to allow for a splendid 45-foot Cinemascope screen.

In the interior, use was made of materials unheard of before the war, the lower parts of the auditorium walls being covered with a type of washable mock-leather and the upper parts finished in a light mushroom-toned satinised paint. The lighting system, made up of dimmable fluorescent tubes, was the largest of its kind since the idea's introduction a few years previously at the Royal Festival Hall, London. In the ceiling above the centre stalls and balcony were set distinctive saucer-style light fittings, and in the side walls were little lamps with star-shaped shades. A star pattern was also used to break up the otherwise plain surfaces of the walls in the proscenium area. The sound system was only the second example so far of the Perspecta Company's new stereo model, the first being at the Empire, Leicester Square. During the Regal's first two weeks, circuit organist Hubert Selby entertained at 'the wonder electronic organ', a Hammond organ with illuminated surround, placed on a little platform in front of the stage.

Besieged by autograph hunters on the opening night, Richard Todd was pressed by the *Evening Express* reporter 'Kirsteen' to say something special about Aberdeen girls—especially the twelve chosen in the beauty contest, at which he had been among the judges. Diplomatic fellow that he was, his answer was just 'Lovely girls are lovely girls wherever you go!'

The practical Kirsteen could find around the Regal plenty of things that she considered the housewife would 'find worth noting.' Such features as wall coverings received mention, particularly those in the ladies' room, wherein could be found an example of the new tweed-like finishes that were just coming on the market. Perhaps her most revealing remark concerned the foyer ceiling, finished in 'a delightful patch of sky blue paper, decorated with tiny stars, which could look well in any small hall or passage at home'. There is such a thing as reading too much into a perfectly innocent statement, but would anyone have written in such terms about the Regent, the Capitol, or the Astoria two decades before? Times had clearly changed.

Despite a slight disturbance in sightlining brought about by the compromise nature of its interior, the Regal was a good (and, indeed, rare) example of a cinema built essentially new in the period immediately before serious decline set in. It embodied some 'traditional' practices of the 1930s, but used them in a new way—for instance, the concealed lighting system in the foyers extended right into the Union Street entranceway and even appeared under-foot in a thick glass 'illuminating doorstep' through which shone the titles of the day's programme.

A large canopied entrance on the Shiprow gave access to the stalls foyer, which could also be reached from Union Street via various lobbies and doors. The foyer even had a little balcony where patrons could linger, perhaps to peruse the latest edition of the monthly house magazine 'ABC Film Review', available for 6d. A signalling system gave complete coordination between the front and side payboxes, and neither entrance was allowed priority over the other.

Manager at the Regal was Mr J.L. Laing, who had come into the trade in 1923 as operator at the Maryhill Picture House, Glasgow. From there he had worked his way up via the Star, Maryhill and the Blythwood Cinema (one of the first Glasgow suburban houses to have talkies) to the post of chief operator at the New Star, Maryhill in 1930. From there he went to the large Paramount (now Odeon), Renfield Street, when it opened in 1934. Entering cinema management, he was given charge of the Ascot, Anniesland. During the war he was in the Navy, commanding the Admiralty Submarine Battery Station at Elderslie, then on demob he was appointed manager of the Olympia, Bridgeton. Next came the palatial Ritz, Edinburgh, and then to Aberdeen for the first few years of the Regal.

ABC's arrival in the city made life more difficult than ever for local inde-pendents. The Capitol lost the MGM new releases with which it had for so long led the field. Meanwhile the public's defection to television increased dramatically after the advance announcement of the city's first-ever television transmission, a play entitled 'A Nest Of Singing Birds', to be relayed from the hall of Fonthill Barracks on Tuesday 14 December 1954 at 7.30 pm. In its

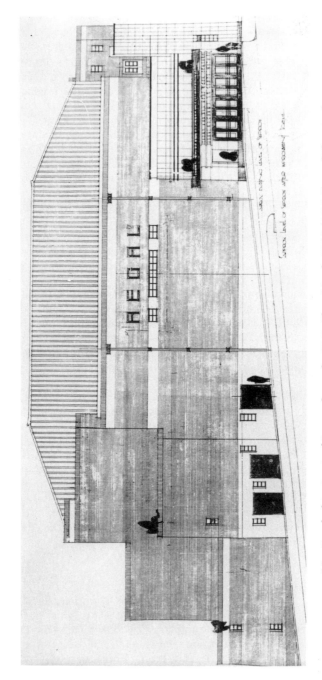

93   Regal, elevation to shiprow, drawn by W.R. Glen, March 1988 (ADC, Dept of Planning)

94   Regal, intended Union Street elevation, W.R. Glen, March 1938 (ADC, Dept of Planning)

95   Regal, Union Street frontage as completed, 1954 (ADC, Dept of Planning)

cast were several local students, but these were denied their historic debut when the broadcast had to be cancelled following rain damage to the temporary transmitter at Schoolhill, Portlethen. It was only a transitory setback. Television broadcasting from Aberdeen, together with improved reception all over the area, began a few months later when the permanent relay station at Oldmeldrum came into service. Back in 1923, cinema exhibitors had worried about the advent of radio; now, thirty years or so later, here was the same threat again, made all the greater by the current swing away from cinema-going on both sides of the Atlantic and the consequent atrophy of movie-making in America. All that the picture trade could do was to carry on and hope for the best.

One of the many new educational measures introduced in the decade following the Second World War was a Cinema Trade Apprenticeship Scheme, spearheaded in Aberdeen and much envied by other Scottish local authorities. Chief instructor was the Capitol's chief operator Bert Ewen, and an annual prize-giving was held at the Trades College with awards presented to the most able students, often in the presence of their managers. Despite the credit that good performance on the course brought to the cinemas where the students worked, not everybody was so pleased. Some 'chiefs' were greatly irked when zealous young apprentices came back and began telling *them* what to do. There was friction, and this, combined latterly with the presence of a rowdy element in the classes, is held to have contributed to the demise of the scheme after a few years.

By 1955, hire purchase was bringing within general reach not only television sets but also electric record players and radiograms. The pop music industry was burgeoning, and before long the new LP record and 45 rpm 'single' would completely oust the long-established shellac '78'. The Rock 'n' Roll era had arrived, and youngsters of the time were just as likely to want to sit and listen to Bill Haley as they were to go to the pictures.

The cinema trade fought back with modernisations, rationalisation of circuits and the introduction of such new lines as foreign connoisseur films. In 1950, interest had been expressed by an unnamed Aberdeen exhibitor in putting on films of this kind. In October 1951 the Odeon had shown the French comedy *Clochemerle*, subtitled in English, but although the experiment went over well it was not repeated. Now, however, Continental films were a much more commercially attractive prospect, and the first Aberdeen proprietor to take them up on a regular basis was Ernest Bromberg, who in 1949 had sold the Palais and moved back to London, but had retained ownership of the News Cinema. Through contacts in the film import business, he was in a position to obtain the pick of the best Continental releases, and after successfully trying these in Glasgow he returned temporarily to Aberdeen to reopen the News Cinema as the NEWCINE CONTINENTAL on 4 April 1955. First film under the new policy was *The Sheep Has Five Legs*, featuring French comedian Fernandel playing five separate roles. With its French dialogue and English subtitling, it proved popular enough to be retained for a second week. Supporting programmes still consisted of sport and interest items, so the old touch had not been completely lost.

The previous summer season had been Messrs Donald's last at the Beach Pavilion, which thereafter entered upon chequered times. Extensive alterations as a nightclub during the 1970s have completely obscured its former identity, but the Inversnecky Café still remains close by as a reminder of Harry Gordon and the old days.

When the Donald summer shows resumed on Monday 4 July 1955, they did so at the Capitol with artistes secured through the agency of impresario Harold Fielding, who had provided some of the acts for the Beach Pavilion. This new series of variety shows, which changed every week, was given the name 'Music For The Millions', and its first bill featured comedian Ted Ray, vocal group the Coronets, impressionist George Meaton, and a resident troupe of twelve Tiller Girls. Over the remaining four weeks of the season, guests included Peter Brough and Archie Andrews, Ronald Chesney (during whose novelty act hundreds of tiny harmonicas were handed out to the audience), the Tanner Sisters, Beryl Reid, Rawicz and Landauer, popular broadcasters the Hedley Ward Trio, Vic Oliver, Shirley Eaton, Jon Pertwee, and Miki & Griff. Coincidentally, organist George Blackmore made his one-hundredth BBC broadcast (and fortieth from Aberdeen) on the first day of the series.

In an earlier chapter we saw how malicious gossip caused trouble for the Palace just after its reopening in 1931. History repeated itself in October 1955 when it came to the attention of the Regal's manager, Mr Laing, that there were circulating some rather nasty rumours concerning his cinema. Just as with the Palace, no-one knew where these rumours came from, but he'd said that she'd said that there was *something funny* about the place, and of course there's no smoke without fire...

At first, Mr Laing paid no heed to the gossip, but far from abating, it gained such momentum that before long it was being exchanged and embroidered in virtually every place in the city where people gathered. When the Regal's attendances began to suffer, the time for silence was over and Mr Laing enlisted the power of the press. The *Evening Express* took up the cudgels with its own three-week survey of the affair, the findings of which were published in the issue for 4 November, 1955.

They make extraordinary reading. Most persistent amongst the gossip was that the Regal was 'full of bugs', but there was a wide choice of other stories as well. It was variously rumoured that slides were being flashed on the screen announcing the cinema's closure for three months, that contractors had been approached for replacement of the whole interior, that the building was to be changed into a dance hall, that the entire staff was to be paid off or transferred, that a cleaner's sister had reported that bugs were coming in through the roof because the cinema was built on old sites, that the place was closing for a week for fumigation, and that posters had gone up in schools advising children against going to the Regal until further notice. The chief operator was amazed to learn of his supposedly having been turned out of his lodgings on account of the infested state of the cinema, and a cashier noted how an acquaintance intentionally kept her distance when sharing a seat on a bus!

With the headline 'Is Your Face Red?' the *Evening Express* of 4 November, 1955 exposed the stories for the fiction that they were. The Regal management consulted Aberdeen's Chief Sanitary Inspector, Mr Parry, and (after, it has been said, some unpublicised preventative work just to make doubly sure!) a strongly-worded statement was published making clear that the cinema had been given a clean bill of health. A warning was also given that should information reach the company enabling action to be taken against the rumours' perpetrators, there would be no hesitation in doing so. All of a sudden things went quiet, attendances began to recover, and soon the matter was forgotten.

Much commented on by cinema-goers was the rapid spread of 'X'-certificate films, a designation created in 1951 by widening the scope of the old 'H' Horror category in response to the increasing emphasis on sex. At that time 'X' films (barred to under-16s) had been relatively few and far between, but as the movie industry's malaise deepened and film makers and exhibitors looked increasingly to the younger audience with money to spend, they became all-pervasive. By 1957 there would be quite justifiable complaints that they were crowding out everything else. Traditional cinema patrons quickly became alienated and drifted away—to television.

Chapter 14

Teds And Television   1956—1958

In January 1956, with Aberdeen's television link a few months in operation, the *Evening Express* Bon-Accord Gossip reporter went the round of local cinema managers to find out just how concerned they were at the rise of television in the city. The answer was 'not very much', with the emphasis on the 'very'. It was a widely-held view that after an initial burst of enthusiasm for TV (during which cinema attendances had certainly been affected) Aberdonians were returning to the big screen. Further factors cited as contributing to the temporary desertion of cinemas were the widespread purchase of television sets, which took up money otherwise spent on entertainments, and the public's choosiness—nothing new in Aberdeen, as Jack Wright of the Capitol pointed out!

If picture-going was holding its own in town, outwith the city it was still thriving. On 5 March 1956, Messrs Donald bought the Victoria Cinema, West High Street, Inverurie, from Mr Stephen Young of Monymusk. Built in 1935 for Mr Young's father, the Victoria was designed by T. Scott Sutherland—his next cinema commission after the Astoria. Mr Young senior, after years of unopposed operation in the Town Hall, had got wind of other exhibitors' interest in Inverurie and had quickly secured a site on the town's main thoroughfare. The plans were drawn up and construction began, but the building was only half finished when the money ran out. Sutherland suggested forming a limited company to borrow the rest of the capital on high interest debentures. The result was a company named Inverurie Picture House Ltd, but it was not floated on any outside loan; it was floated on a public issue of shares, major holder of which was the inveterate entrepreneur Mr Sutherland, who also became the company's chairman.

The Victoria paid for itself within five years, and when (much later) Mr Young died, his place was taken by his son, who proved a good businessman. Gradually, minority shareholders were bought out and the outlay on the cinema was doubled. Connected for some years (presumably by way of a film booking arrangement) with the Glasgow-based A.G. Matthews Circuit, this pleasant little 500-seater passed to the control of Messrs Donald through Aberdeen Picture Palaces, and was immediately improved by the addition of Cinemascope facilities and new equipment. Still very much alive, it now offers a combination of films and Bingo.

As a further indication of the support for pictures in outlying areas, we may note that as late as 1955 the former St Andrew's Church, Ellon, became a cinema—an echo of earlier days when the setting up of picture houses in such buildings was commonplace. Also not to be forgotten is the Glen Cinemas company of Mr Arnold M. Burns of Aberdeen. Established in 1936, Glen Cinemas were, by the mid-1950s, operating in public halls in Banchory, Culter, Ellon, Insch, Strichen, New Pitsligo, Alford, Bucksburn and Inverurie (Town Hall), with more distant branches at the Normand Cinema, Dysart, and the Palladium, Gallatown, Kirkcaldy. They varied in capacity from 200 seats (Insch) to 500 (Inverurie and Bucksburn), and perhaps the best remembered among those in the immediate Aberdeen area was the one in the old Shepherd's Hall (better known as the Argosy Ballroom), Bucksburn. Longest-lived was that at Culter Community Centre, which survived until November 1961.

In November 1955, work started on the modernisation of one of Aberdeen's earliest purpose-built cinemas, the 1914 Gaumont/Picture House in Union Street. Its entranceway was given a face-lift by the covering over of the old walls, woodwork and pillars with fresh new wooden panelling, and by the addition of a large canopy with batteries of warm, bright lights.

The refitted foyer was decorated in bold red, set off with details in turquoise, black and white. The new circular ticket desk and confectionery counter gleamed with chrome and brass, and luxurious tinselled curtains shimmered at the balcony doors. The whole illumination scheme had, to quote the *Evening Express* of 19 April 1956, been carefully worked out

> ....to provide a graded scale of light from the entrance's spotlights, through the bright rectangle of light from the corrugated plastic ceiling over the entrance doors to the large rings of metal reflector lights suspended from the two coloured ceilings of the foyers.

The auditorium was repainted in neutral tones and was fitted with large circular lighting chandeliers echoing those in the foyer. The seating was renewed for, reportedly, the fourth time in as many decades, and up-to-date projection equipment was installed—only the third set since 1914! A new wide screen and curtains took up the entire end wall area, completely covering the old proscenium. Upstairs, out of the public's view, the offices were extended, taking over part of the picture gallery. The cheerful new-look Gaumont was finished on Tuesday, 19 April 1956, the day of screen star Grace Kelly's wedding into the Royal Family of Monaco.

At the former News Cinema, the day of the Continental film seemed to be drawing to a close. In January 1956 the house's name changed from Newcine Continental to NEWCINE NEWS AND SHORTS CINEMA, and the following month News subjects returned daily until 7 pm., giving place, after an hour's break, to

Continental programmes. Whether through lack of demand, lack of good material, or both, the number of Continental features dwindled even further in the course of just a few weeks, and their place was taken by some of the best feature films of the past few years. That April, News Cinema programmes made a complete return, and finally on 3 December 1956 the little cinema reverted to its original name—all in the face of the growth of TV news broadcasting which would in just a few years make newsreels and News Cinemas redundant.

In international affairs, 1956 was the year of Suez, petrol crisis and the crushing of the Hungarian rebellion. At home in Aberdeen, 'Syncopating Sandy' made the headlines through his marathon piano-playing bout at the Music Hall that November, and the Music Hall was also the venue for the city's first Rock 'n' Roll sessions, all duly supervised by Council officials.

These were anxious times for the cinema world, with attendances down 25 per cent on 1949 levels and a list of no less than 179 houses ready for closure, 79 of them Rank's. A new BBC radio series of soundtrack snippets from the latest films won the approval of the trade, but the same could not be said of another innovation announced for that year—the televising of football matches. Alarmed cinema proprietors joined with their employees' Union (by then called the National Association Of Theatre And Kine Employees) in sending telegrams of protest to the representatives of the Football League as they met in Manchester to consider rival offers from BBC and ITV. Saturday night matches on television would, it was feared, be the final straw not just for the many provincial cinemas that relied on weekend takings, but for the entire British film-making industry as well. Already, rising costs and continuing high Entertainments Tax had led to widespread increases in seat prices (those at the Donald cinemas went up by between 3d. and 6d. that July, making the cheapest seats 1s. 10d. instead of 1s. 6d., and the dearest 4s. instead of 3s. 9d.) and the trade's apprehension was understandable, but fortunately the relaying of football matches did not bring the jdire consequences that some had predicted.

1956 saw the deaths of James Clapperton (lawyer and secretary to Aberdeen Picture Palaces throughout its existence as an independent company) and, on 29 October, of Joseph (Joe) Milne, manager of the Majestic and long-time stalwart of the Donald organisation. Full responsibility for the daily running of the Majestic passed to Mr Milne's assistant, Charles Elder, who, having worked his way up through the ranks there, was to remain as manager for the rest of the cinema's life.

Stars of the Capitol's second 'Music For The Millions' series included Arthur Askey, Terry Thomas, Rawicz & Landauer, David Whitfield, Chic Murray and Maidie, Kay Cavendish, Arthur Haynes, Vic Oliver, Michael Holliday, and Semprini. Charlie Chester's TV competition show paid a visit, complete with full cast and a 71 guinea television set for some lucky winner.

In the matter of films, cross-town linking of programmes on the Donald circuit had died out over 1955 and most cinemas were now entirely separate. The Capitol was still able to offer some very prestigious first-runs—the Scottish premiere of *Carousel* that June, *Love Is A Many Splendoured Thing*, starring William Holden, which did good business over a fortnight's showing at New Year 1956-57, and *The King And I*, which ran for two weeks from 29 October, with organ interludes by George Blackmore. At the Odeon that February, a real cockleshell boat was set up in the foyer for the showing of the film *Cockleshell Heroes*.

The old Hollywood was quickly fading, and a new realism in film-making had begun. With this came a new kind of hero, typified by James Dean in his roles as the moody rebel. Also, the province of the film star was now being invaded by the pop singer. Bill Haley And His Comets had consolidated the success of their first hit record, 'Shake Rattle And Roll', with the teen anthem of the mid-1950s, 'Rock Around The Clock', first heard over the credits of a film called *Blackboard Jungle*. Haley and his one-time Country & Western band had become hot property, and the next step for them was to make a full-length showcase feature film, entitled *Rock Around The Clock*. A mixed bag of musical numbers, minimal plot and big rock finale, *Rock Around The Clock* did well on its UK release in 1956, although rough scenes at some early showings put many members of the cinema trade against it. Youngsters revelled in this new outlet for their rebellious energies in what were otherwise rather hidebound times, and sometimes these rebellious energies were apt to get out of hand. At one cinema, seats and fittings were demolished as teenagers danced in the aisles. Elsewhere there was rowdyism and trouble with Teddy-boys (or at least that was who got the blame), and as a result the film was banned altogether in several towns and cities.

When it became known that Aberdeen's first showing of *Rock Around The Clock* was scheduled for the Gaumont on Monday 10 September 1956, the cinema's manager, Mr Miller, was interviewed by the *Evening Express'* reporter John Lodge to find out his reaction to the prospect. He expressed no great concern; in common with colleagues in other places where the film was shown, he had taken the precaution of arranging, in the event of any disturbance, for an appearance by some special live guests—the local constabulary. Still, John Lodge expressed the hope that such optimism would not prove misplaced; by the following Saturday, he suggested, Mr Miller would at the very least be well acquainted with the new definition of the word 'cat'!

John Lodge's report of the opening of *Rock Around The Clock* (printed in the *Evening Express* of 11 September 1956) is well worth quoting at length:

'We're gyan awa' back. Turn aff the soun' wid 'e? We'll be back', snorted an angry youngster last night outside the Gaumont. He had just been jiving in the aisles with another boy, his face twisted, eyes popping, and hands shaking wildly.

This wasn't Rock 'n' Roll hypnotism. It was nothing else than exhibitionism, where the few found they just had to go one better than their hand-clapping, singing buddies in the stalls.

I sat through two performances of Bill Haley And His Comets. As a film, it is rubbish. As a box-office draw it is terrific. Crazy mixed-up kids? For my money they are ill-mannered youths who went to the Gaumont determined to cause a sensation. Almost twenty specimens left their seats in the front stalls and held hands, flailing their arms and legs about like a crowd of dervishes doing a war dance.

They were politely ignored by the management—but the sound was turned off if they became too bad. This happened several times during the show, but nothing could be heard for the last three minutes when a Rock 'n' Roll jamboree was being shown. It became impossible to watch the extras dancing in this American film. Instead, first one youth of about fourteen got up on to the stage, and, silhouetted against the bright light, stuck a finger up in the air and—eyes popping—waggled across the stage. Then, as if rehearsed, as soon as he reached ground level, four more boys got up on to the stage, and at equal spaces faced the audience, hands stretched high into the air and mouths open.

I sat immediately behind this crowd of youths through both evening shows, and the 6.15 performance produced little more than an occasional murmur. Once over, they became impatient again for Haley's Comets and Freddy Bell and the Bellboys, who screamed out the insistent rhythm.

The audience liked it. At times it reminded of the old-fashioned music hall where the villain of the piece was booed off stage. For *Rock Around The Clock*, a rather thin story, this villain is an attractive scheming woman. By 9.30 an appearance by her was enough to start the audience booing. Chanting 'We want Haley', a small group in the front stalls did at one time drown the soundtrack with their version of 'Rock Around The Clock'. And as the film neared its climax, more and more youths joined the jiving in the aisles. An usherette went along to try and persuade them to go back to their seats. Her pleas were drowned with a torrent of abuse.

The article concluded with an account of how, the previous night, police had had to use batons to shepherd a 1,000-strong crowd of screaming, jiving teenagers through the centre of Bootle, Lancashire, after 500 of them had been to see the film, how at a Lewisham cinema about fifty youths had been forcibly ejected by police and staff, and how in Manchester light bulbs had been thrown from the balcony and a fire hose sprayed about the hall. It came as rather a relief when the Gaumont's week of *Rock Around The Clock* passed without serious incident.

In the history of Aberdeen's growth and development, the 1950s was an important period. Long-awaited new housing estates spread into what had formerly been open country on the outskirts of town, easing overcrowding and allowing much sub-standard city-centre property to be done away with, but by 1957 the steady exodus from the inner city area was beginning to tell on traditional small shops and businesses. It also carried serious long-term implications for cinemas, but Aberdeen's picture establishment was not too downhearted. As the war-damaged Gallowgate U.F. Church was being demolished in January 1957 there was speculation that stone from it might be reused in the construction of a new cinema on a site that Messrs Donald had acquired at the top of Kincorth Hill.

Rank, after having renovated the Gaumont, next turned to the modernisation of the Odeon, on which work began early that same year. Among the improvements carried out was the replacement of the old and troublesome lighting system (always impossible of access for maintenance) with a new fluorescent system requiring, it was claimed, only two-thirds of the previous number of light sources. Also added was a Plenum plant, one of the few modern refinements missing from the original design. It was proudly reported that since 1932 the Odeon had required only one reseating, two recarpetings and refloorings of the foyer, and three redecorations—quite remarkable considering that the building had been in constant use for so long.

The Odeon's refurbishment came at an appropriate time, as Monday 23 February 1957 marked its 25th anniversary. Of the contractors concerned in its construction, A.B. Robertson, Calder & Henderson, George Bisset and James Scott were still in existence, and placed special advertisements in the local newspapers. A large anniversary cake was displayed in one of the foyer kiosks before being presented to the Women's Volunteer Service.

Central to the celebrations was an evening gala screening of one of the latest releases, Dean Martin and Jerry Lewis in *Hollywood Or Bust*. Invitations were sent to the Lord and Lady Provost and to T. Scott Sutherland, but unfortunately none of these were able to attend. Something else had to be found to add a fillip to the occasion, and so a special message of congratulation from Muriel Pavlow, co-star with Kenneth More in *Reach For The Sky*, was played over the cinema's sound system, adding a unique touch to the Odeon's very happy birthday.

The Regal, meanwhile, gained distinction of sorts when, in January 1957, it became one of probably rather few cinemas to be attacked by an angry bullock. Escaping from the slaughter-house, the animal led its pursuers a merry chase around the centre of town. Entering the Regal's car park, it took a run at the doorways before heading off again through the busy city streets to the Broadford Works in Maberly Street, where it was finally recaptured!

At the Capitol, that summer's 'Music For The Millions' started on 1 June with Tommy Steele And The Steelmen plus Mike & Bernie Winters. In connection with this show the Evening Express organised a Teenage Party, for which young people were invited to apply for free tickets and meet Tommy in person. Several more parties followed, the next being for Frankie Vaughan, who arrived on 22 July and, as a great champion of the youth movement, lost no time in visiting Aberdeen Lads' Club. Local youth clubs arranged their own party to meet Frankie, whose diary contained a further appointment while in town—a private showing, at the Regal, of *The Dangerous Years*, in which he played his first starring role—as a Teddy-Boy from his native city, Liverpool. Quite a crowd turned out to see him, including a good number of the city's 'Tedsers'. Among the other guest stars that season were Petula Clark, the ever-popular Chic Murray and Maidie, Al Koran the mind-reader, Eve Boswell, Rawicz & Landauer once again, and Bill Maynard, who, as 'TV's

Sweater Boy', strolled on stage dressed in a large yellow sweater, beamed at the audience and remarked cheerily 'You can't switch me off tonight!'

Missing from the musical scene by this time was George Blackmore who, uneasy at the downward trend in the cinema business, departed in May 1957 for pastures new. During the first 'Music For The Millions' series George, as general musical director, led the twelve-piece pit orchestra, playing the ballroom's Hammond organ which had been brought in because of its immediacy for stage work. Leading an orchestra whilst playing the organ was no easy task, but for the 1956 season George was permitted to pay fuller attention to his keyboards through the appointment of Aberdonian Jimmy Miller (formerly of the RAF Squadronaires dance band) as orchestra conductor. Harold Fielding, who regularly travelled north to supervise the Aberdeen shows, was impressed with George's work, and tempted him away to Bournemouth to accompany a variety season over the summer of 1957. Next, George joined the London music publishing firm of Bosworth as composer and arranger, but after a while returned to full-time playing, first as demonstrator for electronic organ manufacturers and then in a freelance capacity. He is still to be heard frequently on the air, and remains in demand for pipe and electronic concerts both at home and abroad, among his many ports of call in recent years having been his old home ground, the Capitol!

The Gaumont was the venue, in July 1957, for the annual *Evening Express* Personality Girl competition, won that year by local contestant Yan Gillan. The prizes consisted of a trip to London to meet show business stars and (more immediately) a large Helena Rubinstein Beauty Box. Making the presentation of the box was none other than Mary Garden. When Miss Garden retired from the opera stage in 1934, she commenced an association with Hollywood, joining MGM as voice scout (one of her discoveries being Nelson Eddy) and as adviser for opera scenes. On her return to Aberdeen in 1939 she was acknowledged as one of the city's most famous daughters, and found herself frequently called upon to officiate at such public occasions as this.

A small but regal figure, Miss Garden, for all her past international fame, never lost her down-to-earth touch. As highly thought of by doorman and taxi-driver as by the upper echelons, she was something of a regular at the Gaumont, where she would invariably be ushered to her seat by the cinema's commissionaire George Repper, himself a great favourite with the public. Mr Repper had seen service in the Indian Police and as a mental nurse before taking up his post at the Gaumont in 1940. From then until his retirement in 1964 he was a popular and familiar figure to all as he shepherded queues, attended to patrons, and conversed cheerfully with customers as they came and went. Mary Garden eventually went to live with relatives outwith the city; she died in 1967 at the age of 92.

Typical film fare of 1957 was Elvis Presley's *Love Me Tender* (Scottish-premiered at the Capitol in January), Bill Haley once again in *Don't Knock The*

Rock, and Tommy Steele in *The Tommy Steele Story*. For those preferring something more conservative, there were Brando and Sinatra in *Guys And Dolls*, Gordon Macrae, Gloria Grahame and 1930s comedienne Charlotte Greenwood in *Oklahoma*, Howard Keel and Ann Blyth in *Kismet*, and Doris Day in *The Pajama Game*. Among the non-musical subjects, Marlene Dietrich starred in *The Monte Carlo Story* and Marlon Brando in *Teahouse Of The August Moon*, while Peter Cushing was ever his adorable screen self in *The Abominable Snowman*. The Disney studio had been busy on another craze of the time with *Davy Crockett And The River Pirates*, and there were still plenty of Coopers, Flynns, Crosbys and Bogardes. Aberdeen Town Council dabbled in film-making that year, sponsoring a promotional tourist-trade production entitled *The Silver City*. This was premiered at the Capitol on Friday, 21 June before a distinguished company that included the Lord Provost and Mr (later Sir) Hugh Fraser. Copies of the film still survive to remind us of Aberdeen as it was in those days.

However old-hat such things as cinema organs may have seemed to the young hep-cat generation, the Capitol and Astoria might still have had a resident organist if a suitable one could have been found at reasonable outlay. Since the departure of George Blackmore neither organ had been featured at all, but January 1958 saw the brief return of a well-known face from the past—Bobby Pagan. Bobby had always retained an interest in Aberdeen, making a point of dropping in to see George Blackmore whenever visiting the area. The main reason for his prescence in the city on this occasion was an engagement as musical director for a three-week run of Johnny Victory variety shows at the Tivoli, but he took the opportunity of arranging to play at the Astoria at 3 p.m. and 8 p.m., and at the Capitol at 7 p.m. daily throughout his stay. The response was good and Bobby enjoyed himself, although the choosing of music for the Astoria during his final week must have been a little tricky—the film programme was a double billing of *Daughter Of Dr Jekyll* and *The Disembodied*! (How does one follow that?)

When Bobby left (rather reluctantly) to fulfil an engagement as musical director for entertainer Jimmy Logan, he was heavily tipped to return as organist at the two cinemas, but this turned out to be mere speculation. It was not until the end of 1958 that the organs were heard again, this time in the hands of a former George Blackmore pupil, 23-year-old student teacher Duncan Sinclair. Duncan's Thursday 'Music Nights' at the Capitol and Saturday sing-song spots at the Astoria were well received, but studies called. In February 1959 the organs fell silent again, and from then on their playing in public on a professional basis was abandoned altogether.

Jimmy Edwards appeared at the Capitol in 'Whacko Aberdeen', part of the 1958 'Music For The Millions' season. Because he had been Rector of the

96   A wave from Duncan Sinclair at the organ of the Capitol (*EE* 5 Dec. 1958)

University in 1953, a visit in the capacity of entertainer had been held off at his own request, but happy memories were undimmed, and University organisations were quick to re-establish contact with him. Other 'Music For The Millions' stars in 1958 were Guy Mitchell and Tommy Steele, both of whom hosted Teenage Parties that summer, Tommy demonstrating to his young guests a little-known and highly amusing sideline of hypnotism. Jimmy Young displayed (in the words of the *Evening Express*) the 'granite-like power of his larynx', Chic Murray was back once again, Hughie Green presented an edition of his TV and Radio Luxembourg show 'Double Your Money', and Joe 'Mr Piano' Henderson played his popular numbers. Singer Petula Clark's act included a number called 'The Lollipop Song', in which she carried a basket of lollies for throwing to children in the audience. Due to the remoteness of the Capitol's stage, however, it was considered better to simply hand the sweets out as the audience left after the show! Musical director that year was Robert Leys, a former pupil of F. Rowland Tims. Expressing an interest in the Capitol's Compton organ, he was given permission to practise on it privately— an association which lasted for twenty years.

Well may the period 1957-58 have been described by a cinema trade spokesman as one of 'gloom and foreboding'. Cinema attendances throughout Britain continued to dwindle, while hopes of a substantial reduction in Entertainment Tax were dashed the 1957 Budget, in which tax on live theatres was completely removed but that on cinemas hardly touched. It was to be 1960 before, too late, the duty was finally abolished.

According to figures released by Rank in 1957, ticket sales had sunk in the space of two years from 1,001 million to 915 million, and the final figure for 1958 was expected to be somewhere in the region of 750 million. As film studios felt the pinch, so the number of major releases continued to drop. Real profit to Rank had fallen drastically and was still going down. When J. Arthur Rank became head of Gaumont British and Odeon it had been on the understanding that the two companies would be run separately. That, however, was in 1941. Now, with the continuing deterioration in trading conditions, it was considered necessary to further trim the two circuits and to fully amalgamate what was left of them under the umbrella of 'The Rank Organisation'. Sixteen Rank houses had closed in 1957 and the axe was poised over a further eighty for 1958, the usual policy being to close Gaumonts where they existed along with Odeons, although occasionally it was the Odeon that was dispensed with and the name transferred to the other house.

Attractive offers for prime sites accounted for more than a few further closures, and before long an increasing number of urban districts (and even smaller towns) found themselves without any cinema at all. Some cinemas ended up as dance halls, bowling alleys or Bingo halls, while others remained in business through the introduction of a mixture of films and Bingo.

Scotland's annual cinema attendance figure had fallen from 15,000 million in 1948 to 7,000 million, with further losses expected. No wonder that Herbert J. Green appealed against a rates assessment of £11,000 per year on George Green Ltd's seven Glasgow cinemas. Aberdeen, for its part, had so far weathered the storm, but sooner or later change would be on the way.

Chapter 15

Bingo, Ballrooms And Bowling   1959—1963

For some time, Messrs Donald had been considering giving up the Playhouse, still held on lease by Aberdeen Picture Palaces from its long-time owners, builders James Scott, whose offices occupied the upper part of the old Union Street premises. The Playhouse could well have ended up as Aberdeen's first casualty of the decline, but instead, on 3 February 1959, it bounced back as the PLAYHOUSE CONTINENTAL with Fernandel in *The Virtuous Bigamist*, and Sophia Loren in *Lucky To Be A Woman*. Admission prices were now 2s. 6d. for Stalls and 3s. 6d. for Balcony (considerably higher than their previous modest levels), but the experiment proved worthwhile.

By this time, the word 'Continental' had begun to imply 'X-certificate Continental'. This spicier class of material was found to bring in money, and despite accusations of sex-peddling an increasing number of cinema proprietors were taking it up. On Monday 8 May, the News Cinema underwent another change of name, this time to the CURZON—called, presumably, after the influential small luxury cinema (since replaced) in Curzon Street, London. Whatever Ernest Bromberg's personal attitude to the new generation of Continental pictures, he started as he meant to continue, with the gala opening of a new release entitled *Around The World With Nothing On*. This great opus was proudly announced as having been made in Eastman Colour—chiefly pink, one imagines, with blue tinges for episodes in the cooler climes.

Also in May 1959 it was decided by the Rank Organisation that the Odeon was to be Scotland's third cinema to present films made in the latest extra-wide screen process, TODD-AO. Developed by the American Optical Company from the ideas of showman Mike Todd, and launched in the UK with the film version of the Richard Rodgers musical *South Pacific*, TODD-AO used a special camera to expose a 70 mm-wide film (twice the standard width), giving more or less wrap-round vision. Magnetic soundtracks replaced the standard optical ones as a vehicle for high-quality six-track stereo sound.

The Odeon was closed for about a fortnight, during which the old pro-scenium arch and stage were removed in favour of a huge screen and an even larger set of gold tab curtains, on to which shone a battery of floodlights mounted on the front of the balcony. Its modernised and redecorated interior a blaze of illumination, the 'new' Odeon reopened on Monday 8 June 1959 with a three-month season of *South Pacific*, each performance including an electronic organ interlude by George Sievewright. An entranced public proclaimed it quite the show of the year.

At the other end of town, the aged Casino, its business badly affected by depopulation of the area, looked as if it might be about to experience a dramatic change in its fortunes. There now ran past its doors the long-awaited Beach Boulevarde (opened by the Queen Mother on 25 May 1959), and a rich new vein of passing trade seemed assured. APP's enlargement plan for the building had long been abandoned because the adjacent ground that would have been required had been partially built over, but on 15 March 1959 the 'Casash' closed for thorough renovation. Its entranceway was brightened up and modernised, and a brand new canopy and sign fitted. The layout of its 800 seats was improved, and all interior decorative detail streamlined. On Monday 7 June it reopened to the public, but the fates proved fickle. Perhaps the proximity of the new first-run Regal steered the holiday crowds away; the expected extra business never materialised, and by September it was clear that all the trouble and expense had been for nothing. After the last house on Saturday 3 October 1959, Messrs Donald shut up shop and advertised the premises for sale.

The massive Rank circuit cuts of the previous couple of years had so far bypassed Aberdeen, but after the Odeon's £25,000 face-lift (costing more than half of what was spent on putting up the building!) and the similar treatment of the Gaumont, the Palace was left an unrenovated also-ran. No-one was unduly surprised when a press release of 31 August 1959 proclaimed that the Palace's cinema days were to end. Further details were not divulged until October, but then it emerged that unlike the many cinemas that had been sold off for their sites or had been turned into Bingo halls (still a thing of the future in Aberdeen), the Palace was to become a Top Rank ballroom—one of only three such conversions by Rank so far that year.

The Palace's last film show took place on Saturday 14 November 1959, when on screen was Jaques Tati in *My Uncle Frank*. Thereafter the cinema's staff of thirty were redistributed locally and the Boys & Girls Club wound up. Soon, contractors arrived to alter the already much-rebuilt theatre once again, replacing its raked floor with a new sprung one at street level and creating a false ceiling by extending the balcony along the entire length of the former auditorium. Where the stage had been was built a raised soda bar, entered from the dance floor, and opposite the entrances (themselves reduced somewhat from the original five sets of double doors) was erected a band platform. The old balcony foyer became a café. The new Palace Ballroom was launched on Thursday 24 March 1960 as Aberdeen's largest dance hall, continuing in more or less that form (but with licensed bars replacing the café and soda bar) until 1976 when the live band was dispensed with and, following modern trends, the hall became first Fusion and then Ritzy's Discotheque. Meanwhile, above the false ceiling, the upper part of the old Palace still exists more or less intact.

Among the better remembered screen titles of 1959 were *Some Like It Hot* starring Marilyn Monroe, Tony Curtis and Jack Lemmon, and *I'm All Right, Jack* starring Ian Carmichael, Terry Thomas and Peter Sellers. Audrey Hepburn and Peter Finch's very successful *Nun's Story* spent a fortnight at the Regal, with interludes by Rex Griffiths (one of a small team of organists still retained by ABC) at a Compton 'Melotone' electronic organ. *Gigi*, starring Leslie Caron, Maurice Chevalier and Louis Jordan, showed for no less than five weeks at the Majestic up until the end of April, also with organ interludes, played this time by Robert Leys. Some may remember the large cut-out canopy display which caused tense moments through its proclivity for blowing down!

Due mainly to rising costs, the days of the big variety show were numbered, and 1959's 'Music For The Millions' season was the last. To the Capitol's stage came Bob Monkhouse, the Beverley Sisters, Eddie Calvert, Jimmy Young, Margo Henderson, Rawicz & Landauer, Jon Pertwee, Alma Cogan and Ronald Chesney, with the return of George Blackmore as musical director.

'Change and decay in all around I see' is a phrase that may have sprung quite readily to mind for those involved in cinema exhibition in this country during the early 1960s, but yet that period was a fertile one for film-making, especially features aimed at the younger generation. A new wave of stars and producers was on its way, turning the old ideas upside down as the industry reshaped itself for a future in which its importance as a national entertainment would be greatly diminished.

On the Aberdeen cinema scene, the new decade began in a quiet enough way with no startling developments, but 1961—the year of Yuri Gagarin, the Twist, Scotland's new 10 o'clock licensing hours, and the founding of CND—turned out to be the year of the Bingo Hall. Under the name 'Housey-Housey', Bingo had enjoyed great popularity with American servicemen during the Second World War. With its new title, it had made a triumphant sweep of the States, ousting pictures in a great number of movie houses. Successful try-outs by Rank and a few independents during the late 1950s had caused some apprehension in the British cinema trade; now, in the affluent 1960s, Bingo was to become as much of a craze in this country as it was in the USA.

So far, Aberdeen's city authorities had not viewed the idea of Bingo with much favour, but in 1961 the empty Casino was sold for Bingo purposes to local bookmakers James Rennie and Arthur Forbes. A gaming licence was applied for and, after much deliberation, granted. On Sunday 26 September 1961 a queue of 400 awaited the opening of the doors for the first session. Inside, silver screen had given place to £400 worth of American-style Bingo board, and every night of the week, to the subdued music of an electronic organ, the money rolled in and the lucky winners gleefully claimed their prizes. Although following the inevitable complaints Sunday play was soon dropped, membership of the Casino Bingo Club rose to 10,000 within three weeks, some participants reportedly travelling regularly from Arbroath, Montrose, Wick and even Kirkwall. The small former cinema was bursting at the seams, with between 300 and 400 would-be players having to be turned away every night, and it was clear that larger premises would have to be found. Enquiries were made, with results that we shall presently see.

New ground had meanwhile been broken at the Capitol in the presentation, on the night of 21 February 1961, of its very first live pop concert—the second edition of Jack Good's 'Rock n' Trad Spectacular'. On stage were Billy Fury, Tommy Bruce, Mark Wynter, Joe Brown, and an assortment of lesser lights. Later in the year the Capitol hosted a short season of the recently established 'White Heather Club', starring, among others, the Joe Gordon Folk Four, Robert Wilson, Jimmy Shand Jnr, and Sydney Devine.

The Playhouse shed its Continental role in 1961, and at Christmas the Curzon reverted once again to its old function, as the CURZON CARTOON COMEDY CINEMA, charging 1s. 6d. (children 1s.) for a 75-minute programme.

Charlton Heston's epic *Ben Hur* had its first Aberdeen showing not, as might have been expected, at the Odeon or the Regal, but at the huge Kingsway, where it showed daily between the end of June and the beginning of September 1961. This, the only film season in the Kingsway's history, was surrounded by much hoop-la, even down to the printing of cut-out booking forms in the local papers. With the major circuits now soaking up practically every new film release of consequence, *Ben Hur* was a rare capture for 'outsiders'; it was in fact to prove the last large independent scoop in Aberdeen where, as a result of the above monopoly, the Donald cinemas and their subsidiaries were having to get by almost entirely on second runs of pictures whose box-office potential had been milked dry over two, three, or more weeks at the Regal or Odeon. The effect of this plus the general downturn in cinema-going is reflected in the city's rates assessment revisions that April. Calculated partly on business turnover, these reduced the first-run Regal to £2,955 per annum from £3,250 the previous year, with the other cinemas falling back in stages thereafter. Last of all was the poor old Astoria, slashed to a mere £830 as compared with £1,400 in 1960. The trade's discomfiture was compounded by the opening, on 30 September 1961, of Grampian Television in Scotland's first purpose-built TV studio, on the site of the old tram depot in Fountainhall Road.

The Kingsway's brief moment of glory turned out to be its swan-song. As we have already seen, the Casino was much too small for its new role. Where better to negotiate for than the 2,300-seater in Frederick Street, scarcely a stone's throw away? Messrs Donald may not have felt disposed towards selling their property, but lease to another (non-cinema) concern was a different matter, and on Thursday 19 January 1962 was announced the start of a dialogue that soon led to agreement.

On Saturday 3 February the film *Warlord Of Crete* brought the Kingsway's days as a cinema to a close, although all operating box equipment was left *in situ*. Ever since then, the Kingsway has been Aberdeen's largest Bingo hall, run until recently by Messrs Donald themselves, who assumed control of the Casino Bingo company when, after some years, the lease arrangement was dissolved by mutual agreement and the original promoters were given alternative premises—the former Donald's Ballroom in North Silver Street, empty since its closure in 1959. In 1980 the Kingsway received the additional facility of a lounge bar, converted from former adjacent shops. The old North Silver Street Hall, meanwhile, functioned under a succession of Bingo ownerships until about 1979 when it finally closed and was sold. In 1984-5, after years of disuse, it was converted into flats.

As for the Casino, a suggestion was made by the Bingo men, just prior to their move to the Kingsway, that a fund be set up to secure it for Aberdeen Lad's Club, which was then being forced to quit its old Gallowgate quarters. For the sum of £30,000 an adjacent building, also owned by the Bingo Club and suitable for conversion to a gym, would be thrown in, but this laudable proposal foundered when it transpired that the whole block had been earmarked for redevelopment by the Town Council. The old cinema was compulsorily purchased, and ended its days as a council store, becoming increasingly delapidated until it was finally demolished in 1971. Demolished at the same time was the former Star, its red 'star' window still *in situ*. The sites of both buildings are now occupied by a complex of low-rise flats.

In 1962, after decades of campaigning by the cinema trade, Aberdeen's picture houses were given permission to open on Sundays, one at a time on a rota basis. On 24 March that year, ABC rationalised the name Regal out of existence, substituting the standard title, ABC, which lasted for twenty-five years. Films ranged from Leslie Phillips' *In The Dog House* and Charlie Drake's *Petticoat Pirates* to Kirk Douglas, Olivier and Laughton's *Spartacus*. Hayley Mills played a double role in *The Parent Trap*, Vincent Price starred in *The Pit And The Pendulum*, and Warren Beatty made his screen debut in *Splendour In The Grass*. A furore was caused by the daring *Lolita*, and pop-stars were to the fore with Cliff Richard in *The Young Ones*, Elvis Presley in *Blue Hawaii*, Billy Fury and Bobby Vee (both soon to disappear over the Liverpool beat precipice) in *Play It Cool*, and Adam Faith displaying considerable acting talent in *Mix Me A Person*. James Stewart and John Wayne were in *The Man Who Shot Liberty Valance*, and Herbert Lom was the third *Phantom Of The Opera*. *Dr No*, first in the long line of James Bond spy-thrillers, opened at the Odeon on Monday 5 November, immediately setting a standard in its glossy sophistication.

After Bingo came another new craze—ten-pin bowling. An old garage in Loch Street was acquired by a company called Granite City Bowling Lanes (Aberdeen) Ltd (a director of which was T. Scott Sutherland), and was converted into the Granite Bowl, opening in December 1962. It soon had a rival.

97   The Regal becomes the ABC, July 1963 (ADC, Dept of Planning)

Back in 1960 there had been a rumour concerning the possible sale or lease of the City Cinema to Weston's Supermarkets. Denied by Messrs Donald, the rumour died a natural death, but on 18 June 1963 came the news that the City was now indeed to close as a picture hall. Associated British Cinemas (ABC) was diversifying into ten-pin bowling, and had initially been looking

98   T. Scott Sutherland

towards obtaining space on one floor of the new Shiprow Car Park. Hours
restrictions made this idea impracticable, but just the right kind of premises
were found in the City, on which a 35-year lease was negotiated. On 20 July
1963 the City's curtains closed for the last time with *Sign Of The Pagan*,
starring Mickey Rooney and Anthony Quinn, and in the ensuing £300,000
conversion the cinema interior disappeared completely to make way for two
floors of bowling alleys.

Ironically, the celebrity guests at the opening of the new ABC Bowl (now
called the Aberdeen Bowl) on 1 May 1964 were Jess Conrad, Oliver Reed and
Julia Foster—all film stars! Announcement of the City's impending closure
came only days after the death, on 13 June 1963, of its architect, T. Scott
Sutherland—part-instigator of the introduction to Aberdeen of the very pastime that was to bring about the demise of this particular brainchild. Not that
Sutherland, hard-headed businessman that he was, would have been likely
to regret too much the City's disappearance in favour of a new and much
more profitable alternative! Proprietorship of the Bowl passed to EMI Leisure
in the 1970s, then to Trust House Forte and, more recently, First Leisure
Corporation. Its interior and equipment have undergone much renewal and

renovation in 1987, and has never looked better. The building still belongs to Aberdeen Picture Palaces.

More links with the old way of things were broken by the death of the Capitol's architect A.G.R. MacKenzie in March 1963, and by the closure of the Tivoli Theatre that September. The Tivoli's subsequent sale to a Bingo promoter did at least serve to safeguard a fine example of the work of Frank Matcham— foremost theatre architect of late Victorian and Edwardian times, and designer also of the present His Majesty's Theatre.

On 11 October 1963 Ernest Bromberg announced from London the coming sale of the News Cinema/Curzon to Singleton's of Glasgow, a firm which had been in business since 1911 when it bought a hall from J.J. Bennell. Simultaneously, Singleton's arranged to acquire the Palais from dancing teacher Lex Henderson who had purchased it from Bromberg when the latter quit Aberdeen in 1949. Bromberg came North on 25 October to settle the cinema's affairs and to have a last look around before returning to the financier's business that he continued until his death in April 1973. On Saturday 2 November the Curzon closed for renovation and to begin a new phase in its existence.

Chapter 16

Decline But Not Fall   1964—1987

On Wednesday, 22 January 1964 the former News Cinema came back to life under the name of COSMO 2, Cosmo 1 being the former King's, Glasgow, then owned by Singleton's and now (1987) belonging to the Scottish Film Council. Olmi's *Il Posto* was the film chosen to inaugurate what was now more than ever a specialist house. Other features in the Cosmo's earlier days included *Black Orpheus* and the Salzburg Festival production of the Mozart opera *Don Giovanni*.

The Capitol hosted another big pop concert on 22 March, this time featuring the Searchers, Bobby Vee, Dusty Springfield, and Big Dee Irwin of 'Swingin' On A Star' fame. A follow-up show on 19 May brought the Silhouettes, the highly athletic Freddie And The Dreamers, Peter And Gordon, Mark Peters, Dave Berry, The Five Embers, Millie and—most of all—The Rolling Stones, then assiduously cultivating their image as Peck's (or rather their manager Andrew Oldham's) Bad Boys. The police had to be called in to control the crowds outside the Capitol that night, and Messrs C. Bruce Miller, at whose George Street shop Millie made a personal appearance to sign autographs, ended up with their own souvenir of the occasion—a bill for the replacement of one of their plate-glass windows, broken in the crush!

The concert itself played to a rather mixed reception. Dave Berry's 'creepy' gimmick of slinking on to the stage from behind the scenery seems to have made little impression, while Peter And Gordon were considered to lack movement and audience contact. The show's real hit was Freddie And The Dreamers, who made their greatest impact on the older audience at the second house. Grown men were seen to jump out of their seats, shouting and waving their arms at the madcap antics of Freddie as he cavorted about the stage!

Much publicity was given to reports of a move to bring the Beatles to the Capitol, but unfortunately these negotiations did not survive their preliminary stages. 'The Top Beat Show', which ran at the Capitol for five days from 20 July, had at the top of its bill Gerry And The Pacemakers and Sounds Incorporated, and also featured a variety of other groups. Later in the year 'The Billy J. Kramer Beat Show' featured Mark Wynter and a variety of lesser-known acts, including Johnny And The Copycats from Buckie.

Those were the days of the Gordon Lonsdale spy scandal, Mod and Rocker battles at Margate, Gonk dolls, the beginning of the conflict in Vietnam, and the election of the first Harold Wilson government. In Aberdeen they are remembered for something else—an outbreak of typhoid fever, which began

316

when one defective tin of corned beef was unwittingly sliced up and sold over the counter of Low's Supermarket at the west end of Union Street. As this dangerous disease spread throughout the city over late May and early June 1964, cinema and theatre attendances plummeted and major film bookings had to be postponed until conditions returned to normal.

Feature films of the day comprised a good mix of the typical and the memorable, with Albert Finney in *Tom Jones*, Sellers at his most hilarious in *The Pink Panther*, darling of the day Rita Tushingham in *The Leather Boys* and *No Place To Go*, Elizabeth Taylor and Richard Burton's *Cleopatra*, which played for a long season at the Odeon, Stanley Baker in *Zulu*, and Cliff Richard And The Shadows in *Wonderful Land*. The Beatles' first film *A Hard Day's Night* opened at the Gaumont on 3 August, Bond was back in *Goldfinger* that October, Elvis Presley was in *Roustabout*, and among the large number of 'family' films in evidence that Christmas was the one with the biggest musical title theme of all—*The Big Country*.

The film-making boom of the early 1960s was abating, but a good selection of material reached Aberdeen in the course of 1965—*The Carpetbaggers*, Sellers' *Only Two Can Play*, Melina Mercouri and Peter Ustinov's *Topkapi*, Burton and O'Toole in *Becket*, Anthony Quinn in *Zorba The Greek*, Gerry And The Pacemakers in *Ferry Across The Mersey*, and Peter Sellers' masterful follow-up to *The Pink Panther*, *A Shot In The Dark*. Morecambe & Wise were in *The Intelligence Men*, the Beatles were back in the relatively plot-free but highly entertaining *Help*, The Dave Clark Five were on the pop-film band-wagon with *Catch Me If You Can*, Taylor and Burton starred in *The Sandpiper*, Jane Fonda was *Cat Ballou*, 'Tush' Tushingham was bait for young chauvinists Ray Brooks and Michael Crawford in *The Knack*, and Robert Vaughn followed in the wake of Bond with the first spin-off of the 'Man From UNCLE' series, *Spy With My Face*.

On the evening of Thursday, 17 June 1965 the Capitol reverberated once again to the sound of the Rolling Stones. The scenes inside the auditorium were by no means as unruly as some that had occurred at the group's shows, but reports of frenzied fans jumping on seats, tearing their hair, running about in the aisles, weeping, struggling with police, and generally exhibiting every sign of mass hysteria, seem to have come as something of a shock in a city not used to such excesses. Whether by reason of this, the cost of touring, or perhaps simply because the theatre was not at that time geared for dealing with stage shows on a regular basis, it was to be close on another decade before the Capitol ran another pop evening!

Amid all the films of 1966 there was one that stood head and shoulders above the rest, not only as a tremendous box-office success but also for its long-term appeal and durability where so many of its contemporaries are already forgotten. No matter how thoroughly society may have been invaded by pop culture, this film contained nothing trendy, outrageous or controversial, and there was only one guitar in it. Its title was *The Sound Of Music*, and it was shown at the Odeon over a marathon season which began on 4 April 1966 and continued until 7 January 1967—an all-time record for Aberdeen. It scored success after success on return showings up until the time of the sale of its exhibition rights to television in the 1980s, and even that may not be the end of the story.

The end of the story it was for the fine Astoria, Kittybrewster, which for years had been struggling against ever-lengthening odds. It closed on Saturday 13 August 1966 after the last showing of Paul Newman and Lauren Bacall's *The Moving Target*, and reopened on 29 August as a Bingo hall. The resumption of films was not ruled out should trading conditions improve, but for the present it was to be Bingo all the way. There were generous prizes to be won, and as the game was reaching the peak of its national popularity the move ought to have been a successful one, but it seems that nothing could ever be assumed as far as the Astoria was concerned. Not even Bingo could bring its public back, and at the end of the year Messrs Donald reluctantly threw in the towel. The Astoria's site was sold for redevelopment as a shopping complex. All removable fittings and materials worth keeping were salvaged, and in April 1967 demolition began on what was little more than an empty shell.

In a way, the Astoria had the last laugh. If the demolition men expected an easy job, they were disappointed. The mix for the concrete parts of the

99   The Astoria becomes a Bingo hall, 1966 (Michael Candy)

building had been so good that they presented a rock-like mass, the breaking up of which took a great deal of time and effort. Eventually a side wall was breached so that bulldozers and lifting plant could be brought in, but it was only after weeks of steady battering that at length the structure disappeared. A picture comes to mind of the shade of the late T. Scott Sutherland standing somewhere just out of sight, watching operations with wry amusement and not a little satisfaction. Just to add to the difficulties, a natural spring that still runs beneath the site had to be kept constantly pumped to avoid flooding. Throughout the life of the cinema above it this pump had been controlled from the operating box, wherein was a large red-painted mains switch conspicuously marked 'Do Not Switch Off'!

One item from the Astoria that immediately went to a new home was its Compton organ. The news that the cinema was to close caused some apprehension among local enthusiasts as to the fate of the instrument. Luckily, Robert Leys, who had by then become head music teacher at Powis Academy, was on hand to initiate and carry out a most unusual and interesting school project—the re-installation of the organ in the Academy's assembly hall. After preliminary discussions with the authorities and with Messrs Donald, permission was granted and money was put up. Under the guidance of Mr Leys, teams of pupils descended on the Astoria, taking out all the organ's pipes, carefully wrapping them for storage, unsoldering and labelling the hundreds of electrical connections, dismantling the larger components and lugging them out of the lofty chambers. In the course of this operation there came to light, in a dusty corner, an ancient bottle of Sloane's Liniment, still with quite some pep left in it. The provenance of this unlikely find remains a mystery to this day.

After much preparation, the instrument, restored and refurbished by staff and pupils, was set up again in two chambers created under the hall stage, with the console (reclothed in a new and less bulky wooden surround) in front of the stage on the right. The lighting equipment from the console's original glass surround was not wasted. Still under the player's control, it now illuminated the spaces behind the grillework in the front of the stage, through which the organ spoke.

The opening concert was performed by George Blackmore on Monday, 7 March 1969, and for the next thirteen or so years the organ served the school well. After the departure (in the late 1970s) of Robert Leys for a new teaching post in the South, it was looked after by enthusiastic members of staff and remained in regular use for teaching purposes. It would almost certainly have come to the fore again in a public capacity had not disaster struck on the night of Saturday, 20 November 1982, when, in an act of grossest vandalism, a youth (still under education at the Academy) broke into the building and set fire to the hall and adjoining staff rooms. Due to the hall's central position, the outbreak went unnoticed until it had taken a firm hold. Thanks to the efficiency and speed of Aberdeen's Fire Service the rest of the school was saved, but the next morning all that remained of one of the city's best-appointed school halls was four blackened walls and a pile of smoking debris. No-one would have known that there had ever been an organ there.

Returning to 1966, on Saturday, 24 September the Torry Cinema was the next to bow out, having become uneconomic to run. After the failure of Bingo at the Astoria, the gaming equipment had been moved from there to Torry, but no sooner had it arrived than a good offer was received for the Crombie Road site. The 'Torryer' never re-opened, and now a block of shops stands in its place.

Teenagers of 1966 may recall the coming of another competitor for Aberdeen's embattled cinema trade—'The Place', a beat club which opened in the former Melville Church at the corner of Skene Street and Rose Street. An ambitious affair with a boutique and coffee shop, it provided a platform for many aspiring young groups as well as opportunities to hear better-known ones, but before many months had passed the concern petered out. Next owners of the building were none other than Messrs Donald, for whom it became a store and maintenance depot. It remained as such until 1982 when it was sold once again and its interior rebuilt as a most interesting and unusual block of flats.

September of the Flower Power year 1967 brought a rare instance of the exercising of local censorship on a film. James Joyce's *Ulysses*, planned for showing at the ABC, gained the distinction of being banned by Aberdeen's magistrates, and not even a substantial *Evening Express* article by the ABC's manager, Mr Geoffrey Ramsden (head of Aberdeen CEA), arguing the case for allowing the film to be shown, could make them change their minds. Mr Ramsden was even supported by an outspoken member of the clergy, but banned the film was and banned it stayed. There still exists a local censorship committee which can be called upon to rule on any picture considered to be of an explicit nature, and which lacks a Board Of Censors certificate.

And so to the sobering 1970s, in the course of which the UK cinema trade underwent more upheaval and contraction than ever. Films came and went in waves of fashion—Kung-Fu extravaganzas in the early part of the decade, the super-goriness exemplified by *Straw Dogs*, dire visions of the future in *A Clockwork Orange*, amazing science-fiction adventures in *Star Wars* and *Close Encounters*, and tear-jerkers pure and simple such as *Love Story*. Lineal descendents of the musicals of Busby Berkeley and Fred Astaire were the disco-dancing *Saturday Night Fever* and *Grease*, a light-hearted backward glance at the 1950s. In accordance with the more down-to-earth outlook of the times, 'family' films were much more in evidence than during the arty 1960s, and it is also interesting to note that for the first time films came to be advertised by means of the cinema's old *bête noir*, television!

The Astoria's disappearance was followed by a period of calm, but when further change came it did so with a rumble. On Saturday 16 January 1971, with the film *Where Eagles Dare*, the Cinema House, off the beaten track in

Skene Terrace, closed just a few months short of its 61st year of operation. The Bingo licence that it had held since 1970 was invoked and, as at the Kingsway, the old projection equipment was mothballed. Blame for the closure was laid squarely at the door of the film industry, and once again it was stressed that a return to cinema shows might not be ruled out should there be adequate demand in the future.

As a Bingo hall, the Cinema House ran in tandem with the Kingsway. It was rechristened CASINO BINGO in September 1981, with a new exterior sign; the large outside board is also recent, replacing the original programme board which blew down about 1978. As one of the few remaining picture halls of its age and type in Scotland, it remains an historic building in its own right. The tiny cramped operating box, from which the screen could only be viewed by squeezing in between the projector and the side wall, still remains perched in the back of the balcony, and also visible in the auditorium is the acoustic baffling added when talkies arrived in 1930. Upstairs, the old secondary Union Hall is also unchanged. It was often used as a rehearsal room for productions at His Majesty's Theatre, itself sold in 1974 to the Town Council. (Beautifully restored in 1982, the Theatre retains its long-standing links with the Donald family through the retention of Messrs Peter Donald (II) and James Donald (III) as managers.)

Early in the 1970s, it was further decided by Messrs Donald that either the Capitol or the Majestic would have to go. For reasons which will soon become apparent, it was the Majestic for which redevelopment plans were intimated in October 1972. Caledonian Theatres was wound up, and the Majestic closed on Saturday, 29 September 1973 after the last showing of *Kelly's Heroes*. As usual, any useful fittings were rescued, but the front display letters were left, providing the demolition squad with lots of absorbing spelling exercises, not all of them entirely polite.

The Majestic may have been T. Scott Sutherland's *magnum opus*, but it presented nothing like the resistance encountered at Kittybrewster, and within two or three weeks it had completely vanished. Its removal clearly exposed the roof-line of the old La Scala and the blocked-up former entrance to the Chintz Room above the neighbouring Clydesdale Bank (regrettably lost in the redevelopment scheme). Whether by chance or design, the name of the Majestic's original owners lives on in the building's successor, Caledonian House, which contains shops, a new bank and some departments of British Telecom.

The major circuits of Rank and ABC were by now being steadily thinned out, with most of the remaining houses converted into double or, more commonly, triple auditoria. Over the 1970s this policy gathered momentum, and a special department was set up within the Rank Organisation to examine the possibilities of redundant cinema sites which might be profitably redeveloped on behalf of the company itself. Pre-oil Aberdeen, with its widely-publicised property boom, was just the sort of place for such a redevelopment, and only

100   The end of the Majestic, October 1973 (James Brooks)

101   The Gaumont interior, 1973 (Michael Thomson)

a month after the announcement of the Majestic's forthcoming demise it was disclosed that plans had been submitted for a new block of shops and offices on the site of the Gaumont—a piece of news not entirely unexpected in local cinema circles.

The former Picture House's last night came on Saturday, 6 October 1973 when the main film was Paula Wilcox and Richard Beckinsale in *The Lovers*. Attendances were good, whether through feelings of nostalgia or whether through the mention in a press report that there might be a 'pleasant surprise' awaiting patrons that evening. There were in fact no hand-outs, but perhaps on reflection the sight of a full house was surprise enough!

Formalities over, the brick-built structure was soon removed, leaving only the Union Street granite frontage which the authorities insisted be retained. On the gable wall of the next-door building in Windmill Brae could be seen the outlines of the small houses that had stood there before 1914, an age away. The cinema site lay empty for a while because of the financial recession of 1974-75 and the consequent uncertainty over occupancy of the new building, but in 1976 the gap was filled by the present attractive Job Centre and shop.

Since the late 1960s the Playhouse's staple fare had consisted of what one might term 'Continental' pictures, but by 1973 the profitability of even these was being seriously eroded by spiralling costs. It seems probable that the Playhouse's days would have been numbered even if Messrs Scott the builders had not decided to erect new premises in Union Glen and to dispose of their Union Street property. At the end of 1973 the Playhouse's lease was terminated, and on Saturday 9 May 1974 it closed. Messrs Donald expressed interest in buying the Playhouse block (although they declined to comment on whether cinema activities would continue there) but in the event ownership of the building passed to Devanha Properties Ltd. After lying empty for a few months the Playhouse was demolished to make way for a new block of shops and offices.

As the size of the Donald/APP circuit decreased, staffing underwent a reshuffle. On the closure of the Majestic and (later) the Playhouse, several employees were transferred to the Capitol, among them the Majestic's manager, Charles Elder. Jack Wright, who, having witnessed fashions come and go at the Capitol over four decades, must have been Aberdeen's longest-serving manager in any one cinema, was moved to the Playhouse to supervise its running-down. There he succeeded Peter Donald (II), who had gone to be Assistant Manager at His Majesty's Theatre. After the Playhouse closed, Mr Wright remained with the company for a while as part-time peripatetic relief manager, and every now and then his familiar figure could be seen in its old place at the top of the Capitol's main stairway. Deteriorating eyesight forced him to retire completely after a couple of years, and he and his wife Dorrie subsequently moved south to Twickenham so as to be closer to their family. Mr Wright died in May 1987 at the age of 81, and it is fitting that he was accorded a brief obituary in the newspapers of the city where he spent most of his career. It is also pleasant to note that in 1986 he was able to pay a short return visit to Aberdeen, and to drop in at his old Capitol once again.

Early in 1974, hotelier Stewart Spence and his business partner Ian Donald (son of Richard M. Donald) took a lease on the former Capitol café. The café had been redecorated and rearranged in 1959 when the catering contract passed to the local firm of Nixons, but it had gone out of use in 1967. A drinks licence had been granted in 1968, and this was taken up by Messrs Donald and Spence. Further alterations were put in hand to turn the area into a comfortable little restaurant and bar. The bar counter was placed across the right hand wall where the old orchestra platform had been (the top of the alcove was left visible above and behind the canopy) and all walls were redecorated in warm pink with a black dado, nicely offsetting the superb art

102 The Playhouse, Union Street, June 1973 (the old central ticket office was removed during the 1950s) (Michael Thomson)

103   The Playhouse interior, 1973 (Michael Thomson)

deco mirrors, the large opalescent white glass light fittings and the fanciful window pelmets which, like most of the woodwork, were painted white. In accordance with the restaurant's cinematic connections, the front of each menu card carried a silhouette of Charlie Chaplin. Of the Capitol's good but unpretentious cuisine the most outstanding features were salads, home baking and excellent morning coffee. In theory, it was possible to float between cinema, restaurant and bar for a whole day without leaving the building!

In the summer of that same year, an appearance by the then immensely popular Bay City Rollers marked the beginning of a regular policy of live shows at the Capitol, using the stage facilities that had largely determined the building's survival when the choice had to be made between it and the Majestic. Seeing Aberdeen as now being a worthwhile prospect, agents and promoters readily added an extra date to tours taking performers to Edinburgh and Glasgow. Messrs Donald, for their part, had the stage extended in 1975 by the building of a semi-circular apron over the old orchestra pit. Trap doors were provided to allow the organ console to rise through the floor, and a large set of curtains (since removed because of technical difficulties) was installed on runners suspended from above the sounding-board, closing over the front of the apron when the full stage was in use. The organ, now watched over by local enthusiasts in conjunction with the management, is the last in a Scottish cinema and is among very few in the whole of Britain that remain in their original settings.

While the Capitol's interior has changed a little over the years (its original silver decorations, which had become tarnished, were refinished in gold when the auditorium was redecorated around the time of the Coronation), its significance as a building of historical and architectural interest was officially recognised in 1976 when, at the behest of the Secretary Of State For Scotland, it became one of only a small number of British cinemas to be accorded a category B listing for statutory protection. No building so listed can be demolished or altered without the consent of the local authority or, if necessary, the Secretary Of State For Scotland. In the Capitol's official description, special mention is made of its 'restrained art-deco' interiors, now very rare.

The statutory listing of cinemas has followed a general reappraisal of the art and architecture of the inter-war period, and the realisation that they are as much a part of the country's heritage and social history as is any other type of public edifice. Among those listed further south are the Granada, Tooting and the Astoria (now Rainbow pop concert hall), Finsbury Park, London; in Scotland the Playhouse, Edinburgh, the superb 1920s Caley, Lothian Road, Edinburgh, the Odeon (formerly New Victoria), Clerk Street, Edinburgh, the Salon, Glasgow and the Kinnaird, Dundee have also been so treated.

In April 1977, soon after its addition to the statutory list, the Capitol was the subject of an application from would-be developers seeking outline permission to demolish both it and the adjoining Bell's Hotel (then on the market for between £800,000 and £1,000,000) in favour of a shop and office block. The first that Messrs Donald heard of this was in the next day's papers; no approach had been made to them, and neither had any drawings for a new building been lodged with the city authorities. Also, before long the developer's supposedly high bid for the hotel was substantially reduced. Bell's Hotel stayed in the Bell family, and the Capitol, which in any case was not on the market, continued on its way.

Competition from nearby restaurants and food takeaways brought about the Capitol restaurant's closure in September 1977. The whole bar-restaurant area was made over to bar space, and the seating was rearranged to give a large crush area for concert-nights. If the beautifully made solid wood and criss-cross stainless steelwork doors to the bar seem familiar to cinemagoers of past years, this may be because they are from the Astoria, ideally suiting their new surroundings. Some of the wood-finish panelling in the bar also came from the Astoria, and (amazingly in these days of planned obsolescence) still looks perfectly fresh.

The Capitol's exterior remains unaltered except for the covering over with poster-boards (in September 1976) of the elegant solid wooden 'Capitol' sign above the outside doors—made necessary by the lack of display space in the entranceway—and the disappearance of the old neon-work. The main sign, unlit for several years, was damaged in a gale in October 1973, and was reinstated in plain white letters. The vertical signs on either side, long out of use, were removed in March 1986. Shortly after the Capitol's regular stage show policy began, the floodlighting above the canopy was reinstated, but the lamps proved too susceptible to rain-damage. However, the outside foyer and vestibule have been brightened by the addition of extra illumination under the canopy, which itself was refaced in 1983 after having withstood fifty years' exposure to the elements.

When His Majesty's Theatre closed for restoration in October 1980, Bert Ewen returned to the Capitol to give the benefit of his technical experience in the adaptation of the wingless cine-variety stage for the many theatre shows that were to be transferred to it. In collaboration with the Capitol's technical staff under its present chief operator Robert Stewart, HM Theatre's stage manager Edi Swan and his team succeeded in fitting on to the stage some remarkably elaborate presentations. When the Theatre reopened in 1982, Bert remained at the Capitol in a part-time, semi-retired capacity, and was present when Bert Gates' wonder cinema of 1933 reached its 50th anniversary on 4 February 1983. (Marked by prominent reports in the press and by a show featuring the popular group 'Sky' on the day itself, the occasion was celebrated with a convivial gathering for staff and friends a few days later.) Ill health forced Bert's retirement at this time, and his death in early 1984 greatly saddened his many friends and colleagues.

When, in 1979, the Capitol's 'new' manager Charles Elder moved on to take up a position in the licensed trade, his place was taken by Brian Donald, younger son of Herbert M. Donald. Since 1983, house manager has been Mr Arthur Buchanan, one time manager of Cosmo 2, and of long experience in the entertainment business.

Aberdeen's first taste of the triple cinema came on Monday, 8 April 1974 when after several weeks of intensive preparation (during which the cinema still remained open) the ODEON FILM CENTRE came into being. On Monday, 8 July 1974 the ABC also reopened in triple form, both cinemas having been treated in the standard manner of walling off the back stalls and dividing the space thus enclosed to create two little cinemas seating about 150 each. As is normal practice, the former balconies, seating between 500 and 600, are designated 'Cinema One', and are used chiefly for first runs. The smaller cinemas (Two and Three) are used for less commercial attractions, or for the retention of popular features already seen upstairs. Subject to the agreement of film distributors, they can also be used to duplicate the programmes of Cinema One.

At both the ABC and the Odeon, the conventional two-projector system, which requires constant changing-over from one machine to the other, was supplanted by what is known as the 'cakestand', in which all the film that makes up the programme is spliced together in sequence and wound on to a large metal disc. The disc rotates on its side, the film moves through the projector horizontally, and special lenses turn the image the right way up for showing on the screen. A minimum complement of staff is thereby required to work all three sets of equipment more or less simultaneously, aided by time-switches and other automation. Something similar is in operation at the Capitol, where the programme is spliced together on one or two large reels and placed on a 'tower', an upright stand with a film reel and a take-up reel on either side. The tower is fixed behind the projector so that the film passes above the machine before being directed down past its shutter as usual. It is mounted on a swivel so that while one part of the programme is being shown the other can be rewound using a built-in mechanism.

Between 1974 and 1977 there were no further closures among the city's remaining cinemas, but on 6 August 1977 Cosmo 2 shut its doors at only a fortnight's notice. A furious letter from Aberdeen's NATTKE secretary Brian Gascoyne in the *Evening Express* of 10 August accused the cinema industry of being clandestine in its attitude and in its dealings with staff, most of whom were working awkward hours for quite poor pay. By way of an example, attendants were cited as coming out with about £28 gross for a forty-hour week, and it was held by Mr Gascoyne that employers brainwashed their staffs into a 'the show must go on and somebody's got to do it' way of thinking.

The Cosmo had been fulfilling a valuable function through its policy of showing British and foreign films for the connoisseur, paralleling the activities of the old La Scala long before. Its closure was forced by a lack of good foreign material and by the fact that the major circuits, with their triple cinemas, were now picking up on films which would previously have been considered too uncommercial—precisely the sort of material that had sustained the likes of the Cosmo. Mr Ronald Singleton, managing director of Singleton Cinemas, expressed the hope that someone would be able to continue the Cosmo, and suggested that it might be very suitable as a regional film theatre for the Scottish Film Council, which already had the former Cosmo 1 in Glasgow. The Council did want a centre in Aberdeen, but the very small size of the Diamond Street building made it impractical as the kind of cinema and meeting-place that the Council was envisaging. Takeovers by other groups were spoken of, but unfortunately nothing of the kind came about, and after a few weeks during which the Cosmo's only use was for midnight screenings of Chinese films (popular with the staffs of nearby restaurants but not with projectionists, who could never tell which reel was which!) it closed for good. Plans were announced some time later for turning the premises into a restaurant, but again nothing happened. The end came in September 1981, when the former Palais next door, leased by Singleton's to another concern and operating as Satchmo's disco club, was destroyed by fire and the whole of the building was left roofless. At one point a reconstruction plan was spoken of, incorporating the former cinema area, but instead the entire site (apart from a surviving corner block) is now occupied by a car park.

As the 1980s dawned, time was running out for the last of the original Donald cinemas. The Grand Central's simple 1929 frontage, made up of elements of what had been there before plus a plain harled top storey, had been considerably brightened by the cleaning and renewal of its vestibule woodwork in 1973 and the replacement of its old sign four years later with a new fluorescent one. Inside, its 'atmospherics' long gone, the hall was strictly functional, although glimpses of the past could still be seen in ornamental plaster mouldings above the stairways and on the balcony front. In the tiny operating box was a pair of Simplex projectors, inherited from the City and replacing two venerable Kalees. The rewinding room (which also contained the stage curtain controls!) was below the box, from where it was reached by a spiral iron stair.

The Queen's, meanwhile, remained an odd mixture of twentieth century cinematic and nineteenth century Georgian civic architectures, its original function not easy to discern without visualising it with window spaces intact and minus later exterior additions. Its appearance benefited a great deal from the fitting of modern illuminating display panels on the Union Street frontage (replacing the original large poster board which collapsed in late 1979), and the repainting of the exterior woodwork and signs. The large 'Queen's' neon sign, lettered in red with a blue outline and crown, had by that time been inoperative for some time—possibly since the late 1960s.

Both cinemas struggled on until ever-increasing costs, combined with the spread of such pastimes as home computer games and video, finally destroyed their viability. On 17 October 1981 their closure brought to an end the history of James F. Donald (Aberdeen Cinemas) Ltd as picture hall proprietors, although the Aberdeen Picture Palaces subsidiary remains active. The Queen's (its defunct neon sign removed in 1986) stood empty for years awaiting a buyer or lessee. Various uses for it were proposed by interested parties, but with no result. Eventually, Messrs Donald took the building in hand again, converting it into Aberdeen's latest night-club, under the managership of Ian Donald. A competition was held via local radio to find a name for the club, and the £100 prize-winning entry was 'Legends', a kind of memorial to the many legendary personalities who graced the screen of the Queen's Cinema over nearly seventy years. This pleasant idea had to be abandoned at the last minute when a mobile discotheque in Torry successfully laid legal claim to the name. The exterior neon sign was changed, and in July 1987 the club opened as 'Eagles'!

The Grand Central was demolished in 1984 to make way for housing, as was the neighbouring Ice Rink, another casualty of recent change in entertainment trends. At the Picture House, Stonehaven, a combination of Bingo and films had been introduced in the late 1960s or early 1970s, soon changing to Bingo exclusively. Even this did not reverse the cinema's fortunes, and in the early 1980s Messrs Donald made an application for change of use of the building or land—essential before any redevelopment could take place or the site made attractive to buyers. In the event, any private plans were pre-empted by a compulsory purchase order from Kincardine District Council, and in the summer of 1982 the Picture House closed. It lay derelict until its demolition in June 1986.

Change has taken place within the Donald organisation itself. In the Spring of 1977 Herbert W.G. Donald, elder son of Herbert M. Donald, joined the family firm in a managerial capacity. Previously concerned with concert promotion in London, he holds special responsibility for the Capitol's live entertainments. In 1979 the distinctive red neon sign above the optician's shop in Back Wynd went out for the last time as Herbert Donald senior, supervisor of the family's Union Street. cinemas, took his retirement from business.

Property seems to have been a fairly regular sideline for both Aberdeen Picture Palaces in its original form and for James F. Donald (Aberdeen Cinemas) Ltd, in whose affairs it has come to play a major role. The story is told of how one day about 1930 James Donald senior, meeting by chance his North Silver Street neighbour, the auctioneer James Milne, enquired casually of Mr Milne as to where he was bound for just then. Mr Milne answered that he was off to auction the old Sick Children's Hospital in Castle Terrace. James Donald went along, and by the end of the day the building was his. (It later was to become the premises of the celebrated 'Cocky' Hunter.) James Donald's acquisition of the old hospital marked the company's entry into a line of business which has attained enough importance for offers to be constantly received from parties interested in buying one piece of property or another.

Indeed, at least one major take-over bid has been attracted from the south. In the morning papers of 5 March 1983, before Messrs Donald had as much as received their official letters on the matter, there appeared headlines proclaiming a £1,890,000 offer for Aberdeen Cinemas Ltd from a business consortium called Legibus 200, headed by the Dunton Group of Chesham, Buckinghamshire. This consortium, the story ran, planned to inject the Donald firm with 'more aggressive' management policies, expand its Bingo interests and (perhaps a little more to the point) redevelop some of its properties for housing and/or offices. (This seemed to ignore the fact that the Grand Central and Ice Rink, standing on prime sites in an area zoned by the local authority for residential development, were already being sold to the building firm of Barratt!)

Dialogue had in fact been going on between Messrs Donald and the Dunton group for about two years, and Dunton was confident of being able to interest a sufficient number of Donald family share-holders to allow it to take full control, but a statement issued by Herbert W.G. Donald on the following Tuesday gave a different picture:

> The offer was made direct to shareholders without prior board consultations and does not therefore carry the recommendation of the directors.
>
> Any statements made to the Press have therefore been made by individuals as shareholders and not on behalf of the board.
>
> As this is a family-owned private company the board does not intend to issue any statements other than to say that while it is premature to forecast the outcome of the bid, it is already clear that it will not be accepted by a substantial number of shareholders.

Dunton reiterated its certainty that the offer would find favour, but the deadline of 25 March came and went with no agreement. When news of the bid broke, the *Press & Journal* contacted James Donald of His Majesty's Theatre, who confirmed that share-holders were indeed interested in selling, but added that there had been a number of parties who would like to take over the company, and that it might not necessarily be the Dunton Group to whom the shares would go.

The truth of this statement shortly became apparent. By the time that the Wednesday evening papers were on the stands it had been officially intimated that there was indeed another contender for control of the firm—senior partner Richard Donald. In a complicated move requiring the approval of the Inland Revenue, his proposal was to use the company's own money in buying out fifteen of its sixteen shareholders. Dunton extended its deadline, but to no avail. At a reported £120 as against the rival's £135 bid for each of the 14,000 shares, it was Mr Donald who won through, securing full control over all aspects of the firm's activities. What the plans will be for James F. Donald (Aberdeen Cinemas) Ltd in its new form will doubtless become clear

104   The Kingsway, October 1987—renovation is under way in the auditorium (Alex Garden)

in due course, but it seems likely that property and the new incarnation of the Queen's will figure largely in its dealings. Aberdeen Picture Palaces was not involved in the transaction, and remains unaffected.

Bingo is no longer one of Aberdeen Cinemas' interests; on 22 December 1986 an announcement was made that the former Cinema House and the Kingsway had been bought over by the large Nottingham-based company Coral Social Clubs. Interviewed by the *Evening Express*, Richard Donald, in confirming the sale, expressed some sadness at parting with the halls, especially the Cinema House, which he had managed as a lad. However, change is inevitable, and since the purchase Coral has put into effect an ambitious renovation and upgrading plan for the Kingsway, which will become an excellently-appointed modern entertainment centre.

The ABC triple cinema ran on steadily with little stir over the years, although during the late 1970s or early 1980s some interesting experiments were tried using special earthquake devices that made the whole place seem to tremble during big disaster scenes! It was also in the ABC's highly-automated operating boxes that Aberdeen's first Dolby sound system was installed, much improving the playing quality of optical soundtracks, which are less prone to damage than magnetic ones, and have been generally re-adopted by film studios.

During the 1970s, ABC Cinemas became an arm of the large EMI multi-entertainments group, which got into difficulties during the early 1980s and was sold to the prosperous Thorn electrical company. Thorn's primary interest was undoubtedly in the recording and electrical side of EMI, but at the time of the take-over it was stated that the EMI group would be kept together, although the performance of all of its areas would be closely scrutinised. The ABC chain's new owners were not really an entertainment concern, and could hardly have felt much enthusiasm for their role as cinema proprietors, especially considering present-day trading conditions. In 1985, as had been widely expected, ABC Cinemas was offered for sale, attracting a bid from its arch-rival, Rank. For a while it looked as if a management buy-out might succeed, but in 1986 the chain became part of the American-based Cannon company, which already had extensive cinema interests in the UK. In June 1987 the familiar ABC sign (the third to go up in succession to the old Regal one) gave place to the Cannon logo. It is understood that staffing remains unchanged at the time of writing, and that the technical team is still under the direction of 'chief' Cliff Walker.

In 1981, the Rank Organisation settled on a list of twenty-nine houses that were considered unprofitable and were to be dispensed with. This was only part of an even larger list that had originally been under consideration, and one of the closer-run reprieves had been Aberdeen's Odeon. The axe having swished by its battlements, Jack Poole's Regent was able to celebrate its 50th birthday in style with a special gala evening on Saturday 13 March 1982. Main attraction was the provincial premiere of the award-winning film *On Golden Pond*, starring Henry Fonda and Audrey Hepburn.

Vintage material that the management had hoped to include in the programme proved hard to find, but enough was come by to put together a unique second feature—an assemblage of clips and trailers from some of the Odeon's major film successes of the past five decades. The sight of James Cagney, Humphrey Bogart and Bette Davis on the large screen was quite a revelation after a staple diet of television re-runs; full credit must go to the Manager and Assistant Manager of the time, Messrs Anthony Goodman and George Raitt, supported by their able operating staff under 'chief' Bill Cowie, for a well-crafted and imaginative presentation.

Guest of honour that night was J.K.S. Poole, returning to his old cinema for the first time since 1936 to reminisce briefly on his Aberdeen days and to cut the anniversary cake. At that time, Mr Poole was still active in the cinema trade, providing imaginative programming (often with the connoisseur in mind) at the Cameo, Tollcross, Edinburgh, a cinema which possessed a little-known historic link with Aberdeen.

When, back in 1934, the Picture House's manager, Thomas Lunn, left for Edinburgh, it was to take over the Cameo, which was then named the Kings. It seems that he found his new business hard going; war-time and the immediate post-war boom kept the place alive, but by 1947 the King's was on its last legs both financially and structurally. Mr Poole, who knew Mr Lunn and his wife fairly well, happened to hear indirectly that they were planning to sell the cinema and emigrate to Canada. Having returned from war service with ideas on breaking into the Continental and specialist film market, he could not miss this opportunity, and in March 1949 the old Kings, restored and modernised, re-opened under his ownership as the Cameo.

'Jim' Poole, on the death of his father, became head of the company, presiding over its affairs initially from the Synod Hall, then later from a new office which occupied a flat in the tenement block next door to the Cameo. Every wall of this office seemed to carry some piece of memorabilia, especially of the family's sixty years at the Synod Hall, terminated in 1965 when the City Council, who owned the building, had it demolished to make way for Edinburgh's celebrated non-existent opera house.

The author was in Edinburgh in the summer of 1982 when the newspapers announced the abandonment of the latest plan for a prestigious hotel on what was to have been the Opera House site. The thought immediately occurred that Mr Poole would probably also be reading that report; a few days later, on 12 July, the letters page of *The Scotsman* carried a missive (or missile) from the Cameo describing the long saga of the Opera House as 'possibly the all-time record of farcical civic ineptitude, repeated council after council'. After 17 years' reticence on the matter, Mr Poole now told how, thinking that the well-known Synod Hall site would still be used to entertain Edinburgh in one way or another, a seat had been presented by the family for placing opposite it, in memory of Jack Poole. 'Wherever my father is now,' the letter concluded, 'he must be laughing his head off, and we are very tempted to request the transfer of the Poole seat to opposite the City Chambers—The House Of Comedy.'

Increase in local competition following upon the tripling of Edinburgh's Odeon in 1981, and the opening of the new specialist Film Theatre in nearby Lothian Road, had no immediately disastrous effect on business at the Cameo, but these events combined with a concurrent paucity of new feature films made Mr Poole think that perhaps, at years that were after all upward of three-score-and-ten, the time had come for him to retire. The Roxy had been sold some years previously because, typically, Mr Poole preferred his first love, the cinema, to any Bingo. With the Cameo's closure in September 1982, Poole's Entertainments finally reached the end of the line. For nearly four years the Cameo lay dormant, with 'for sale' signs above its entrance, but just in time for the Edinburgh Festival of 1986 it at last changed hands and is continuing as a cinema.

On hearing of J.K.S. Poole's retirement, the Scottish Cinema Exhibitors Association arranged a presentation in recognition of his service to the indus-try—a fitting tribute to one of its most popular and highly-respected members. On the train back from Glasgow where the function was held, Mr Poole chanced to pick up a copy of the latest edition of Punch, and, leafing through it, found to his surprise a substantial article on his own family and their Myriorama!

One invitation to the Odeon's celebration that unfortunately could not be accepted was that sent to its former manager, Mr Wilfred Pryor, who had been associated with the house from its very beginnings until 1972. Those who attended 'The Mickey' (as the Saturday morning children's shows were known from time immemorial) during the 1950s and 1960s must surely remember the kindly gent who, at the end of each performance, stood spotlit at the microphone by the right hand corner of the front stalls, sending his young audience home with his regular parting phrase—'...and mind how you go.' A man of varied talents, Mr Pryor was for many years organist of Union Grove Baptist Church, while at home he found time for interests in electronics and watchmaking. He lived in quiet retirement, and was in very indifferent health for some time before his death in late 1982.

Another long-serving member of the Odeon's staff was its first chief operator James 'Jimmy' Ross, who also died in 1982. He came into the trade in 1926 as a page-boy at the Picture House (Gaumont), where he worked his way up to the post of chief, supervising the installation of talkies when these arrived. Moving to the Odeon/Regent for its opening, he remained there for 41 years. Interviewed by the press at the time of his retirement in 1973, he recalled the early days of talkies when queues for the Picture House stretched right along Union Street every night. His most salient memory of more recent times was of the impact made by The Sound Of Music. Bus parties came from as far away as Dundee and Inverness, some folk were brought in wheelchairs, and others had to be carried into the place, so determined were they to see the film. *The Sound Of Music* also brought to the Odeon people who had never been to a cinema before in their lives!

When the Odeon's auditorium was divided in 1974, the front stalls were left as before, but, lacking an easy entrance or exit, they could not be opened to the public, even though a busy first-run put space in Cinema One at a premium. An access corridor has therefore been added on the North side of the building, and now the area is in regular use. The front canopy was remodelled in 1959, and further work was done in the late 1960s. A fuller refurbishing of the canopy was carried out at the time of tripling, then in 1977 or 1978 it was modernised by the addition of the circuit's stock fluorescent lighting and movable display letters. At about the same time the old lamps on either side of the entrance and the large hoarding above the right hand wing of the frontage were removed. The granite-work was cleaned and the terracotta decoration replaced where necessary, leaving the frontage looking as good as new. In the summer of 1978 the old threepenny-piece 'Odeon' sign was replaced by lettered fluorescent squares attached to the upper stonework of the frontage. While this arrangement is undoubtedly neat and perfectly suits the building, the author has to confess to a hankering for

105   The Odeon prior to alteration, August 1973 (Michael Thomson)

those winter nights of old when the vista down Union Grove culminated in a great orange-red flare suffusing the mist and unmistakably proclaiming 'Cinema'!

A video lending library was added in 1985; in 1986 the Odeon was further improved by a general freshening of decor and the carpeting of all public areas. Consideration was given to flooring over the area of Cinema One from the former balcony to the screen, but this was not carried out. Prior to the Odeon's tripling, experiments were tried with no-smoking areas in the auditorium. Now, since the 1986 refurbishment, all three cinemas are designated No-Smoking—a trend which has also been followed by Cannon.

And so we come to the end of our narrative. As to the future, who knows? Will cable television and video destroy the cinema altogether, as some would have us believe? Perhaps, but then the sound cassette was supposed to kill off the LP record, and quadrophonic sound was supposed to make stereo a thing of the past. Besides, if there were no cinemas to act as a market place

106   The former Globe, Nelson Street, before renovation, 1972 (Michael Thomson)

for new films and to encourage investment in their making, what sort of offerings would we be presented with? There is only one way to find out what will happen next—be there!

For now, stand on Union Bridge, especially on a damp day when the slates are darker, and look very hard at the roof of what was once the Trades Hall (substantially altered within during a long period as a carpet warehouse). You may just discern traces of two sets of large white letters superimposed one above the other. One set reads 'Belmont', while under it can still be vaguely picked out 'Coliseum'.

We have already mentioned the survival of the Cinema House, formerly the Picturedrome. On the corner of Nelson Street and Mounthooly you will still find the old Globe Picture Playhouse, commendably smartened up by its present occupiers. At the back of the building can still be seen the brick stage wall (now harled), the ventilation louvres installed for Bert Gates all those years ago, and the little built-out slated box that was added to accommodate the talkie speakers in 1930.

Finally, it is still a fact that Aberdeen sees film releases well in advance of many other Scottish centres, a tradition that can be traced all the way back to Bert Gates and his 'Starrie'—and isn't that, to use a well-worn metaphor, just about 'where we came in'?

Appendix 1

The Great Jam-Jar Controversy

One of the most popular stories about cinema-going during the 1920s and 1930s of this century concerns the admission of children in return for either one or two returnable glass jam-jars. This practice seems to have been widespread in Scotland, and would appear to have begun around the time of the First World War. Certainly as old is the famous story about the little boy who tenders a shilling piece at the cash desk and receives eleven jam-jars as change—it appears in one issue of the *Evening Express* as far back as March 1921!

During the hard times that followed the First World War, every penny counted and it made sense for cinema proprietors in less well-off city areas to allow some bartering of these jars, which could later be reclaimed for a sum equivalent to that of an admission ticket. When the practice ceased in Aberdeen is not clear, but one might guess at around 1935 when the worst of the Depression was past. It may well have continued considerably longer in some other towns.

In her excellent survey of the cinema in Scotland *Pictures Past*, Scottish Film Council archivist Janet McBain expresses some doubts about the veracity of the entire jam-jar saga, but when this was pointed to in the Aberdeen press review of her book (*Evening Express*, 24 August 1985), readers were quick to set the record straight.

Mr Albert Annand of Aberdeen recalled having had many a jam-jar's worth at the 'Starrie', where the jars were collected by the cashier and a male attendant, and stacked into wooden crates beside the kiosk. The date that Mr Annand gave for this was 1928-1930.

Mrs Ethel Kilgour, also of Aberdeen, remembered jam-jars at the Star, and more:

I was initiated into the wonder of the cinema via the Star Picture House, known as the 'Starrie', in Park Street. The year was 1925 and the talkies hadn't been invented. I was too young to be able to read the captions and 'blurbs' on the screen, but from then on through my childhood years, the Saturday matinee 'tuppenny rush' was a must for me and my chums from the Footdee district.

I saw the genius of Charlie Chaplin, laughed at Harold Lloyd and Buster

Keaton, and thrilled to the bravery of Tom Mix the cowboy star. When Tom Mix was chasing the Indians, the lady who played the piano accompaniment to all the films from her seat in front of the stage had to labour for her pay, as she had to keep in time with the galloping horses. There was always a moral in these films, for the 'goodies' always won—the 'baddies' never did.

The cinema itself was very basic. Seats were long wooden forms with backs from which most of the varnish had been worn off. The floor was of wood, so if the film broke down, as it frequently did, the noise of stamping feet was deafening. One side of the cinema had three or four very tall windows, and blinds had to be drawn before each performance. This task was done by the head attendant or 'checker', as they were called. He was dressed resplendently in a plum-coloured uniform, with lots of gold braid and a 'cheese-cutter' hat. I remember him very vividly as he looked so much like King George V, beard and all, and he had a very regal air as he walked slowly to each window and lowered the long navy-blue canvas blinds. As each blind was lowered, a thunderous cheer went up from the audience, as by this time excitement was at fever pitch. The last blind down, the lights went out and the piano accompaniment began.

In the programme, there was always a serial like the Red Phantom, with a cliffhanger ending which enticed the youthful audience back for more. During the films, the checkers had a busy time keeping order. If some of the kids got out of hand, a torch was shone on them, with the curt order 'keep quiet or out you go!'

To freshen the somewhat fetid air, scented water was sprayed over the audience from a long brass-handled spray by one of the checkers. On Hogmanay, a special matinee was given and everybody got an apple and an orange on entry to the cinema. The checkers were so pelted with orange peel and apple cores, and indeed with orange juice rained down on them from the balcony, that the format was changed to an apple and an orange going OUT.

When, in 1929, talking pictures began, we couldn't understand what the actors were saying, never having heard Americans speak, but soon we were saying 'OK baby' in a poor imitation of the stars who we so adored from our seats in the 'Starrie'. It was a great little cinema, jam-jar entry fee and all, and it was a form of escapism for so many children in a world so depressed between the wars.

Appendix 2

Memories Of The Woodside 'Rinkie'

ANDREW DURWARD

For World War One youngsters of Woodside, nothing could beat the 'Rinkie'. It was named after a one-time roller skate venture in a single storey building which, although much altered, still remains. Sited at 705 Great Northern Road, it attracted hordes of youngsters who were held spellbound by cowboy Bill Hart and by the never ending 'to be continued next week' serial with Eddie Polo in 'The Broken Coin'.

All this world of fantasy attracted our hard-gotten Saturday penny, and there were tunes from a tinny piano to fill in the frequent film breaks. A breakdown of the projector (usually at the most exciting part of the film) meant instant uproar in the audience. Stamping on the wood floor, shouting and whistling—complete bedlam until the show restarted. We didn't know who owned the cinema, but it did get to be known that the films were passed from town, reaching the 'Rinkie'—hopefully—in time for the performance. Late arrival of reels meant sure trouble from an impatient audience.

The hard wooden seating and cold comfortless building did in no way affect our enjoyment. We did not mind; it was new, exciting and we were happy. Well do I remember the posters pinned around the walls: 'Anyone Stamping, Shouting, Swearing, Fighting or Spitting will be Ejected'. As youngsters of seven plus years of age we did not understand the meaning of the last word, so little heed was given to the rest.

The 'Rinkie' brought enjoyment to many in Woodside, yet somehow always appeared to be struggling for survival. Latterly the management resorted to part-film part-touring company performances, along with an early version of 'Opportunity Knocks', or Talent Spotting as it was then. Highland dancing, singing, music, etc., vied with each other as budding 'star' acts, all in an endeavour to regain falling support.

Latterly, the Saturday matinees brought the main money income of the week, with gimmicks such as balloons, windmills and sweeties to entice the youngsters. Finally the attractions of more comfortable entertainment along with cheap tramcar fares finished off the Rinkie's support. Around 1922, just at the time that I left school, the cinema closed, never to reopen.

Bibliography

The reader may find the following books of interest as a source of background information:

ATWELL, David, *Cathedrals Of The Movies: A History Of British Cinemas And Their Audiences* (Architectural Press 1980)

BLUM, Daniel, *A Pictorial History of the Silent Screen* (Hamlyn 1962)

—— *A Pictorial History of the Talkies* (2nd edn, Hamlyn 1974)

FIELD, Audrey, *Picture Palace: A Social History Of The Cinema* (Gentry 1974)

GRIFFITH, Richard and MAYER, Arthur, *The Movies* (Rev edn, Spring Books 1971)

HALL, Ben M., *The Best Remaining Seats* (1961) Reissued as *The Golden Age Of The Movie Palace* (Clarkson & Potter, New York, 1975)

McBAIN, Janet, *Pictures Past: Scottish Cinemas Remembered* (Moorfoot 1985)

MELLOR, G. J., *Picture Pioneers: The Story of The Northern Cinema 1896-1971* (Frank Graham 1972)

PERRY, George, *The Great British Picture Show* (Granada 1975)

RICHARDS, Jeffrey, *Age Of The Dream Palace; Cinema And Society In Britain 1930-1939* (Routledge 1984)

SHARP, Dennis, *The Picture Palace* (Hugh Evelyn 1969)

SHIPMAN, David, *Story Of The Cinema* (Hodder & Stoughton 1982)

SHIPMAN, David, *Story Of The Cinema Vol II* (Hodder & Stoughton 1984)

Index